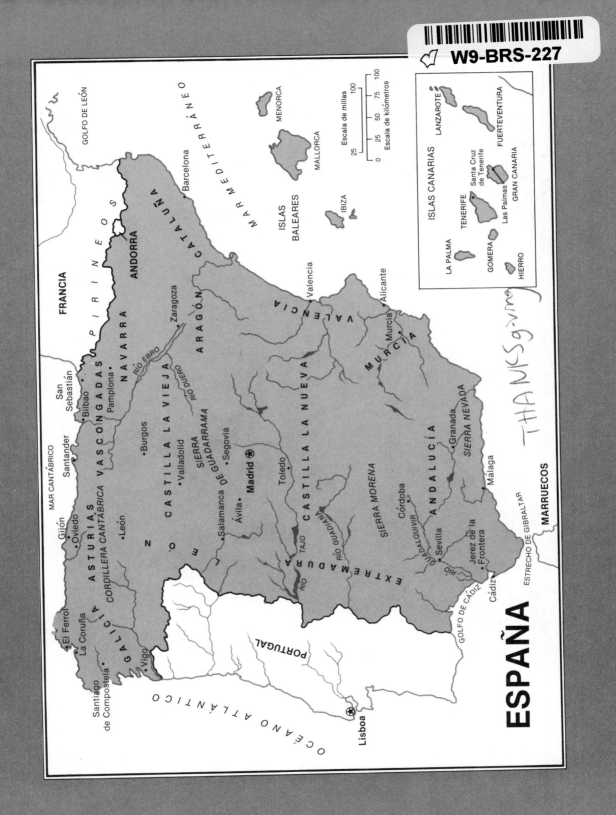

ESPAÑA

THANKSgiving

FRANCIA

P I R I N E O S

ANDORRA

CATALUÑA

Barcelona

GOLFO DE LEÓN

MAR MEDITERRÁNEO

MENORCA

MALLORCA

IBIZA

ISLAS BALEARES

Escala de millas
Escala de kilómetros

NAVARRA

Zaragoza

ARAGÓN

Pamplona

San Sebastián

Bilbao

VASCONGADAS

RÍO EBRO

RÍO DUERO

Valencia

VALENCIA

Alicante

Murcia

MURCIA

Santander

MAR CANTÁBRICO

CORDILLERA CANTÁBRICA

ASTURIAS

Gijón

Oviedo

León

Burgos

Valladolid

CASTILLA LA VIEJA

SIERRA DE GUADARRAMA

Salamanca

Segovia

Ávila

Madrid

Toledo

CASTILLA LA NUEVA

RÍO TAJO

RÍO GUADIANA

EXTREMADURA

SIERRA MORENA

Córdoba

GUADALQUIVIR

Sevilla

RÍO

Jerez de la Frontera

ANDALUCÍA

Granada

SIERRA NEVADA

Málaga

ESTRECHO DE GIBRALTAR

MARRUECOS

Cádiz

GOLFO DE CÁDIZ

GALICIA

El Ferrol

La Coruña

Santiago de Compostela

Vigo

OCÉANO ATLÁNTICO

PORTUGAL

Lisboa

ISLAS CANARIAS

LANZAROTE

FUERTEVENTURA

LA PALMA

TENERIFE

Santa Cruz de Tenerife

GRAN CANARIA

Las Palmas

GOMERA

HIERRO

¿Habla español?

ESSENTIALS

FOURTH EDITION

Teresa Méndez-Faith
Saint Anselm College

Mary McVey Gill

Harcourt Brace Jovanovich College Publishers
Fort Worth   Philadelphia   San Diego
New York   Orlando   Austin   San Antonio
Toronto   Montreal   London   Sydney   Tokyo

Publisher *Ted Buchholz*
Senior Acquisitions Editor *Jim Harmon*
Senior Developmental Editor *Sharon Alexander*
Production Manager *Annette Dudley Wiggins*
Cover Design Supervisor *Serena L. Barnett*
Cover Design *Margaret E. Unruh*
Text Design *York Production Services*
Text Illustrations *York Production Services*
Photo Research *Judy Mason*
Editorial, Design & Production *York Production Services*

Harcourt Brace Jovanovich, Inc. would like to thank Edward David Allen, Professor of Education at The Ohio State University, for his guidance and inspiration over the life of *¿Habla español? Essentials* and for his valuable work on previous editions.

Printed in the United States of America

Library of Congress Cataloging-in-Publication Data

Méndez-Faith, Teresa.
    Habla español?—Essentials 4th ed. / Teresa Méndez-Faith, Mary
McVey Gill.
        p. cm.
    Rev. ed. of: Habla español? / Edward David Allen, Teresa Méndez-Faith,
Mary McVey Gill. Essentials 3rd ed. ©1986.
    1. Spanish language—Textbooks for foreign speakers—English.
I. Gill, Mary McVey. II. Allen, Edward David, 1923–   Habla
español? III. Title.
BX2350.M542   1989
248.3—dc20

89-39807
CIP

ISBN 0-03-030037-1
    2 3 4   039   9 8 7 6 5 4

Harcourt Brace Jovanovich, Inc.
The Dryden Press
Saunders College Publishing

Photographic credits appear on page x.

Preface

his Fourth edition of *¿Habla español? Essentials* reflects the comments and suggestions of professors across the country who used the third edition with great success in their classrooms. The fourth edition was designed to give instructors as much freedom and flexibility as possible in creating their own courses and to respond to comments and suggestions from reviewers.

New to this Edition

The fourth edition of *¿Habla español? Essentials* has the following new features:

1. There are a variety of new exercises and activities.
2. Many dialogues and readings have been revised or updated. Each chapter now focuses on a specific country or region on the Spanish-speaking world.
3. Relative pronouns and the progressive tenses are now introduced earlier. The future and conditional are introduced before the chapter on the subjunctive in adverbial clauses and used in that chapter.
4. English translations of the minidialogues have been eliminated from Chapters 13–18 to provide additional reading practice.
5. There is more realia in this edition.
6. In the Spanish-English end vocabulary, chapter numbers have been indicated so students and instructors can tell where words were first introduced.
7. The workbook/lab manual has been revised and now includes answers to the exercises in the back of the text.

A detailed description of other ancillary materials (video, testing program, transparencies, software, and situation cards) to accompany *¿Habla español? Essentials* is contained in the preface to the instructor's annotated edition.

Organization

The fourth edition consists of a preliminary chapter and eighteen chapters, three self-tests, and eight illustrated readings. The preliminary chapter emphasizes pronunciation and presents classroom expressions, salutations, and simple vocabulary and structures to allow the students to introduce themselves. Each of the following eighteen chapters is divided into four parts, as follows:

1. An illustrated chapter opener including an exercise and a series of questions to introduce the theme vocabulary;

2. Three to five grammar topics, each introduced by a minidialogue and accompanied by exercises ranging from simple to more challenging, including a variety of contextualized exercises and personalized questions;
3. A longer dialogue combining the structures of the chapter, followed by comprehension questions and cultural notes;
4. A *Funciones y actividades* section, which discusses and summarizes the language functions of the chapter and provides a variety of activities to practice the chapter functions, structures, and vocabulary.

There are three self-tests, one after every six chapters, designed to review key points; students may do these on their own or in class. After every even-numbered chapter except the last one there is an illustrated reading on Hispanic culture.

Flexibility

There are many optional features of the text, which an instructor can use or not use, depending on individual preference. For instance, the self-tests and illustrated readings are optional. Similarly, the *Funciones y actividades* sections can be skipped if necessary because of limited time, as can the long dialogues. Conversely, if time permits, the *Preguntas* and *Funciones y actividades* can be expanded on in a wide variety of ways.

Supplementary Materials

This text may be used in conjunction with the *Manual de ejercicios y laboratorio* and the tape program, both of which have been revised to reflect the changes in the new edition. Each chapter of the manual contains oral and written exercises that correspond to the equivalent chapter in the text. The workbook section provides additional practice of the grammatical structures and vocabulary through a variety of written exercises. Each laboratory session is approximately 40 minutes and includes pronunciation exercises, additional grammar exercises, and a wide variety of listening comprehension activities designed to teach the student to understand spoken Spanish.

Acknowledgments

The authors would like to thank Sharon Alexander of Holt, Rinehart and Winston for her careful reading of the manuscript. We are also grateful to Marilyn James of York Production Services for taking the manuscript through production, and to Ray Faith for his careful and painstaking work on the computerized *Vocabulario español-inglés*.

Special thanks are also due to the following reviewers, whose comments, both positive and critical, were of great help in the revision of this text: Robert Anderson, California State University, Stanislaus; Pilar Ara, Pasadena City College; Walter Borenstein, State University of New York at New Paltz; B. Brant Bynum, Converse College; Alexander Callaghan, Grand Rapids Community College; Jane E. Connolly, University of Miami; Aleta Davis, California State University, Long Beach; Agnes L. Dimitriou, University of California, Berkeley; Susana Duran, Gulf Coast Community College; Beatriz G. Faust, Houston Community College; Rosa M. Fernández, The University of New Mexico; David W. Foster, Arizona State University; Robert M. Gleaves, University of North Carolina at Charlotte; Rita-Marie Maisonneuve, Middle Tennessee State University; Eleanor H. Miller, Norfolk State University; Ada Ortuzar-Young, Drew University; Marie S. Rentz, University of Maryland; Alice H. Reynolds, North Georgia College; Stanley L. Rose, University of Montana; Nancy Shumaker, Georgia Southern College; Rogelio A. de la Torre, Indiana University at South Bend.

Contents

Appendix I

Appendix II

Appendix III

Appendix IV

PHOTO CREDITS

Page 5—© Robert Frerck, Odyssey/Frerck/Chicago; Page 16—© 1988, Stuart Cohen, Comstock; Page 33—© Chip Peterson; Page 37—© Chip Peterson; Page 49—© Robert Frerck, Odyssey/Frerck/Chicago; Page 56—© Owen Franken, Stock Boston; Page 61—© 1978, F. Gohier, Photo Researchers, Inc.; Page 61—© Chip Peterson; Page 73—© Robert Frerck, Odyssey Prod.; Page 75—© Owen Franken, Stock Boston; Page 77—© Walter R. Aguiar; Page 80—© Robert Frerck, Odyssey/Frerck/Chicago; Page 99—© 1987, Peter Mentzel, Stock Boston; Page 104—© Robert Frerck, Odyssey/Frerck/Chicago; Page 104—© Robert Frerck, Odyssey/Frerck/Chicago; Page 105—© 1988, Ulrike Welsch; Page 105—© Robert Frerck, Odyssey/Frerck/Chicago; Page 120—© Beryl Goldberg; Page 121—© Mimi Forsyth, Monkmeyer Press; Page 134—© Larry Kolvoord, Viesti Associates, Inc.; Page 141—© Deborah Davis, PhotoEdit; Page 147—© 1989, Stuart Cohen, Comstock; Page 148—© Robert Frerck, Odyssey Prod.; Page 148—© Bob Daemmrich Photography; Page 162—© Peter Menzel, Stock Boston; Page 167—© Robert Frerck, Odyssey/Frerck/Chicago; Page 186—© Robert Frerck, Odyssey/Frerck/Chicago; Page 188—© 1989, Southern Stock Photos; Page 189—© Robert Frerck, Odyssey/Frerck/Chicago; Page 194—© Robert Fried, Robert Fried Photography; Page 194—© Walter R. Aguiar; Page 195—© Walter R. Aguiar; Page 195—© Robert Fried, Robert Fried Photography; Page 208—© Robert Frerck, Odyssey/Frerck/Chicago; Page 208—© Peter Menzel, Stock Boston; Page 220—© Larry Mangino, The Image Works; Page 223—© 1989, Stuart Cohen, Comstock; Page 229—© Metropolitan Museum of Art; Page 230—© Robert Frerck, Odyssey/Frerck/Chicago; Page 236—© Eric Carle, Stock Boston; Page 237—© Robert Frerck, Odyssey/Frerck/Chicago; Page 238—© Robert Frerck, Odyssey/Frerck/Chicago; Page 252—© Robert Frerck, Odyssey/Frerck/Chicago; Page 273—© Robert Frerck, Odyssey/Frerck/Chicago; Page 275—© Marvullo; Page 279—© Robert Frerck, Odyssey Prod.; Page 280—© Walter R. Aguiar; Page 281—© Art Resource—New York; Page 281—© Bradley Smith, Photo Researchers, Inc.; Page 301—© Peter Menzel, Stock Boston; Page 302—© Joe Viesti, Viesti Associates, Inc.; Page 313—© Beryl Goldberg; Page 317—© Katherine McGlynn, The Image Works; Page 321—© Murray Greenberg, Monkmeyer Press; Page 329—© Joe Viesti; Page 329—© Robert Frerck, Odyssey Prod.; Page 345—© D. Donne Bryant, DDB Stock Photo; Page 352—© Museum of Modern Art of Latin America; Page 364—© Walter R. Aguiar; Page 370—© Walter R. Aguiar; Page 371—© Robert Frerck, Odyssey/Frerck/Chicago; Page 382—© 1987, Peter Menzel; Page 384—© Walter R. Aguiar; Page 387—© 1987, Rob Crandall, Stock Boston; Page 396—© Beryl Goldberg; Page 408—© Jeanne White, Photo Researchers, Inc.

¿Habla español?

ESSENTIALS

FOURTH EDITION

o gusto, señora
ía.

En la sala de clase

Capítulo preliminar

Greetings
Classroom Expressions

PREGUNTAS

1. ¿Cómo se llama la profesora?*   **2.** ¿Cómo se llama la señorita?   **3.** ¿Cómo se llama el señor?   **4.** ¿Cómo se llama usted? (Me llamo...)

---

* Note that an inverted question mark precedes Spanish questions. This is to let the reader know that a question will follow. Similarly, an inverted exclamation mark precedes exclamations: **¡Bravo!**

The sounds of Spanish: vowels

A. Vowels

There are five simple vowel sounds in Spanish, represented by the letters *a, e, i* (or *y*), *o,* and *u*. In the following examples, the stressed syllables—the syllables that are more forcefully pronounced—appear in **bold** type.

a   This vowel is similar in sound to the first vowel of *father,* but it is more open, tense, and short than that of English.

         A**de**la, **A**na, Cata**li**na, Marga**ri**ta, ma**má**, pa**pá**

e   This vowel has a sound similar to the first vowel in the English word *ate,* but shorter and tenser, without the glide.

         E**le**na, Fede**ri**co, Te**re**sa, Fe**li**pe

i, y   These letters are pronounced like the second vowel of *police.*

         Mi**guel**, Isa**bel**, Cris**ti**na, Fe**li**sa, sí, y *(and)*

o   The *o* is similar to the English *o* of *so* or *no,* except shorter, without the glide.

         no, **so**lo *(alone)*, **Pa**co, Al**fon**so, Ro**dol**fo, Ra**món**, An**to**nio, Teo**do**ro

u   The *u* is pronounced like the English *oo* in *cool* or *fool* (never the sound of *book* or the *u* in *universal*).

         Su**sa**na, Ra**úl**, Je**sús**, **Úr**sula, univer**sal**

B. Diphthongs

Nearly every vowel in English is actually pronounced as a diphthong—a gliding from one vowel position to another. Spanish vowels, pronounced in isolation, are short and clear, but when two of them occur side by side, a diphthong is sometimes produced, depending on which vowels are combined. There are two weak vowels in Spanish, *i* and *u,* and three strong vowels, *a, e,* and *o.* Two strong vowels together constitute two syllables, or sounds: **le-al.** However, a combination of two weak vowels or of a weak and a strong vowel is a diphthong—a multiple vowel sound pronounced in the same syllable.

ia	Ali**cia**, Pa**tri**cia, San**tia**go
ua	Juan, Jua**ni**ta, E**duar**do
ie	Ga**briel**, **Die**go, Ja**vier**
ue	Con**sue**lo, Ma**nuel**
io	**Ma**rio, An**to**nio, **ra**dio, a**diós**

uo	antiguo (*ancient*), **cuo**ta (*quota*)
iu	vein**tiu**no (*twenty-one*), ciu**dad** (*city*)
ui (uy)	Luis, muy
ai (ay)	**Jai**me, Rai**mun**do, hay (*there is, there are*)
au	**Pau**la, Au**re**lio, Au**ro**ra
ei (ey)	seis (*six*), rey (*king*)
eu	Eu**ge**nio, Eu**ro**pa, feu**dal**
oi (oy)	es**toi**co (*stoic*), hoy (*today*)

EJERCICIO

Conversación.   With a classmate, create a conversation similar to the following one, but use your own names. You might want to ask your instructor if your name has a Spanish equivalent and use that.

Good morning. I'm ——————. What is your name?
My name is ——————.
Glad to meet you, ——————.
Glad to meet you!

Dos amigas españolas

The sounds of Spanish: consonants, word stress, and linking

EL PROFESOR	Buenas tardes, estudiantes.
LOS ESTUDIANTES	Buenas tardes, profesor.
EL PROFESOR	Repitan, por favor: la ventana.
LOS ESTUDIANTES	La ventana.
EL PROFESOR	¿Qué es esto?
LOS ESTUDIANTES	Es la ventana.
EL PROFESOR	Y esto, ¿qué es?
LOS ESTUDIANTES	Es el libro.
EL PROFESOR	¡Muy bien! Y, ¿cómo se dice *door* en español?
LOS ESTUDIANTES	Se dice «puerta».
EL PROFESOR	¡Excelente!

EJERCICIO

¿Cómo se dice en español...?

1. notebook   3. table   5. pencil   7. book
2. blackboard 4. chair   6. professor 8. pen

A. By now you have probably noticed that some consonants have sounds in Spanish that are different from those in English:

b, v   The letters *b* and *v* are pronounced in the same way. At the beginning of a word, they sound much like an English *b*, whereas in the middle of a word, they have a sound somewhere between *b* and *v* in English.

Bogotá, Valencia, Verónica, **bu**rro, Eva, Sebas**tián**

c, z   In Spanish America, the letters *c* (before *e* and *i*) and *z* are pronounced like an English *s*.*

Alicia, Galicia, Cecilia, Zaragoza, La **Paz**, pizarra, **lá**piz

A *c* before *a*, *o*, *u*, or any consonant other than *h* is pronounced like a *k*.

inca, **co**ca, **cos**ta, **Cuz**co, se**cre**to, **cla**se

ch   The combination of *c* and *h*, *ch*, is a separate Spanish letter. It therefore appears separately in word lists and dictionaries, following the letter *c*. The *ch* is pronounced like the same letter combination in English.

choco**la**te, **Chi**le, cha-cha-**chá**

d   The letter *d* has two sounds. Usually, it is similar to the *th* in the English word *then*.

Felici**dad**, **Eduar**do, **Ricar**do, pa**red**, estu**dian**te

After *n*, *l*, or a pause, it is somewhat like a *d* in English, but "softer," with the tongue touching the upper front teeth.

día, don, **Die**go, Mi**ran**da, Ma**til**de

g, j   The *g* before *i* or *e* and the *j* are both pronounced approximately like an English *h*.

Jorge, Jose**fi**na, geolo**gí**a, **Jalis**co, re**gión**, **pá**gina

The *g* before *a*, *o*, or *u* is pronounced approximately like the English *g* of *gate*. In the combinations **gue** and **gui**, the *u* is not pronounced, and the *g* has the same sound as an English *g*.

a**mi**go, a**mi**ga, **gus**to, Mi**guel**, gui**ta**rra

---

*In most parts of Spain, a *c* before *e* or *i*, a *z* before *a*, *e*, *o*, or *u*, and a final *z* are pronounced like a **th** in the English word **thin**. This is a characteristic feature of the Castilian accent.

In the combinations **gua** and **guo**, the *u* is pronounced like *w* in English.

an**ti**guo, Guate**ma**la

h   The Spanish *h* is silent.

Ha**ba**na, Hon**du**ras, Her**nán**dez, ho**tel**, **Hu**go

ll   In most of the Spanish-speaking world, the double *l* (*ll*) is much like the English *y* of *yes*. It is a separate letter of the alphabet, like *ch*.

llama, Va**lle**jo, Se**vi**lla, Mu**ri**llo, **si**lla

ñ   The sound of the *ñ* is roughly equivalent to the English *ny* of *canyon*.

se**ñor**, ma**ña**na, espa**ñol**

q   A *q* is always followed in Spanish by a silent *u*; the *qu* combination represents the sound *k*.

Quito, En**ri**que

r   There are two ways of pronouncing the single *r*. At the beginning of a word or after *l*, *n*, or *s*, it has the same sound as the *rr* (see below). Otherwise, it is an *r* so soft it is close to the *tt* of *kitty* and *Betty* in American English.

Pa**tri**cia, El**vi**ra, tor**ti**lla, Pi**lar**, profe**sor**

rr   The *rr* sound is trilled, like a Scottish burr or a child imitating the sound of a motor. The *rr* sound is represented in two ways in writing: by the *rr* and by a single *r* at the beginning of a word or after *l*, *n*, or *s*.

e**rror**, ho**rror**, ho**rri**ble, **pe**rro (*dog*)*
Rosa, **Ri**ta, Ro**ber**to, **ra**dio, alrede**dor** (*around*), En**ri**que, Isra**el**

x   The *x* in Spanish generally sounds like *ks* in English.

e**xa**men (*exam*), exis**ten**cia

Before a consonant, only the *s* sound is heard.

ex**ter**no, **tex**to

One common exception to this is the word **México**, where the *x* has the sound of an English *h*; this word can also be spelled **Méjico** in Spanish.

---

* Note that **perro** and **pero** (*but*) are very different in sound and in meaning.

B. In Spanish the *ch*, *ll*, and *rr* combinations are considered separate letters of the alphabet; *ñ* is also a letter of the alphabet.

a	a	**h**	hache	**ñ**	eñe	**t**	te
b	be	**i**	i	**o**	o	**u**	u
c	ce	**j**	jota	**p**	pe	**v**	ve
ch	che	**k**	ka	**q**	cu	**w**	doble ve
d	de	**l**	ele	**r**	ere	**x**	equis
e	e	**ll**	elle	**rr**	erre	**y**	i griega
f	efe	**m**	eme	**s**	ese	**z**	zeta
g	ge	**n**	ene				

C. Have you noticed a pattern in Spanish word stress? There are three simple rules for word stress in Spanish.

1. Words ending in a vowel, *n*, or *s* are pronounced with the emphasis on the next-to-the-last syllable.

   cla-ses   **co**-mo   re-**pi**-tan
   A-na   **bue**-nos **li**-bro

2. Words ending in a consonant other than *n* or *s* have the emphasis on the final syllable.

   E-cua-**dor**   pa-**red**   pa-**pel**
   se-**ñor**   us-**ted**   pro-fe-**sor**

3. Words whose pronunciation does not follow the above two patterns have written accents. The emphasis falls on the syllable with the accent.

   ca-**fé**   a-**quí** (*here*)   **Gó**-mez
   in-**glés*** (*English*) **lá**-piz   a-**diós**

For information on how to divide words into syllables, see Appendix I of this text.

D. Linking—the running together of words—occurs in every spoken language. In American English, for instance, *Do you want an orange?* becomes approximately "*D'ya wanna norange?*" Anyone who attempts to speak English exactly as it is written is sure to sound like a computerized toy. Linking in Spanish is influenced by the following considerations.

1. The final vowel of a word links with the initial vowel of the next word.

   Se llama Amalia.   *Her name is Amalia.*

2. Two identical consonants are pronounced as one.

   el libro   los señores

3. A final consonant usually links with the initial vowel of the next word.

   Rafael es un estudiante excelente. *Rafael is an excellent student.*
   ¿Qué es esto?   *What's this?*

---

* Names of languages are not capitalized in Spanish.

A. ¿Cómo se llama usted?   Ask a classmate his or her name. He or she will say it and then spell it, using the Spanish alphabet.

Modelo   ¿Cómo se llama usted?
Me llamo Juan Garza, jota-u-a-ene, ge-a-ere-zeta-a.

B.   Underline the stressed syllable in each word.

1. To-le-do
2. Hon-du-ras
3. us-ted
4. Bra-sil
5. cua-der-no
6. Ra-mí-rez
7. u-ni-ver-sal
8. E-cua-dor
9. pa-red
10. Tri-ni-dad

C.   ¿Cómo?   Work in pairs. One student spells a Spanish word and the other student pronounces it.

Modelos   ele-a acento-pe-i-zeta → **lápiz**   ese-e-eñe-o-ere → **señor**

Estar and subject pronouns

SR. HERNÁNDEZ	Hola, María. ¿Cómo *estás*?
MARÍA	*Estoy* muy bien, señor Hernández, gracias.
SR. HERNÁNDEZ	Y la familia, ¿cómo *está*?
MARÍA	Papá y mamá *están* bien. Y *ustedes*, ¿cómo *están*?
SR. HERNÁNDEZ	*Nosotros estamos* bien, gracias.
MARÍA	¡Qué suerte!... Adiós, señor Hernández.
SR. HERNÁNDEZ	Adiós, María.

A.   Estar (*to be*) is an infinitive verb form. It is conjugated by removing the **-ar** ending and adding other endings to the **est-** stem.

estar					
person		**singular**		**plural**	
1st	yo*	estoy	*I am*	nosotros(-as)	estamos	*we are*
2d	tú	estás	*you are*	vosotros(-as)	estáis	*you are*
3d	él		*he is*	ellos		*they are*
	ella	está	*she is*	ellas	están	*you are*
	usted		*you are*	ustedes		

* Notice that **yo,** the first-person singular subject pronoun, is not capitalized.

B. Subject pronouns are used far less frequently in Spanish than in English, since in Spanish the verb endings indicate the subject of the sentence. Subject pronouns are used in Spanish mainly to avoid confusion or for the sake of emphasis.

Estoy bien.	*I'm fine.* (statement of fact)
Yo estoy bien.	***I'm fine.** (emphatic)*
Él está aquí.	***He** is here.*
Ella está aquí.	***She** is here. (clarification)*

C. There are several ways of saying *you* in Spanish. The familiar singular form, **tú**, is used in speaking to friends, young children, and family members. It corresponds roughly to "first-name basis" in English. Students usually address each other with the **tú** form. The **usted** form is used in more formal situations, such as with older people, people you do not know, or people in authority. Students usually address their teacher with the **usted** form. It uses the same forms as the third-person pronouns because it was originally contracted from **vuestra merced**, *your grace*. If you are in a situation where you are unsure of which form to use, it is usually better to use the **usted** form unless the native speaker requests otherwise.

D. In most parts of Spain, the plural of **tú** is **vosotros** (masculine), **vosotras** (feminine). However, in Latin America, **ustedes** is used as the plural of both **tú** and **usted**.

E. **Usted** and **ustedes** are frequently abbreviated in written Spanish as **Ud**. and **Uds**. or **Vd**. and **Vds**.

¿Ud. está con Manuel?	*You are with Manuel?*
¿Vds. están bien? ¡Qué suerte!	*You are fine? How lucky! (What luck!)*

F. The subject pronouns **él**, **ella**, **nosotros**, **nosotras**, **vosotros**, **vosotras**, **ellos**, and **ellas** show gender, either masculine or feminine. In speaking about two or more males, or a mixture of males and females, the masculine forms **nosotros**, **vosotros**, and **ellos** are used. The feminine forms **nosotras**, **vosotras**, and **ellas** are used only to refer to two or more females.

Ellos (Juan y José) están en Madrid.	*They (Juan and José) are in Madrid.*
Ellos (Juan y María) están en clase.	*They (Juan and María) are in class.*
Ellas (Rita y Teresa) están en México.	*They (Rita and Teresa) are in Mexico.*
Nosotros (Elena, Ricardo y yo) estamos en casa.	*We (Elena, Ricardo, and I) are at home.*

A. Los pronombres. (*Pronouns.*)   Read each of the following phrases and then provide the corresponding subject pronouns. Your instructor may have you work with a partner.

Modelos   Sara y Pepe → **ellos**
tú y el profesor → **ustedes** (or **vosotros,** in Spain)

1. Josefina
2. Carlos
3. Carmen y Beatriz
4. Eduardo y yo
5. Elena y yo
6. Víctor y el señor Gómez
7. Amalia, Alicia, Ana y Arturo
8. tú y Marta
9. tú y yo
10. la señorita Alfonsín

B. ¿Tú, usted o ustedes? Which subject pronoun should be used when speaking to each of the following persons?

Modelos   Pepe → **tú**
el señor López → **usted**
la señora Ruiz y Susana → **ustedes**

1. el profesor
2. Juanita
3. tú y Juanita
4. el señor y la señora Méndez
5. la señorita Pérez
6. los estudiantes
7. el presidente
8. Juan Antonio

C. La señora Ramos.   Mrs. Ramos always likes to know where everyone is and how they are. Answer her questions in the affirmative and use subject pronouns, as in the example.

Modelo   ¿Eva está en Guatemala? **Sí, ella está en Guatemala.**

1. ¿Susana y Jorge están en Madrid?
2. ¿Pedro está en Los Ángeles?
3. ¿Alberto y Elena están aquí?
4. ¿Usted y Ricardo están bien?
5. ¿Eva y Luisa están con Marta?
6. ¿Tú y Alicia están bien?
7. ¿La señora López está en Barcelona?
8. ¿Ustedes están en casa?

D. Imaginación y lógica.   Make complete sentences, combining each of the subjects on the left with an appropriate ending on the right.

usted	están en México
vosotros	estoy bien
papá y yo	está en San Francisco
Cecilia y mamá	estás aquí
tú	estamos en casa
yo	está con Pablo
la familia de Teresa	estáis en España

Hi, —————. How are you?
I'm fine, thanks. How is the family?
Mom and Dad are fine. They're in ————— (name of city).

Negation

To make a sentence negative, place **no** before the verb.

¿Sí o no?   Answer **sí** if the statement is true and **no** if it is false.

Modelos   La ventana está en la pizarra.
No, la ventana no está en la pizarra.

La Paz está en Bolivia.
Sí, La Paz está en Bolivia.

1. Nosotros estamos en el hospital.
2. El profesor (la profesora) se llama Pablo Picasso.
3. Madrid está en España.
4. Caracas está en Colombia.
5. *Chair* se dice «silla» en español.
6. El presidente de México se llama Fidel Castro.
7. Nosotros estamos en casa.
8. *Paper* se dice «papel» en español.
9. La pizarra está en la mesa.
10. Buenos Aires está en Chile.

 # Yes/No questions and Spanish word order

Juan está en casa.

¿Está Juan en casa?
¿Juan está en casa?

Spanish word order is especially flexible in questions. To distinguish yes/no questions from statements of fact, the voice must rise at the end of the sentence. The most common way of asking a question is to invert the normal order of subject and verb:

Ellos están con Marta. ¿Están ellos con Marta?   *Are they with Marta?*

Ana está en clase. ¿Está Ana en clase?   *Is Ana in class?*

Sometimes, however, the normal word order for statements is used in a question, but the voice rises at the end of the sentence to make it clear that a question is being asked.

¿Ellos están con Marta?   *They're with Marta?*

¿Ana está en clase?   *Ana is in class?*

In negative questions, **no** normally precedes the verb.

¿Juan no está en casa?   *Juan isn't home?*

¿No está Juan en casa?   *Isn't Juan home?*

EJERCICIO

¿Cómo? No comprendo muy bien...   Imagine that a friend of yours is telling you the latest news and you are not sure if you heard him or her correctly. Ask questions in two ways to confirm the information.

Modelo   El profesor se llama Antonio García.
¿El profesor se llama Antonio García?
¿Se llama Antonio García el profesor?

1. Carmen está en España.
2. Paco está con el profesor.
3. Nosotros estamos muy bien.
4. Los estudiantes están en clase.
5. Ella no está en casa.
6. La Paz está en Bolivia.
7. Santiago no está en Colombia.
8. Diego y Miguel están en Madrid.

Study Hints: Getting Organized

Welcome to first-year Spanish! Here are some hints for a successful language-learning experience:

1. Become familiar with your textbook: the table of contents, the index, and the appendixes—including the vocabulary.

2. Use a loose-leaf binder or other notebook to organize your class notes, handouts, workbook exercises, and other materials.

3. Make charts, lists, and flashcards to help you organize the materials you are studying. Index cards can be carried around easily and studied when you have a few minutes to spare.

4. Review frequently—daily, if possible—and work with someone else if you can, even someone who does not know Spanish. If possible, however, try to find a native Spanish speaker or an advanced Spanish student. If your school has a department of English as a second language, there may be someone who would be willing to give you help in Spanish in exchange for help in English.

Una sala de clase de la Universidad Nacional Autónoma de México

Cognates

Cognates are words that are similar in spelling and meaning in two languages. Some Spanish cognates are identical to English words:

chocolate	final	capital
doctor	horrible	lunar

Sometimes the words differ in minor or predictable ways.

1. Except for *cc, rr, ll,* and *nn,* double consonants are not used in Spanish.

   oficial *official*   profesor *professor*

2. Many English words beginning with *s* have cognates beginning with *es.*

   especial *special*   español *Spanish*
   escuela *school*   esquí *ski*

3. The endings **-ción** or **-sión** in Spanish correspond to the English endings *-tion* or *-sion.*

   constitución   nación   televisión

4. The Spanish ending **-dad** corresponds to the English *-ty.*

   actividad   realidad   universidad

5. The Spanish endings **-ente** and **-ante** generally correspond to the English endings *-ent* and *-ant.*

   presidente   accidente   restaurante   importante

FUNCIONES Y ACTIVIDADES

Greetings

In Spanish, as in English, there are many ways to say the same thing, some more formal than others and some appropriate only to very specific circumstances. In the **Funciones y actividades** sections, you'll see different ways to express the same language functions, or uses—in this case, greetings. What do you say to someone to open a conversation? That depends on the circumstances.

1. With a friend or in an informal situation:

Hola, Miguel. ¿Cómo estás?   *Hi, Miguel. How are you?*
Hola. ¿Qué tal?   *Hi. How's it going?*

¿Qué tal? has many uses and meanings. Basically, it just means *How are things?* But combined with other words, it has other meanings; for instance, **¿Qué tal el examen?** *How did the exam go?*

2. With a stranger or in a more formal situation:

Buenos días. ¿Cómo está?   *Good morning. (Good day.) How are you?*
Buenas tardes.   *Good afternoon.* (until about sunset)
Buenas noches.   *Good night.* (after sunset; used mainly upon retiring)

3. You meet someone for the first time:

Hola. Me llamo...   *Hi. My name is...*

And what do you say in response to the question **¿Cómo está(-s)?** Here are some possible answers:

Muy bien, gracias.	*Very well, thanks.*	Bien.	*Good. Okay.*
No muy bien.	*Not too well.*	Más o menos.	*So-so.* (literally, "More or less.")
Así-así.	*So-so.*	Mal.	*Bad.*

When meeting someone for the first time, you can say:

Mucho gusto.   *Glad to meet you.*

A. Situaciones. With a partner, create short conversations for the following situations.

1. You are meeting someone for the first time. Greet the person and introduce yourself in Spanish. Ask his or her name and, when he or she answers, say, "Glad to meet you."
2. You meet a friend on the street. Say hello and ask how things are going ("How are things?"). Your friend responds, "So-so." He or she asks you how the exam went. "Badly," you say. "How's the family?" you ask, and

he or she replies that they are well. You say, "What luck!" Both of you say good-bye.

B. Una expresión apropiada. Give an appropriate expression for each drawing. Refer to the **Vocabulario activo** at the end of this chapter for help.

1. (a)
2. (b)
3. (c)
4. (d)
5. (e)
6. (f)

Classroom expressions

Each of the following classroom expressions in Spanish contains at least one cognate. You don't need to memorize these expressions, but you should be able to understand them when your instructor uses them. Match the Spanish expressions with their English equivalents.

1. Repitan, por favor.
2. No comprendo.
3. En voz alta.
4. Conteste en español.
5. Abran el libro en la página 10.
6. Muy bien. Excelente.

a. I don't understand (comprehend).
b. Open your books to page 10.
c. Repeat, please.
d. Very good. Excellent.
e. Out loud (in a loud voice).
f. Answer in Spanish.

VOCABULARIO ACTIVO

Cognados *Cognates*

la clase	el, la estudiante	la familia*	la lección
el español	excelente	el hospital	el profesor,
			la profesora

En la sala de clase (*In the classroom*)

el cuaderno	*notebook*
el lápiz	*pencil*
el libro	*book*
la mesa	*table*
la página	*page*
el papel	*paper*
la pared	*wall*
la pizarra	*blackboard*
la pluma	*pen*
la puerta	*door*
la silla	*chair*
la ventana	*window*

Otras palabras y frases (*Other words and phrases*)

aquí	*here*
bien	*okay, well*
la casa	*house*
en casa	*at home*
¿Cómo se dice...?	*How do you say . . . ?*
con	*with*
de	*of, from*
Es...	*It's . . .*
estar	*to be*
estar bien (**mal**)	*to be well (unwell)*
¿Qué es esto?	*What is this?*
¡Qué suerte!	*What luck!*

Se dice...	*You say . . .*
o	*or*
el señor	*man; sir; Mr.*
la señora	*lady; ma'am; Mrs.*
la señorita	*young lady; miss; Miss*
sí	*yes*
y	*and*

Expresiones útiles (*Useful expressions*)

Así-así.	*So-so.*
Buenos días.	*Good morning. Good day.*
Buenas tardes.	*Good afternoon.*
Buenas noches.	*Good night.*
¿Cómo se llama...?	*What is the name of . . . ?*
Más o menos.	*More or less. So-so.*
Me llamo...	*My name is . . .*
Conteste, por favor.	*Answer, please.*
Mucho gusto.	*Glad to meet you.*
Por favor.	*Please.*
Gracias.	*Thank you.*
Muy bien.	*Very good. Well.*
¿Qué tal?	*How are things? How's it going?*
¿Qué tal el examen?	*How was the exam?*
Repitan.	*Repeat.*
Hola.	*Hello. Hi.*
Adiós.	*Good-bye.*

* In the vocabulary lists in this text, definite articles (**el, la, los, las**) are given with all nouns to indicate gender.

> **Don't forget:**
> Subject pronouns, page 10.

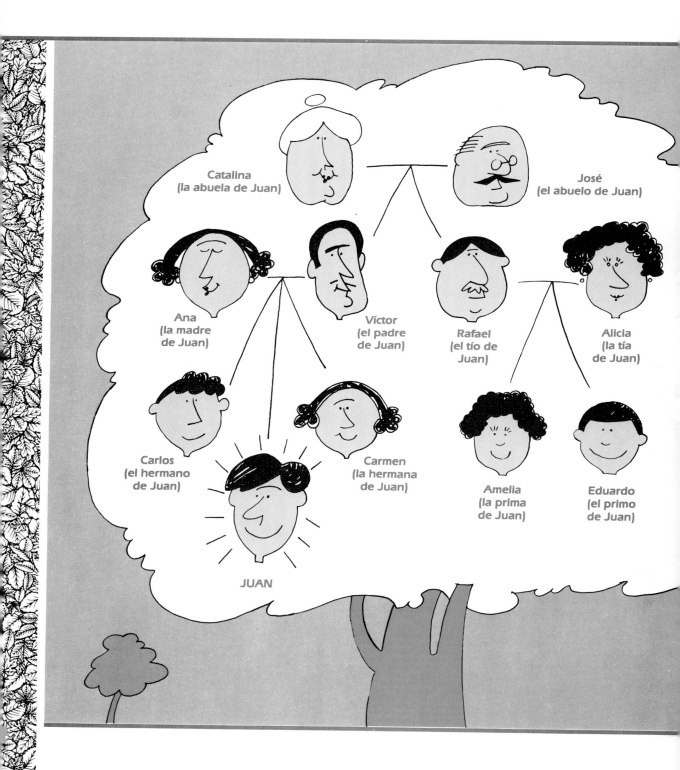

La familia ———————————— 1

Asking for Information
Using the Telephone
Ending a Conversation

EJERCICIO

Choose the correct answer.

1. Catalina es (*is*) la (abuelo, abuela, tía) de Juan.
2. Carlos y Carmen son (*are*) los (tíos, hermanos, primos) de Juan.
3. Carmen es la (hermana, tío, prima) de Eduardo.
4. Víctor es el (padre, primo, hermano) de Rafael.
5. Rafael es el (padre, tío, abuelo) de Eduardo y Amelia.
6. Rafael y Alicia son los (tíos, abuelos, primos) de Juan.

PREGUNTAS

1. Ana y Víctor son los padres (la madre y el padre) de Juan. ¿Cómo se llaman los padres de Amelia?   **2.** Catalina es la esposa de José. ¿Cómo se llama el esposo de Alicia?   **3.** ¿Cómo se llaman los primos de Carmen?   **4.** ¿Cómo se llama la madre de Víctor y Rafael?   **5.** Eduardo y Amelia son los hijos de Rafael y Alicia. ¿Cómo se llaman los hijos de Ana y Víctor?

The present tense of regular *-ar* verbs

En la Universidad de Madrid.

ANDREA ¿Tú también *estudias* sociología, Susana?

SUSANA Sí, ahora *estudiamos* la familia hispana en la clase de «Familia y sociedad».

ANDREA ¿Sí? ¡Qué interesante! Yo *busco* información sobre «la liberación de la mujer». *Necesito* un libro... o ¿*habláis* vosotros en clase sobre la situación de las mujeres en España? ¿Cómo se llama el profesor de sociología?

SUSANA La profesora, Andrea. Se llama Graciela Villegas y mañana *habla* sobre la situación de las mujeres aquí en España. ¡Qué suerte!, ¿no? ¿Por qué no *visitas* la clase?

---

1. ¿Estudia sociología Susana?   2. ¿Ahora estudian «la liberación de la mujer» en clase?   3. ¿Busca Andrea información sobre los profesores en España? 4. ¿Mañana hablan sobre la situación de las mujeres en México?

A. Verbs that end in **-ar** in Spanish are referred to as **-ar** verbs. Regular **-ar** verbs are conjugated by removing the infinitive ending **-ar** and replacing it with the endings **-o, -as, -a, -amos, -áis, -an.*** **Hablar** (*to speak*) is a regular **-ar** verb:

hablar (*to speak*)			
yo	habl**o**	nosotros(-as)	habl**amos**
tú	habl**as**	vosotros(-as)	habl**áis**
él		ellos	
ella	habl**a**	ellas	habl**an**
usted		ustedes	

At the University of Madrid. ANDREA: Are you studying sociology too, Susana? SUSANA: Yes, now we're studying the Hispanic family in the class "Family and Society." ANDREA: Yes? ("Really?") How interesting! I'm looking for information about the liberation of women (women's lib). I need a book . . . or do you talk in class about the situation of women in Spain? What is the sociology professor's name? SUSANA: The woman professor, Andrea. Her name is Graciela Villegas, and tomorrow she's talking about the situation of women here in Spain. What luck, right? Why don't you visit the class?

* **Estar**, which you saw in the preliminary lesson, is an irregular **-ar** verb; that is, it has its own special forms.

B. Other common regular **-ar** verbs are:

buscar	*to look for*	**llevar**	*to carry; to take*
desear	*to want*	**mirar**	*to look (at)*
escuchar	*to listen to*	**necesitar**	*to need*
estudiar	*to study*	**pasar**	*to pass; to spend (time)*
hablar	*to speak, talk*	**viajar**	*to travel*
llegar	*to arrive*		

Nosotros buscamos un hotel.	*We're looking for a hotel.*
Papá no desea viajar a Sudamérica.[†]	*Dad doesn't want to travel to South America.*
El esposo de Graciela necesita un pasaporte.[††]	*Graciela's husband (the husband of Graciela) needs a passport.*
¿Llevas los libros?	*Are you carrying the books?*
El niño mira por la ventana.	*The child is looking out the window.*

C. Notice that the present tense in Spanish can have more than one English equivalent.

Hablo español. $\begin{cases} I\ speak\ Spanish. \\ I\ do\ speak\ Spanish. \\ I\ am\ speaking\ Spanish. \end{cases}$

D. The present tense is also often used in place of the future tense to imply that the action will take place in the immediate future.

Estudian con nosotros hoy.	*They're studying (will study) with us today.*
El hermano de Juan lleva un regalo también.	*Juan's brother is taking (will take) a present, too.*

E. Verbs of motion, such as **viajar** and **llegar**, require the preposition **a** before a noun that indicates a destination, but not otherwise.

Ellos no viajan a Los Ángeles; viajan a Nueva York.	*They're not traveling to Los Angeles; they're traveling to New York.*
Las dos hermanas viajan por avión.	*The two sisters are traveling by plane.*
El avión llega a Madrid hoy.	*The plane arrives (is arriving, will arrive) in Madrid today.*

[†] Notice that an infinitive can follow a conjugated verb directly.
[††] The preposition **de** (*of* or *from*) is used to show possession in Spanish; for instance, to say "Graciela's husband," you say **el esposo de Graciela** (*the husband of Graciela*).

A. Nosotros dos.   Francisco is taking his twin brother Alejandro to class today. Change his statements about his usual routine to include Alejandro.

> Modelo   Llevo los libros a la universidad.
> **Llevamos los libros a la universidad.**

1. Busco la clase de español.
2. Necesito un cuaderno.
3. Llego a la clase.
4. Miro el libro.
5. Estudio la lección.
6. Hablo con el profesor.

B. Un fin de semana típico.   Carmen is telling a cousin how she spends a typical weekend and asking how some of their other relatives spend it. Answer her questions in the affirmative, as her cousin would.

> Modelo   Miro televisión. ¿Y Juan?
> **Juan también mira televisión.**

1. Hablo con los amigos. ¿Y ustedes?
2. Escucho la radio. ¿Y tía Marta?
3. Viajo a la capital. ¿Y los primos?
4. Llevo regalos a los abuelos. ¿Y tú?
5. Estudio español. ¿Y los hermanos de Raúl?

C. Imaginación y lógica.   Take one word or phrase from each column to form original sentences. Be sure to use the correct form of the verb in the second column. Use each subject at least once.

> Modelos   **El estudiante habla muy bien el español.**
>
> **El estudiante desea escuchar radio.**

yo no	viajar	el hotel
los abuelos	hablar	la cámara
el profesor	llegar	por avión
tú	buscar	escuchar radio
el estudiante	desear	muy bien el español
nosotros no	necesitar	a España hoy
Tom y Brenda	mirar	hablar con papá y mamá

D. En acción. Describe to a classmate what the following people are doing. Use the words **estudiar, mirar, hablar español, llegar a casa, buscar, necesitar el pasaporte, viajar, pasar.**

1. Pablo, Ana y Felipe...

2. Nosotros...

3. El abuelo...

INMIGRACIÓN

4. Tía Teresa...

5. Tú...

IBERIA

6. Papá...

E. Traducción. Give the Spanish equivalent of the following sentences.

1. I study Spanish.
2. We are looking for a pencil.
3. Uncle Jorge travels a lot.
4. You (**tú**) are carrying the present.
5. Do you (**usted**) need the book?
6. Are you (**ustedes**) visiting the class?
7. Grandpa wants to travel.
8. Mom and Dad arrive today.

PREGUNTAS

1. ¿Estudia usted español? ¿Desea usted hablar bien el español? **2.** ¿Hablamos español ahora? ¿Habla mucho el profesor (la profesora)? **3.** ¿Lleva usted los libros a clase? **4.** ¿Viaja usted mucho? ¿Desea viajar a España? ¿a México? ¿a Sudamérica? **5.** ¿Mira mucho la televisión? ¿Escucha mucho la radio?

 ## Articles and nouns: gender and number

En el aeropuerto de Barajas, en Madrid.

AGENTE Buenos días. *Los* pasaportes, por favor.
RAMÓN *Un* momento... aquí están.
ISABEL Ramón, ¿dónde está *la* cámara? ¿Y *los* regalos para *las* hijas de Juan?
RAMÓN ¡Dios mío! ¡Están en *el* avión!

1. ¿Necesita los pasaportes el agente? 2. ¿Lleva los pasaportes Ramón? 3. ¿Dónde están la cámara y los regalos para las hijas de Juan? 4. ¿Dónde están Isabel y Ramón?

A. In Spanish all nouns are either masculine or feminine. An article in Spanish is also either masculine or feminine, to reflect the gender of the noun it modifies. The definite article has four forms:

	Singular		**Plural**	
Masculine	**el** regalo	*the gift*	**los** regalos	*the gifts*
Feminine	**la** cámara	*the camera*	**las** cámaras	*the cameras*

B. The indefinite article in Spanish also has four forms:

	Singular		**Plural**	
Masculine	**un** primo	*a cousin*	**unos** primos	*some (a few) cousins*
Feminine	**una** familia	*a family*	**unas** familias	*some (a few) families*

Notice that **unos** (**unas**) can mean *some* or a *few*.

C. Most Spanish nouns ending in **-o** in the singular are masculine. Most nouns ending in **-a** in the singular are feminine.

el aeropuerto	*the airport*	la farmacia	*the drugstore, pharmacy*
el abuelo	*the grandfather*	la abuela	*the grandmother*

Some exceptions are **el día** (*the day*), **el problema** (*the problem*), and **la mano** (*the hand*).

D. With nouns that do not end in **-o** or **-a** in the singular, it can be helpful to learn the definite article when you learn the noun. Notice that most nouns ending in **-dad** and **-ión** are feminine. (**El avión** is an exception.)

el hotel	*the hotel*	la verdad	*the truth*
el viaje	*the trip*	la dirección	*the address*
el inglés	*English*	la ciudad	*the city*
el restaurante	*the restaurant*	la capital	*the capital (city)*

E. The gender of many nouns that refer to people can be changed by changing the noun ending and the article.

el primo	*the (male) cousin*	la prima	*the (female) cousin*
el señor	*the man, gentleman*	la señora	*the woman, lady*
un hijo	*a son*	una hija	*a daughter*
un amigo	*a (male) friend*	una amiga	*a (female) friend*

However, for some nouns the ending does not change, and so the gender of the person the noun refers to is shown by the gender of the article.

un turista	*a (male) tourist*	una turista	*a (female) tourist*

F. The plural of most nouns ending in a vowel is formed by adding **-s**: **libro**, **libros**; **mesa**, **mesas**; **viaje**, **viajes**. The plural of most nouns ending in a consonant is formed by adding **-es**: **hotel**, **hoteles**; **ciudad**, **ciudades**; **dirección**, **direcciones**.* A final **z** must be changed to **c** before adding **-es**: **lápiz**, **lápices**. The masculine plural of nouns referring to people may include both genders.

el niño	*the boy*
el señor González	*Mr. González*
el tío	*the uncle*
los niños	*the boys* or *the boys and girls*
los señores de González	*Mr. and Mrs. González*
los tíos (el tío y la tía)	*the aunt and uncle*

---

* Notice that there is no accent mark on **direcciones**, since the emphasis falls naturally on the next-to-the-last syllable.

G. The definite article is used with titles such as **señor**, **señora**, or **señorita** when you are talking or asking about an individual.

Un estudiante habla con el señor Martínez.	*A student is talking to Mr. Martínez.*
El doctor García necesita unas semanas de vacaciones.†	*Dr. García needs a few weeks of vacation.*

The definite article is not used with titles when you are speaking to the person directly.

Buenos días, señor Martínez.	*Good morning (Good day), Mr. Martínez.*
¿Cómo está usted, doctor García?	*How are you, Dr. García?*

EJERCICIOS

A. Preguntas y respuestas.   With a classmate, create questions and answers by replacing the nouns with the cues suggested.

Modelo   Estudiante 1:   **¿Están aquí *los turistas*?**
Estudiante 2:   **No, los turistas están en *la ciudad*.**

Estudiante 1	*Estudiante 2*
1. pasaportes	hotel
2. aviones	aeropuerto
3. estudiantes	clase
4. profesores	universidad

Modelo   Estudiante 1:   **¿Buscas *un lápiz*?**
Estudiante 2:   **No, busco *una pluma*.**

Estudiante 1	*Estudiante 2*
1. farmacia	restaurante
2. cuaderno	libro
3. regalo	cámara
4. papel	pizarra

B. ¿Qué necesitan...?   Marta and the Garcías have a list of things they need. Tell what they need, following the model.

Modelo   silla
Marta necesita una silla. Los García necesitan unas sillas.

1. cuaderno	5. libro
2. lápiz	6. mesa
3. pluma	7. cámara
4. papel	8. semana de vacaciones

---

† *Vacation* (singular) in English is always expressed by **vacaciones** (plural) in Spanish.

C. Formación de frases.   Make up sentences using the following words. Provide the definite articles, as in the model.

Modelo   abuelo de Pablo / hablar / con / señorita González
El abuelo de Pablo habla con la señorita González.

1. niño / buscar / regalo
2. doctor / viajar / a / ciudad
3. estudiantes / hablar / con / profesor
4. mamá de Ana / llevar / pasaportes
5. tú / estudiar / lecciones
6. nosotros / mirar / pizarra
7. primo de Juan / llegar / a / capital
8. turistas / estar / en / hotel

D. Traducción.   Give the Spanish equivalent of the following sentences.

1. Mr. Gómez is looking at the notebook.
2. Dr. García, how is the boy?
3. Mrs. Rodríguez is spending three days in Spain with a friend.
4. How are you, Miss Vega?
5. She travels to the city with the family.
6. Professor Martínez wants to speak with the students.

Cardinal numbers 0–99; hay

Hotel Santa Cruz

Avenida Lope de Vega 55

41   82   69

Direcciones y teléfonos de interés

Urgencias	Teléfonos		
Policía	091		
Doctor	42	10	35
Taxi	41	50	86
Restaurante Santa Cruz, Avenida Lope de Vega 57	41	55	08
Salón de belleza Santa Cruz, Avenida Lope de Vega 60	54	69	81
Oficina de turismo, Avenida Toledo 65	41	16	02
Aerolíneas Iberia, Plaza Mayor 3	55	91	83
Farmacia José Antonio, Avenida Toledo 74	23	31	75

direcciones *addresses*   **urgencias** *emergencies*   **el salón de belleza** *beauty salon*
las aerolíneas *airlines*

1. ¿Hay (*Is there*) un restaurante en la Avenida Lope de Vega? ¿Cómo se llama?
2. ¿Hay una farmacia en la Avenida Toledo? ¿Cómo se llama?   3. ¿Está la oficina de turismo en la Plaza Mayor?

A. Cardinal numbers 0–99.

0	cero	14	catorce	28	veintiocho
1	uno (un, una)	15	quince	29	veintinueve
2	dos	16	dieciséis	30	treinta
3	tres	17	diecisiete	31	treinta y uno
4	cuatro	18	dieciocho		(un, una)
5	cinco	19	diecinueve	32	treinta y dos
6	seis	20	veinte	33	treinta y tres,
7	siete	21	veintiuno (-ún, -una)		*etc.*
8	ocho	22	veintidós	40	cuarenta
9	nueve	23	veintitrés	50	cincuenta
10	diez	24	veinticuatro	60	sesenta
11	once	25	veinticinco	70	setenta
12	doce	26	veintiséis	80	ochenta
13	trece	27	veintisiete	90	noventa

Notice the accents on **dieciséis**, **veintidós**, **veintitrés**, and **veintiséis**, all of which end in **-s**. The compound **veintiún** also takes an accent. **Uno** becomes **un** before a masculine noun and **una** before a feminine noun.

B. **Hay** is the impersonal form of **haber**; it means *there is* or *there are* and can be used with singular or plural nouns.

Hay treinta y una personas en la sala de clase.	*There are thirty-one people in the classroom.*
Hay siete días en una semana.	*There are seven days in a week.*
Hay un hotel en la Avenida Balboa.	*There is a hotel on Balboa Avenue.*
Hay veintiún hombres aquí.	*There are twenty-one men here.*

EJERCICIOS

A. Cero, uno, dos, tres... Count to fifty, each student taking a turn. Then count to fifty by twos, by threes, by fives, and by tens.

B. Números y más números... Read each of the following expressions.

1. 11 hombres
2. 81 libros
3. 52 semanas
4. 1 avión
5. 70 primos
6. 31 ciudades
7. 45 mujeres
8. 90 universidades
9. 65 páginas
10. 28 pasaportes

C. ¿Verdadero o falso? If the statement is true, say **Verdadero**. If it is false, say **Falso** and restate it, giving the correct answer.

Modelo Hay tres estudiantes en la clase.
Hay veintiún estudiantes en la clase.

1. Hay cinco profesores en la clase.
2. Hay doctores en un hospital.

3. Hay quince sillas en la clase.
4. Hay una pizarra en la pared.
5. Hay veinticuatro horas (*hours*) en un día.
6. Hay tres ventanas y cuatro puertas en la clase.
7. Hay aviones en un aeropuerto.
8. Hay pasaportes en una farmacia.
9. Hay veinte días en abril (*April*).
10. Hay nueve días en una semana.

D. En el hotel. Look at the hotel directory from the Hotel Santa Cruz at the beginning of this section. In pairs, ask and give addresses and phone numbers.

Modelo   Estudiante 1:   **¿Hay una farmacia en la Avenida Toledo?**
              Estudiante 2:   **Sí, la Farmacia José Antonio está en la Avenida Toledo, número 74.**
              Estudiante 1:   **¿Número de teléfono?**
              Estudiante 2:   **23 31 75.**

E. Entrevista. (*Interview.*) In pairs, ask and give your own addresses and phone numbers. You can make up the information if you like. Give the numbers in groups of two when possible.

Modelo   Estudiante 1:   **¿Dirección?**
              Estudiante 2:   **101 (Uno cero uno) Walnut.**
              Estudiante 1:   **¿Teléfono?**
              Estudiante 2:   **323–0985. (Tres veintitrés cero nueve ochenta y cinco.)**

Interrogative words and word order in questions

En el teléfono, en la Avenida Toledo, en Madrid.

SRA. RIBERA	Dígame.
MIGUEL	Hola. ¿Está Teresa en casa?
SRA. RIBERA	Sí..., pero *¿quién* habla?
MIGUEL	Habla Miguel.
SRA. RIBERA	¡Ah, Miguel! Un momento, por favor.
TERESA	Hola, Miguel, *¿Cómo* estás?
MIGUEL	Bien, gracias. ¿Estudias ahora?

Un muchacho madrileño habla por teléfono.

TERESA	Sí. Estudio con Adela. ¿Deseas estudiar con nosotras?
MIGUEL	Sí. Paso por ahí en unos minutos, ¿de acuerdo?
TERESA	De acuerdo. Hasta luego.
MIGUEL	Adiós.

1. ¿Quién (*Who*) desea hablar con Teresa?   2. ¿Está Teresa en casa?   3. ¿Cómo está Miguel?   4. ¿Con quién estudia Teresa?   5. Miguel desea estudiar con ellas, ¿verdad?   6. ¿Cuándo pasa Miguel por la casa de Teresa?

On the telephone, on Toledo Avenida in Madrid. MRS. RIBERA: Hello. (literally, "Tell me.") MIGUEL: Hello. Is Teresa home? MRS. RIBERA: Yes . . . but who is this? MIGUEL: This is Miguel speaking. MRS. RIBERA: Oh, Miguel! Just a minute, please. TERESA: Hello, Miguel. How are you? MIGUEL: Fine, thanks. Are you studying now? TERESA: Yes. I'm studying with Adela. Do you want to study with us? MIGUEL: Yes. I'll come by there in a few minutes, okay? TERESA: Fine. See you later. MIGUEL: Good-bye.

A. Statements can be made into questions by adding "confirmation tags," such as **¿de acuerdo?**, **¿verdad?**, or **¿no?**.

Estudiamos ahora, ¿de acuerdo?	*We'll study now, okay?*
Ustedes viajan a España, ¿verdad?	*You are traveling to Spain, aren't you?*
Abuela llega hoy, ¿no?	*Grandmother is arriving today, isn't she?*

> **¿No?** is not used after a negative sentence. Notice that **¿de acuerdo?** (*okay?*, *agreed?*) is most often used when an action is proposed.

B. Questions can also be formed with interrogative words. Some common interrogative words are:

¿Cómo?	*How?*	**¿Por qué?**	*Why?*
¿Cuál? ¿Cuáles?	*Which? Which one(-s)? What?*	**¿Qué?**	*What?*
¿Cuándo?	*When?*	**¿Quién? ¿Quiénes?**	*Who? Whom?*
¿Dónde?	*Where?*		
¿Adónde?	*To what place? Where?*		
¿De dónde?	*From where?*		

Note that **¿Por qué?** is two words; **porque** (*because*) is one word:

¿Por qué no viajas a Barcelona?	*Why aren't you traveling to Barcelona?*
Porque ahora necesito estar en Madrid.	*Because I need to be in Madrid now.*

C. The word order for Spanish questions is interrogative word + verb + subject (if any) + remainder (if any). The voice normally falls at the end of a question with an interrogative word.

¿Cómo viajan los señores a Segovia?	*How are the gentlemen traveling to Segovia?*
¿Qué buscan los niños?	*What are the children looking for?*
¿Por qué estudias francés?	*Why are you studying French?*
¿Quién (*singular*) visita la clase?	*Who (singular) is visiting the class?*
¿Quiénes (*plural*) estudian inglés?	*Who (plural) is studying English?*
¿Dónde están los libros? —¿Cuáles?	*Where are the books? —Which ones?*
¿Adónde viaja tío Juan?	*Where is Uncle Juan traveling?*
¿Cuál es el avión a Sevilla?	*Which one is the plane to Seville?*

D. Notice that question words always have a written accent and that both **¿quién?** and **¿cuál?** have plural forms. **¿Quién (quiénes)?** is also used after prepositions:

¿A quién escuchas?	*To whom are you listening?*
¿Con quién estudias?	*With whom are you studying?*

EJERCICIOS

A. ¿Verdad...? You and a classmate are preparing for a test and are a little unsure about the following information. Ask for confirmation by adding **¿no?**, **¿verdad?**, or **¿de acuerdo?**, as appropriate.

Modelo Granada está en España.
Granada está en España, ¿no?

1. Ahora estudiamos el vocabulario activo.
2. *City* se dice «ciudad» y *trip* se dice «viaje» en español.
3. El libro se llama *¿Habla español?*.
4. Sevilla no está en México.
5. Miramos la televisión.
6. En Puerto Rico no hablan francés.

B. ¿Qué información necesita? Use the following interrogative words to form questions that will correspond to the answers given. Follow the model.

Modelo **¿Qué?**
Pablo busca el pasaporte.
¿Qué busca Pablo?

1. **¿Qué?**
   a. Miguel busca los libros.
   b. Ana y José estudian francés.
   c. María necesita un pasaporte.
2. **¿Quién? ¿Quiénes?**
   a. Miguel busca los libros.
   b. Ana y José estudian francés.
   c. María necesita un pasaporte.
3. **¿Con quién? ¿Con quiénes?**
   a. La señora Rodríguez está con los niños.
   b. Viajan con el profesor.
   c. Juan estudia con Manuel.
4. **¿Dónde? ¿Adónde?**
   a. Estela está en la universidad.
   b. Viajan a Madrid.
   c. Felipe está en Barcelona.
5. **¿Cuándo? ¿Cómo?**
   a. El avión llega en un momento.
   b. Me llamo Marta Hernández.
   c. Llegamos en unos minutos.
6. **¿Por qué?**
   a. No están aquí porque están en clase.
   b. Llevan los pasaportes porque viajan a Bolivia.
   c. Busca un teléfono porque desea hablar con Teresa.

C. Conversación. Complete the following conversation between Pedro and Miguel with the appropriate interrogative words.

MIGUEL	Hola, Pedro. ¿——————— estás?
PEDRO	No muy bien, Miguel. ¿——————— es (*is*) el examen de geografía (*geography exam*)?
MIGUEL	Mañana. ¿Deseas estudiar con nosotros?
PEDRO	¿Con ——————— estudias?
MIGUEL	Con Teresa y Adela.
PEDRO	¿——————— estudian hoy?
MIGUEL	Hoy deseamos estudiar Costa Rica.
PEDRO	Costa Rica..., ¿——————— está Costa Rica?
MIGUEL	En América Central.
PEDRO	¿Y ——————— se llama la capital de Costa Rica?
MIGUEL	¡San José! Pedro, tú necesitas estudiar mucho, ¿no?

D. Entrevista. (*Interview.*) Ask a classmate the following questions in Spanish. Some possible answers are given on the right. Your classmate should answer without looking at the book.

1. what his or her name is	Me llamo Martín (Laura).
2. with whom he or she studies	Con un(-a) amigo(-a).
3. where he or she wants to travel	A México.
4. with whom he or she wants to travel	Con Madonna (Michael J. Fox).
5. what he or she needs	Una semana de vacaciones.

Madrid, capital de España

En un avión. Los señores García, de La Paz, Bolivia, viajan a Madrid a pasar dos semanas con la familia de la señora García.

LA MADRE	En treinta minutos llegamos a Madrid. ¡Jesús,[1] los pasaportes! ¡Ah!, están aquí. Tú llevas el regalo para Isabel, ¿verdad?
EL PADRE	Sí, aquí está. Cálmate,° por favor.
PEPITO	Mamá, ¿dónde está la casa de abuela y de tía Isabel?
LA MADRE	¿Cómo?[2] ¡Ah!... está en Madrid, hijo.
PEPITO	¿Y dónde está Madrid?
EL PADRE	Pepito, mamá está muy nerviosa.° Tú hablas con papá, ¿de acuerdo? Bueno, la ciudad de Madrid está en España, como la ciudad de La Paz está en Bolivia. El rey° Juan Carlos[3] está en Madrid.
PEPITO	¿Y dónde está España, papá?
EL PADRE	España está en Europa.
PEPITO	¿Y dónde estamos nosotros ahora?
EL PADRE	Estamos en un avión y también estamos en Europa.

El Palacio Real de Madrid, España

PEPITO	¿Por qué?
EL PADRE	Porque... pues⁴... ¡porque sí!° Pepito, ¿por qué no miras por la ventana? Necesito unos minutos de paz°.
PEPITO	Pero La Paz está en Bolivia, papá...
EL PADRE	¡Señorita! (*a la aeromoza°*) Señorita, por favor, ¿cuándo llegamos?
LA AEROMOZA	Llegamos en dieciocho minutos, señor...

En el aeropuerto de Barajas, en Madrid.

DOÑA⁵ ISABEL	Hola, Catalina. ¿Qué tal el viaje? Y tú, Pepito, ¿cómo estás?
PEPITO	Bien, gracias. Pero, ¿dónde está papá?
LA MADRE	Está en la farmacia. Busca un tranquilizante°.
DOÑA ISABEL	¡Qué lástima!° Está nervioso por el viaje, ¿no?

Cálmate *Calm yourself*	**nerviosa** *nervous*	**el rey** *king*
¡porque sí! *because it's so!*	**paz** *peace*	**la aeromoza** *stewardess*
tranquilizante *tranquilizer*	**¡Qué lástima!** *What a shame!*	

PREGUNTAS

1. ¿Adónde viajan los señores García? **2.** ¿Quién lleva los pasaportes? ¿y el regalo para Isabel? **3.** ¿Dónde está Madrid? ¿y España? **4.** En el avión, ¿a quién llama el señor García? **5.** ¿Está la abuela de Pepito en el aeropuerto? ¿y la tía Isabel? **6.** ¿Con quiénes habla doña Isabel? ¿Está el señor García con ellos? **7.** ¿Dónde está el señor García? ¿Qué busca él? **8.** ¿Por qué no está bien el señor García?

Notas culturales

1. Expressions such as **¡Jesús!** and **¡Dios mío!** are commonly used in Spanish and are not regarded as blasphemous or coarse.

2. When a Spanish speaker does not hear or understand something, he or she usually indicates this by saying **¿Cómo?**, whereas in English it is common to say *Huh?*, *What?*, or *Excuse me?* Other ways to express incomprehension are discussed in the **Funciones y actividades** section of Chapter 3.

3. Spain is a constitutional monarchy, which has a king (Juan Carlos de Borbón) and queen (his wife Sofía). It has a parliament (called **las Cortes**), divided into two chambers, a senate and a house of representatives. There is also a president, who has most of the political power. The system is similar to that of Great Britain.

4. **Pues** and **bueno** are often used in Spanish when a person is momentarily at a loss for words. English speakers most often say *well*, *uh*, or *um*. Other ways to express hesitation are discussed in Chapter 7.

5. Spanish has two titles, **don** and **doña**, which are used only with first names. Originally titles of nobility, they are now used to show respect to someone of higher social position or to an older person. They are capitalized only at the beginning of a sentence.

FUNCIONES Y ACTIVIDADES

In this chapter, you have seen examples of the following language functions, or uses. Here is a summary and some additional information about these functions of language:

Asking for information

To ask for information, you can use confirmation tags or interrogative words, as you have seen in this chapter.

Confirmation tags:

¿de acuerdo?   **¿verdad?**   **¿no?**

Remember that **¿no?** is not used after a negative sentence and that **¿de acuerdo?** is often used when some kind of action is proposed. In Spanish, just as in English, these tags can be used when you simply want to confirm an answer (that you think you know) or when you do not know the answer to your question. Remember, too, that the most common way of asking yes/no questions is to invert the normal order of the subject and verb:

¿Viaja usted a Sevilla mañana?

Interrogative words:

Review the interrogative words on page 34 of this chapter.

Using the telephone

In the conversation at the beginning of Section IV, Mrs. Ribera (who is Spanish) answers the telephone by saying, «**Dígame**.» In Mexico and Central America, however, people are likely to say «**Bueno**,» and in some areas you may hear «**Aló**.» The most common expression is «**Hola**.» Notice that Mrs. Ribera asks who is calling by saying «**¿Quién habla?**,» but she might also say «**¿De parte de quién?**» (*On behalf of whom?*). With either question, you may say **Habla** and then your name—for example, «**Habla Ana**.» *This is Ana (Ana speaking).*

Ending a conversation

Adiós.   *Good-bye.*
Hasta luego.   *See you later.*
Hasta mañana.   *See you tomorrow.*
Feliz fin de semana.   *Have a good weekend.* (literally, "Happy end of week.")
Bueno, nos vemos.   (Literally, "Well, we'll see each other [soon].")

There are other ways to say good-bye, but the above are the most common. In the southern part of South America, where there has been a lot of Italian influence, people often just say, **¡Chau!**

A. ¿Qué dicen? (*What are they saying?*)   Tell what the people in the following drawings are probably saying.

1.

2.

3.

4.

B. ¿Formal o informal?   Tell which expressions are formal and which are informal. (Formal language almost always involves longer sentences than informal language.)

1. Nosotros estamos bien, gracias. Y usted, ¿cómo está, señorita?
2. Bien, gracias. ¿Y tú?
3. Hola, Roberto. ¿Qué tal?
4. ¿Cómo está usted, doña Carmen?
5. Feliz fin de semana, señor Ortiz.
6. ¿Adónde vas, Julio?

C. La familia.   Complete these sentences about your family.

1. Mamá y papá están ahora en...
2. Mi (*My*) hermano (hermana) se llama... Estudia en la escuela secundaria (la universidad de...) (*high school, the university of...*)...
3. Mi abuelo (abuela) viaja a...
4. Mi familia pasa las vacaciones en...

D. Situaciones.   In small groups, create conversations for these situations.

1. You call up your friend Silvia. Her mother, Mrs. García, answers the phone. She asks who is calling. You tell her your name, and she says, "Just a moment," and calls Silvia to the phone. You ask how Silvia is, and she says fine. You tell her you plan to go by her house in a few minutes, using a confirmation tag to find out if that's okay. She says yes, and you say you'll see her soon. You both say good-bye.
2. You and a friend are on a plane traveling to Madrid. Your friend is very nervous, but you are calm. You talk for a while. Then your friend calls the flight attendant. The attendant asks what you need. You ask when you are arriving in Madrid, and she says that you are arriving in a few minutes. You say "Thank you."

VOCABULARIO ACTIVO

Cognados

las aerolíneas	falso	el inglés	el pasaporte	la televisión
el aeropuerto	la farmacia	la liberación	la radio	el, la turista
la avenida	el hotel	nervioso	el restaurante	la universidad
la cámara	la información	la oficina	la situación	las vacaciones
la capital				

Verbos

buscar	to look for; to search
desear	to want, wish
escuchar	to listen to
estudiar	to study
hablar	to talk, speak
hay (*impersonal form of* haber)	there is, there are
llegar	to arrive
llevar	to carry; to take
mirar	to look at
necesitar	to need
pasar	to pass; to spend time
viajar	to travel
visitar	to visit

La familia

la abuela	grandmother
el abuelo	grandfather
don, doña	titles of respect used with first name
la esposa	wife
el esposo	husband
la hermana	sister
el hermano	brother
la hija	daughter
el hijo	son
la madre	mother
el niño, la niña	child
el padre	father
los padres	parents
los parientes	relatives
el primo, la prima	cousin
la tía	aunt
el tío	uncle

Otras palabras y frases

a	at, to
ahora	now
allí (*or* allá)	there
el amigo, la amiga	friend
el avión	airplane
la ciudad	city
el día	day
¡Dios mío!	My goodness! My God!
la dirección	address
en	in, on, at

el fin de semana	weekend
el francés	French
el hombre	man
hoy	today
mañana	tomorrow
mucho	much; many; a lot
la mujer	woman
muy	very
el número de teléfono	telephone number
para	for; in order to
la paz	peace
pero	but
por	by; for; through; because of
porque	because
la pregunta	question
el regalo	gift
la semana	week
sobre	on, about
también	also, too
la verdad	truth
verdadero	true; real

Expresiones útiles

¿de acuerdo?	okay?, all right?, agreed?
Hasta luego.	See you later.
Hasta mañana.	See you tomorrow.
Feliz fin de semana.	Have a good weekend (literally, "Happy end of week").
¡Qué lástima!	What a shame (pity)!
¿verdad?	right?, true?

Don't forget:
  Definite articles, page 26
  Indefinite articles, page 26
  Cardinal numbers 0–99, page 31
  Interrogative words, page 34

Esteban es
- sociable.
- optimista.
- cortés (*courteous, polite*).
- bueno.
- amable (*friendly*).

Marta es
- intelectual.
- responsable.
- inteligente.
- realista.

El museo e

El avio

Maricruz es
- idealista.
- popular.
- altruista.
- sensible (*sensitive*).

El restaurante es

colombiano.
famoso.
interesante.

chileno.
nuevo (*new*).
grande (*big*).

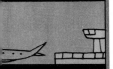

4NTE
4CIONAL

; típicos:
»s mexicanos
oles italianos
* buenos:
ıceses
entinos

legante.   *Wines*
ıoderno.
equeño (*small*).

Descripciones ___ 2

Making Descriptions (1)
Expressing Admiration
Describing Locations

EJERCICIO

Give the opposite of these words:

1. insensible **2.** pesimista **3.** irresponsable **4.** idealista **5.** egoísta (*selfish*)
6. insociable **7.** descortés **8.** malo (*bad*) **9.** viejo (*old*) **10.** aburrido
(*boring*) **11.** pequeño

PREGUNTAS

1. ¿Es idealista Marta? ¿Maricruz? ¿Esteban? **2.** ¿Quién es altruista: Esteban o
Maricruz? ¿Es usted altruista? **3.** ¿Es usted sociable o insociable? ¿optimista o
pesimista? ¿responsable o irresponsable? **4.** ¿Qué adjetivo(-s) asocia usted (*do you
associate*) con Michael Jackson? ¿con Jimmy Connors? **5.** ¿Qué personas asocia
usted con estos (*these*) adjetivos: descortés, idealista, popular, pesimista,
intelectual? **6.** ¿Qué adjetivo(-s) asocia usted con su (*your*) restaurante favorito?
¿con su automóvil ideal?

 ## The verb *ser*

En un café, de Buenos Aires.

PEDRITO	¿De dónde *son* ustedes, señor Larkin?
SR. LARKIN	La doctora Silva y yo *somos* de los Estados Unidos. Yo *soy* de Tejas.
PEDRITO	Usted habla muy bien el español.
SR. LARKIN	Gracias, *eres* muy amable.
PEDRITO	Y usted, doctora Silva, ¿*es* también de Tejas?
DRA. SILVA	No, yo *soy* de California, Pedrito.
PEDRITO	¡De California! De allí también *son* Superman y el ratón Mickey, ¿no...?

---

1. ¿Dónde están Pedrito, el señor Larkin y la doctora Silva?   2. ¿De dónde es el señor Larkin?   3. ¿Habla español el señor Larkin?   4. ¿De dónde es la doctora Silva? Y Pedrito, ¿de dónde es?   5. Según (*According to*) Pedrito, ¿quiénes son también de California?   6. ¿De dónde es usted?

---

ser (*to be*)

yo	soy	nosotros (-as)	somos
tú	eres	vosotros (-as)	sois
él		ellos	
ella	es	ellas	son
usted		ustedes	

Somos estudiantes.	*We are students.*
Eduardo es argentino.	*Eduardo is an Argentinean.*
Ricardo es agente de viajes.	*Ricardo is a travel agent.*

Note that after **ser** the indefinite article is not used with a profession or nationality unless it is modified by an adjective, as you will see later on in the book.

In a café in Buenos Aires. PEDRITO: Where are you from, Mr. Larkin? MR. LARKIN: Dr. Silva and I are from the United States. I'm from Texas. PEDRITO: You speak Spanish very well. MR. LARKIN: Thanks, you're very nice. PEDRITO: And you, Dr. Silva, are you also from Texas? DR. SILVA: No, I'm from California, Pedrito. PEDRITO: From California! Superman and Mickey Mouse are from there too, right...?

A. A que eres de Chile... (*I'll bet you're from Chile...*) Professor Benítez is a specialist in regional accents. Every time she hears someone speak, she guesses where the speaker is from. Make up questions she would ask, following the model.

Modelo   José/España
¿De dónde es José? ¿Es de España?

1. el doctor Lombardi / Argentina
2. los señores García / Cuba
3. Teresa / Paraguay
4. la profesora / Colombia
5. usted / Puerto Rico
6. los amigos de Susana / Chile
7. el profesor / Uruguay
8. ustedes / México

B. ¿Verdadero o falso?   If the statement is true, say **Verdadero**. If it is false, say **Falso** and restate it to make it correct.

1. Buenos Aires es la capital de Bolivia.
2. Yo soy Julio Iglesias.
3. Managua es la capital de Guatemala.
4. Ochenta y cinco más (*plus*) quince son noventa y cinco.
5. Fidel Castro es de Venezuela.
6. Ustedes son estudiantes.
7. Usted es primo (prima) de Jane Fonda.

C. ¿Quién soy? Pues...   Tell a group of three or four classmates a few things about yourself.

Modelos   Estudiante 1: **Soy Catalina. Soy estudiante de español. Soy de California. ¿Y tú?**

Estudiante 2: **Soy Ricardo. No soy de aquí. Soy de Montreal. Hablo inglés y francés. También soy estudiante de español. ¿Y tú?**

D. Personas famosas.   Describe four famous personalities and tell where they are from. Use the list of adjectives below in your descriptions.

Modelo   **Ralph Nader es idealista y sensible. Es de Connecticut.**

pesimista	responsable	amable	cortés
optimista	irresponsable	sensible	descortés
egoísta	idealista	insensible	intelectual
altruista	realista	popular	aburrido

Adjectives

En una avenida de Buenos Aires.

ANA   Allí está Patricia, una amiga de Chile.
NINA   ¿Es *chilena?* Andrés también es *chileno.*
ANA   Patricia es muy *simpática—cortés, sensible, trabajadora...*
NINA   Pues, Andrés también es *simpático—cortés, sensible, trabajador...*
ANA   ¡Una pareja *perfecta!* Quizás Andrés y Patricia...
JUAN   Un momento, chicas. ¡Andrés es hermano de Patricia!

1. ¿Es mexicana Patricia?, ¿y Andrés?   2. ¿Cómo es Patricia?, ¿y Andrés?
3. Según Juan, ¿quién es Andrés?

A. Agreement of adjectives.

1. In Spanish, adjectives must agree both in number and in gender with the nouns they modify. The most common singular endings for adjectives are **-o** (masculine) and **-a** (feminine).

un doctor famoso	*a famous doctor*	una doctora famosa	*a famous doctor*
un estudiante mexicano	*a Mexican student*	una estudiante mexicana	*a Mexican student*
un regalo bonito	*a pretty present*	una ciudad bonita	*a pretty city*
un plato muy delicioso	*a very delicious dish*	una comida muy deliciosa	*a very delicious meal*
un chico indio	*an Indian boy*	una chica india	*an Indian girl*

2. Adjectives of nationality that end in consonants and adjectives that end in **-dor** are made feminine by adding **-a**.

un turista inglés*	*an English tourist*	una turista inglesa	*an English tourist*
un chico trabajador	*a hard-working boy*	una chica trabajadora	*a hard-working girl*

* Remember that the written accent on the last syllable of the masculine form will not be necessary after you change the adjective to the feminine. Note also that adjectives of nationality are not capitalized.

On an avenue in Buenos Aires. ANA: There's Patricia, a friend from Chile. NINA: She's Chilean? Andrés is also Chilean. ANA: Patricia is very nice—polite, sensitive, hardworking... NINA: Well, Andrés is nice too—polite, sensitive, hard-working... ANA: A perfect couple (pair)! Perhaps Andrés and Patricia... JUAN: Just a moment, girls. Andrés is Patricia's brother!

3. With very few exceptions (which are not presented in this book), adjectives that don't end in **-o**, **-a**, or **-dor** have the same forms in the masculine and the feminine.

un examen difícil	*a difficult exam*	una lección difícil	*a difficult lesson*
un chico joven	*a young boy*	una chica joven	*a young girl*
un examen fácil	*an easy exam*	una lección fácil	*an easy lesson*

4. To form the plural of an adjective that ends in a vowel, add **-s**. To form the plural of an adjective that ends in a consonant, add **-es**.

las ciudades grandes	*the big cities*	los pasajeros franceses	*the French passengers*
unos exámenes difíciles	*some difficult exams*	unas lecciones fáciles	*some easy lessons*

B. Position of adjectives.

1. Most adjectives are descriptive—that is, they specify size, shape, color, type, nationality, and so forth. Descriptive adjectives usually follow the nouns they modify.

un hombre hispano	*a Hispanic man*	la chica norteamericana	*the North American girl*
unos señores amables	*some nice gentlemen*		

2. However, adjectives that specify quantity usually precede the nouns they modify.

dos semanas	*two weeks*	mucho progreso	*a lot of progress*
muchos regalos	*many presents*		

3. **Bueno(-a)** (*good*) and **malo(-a)** (*bad*) may be placed before or after a noun.

una buena comida		una mala niña	
una comida buena	*a good meal*	una niña mala	*a bad girl*

4. Before a masculine singular noun, **bueno** is shortened to **buen** and **malo** to **mal**.

un buen restaurante	*a good restaurant*
un mal ejemplo	*a bad example*

Grande becomes **gran** before a singular noun of either gender; it normally means *great* when it precedes a noun and *large* when it follows a noun.

un gran libro	*a great book*
un libro grande	*a big book*
una gran universidad	*a great university*
una universidad grande	*a large university*

EJERCICIOS

A. Los invitados. (*The guests.*)   Ana's friends are giving her a surprise party (for women only). Who will be the guests? Follow the model to find out.

Modelo   una prima (bueno y trabajador)
Una prima buena y trabajadora.

1. una estudiante (español)
2. una profesora (mexicano)
3. una señora (argentino)
4. una mujer (hispano)
5. una gran amiga (italiano)

6. una chica (inteligente y responsable)
7. una doctora (amable y simpático)
8. una señora (elegante y popular)
9. una tía (egoísta y aburrido)

B. Adjetivos correspondientes.   Complete each sentence with the adjectives in parentheses that could modify the person or thing indicated.

Modelo   Estudio en una universidad (buena, grande, joven, chileno, famosa, deliciosa).
Estudio en una universidad buena, grande y famosa.

1. Preparan una comida (sociable, argentina, joven, altruista, típica).
2. Están en un restaurante (grande, colombiana, elegante, nuevo, trabajador).
3. Aquí hay hoteles (típicos, buenos, malos, grandes, pequeñas).
4. Hablan con una pasajera (italiana, inglés, sensible, cortés, simpática).
5. Buscamos una avenida (amable, típica, elegante, pesimista, famosa).

C. Una familia interesante.   The Padillas are an interesting and unusual family. None of the children take after their parents. In fact, they are their exact opposites! Tell what each of them is like, following the models.

Modelos   El señor Padilla es sociable.   La señora Padilla es cortés.
          Los hijos son insociables.   **Las hijas son descorteses.**

1. El señor Padilla es cortés y sensible.
2. La señora Padilla es idealista.
3. El señor Padilla es responsable.

4. La señora Padilla es altruista.
5. El señor Padilla es optimista.

D. ¿Cómo es el amigo (la amiga) ideal?   Describe the ideal friend. Refer to the **Vocabulario activo** for help.

PREGUNTAS

1. ¿Hay buenos restaurantes mexicanos aquí? ¿españoles? ¿argentinos? ¿italianos? ¿Dónde?   **2.** ¿Prepara usted comida típica norteamericana? ¿mexicana? **3.** ¿Cómo es la comida de la cafetería de la universidad? (¿Buena o mala? ¿deliciosa? ¿horrible?)   **4.** ¿Cómo son los estudiantes de la universidad? (¿Inteligentes? ¿responsables? ¿buenos? ¿malos? ¿trabajadores? ¿sensibles? ¿simpáticos? ¿sociables?) **5.** ¿Cómo es la clase de español? (¿Fácil o difícil? ¿interesante o aburrida? ¿grande o pequeña?)

 Ser vs. *estar*

El Teatro Colón de Buenos Aires

En la Avenida Córdoba, en Buenos Aires.

ROBERTO	Por favor, señor, ¿dónde *está* el Teatro Colón?
RAMÓN	*Está* en la Avenida 9 de Julio. Usted no *es* de aquí, ¿verdad?
ROBERTO	No, *soy* turista. *Estoy* aquí con unos amigos. *Somos* de Bariloche y *estamos* perdidos.
RAMÓN	Pues, el teatro no *está* lejos. *Es* fácil llegar allí. *Es* muy grande y *está* cerca de una plaza muy linda.

1. ¿Dónde está Roberto?   2. ¿Está el teatro en la Avenida Córdoba?   3. ¿Quién es Roberto? ¿Con quiénes está él? ¿De dónde son ellos?   4. ¿Cómo es el teatro? ¿Está lejos?

On Córdoba Avenue in Buenos Aires. ROBERTO: Please, sir, where is the Colón Theater? RAMON: It's on 9 de Julio Avenue. You're not from here, are you? ROBERTO: No, I'm a tourist. I'm here with some friends. We're from Bariloche, and we're lost. RAMON: Well, the theater isn't far. It's easy to get there. It's very big, and it's near a very pretty plaza.

A. Ser is used:

1. To link the subject to a noun (or to an adjective used as a noun).

   Silvia es italiana. — *Silvia is (an) Italian.*
   Jorge y Luis son amigos. — *Jorge and Luis are friends.*
   El señor García es agente de viajes. — *Mr. García is a travel agent.*

2. With **de** to indicate origin (where someone or something is from).

   Soy de los Estados Unidos. —¡Bienvenido! — *I'm from the United States. — Welcome!*
   ¿De dónde es el regalo? —Es de México. — *Where is the present from? —It's from Mexico.*

3. To indicate where an event takes place.

   La ópera es en el Teatro Colón. — *The opera is in Colón Theater.*
   La exposición es en el museo. — *The exhibit is in the museum.*

4. With **de** to describe what something is made of.

   ¿Es de oro el reloj? — *Is the watch (made of) gold?*
   La mesa es de madera. — *The table is wooden (made of wood).*

5. With **de** to indicate possession.

   El reloj es de Ricardo. — *The watch is Ricardo's.*
   La cámara es de la señora italiana. — *The camera is the Italian woman's.*

6. With an adjective that is considered normal or characteristic of the subject.

   Marta es trabajadora. — *Marta is hardworking.*
   El señor Torres es amable. — *Mr. Torres is nice.*

B. Estar is used:

1. To indicate location or position.

   El hotel está en la avenida Colón. — *The hotel is on Colón Avenue.*
   Nosotros estamos enfrente de «La Casa Mexicana». — *We are in front of "La Casa Mexicana."*
   Están de vacaciones en Bogotá. — *They are on vacation in Bogotá.*
   ¿Dónde está la agencia de viajes? ¿A la izquierda o a la derecha? — *Where is the travel agency? On the left or on the right?*

2. To indicate the condition of a person or thing at a particular time or with adjectives that are thought of as true of the subject at a particular time, but not always. (This is often the result of a change).

   ¿Cómo estás? —Estoy bien, gracias. — *How are you? —I'm fine, thanks.*
   A veces el aire está contaminado. — *At times the air is polluted.*
   Adela está nerviosa hoy. — *Adela is nervous today (though not always).*

   Otra vez estamos perdidos. — *We are lost again.*

A. ¿Ser o estar? Complete the sentences, using the appropriate forms of **ser** or **estar**.

1. Los profesores ingleses _____ amables.
2. Tú _____ nervioso hoy, ¿verdad?
3. Juan _____ allí otra vez.
4. ¿ _____ el examen de Rubén?
5. Nosotros _____ italianos.
6. Ustedes _____ en la clase de español.
7. Carmen _____ perdida.
8. Yo _____ de la Argentina.
9. La silla _____ de madera.

B. En las nubes. (*In the clouds.*) When Rubén daydreams, he misses half of what is said. He asks questions to confirm what he thinks he's heard. Answer his questions, following the models.

Modelos   ¿Los viajes? ¿interesantes?
Sí, los viajes son interesantes.

¿Tomás? ¿en clase?
Sí, Tomás está en clase.

1. ¿Ricardo? ¿en Bogotá?
2. ¿Los López? ¿de vacaciones?
3. ¿La universidad? ¿grande?
4. ¿Los abuelos? ¿bien?
5. ¿Nosotros? ¿estudiantes?
6. ¿Yo? ¿de Nueva York?
7. ¿Marta? ¿en casa?
8. ¿El reloj? ¿de oro?
9. ¿Tú? ¿nervioso hoy?
10. ¿La ópera? ¿Teatro Nacional?

C. Completar el párrafo. Complete the following paragraph, using the appropriate forms of **ser** or **estar**.

Ahora yo _____ en clase. Pepito _____ en casa porque no _____ bien. Él y yo _____ hermanos; _____ solos (*alone*) porque papá y mamá _____ de vacaciones en Buenos Aires. Ellos _están_ en un hotel muy grande. Mamá dice (*says*) en una carta (*letter*): «La ciudad es muy bonita, pero el aire _está_ muy contaminado. El hotel _es_ moderno. A la izquierda _es_ la agencia de viajes y a la derecha _es_ la casa de los abuelos de Lucía. Ahora nosotros _estamos_ en un restaurante en la Avenida 9 de Julio. Hoy deseamos visitar el Teatro Colón; _es_ muy famoso y _está_ cerca de aquí.» Papá y mamá _están_ muy bien en Buenos Aires. _Es_ un viaje interesante, ¿verdad?

D. Juan Ramírez. Using the words shown, make sentences about Juan Ramírez. Use **ser** or **estar**, as appropriate.

Modelo **Es inteligente.**

1. de Córdoba
2. doctor
3. en el hospital
4. altruista
5. bien

6. argentino
7. de vacaciones
8. en Mar del Plata ahora
9. nervioso
10. amigo del presidente

PREGUNTAS

1. ¿Es usted norteamericano(-a)? ¿Es de Nueva York? ¿de California? ¿De dónde es usted? **2.** ¿Es usted inteligente? ¿trabajador(-a)? ¿optimista? ¿Cómo es usted? **3.** ¿Está usted nervioso(-a) hoy? ¿Por qué? ¿Cómo está usted hoy? **4.** ¿Dónde están los estudiantes que no están en clase hoy? (¿en casa? ¿en la cafetería? ¿en otra clase?) **5.** ¿Está lindo el día?

The contractions *al* and *del*

En un autobús en la Avenida Córdoba.

UNA TURISTA	¿Cómo llegamos *al* Teatro Payró? ¿Por qué no preguntas?
EL ESPOSO	Por favor, señor, ¿dónde está el Teatro Payró? ¿Está cerca o lejos de aquí?
UN SEÑOR	Muy cerca. Está allí a la izquierda, *al* lado *del* Café Córdoba.
LA TURISTA	Gracias, señor. (*al* esposo) ¿Qué tal si bajamos *del* autobús ahora...?

1. ¿Dónde están los turistas? 2. ¿Está el Teatro Payró a la izquierda o a la derecha? ¿Está cerca? 3. ¿Está al lado del café o al lado del hotel?

$$a + el = al \qquad\qquad de + el = del$$

The definite article **el** contracts with **a** to form **al** and with **de** to form **del**. The other articles do not contract.

Las chicas llegan al teatro (a la ciudad, a los Estados Unidos, al país).

Estamos lejos del museo (de la universidad, de los hoteles, de las agencias).

The girls arrive at the theater (at the city, in the United States, in the country).

We're far from the museum (from the university, from the hotels, from the agencies).

EJERCICIOS

A. **¿Verdadero o falso?** Look at the map of South America on page 62. Then react to the following statements with **Verdadero** or **Falso.** If the statement is false, correct it.

```
          NORTE



OESTE              ESTE



          SUR
```

1. La Argentina está al oeste de Chile.
2. Uruguay está al sur del Brasil.
3. El Salvador está en Sudamérica.
4. Ecuador está al norte del Perú.
5. Venezuela está lejos del Paraguay.
6. Colombia está cerca del Uruguay.

B. **Imaginación y lógica.** Form sentences for each group of words, using them in the order given.

Modelo   hotel / izquierda / aeropuerto
El hotel está a la izquierda del aeropuerto.

1. restaurante / lado / universidad
2. hospital / izquierda / farmacia
3. universidad / cerca / teatro
4. museo / derecha / agencia
5. aeropuerto / lejos / ciudad

On a bus on Córdoba Avenue. WOMAN TOURIST: How do we get to the Payró Theater? Why don't you ask? HER ("THE") HUSBAND: Excuse me, sir. Where is the Payró Theater? Is it near or far from here? A GENTLEMAN: Very near. It's there on the left, beside the Córdoba Café. WOMAN TOURIST: Thank you, sir. (to her husband) How about if we get off the bus now...?

1. ¿Desea usted viajar a la ciudad de México? ¿al Perú? ¿Adónde desea viajar? **2.** ¿Lleva usted un pasaporte cuando viaja al Canadá? ¿a la Argentina? ¿a Tejas? ¿a Nueva York? **3.** En la clase de español, ¿está usted cerca o lejos de la puerta? ¿Quién está a la derecha de usted? ¿a la izquierda? **4.** ¿Está la universidad lejos o cerca del aeropuerto? ¿de un buen restaurante?

The personal *a*

El señor mira a la señorita.

El señor mira los precios.

Elena busca al niño.

Elena busca el Hotel Nacional en el mapa (*map*).

The personal **a** must precede a direct object that refers to a person or persons. The direct object is the word that indicates the person or thing that is acted upon (or that receives the action of the verb directly). In the sentence *I give the book to Jim*, *the book* is what is given—it is the direct object. In the sentence *I see Jim*, *Jim* is the person who is seen—he's the direct object. In Spanish, direct objects that refer to people must be preceded by the personal **a**. Compare:

Teresa visita a los señores Navarro.   *Teresa is visiting Mr. and Mrs. Navarro.*
Necesitamos a la doctora.   *We need the doctor.*

but:

Teresa visita el Museo de Historia   *Teresa is visiting the Natural History*
  Natural.   *Museum.*
Necesitamos una casa grande.   *We need a big house.*

Like **visitar**, **mirar**, and **buscar**, the verb **llamar** (*to call*) often requires the personal **a**:

Llama al profesor.   *He (She) calls the professor.*

EJERCICIOS

A. Un detective. Alfonso is an amateur detective. Tell what (or whom) he's looking, using the cues.

> **Modelo**   el hotel / los turistas
> **Alfonso busca el hotel y también busca a los turistas.**

1. la casa de Luis / Luis
2. el pasaporte / una dirección
3. el señor Méndez / un restaurante
4. los abuelos / una mujer italiana
5. las cámaras / los pasajeros
6. los estudiantes / el profesor Ruiz

B. Traducción. Give the Spanish equivalent of the following sentences.

1. Juan looks at Adela.
2. They are looking for a good restaurant.
3. The student visits the museum.
4. I want to visit Mr. Flores.
5. The travel agent is calling the tourists now.

PREGUNTAS

1. ¿Visita usted a unos amigos hoy? ¿al (a la) profesor(-a) de español?   **2.** ¿Llama usted mucho a los amigos? ¿a un(-a) amigo(-a) en particular? ¿A quién desea llamar hoy? ¿mañana? ¿el fin de semana próximo (*next*)?   **3.** ¿Mira usted televisión? ¿Mira a veces (*sometimes*) al presidente en la televisión?   **4.** ¿Necesita usted a veces a los profesores? ¿a un(-a) profesor(-a) en particular?   **5.** Cuando usted está de vacaciones, ¿qué visita? (¿teatros? ¿otras ciudades? ¿otros países?) ¿A quién(-es) visita? (¿a amigos? ¿a parientes? ¿a otras personas?)

Buenos Aires: Bienvenidos al París de Sudamérica

El obelisco de la Avenida 9 de Julio, en Buenos Aires

En un autobús. Los señores Smith están de vacaciones en Buenos Aires. Buscan el Museo de Historia Natural°.

SR. SMITH	¡Dios mío!, el tráfico está horrible y el aire está contaminado.
SRA. SMITH	Es el precio del progreso. Pero los porteños[1] son amables y la ciudad es bonita, ¿no?
SR. SMITH	Sí, pero es muy grande. Estoy perdido... ¿Cómo llegamos al museo?
SRA. SMITH	¿Por qué no preguntamos?
SR. SMITH	Buena idea. (*Habla con un pasajero.*) Por favor... ¿dónde está el Museo de Historia Natural?
EL PASAJERO	Está lejos. Ustedes no son de aquí, ¿verdad?
SRA. SMITH	No, somos ingleses.
EL PASAJERO	¡Ah!, son de Inglaterra°. Pues... bienvenidos al París de Sudamérica. ¿Por qué desean visitar el museo?
SRA. SMITH	Para mirar las exposiciones sobre los animales[2] típicos del país, sobre la cultura de los indios y sobre...
EL PASAJERO	Un momento, por favor. Me llamo Emilio Discotto[3] y soy agente de viajes. Por casualidad° estamos enfrente de la agencia *Viajes Discotto*. ¿Por qué no bajamos?

SR. SMITH	¿Para visitar el museo?
EL PASAJERO	No. Pero es posible visitar una estancia° moderna, visitar a los gauchos[4] y...
SRA. SMITH	Gracias, señor. Otro día, quizás. Hoy deseamos visitar el famoso Museo de Historia Natural.
EL PASAJERO	Bueno, adiós... ¡Y buena suerte!

El señor Discotto baja del autobús. Los señores Smith no bajan.

SR. SMITH	¿Por qué no preguntas otra vez?
SRA. SMITH	Buena idea. (*A un pasajero*) Por favor... ¿dónde está el Museo de Historia Natural?
EL PASAJERO	Está lejos. Ustedes no son de aquí, ¿verdad?...

Historia Natural *Natural History* **Inglaterra** *England*
Por casualidad *By chance* **estancia** *ranch*

PREGUNTAS

1. ¿Dónde están los señores Smith? 2. ¿De dónde son ellos? 3. ¿Qué buscan?
4. ¿Qué pregunta el señor Smith? 5. ¿Cómo se llama el pasajero? 6. ¿Por qué desean visitar el museo los señores Smith? 7. ¿Es agente de viajes el señor Discotto? 8. ¿Adónde desea llevar él a los señores Smith? 9. Al final (*In the end*), ¿llegan al museo? 10. ¿Visita usted museos con frecuencia (*frequently*)?

Notas culturales

1. **Porteño** (literally, *port dweller*) is the usual term for someone who lives in Buenos Aires, Argentina's capital and main port on the Río de la Plata. **Porteños** call their city "the Paris of South America."

2. Because of the variety of its terrain, Argentina has a number of unusual animals, like the **jaguar**; the **cóndor**, the largest bird of flight; and the **carpincho**, the largest living rodent, which sometimes attains a weight of one hundred pounds and in some parts of South America is hunted by the natives for food.

3. If the surname *Discotto* sounds more Italian than Spanish to you, you are correct. A large number of Argentineans are of Italian descent. In addition to Spanish and Italian influence, the British, French, and Germans have also contributed to Argentina's population.

4. The **gaucho**, or Argentine cowboy, is now more a legendary figure than a real one. In the early 1800s thousands of these men led a nomadic life on the **pampas** (*dry grasslands*), living off the wild herds of cattle and horses that had descended from those of the Spanish conquistadors. The word is also used for the descendants of the original **gauchos**, who now work as ranchhands on the large **estancias** (*Argentine ranches*) and preserve some of the old traditions.

FUNCIONES Y ACTIVIDADES

In this chapter you have seen examples of the following language functions, or uses. Here is a summary and some additional information about these functions of language.

Making descriptions (1)

In this chapter you've seen how to use adjectives with both **ser** and **estar**. Consult the **Vocabulario activo** for a complete list of adjectives from this chapter.

Expressing admiration

A common way to express admiration is with an exclamation containing an adjective. To form exclamations, you can use the word **¡Qué...!** + an adjective. The adjective should agree with the noun it describes in gender and number.

¡Qué interesante!   (el libro)   ¡Qué lindos!   (los relojes)

To include a noun in the exclamation, use **¡Qué...!** + noun (+ **más**) + adjective.

¡Qué niño (más) cortés!	*What a polite child!*
¡Qué señora (más) simpática!	*What a nice lady!*
¡Qué chicos (más) trabajadores!	*What hardworking young people!*
¡Qué casas (más) bonitas!	*What pretty houses!*

Describing locations

Here are some prepositions referring to place or position that you have seen so far in this book.

a la derecha	*on (to) the right*	cerca (de)	*near*
a la izquierda	*on (to) the left*	detrás (de)	*behind*
al lado de	*beside, next to*	enfrente (de)	*in front of*
		lejos (de)	*far from*

A. Descripciones. Use **¡Qué...!** + noun (+ **más**) + adjective to describe these pictures. You may want to choose from these adjectives: **grande, pequeño, elegante, delicioso, interesante, difícil, viejo, cortés.**

Modelo

¡Qué pasajeros (más) corteses!

1.
2.
3.
4.
5.
6.

B. Poema. In small groups write a short poem about someone you know. Use the following guidelines if you wish.

Line 1: name of person(-s)
Line 2: two adjectives that describe the person(-s)
Line 3: a place you associate with the person(-s)
Line 4: a descriptive phrase
Line 5: another adjective

La profesora Jones
simpática, inteligente
en la clase
con los estudiantes
paciente

C. En la Avenida Santa Fe. Describe the picture using prepositions. Include answers to the following questions.

El doctor habla con el conductor (*driver*) del autobús. ¿Quién está más cerca de ellos: el policía (*the policeman*) o la señora? ¿Está el doctor a la izquierda o a la derecha del auto? ¿Quién está detrás del auto: la señora o el conductor? ¿Dónde están los pasajeros? ¿Y el conductor?

D. Una foto. (*A photo.*) For this activity, someone should bring to class a camera that develops pictures instantly. Take several pictures of the class, in groups or as a whole, with people in different positions for each. Then, in small groups, describe one of the pictures: **Susan está a la izquierda de Jennifer. Scott está enfrente de Peter; está al lado de Chris...** Then the groups can compare their descriptions.

E. Situaciones. Role-play the following situations.

1. Your boyfriend or girlfriend has called you the following things during a fight: selfish, rude, insensitive, and so on. A friend calls you, and you describe the conversation: _____ **dice que yo soy...** ([name] *says that I am...*). Your friend tells you that these things aren't true—you're not really selfish, rude, insensitive, and so on.

2. You and a friend are on a bus in La Plata, near Buenos Aires. "What a beautiful city!" your friend says. You ask another passenger where the Museum of Natural History is and if it is far. The passenger replies, "No, it's nearby." You have a short conversation with the passenger, who asks you who you are, where you are from, and so forth. The passenger compliments you on your Spanish, and you say, "Thank you, you're very nice." "The Museum of Natural History is there on the left," says the passenger. You say good-bye and get off.

VOCABULARIO ACTIVO

Cognados

el aire	famoso	irresponsable	pesimista
altruista	hispano	italiano	popular
argentino	la idea	mexicano	el, la presidente
colombiano	idealista	moderno	el progreso
chileno	indio	el museo	realista
delicioso	insociable	norteamericano	responsable
el doctor, la doctora	intelectual	la ópera	el teatro
elegante	inteligente	optimista	típico
el estado	interesante	la persona	el tráfico
el examen	internacional		

Verbos

bajar de	to get off
estar de vacaciones	to be on vacation
llamar	to call
preguntar	to ask
preparar	to prepare
ser	to be

Expresiones útiles

a la derecha	on (to) the right
a la izquierda	on (to) the left
al lado (de)	beside, next to
cerca (de)	near
detrás (de)	behind
enfrente (de)	in front (of); across (from), opposite
lejos (de)	far (from)

Adjetivos

aburrido	*boring*
amable	*nice, friendly*
bonito	*pretty*
bueno	*good*
contaminado	*polluted*
cortés	*courteous, polite*
descortés	*impolite*
difícil	*difficult*
egoísta	— *selfish*
fácil	*easy*
grande	(**gran** *before a masculine singular noun*) *big, tall; great*
insensible	— *insensitive*
joven	*young (plural:* **jóvenes***)*
lindo	*beautiful*
malo	*bad; sick*
nuevo	*new*
pequeño	*small, little*
perdido	*lost*
sensible	*sensitive*
simpático	*nice*
trabajador	*hardworking*
viejo	*old*

Otras palabras y frases

la agencia de viajes	*travel agency*
el, la agente de viajes	*travel agent*
el autobús	*bus*
bienvenido	*welcome*
la comida	*food; meal*
la chica	*girl, young person*
el chico	*boy, guy, young person*
la exposición	— *exhibit*
la madera	— *wood*
el oro	*gold*
otra vez	*again, once more*
otro	*other, another*
el país	*country*
el pasajero, la pasajera	— *passenger*
el plato	— *plate; dish*
el precio	*price*
quizás	*perhaps*
el reloj	*watch; clock*
según	*according to*
la vez	*time, instance*

El mundo hispano

Parinacota, volcán de los Andes, Chile

Una playa, en Marbella, España

OCÉANO ATLÁNTICO

FRANCIA

Los Pirineos

• Santiago

Barcelona •

PORTUGAL

Madrid ●

Valencia •

Baleares

ESPAÑA

Sevilla
•

Granada

Cádiz

MAR MEDITERRÁNEO

• Gibraltar

ESTRECHO DE
GIBRALTAR

ÁFRICA

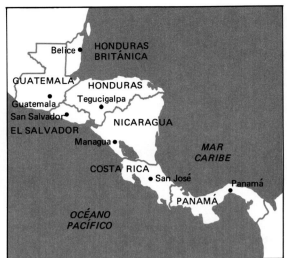

Belice •

HONDURAS
BRITÁNICA

GUATEMALA

HONDURAS

Guatemala •

Tegucigalpa
•

San Salvador •

NICARAGUA

EL SALVADOR

Managua •

MAR
CARIBE

COSTA RICA

• San José

Panamá •

PANAMÁ

OCÉANO
PACÍFICO

ESTADOS UNIDOS

Monterrey
•

GOLFO DE
MÉXICO

La Paz •

MÉXICO

Guadalajara
•

• Jalapa

Mérida •

Península
e Yucatán

México D.F. •

OCÉANO
PACÍFICO

OCÉANO ATLÁNTICO

Caracas •

VENEZUELA

COLOMBIA

GUAYANAS

Quito
•

Bogotá •

ECUADOR

PERÚ

BRASIL

• Lima

Los Andes

La Paz •

BOLIVIA

PARAGUAY

CHILE

• Asunción

ARGENTINA

URUGUAY

Santiago •

Montevideo •

Buenos Aires •

OCÉANO
PACÍFICO

OCÉANO ATLÁNTICO

• Miami

La Habana •

Is. Bahamas

I. de Pinos

CUBA

REPÚBLICA
DOMINICANA

JAMAICA

HAITÍ

San Juan
•

Kingston •

Port-au-Prince •

Santo
Domingo

PUERTO
RICO

MAR CARIBE

As you can see from the accompanying maps, the Spanish-speaking world covers a vast territory: Spain; Mexico; Central America, except British Honduras; Cuba, Puerto Rico, and the Dominican Republic in the Caribbean; and all of South America, except Brazil and **las Guayanas** (Guiana, Surinam, and French Guiana). Consequently, the Spanish-speaking world is one of geographical contrasts. One can travel from the deserts of northern Mexico to the tropical forests of Central America, to the mountainous Andes regions, to the glaciers at the tip of South America. Almost every imaginable climate and terrain are encompassed by **el mundo hispano.**

Here is a short geographical quiz about the Spanish-speaking world. If you don't know the answers, a glance at the maps will provide them.

1. La ciudad de Madrid está: a. en el norte de España   b. en el centro de España   c. en el sur de España.
2. Los Pirineos separan a España de: a. África   b. Portugal   c. Francia.
3. La ciudad de Granada está en Andalucía, famosa por la música flamenca (*gypsy music*). Una ciudad que está cerca es: a. Montevideo   b. Sevilla   c. San José.
4. El estrecho (*strait*) de Gibraltar separa a España de: a. África   b. Portugal   c. Francia.
5. La península de Yucatán está en: a. Chile   b. España   c. México.
6. La capital de Bolivia es: a. La Paz   b. Asunción   c. Quito.
7. Dos islas del Caribe son: a. Cuba y Belice   b. Cuba y Puerto Rico   c. El Salvador y República Dominicana.
8. La capital de Puerto Rico es: a. Managua   b. Jalapa   c. San Juan.
9. La ciudad de Tegucigalpa está en: a. México   b. Perú   c. Honduras.
10. Los Andes están: a. en el oeste de Sudamérica   b. en el centro de Sudamérica   c. en el este de Sudamérica.
11. Argentina está al sur de: a. Uruguay   b. Paraguay   c. Chile.
12. Los dos países sin (*without*) comunicación directa con el Atlántico o el Pacífico son: a. Paraguay y Uruguay   b. Ecuador y Bolivia   c. Bolivia y Paraguay.

1. el policía
   (la mujer policía)

2. el músico
   (la músico)

3. el abogado
   (la abogada)

4. la agente de viajes
   (el agente de viajes)

5. la comerciante
   (el comerciante)

7. el camarero
   (la camarera)

8. la escritora
   (el escritor)

9. el vendedor
   (la vendedora)

AGENCIA DE VIAJES

6. la doctora
(el doctor)

). el ingeniero
(la ingeniera)

Estudios y profesiones

3

Telling Time
Expressing Incomprehension

PREGUNTAS

1. ¿Cuál es la profesión de Bruce Springsteen? ¿de F. Lee Bailey? ¿de Donald Trump? ¿de Benjamin Spock? ¿de Gabriel García Márquez?   **2.** ¿Cómo se llama la persona que trabaja (*works*) en un restaurante? ¿en una boutique? ¿en una agencia de viajes?   **3.** ¿Qué profesión asocia usted con Perry Mason? ¿con Cliff Huxtable (del "Cosby Show")?   **4.** ¿Qué materia (*subject*) asocia usted con Sigmund Freud? (*See next page.*) ¿con Marie Curie? ¿con Miguel de Cervantes? ¿con Margaret Mead? ¿con Albert Schweitzer? ¿con John Locke? ¿con Blaise Pascal? ¿con Margaret Thatcher? **5.** ¿Estudia usted historia? ¿ciencias políticas? ¿español?   **6.** ¿Qué estudia usted? ¿Qué desea estudiar en el futuro?

EJERCICIO

Each of these people is looking for books in the bookstore. Tell what field each is studying.

Modelo   Consuelo busca libros sobre plantas y animales.
             Estudia biología.

1. Adela busca libros sobre las ideas de Carlos Jung.
2. Eduardo busca libros sobre Shakespeare y Cervantes.
3. Felipe busca libros sobre Sócrates y Aristóteles.
4. Ana busca libros sobre las civilizaciones azteca y maya.
5. Manuel busca libros sobre ecuaciones $(24x + 6y = 150)$.
6. Pedro busca libros sobre la estructura del átomo.

Telling time

¿Qué hora es?

Es la una en punto.   **Es la una y cuarto (y quince).**   **Es la una y media (y treinta).**

Son las dos menos veinte.   **Son las dos menos cuarto.**   **Son las cuatro y diez.**

de (por) la mañana

de (por) la tarde

de (por) la noche   ¿A qué hora llega el avión?   **Llega a las diez y cuarto de la mañana.**

De la mañana (tarde, noche) means A.M. (P.M.). **Por la mañana (tarde, noche)** is normally used to talk about time of day. **En punto** means *on the dot*.

A. ¿Qué hora es? Look at the five clocks below and tell the time in Spanish.

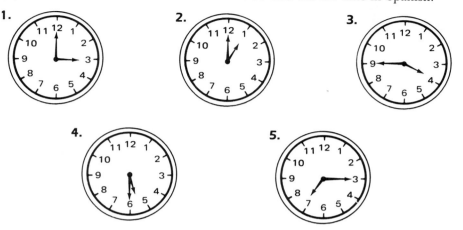

B. ¿A qué hora llega el avión? Using the following chart, tell the arrival time of each of the planes coming from the cities listed there. Airline schedules in the Hispanic world are usually on a twenty-four-hour system, where 12:00 is noon and 24:00 is midnight.

Modelo La Paz / 14:30
El avión de La Paz llega a las dos y media de la tarde.

Ciudad de origen	Hora de llegada (*arrival*)
Buenos Aires	18:30
San Francisco	8:45
Acapulco	22:15
Puerto Rico	9:30
La Paz	14:30
Madrid	6:45
Caracas	17:00

C. Llegadas y salidas. (*Arrivals and departures.*) Write different times, such as 3:00 P.M. or 6:05 A.M., on a sheet of paper and read them to a classmate as if they were arriving and departing flights. Your classmate will write down the times and read them back when the list is complete. **En español, ¡claro!**

PREGUNTAS

1. ¿Qué hora es? **2.** ¿A qué hora llega usted a la clase de español? **3.** ¿Mira usted televisión? ¿A qué hora? ¿Qué programa(-s) mira? **4.** ¿A qué hora llega usted a la universidad? ¿Practica español en el laboratorio? ¿A qué hora? **5.** ¿Estudia usted por la noche o por la mañana? ¿A qué hora?

The present tense of regular *-er* and *-ir* verbs

JUAN   *Lees* y *escribes* mucho, Luisa. ¿Qué *lees* ahora?
LUISA   *Leo* un libro de filosofía y *escribo* notas para una composición.
JUAN   ¿Cómo? No *comprendo. Vivimos* en el siglo veinte. *Debes leer* libros prácticos,
         aprender matemáticas, ciencias de computación, ingeniería o física.
LUISA   Pero Juan, también *debemos* estudiar filosofía. En la filosofía *descubrimos*
         «la verdad en la vida y la vida en la verdad».
JUAN   *Creo* que los filósofos *comprenden* el pasado, pero tú *debes* estudiar para el
         futuro.

---

1. ¿Lee mucho Luisa? ¿Qué lee ahora?   2. ¿Qué escribe Luisa?   3. ¿Qué cree Juan que debemos leer?   4. ¿Qué cree Juan que debemos aprender?   5. ¿Qué descubrimos en la filosofía?   6. ¿Con quién está usted de acuerdo (*in agreement*): con Juan o con Luisa? ¿Por qué?

A. To conjugate regular verbs ending in **-er** or **-ir**, remove the infinitive ending and add the present-tense endings to the stem. The endings are the same for both types of verbs, except in the **nosotros** and **vosotros** forms.

	comer (to eat)	**vivir** (to live)
yo	com**o**	viv**o**
tú	com**es**	viv**es**
él, ella, usted	com**e**	viv**e**
nosotros(-as)	com**emos**	viv**imos**
vosotros(-as)	com**éis**	viv**ís**
ellos, ellas, ustedes	com**en**	viv**en**

JUAN: You read and write a lot, Luisa. What are you reading now? LUISA: I am reading a philosophy book, and I'm writing (taking) notes for a composition. JUAN: What? I don't understand. We live in the twentieth century. You should read practical books and learn mathematics, computer science, engineering, or physics. LUISA: But, Juan, we should also study philosophy. In philosophy we discover "truth in life and life in truth" (*a well-known phrase of the Spanish philosopher Miguel de Unamuno*). JUAN: I think (believe) that philosophers understand the past, but you should study for the future.

B. Other verbs conjugated like **comer** are:

aprender   *to learn*
comprender   *to understand*
creer   *to think, believe*

deber   *should, must, ought to*
leer   *to read*
vender   *to sell*

Debe ser importante. —¡Claro!
Leemos un libro sobre política.
Es bastante interesante.
Creo que Manuela todavía vive cerca
   de la biblioteca.
¿Venden libros de texto en la librería
   de la Avenida Castro?

It must be important. —Of course!
We are reading a book about politics.
It's rather (quite) interesting.
I believe that Manuela still lives near the
   library.
Do they sell textbooks in the bookstore on
   Castro Avenue?

C. Other verbs conjugated like **vivir** are:

abrir   *to open*
decidir   *to decide*
descubrir   *to discover*

escribir   *to write*
recibir   *to receive*

¿Abres la ventana?
¿Cuántas cartas escriben ustedes cada
   semana? ¿Cuántas reciben?*
Deben aprender español si deciden
   vivir en México.

Are you opening the window?
How many letters do you write each week?
   How many do you receive?
You should learn Spanish if you decide to
   live in Mexico.

EJERCICIOS

A. En acción.   Look at the drawings and tell what the people are doing.

1. Susana...

2. Los doctores...

---

* **¿Cuánto(-a, -os, -as)?** is an interrogative word meaning *how much?* or *how many?* It agrees in gender
and number with the noun it modifies, expressed or implied.

3. El señor Ortiz...

4. Los estudiantes...

5. La niña...

6. El señor Montero...

B. Imaginación y lógica. Create as many logical sentences as you can, combining material from the three columns.

Modelos **La doctora Pérez vive en una casa muy moderna.**
La doctora Pérez recibe al abogado Méndez.

ustedes no	recibir	la lección de física
los vendedores	abrir	libros y cuadernos
tú	vivir	en la cafetería de la universidad
el profesor de historia	leer	estudiar
la doctora Pérez	escribir	al abogado Méndez
yo no	aprender	una carta
Ricardo y tú	vender	mucho
nosotros no	deber	en una casa muy moderna
los músicos	comprender	la puerta
el camarero	comer	creer al doctor

C. ¿Dónde vives?   Ask a classmate about what he or she lives near.

Modelo   the university

> Estudiante 1:   **¿Vives cerca de la universidad?**
> Estudiante 2:   **Sí, vivo cerca de la universidad. (No, vivo lejos de la universidad.)**

1. a library
2. a good bookstore
3. the hospital
4. a Mexican (Italian, Spanish, French) restaurant

5. a museum
6. a theater
7. a café (*un café*)
8. a travel agency

Now make a sentence naming several things your classmate lives close to.

PREGUNTAS

1. ¿Lee usted un libro ahora? ¿Cómo se llama?   **2.** ¿Lee usted muchos libros? ¿Lee libros de música? ¿de matemáticas? ¿de ciencias naturales?   **3.** ¿De qué libro o libros aprende usted mucho?   **4.** ¿Cree que la química es aburrida o interesante? ¿Es fácil o difícil? ¿Y la filosofía? ¿Y la literatura?   **5.** ¿Come usted en la cafetería de la universidad? ¿Come bien o mal en la cafetería?   **6.** ¿Escribe usted muchas cartas? ¿muchas composiciones?   **7.** ¿Recibe usted muchas cartas cada semana? ¿De quién(-es)? ¿De dónde?   **8.** ¿Vive usted con un (-a) amigo(-a)?   **9.** ¿En qué ciudad vivimos? ¿En qué estado?

Demonstrative adjectives and pronouns

En la Universidad Nacional Autónoma de México.

BOB   ¡Qué grande es *esta* universidad! *Aquel* mural, ¿de quién es?
PACO   ¿*Aquél* que está en la biblioteca? Es de Juan O'Gorman. Representa la historia de México.
BOB   Y *esas* figuras, ¿a quiénes representan?
PACO   Son indios de siglos pasados. Y *ésas* que están a la derecha son dioses aztecas y mayas.
BOB   ¿Ah, sí? ¡Una inspiración divina para los estudios!

At the National Autonomous University of Mexico. BOB: How big this university is! That mural, who is it by (whose is it)? PACO: That one that is on the library? It's by Juan O'Gorman. It represents the history of Mexico. BOB: And those figures, who do they represent? PACO: They're Indians from centuries past. And those that are on the right are Aztec and Mayan gods. BOB: Oh yeah? Divine inspiration for your (one's) studies!

Mural de Juan O'Gorman en la Biblioteca Central de la UNAM, Ciudad de México

1. ¿Dónde están Bob y Paco?   2. ¿De quién es el mural que está en la biblioteca? ¿Qué representa?   3. ¿A quíenes representan las figuras del mural?

A. Demonstrative adjectives.

1. Demonstrative adjectives are used to point out a particular person or object. They precede the nouns they modify and agree with them in gender and number.

	Demonstrative Adjectives		
	Masculine	**Feminine**	
Singular	este	esta	*this*
	ese	esa	*that*
	aquel	aquella	*that (over there)*
Plural	estos	estas	*these*
	esos	esas	*those*
	aquellos	aquellas	*those (over there)*

Este autobús va muy despacio.	*This bus is going very slowly.*
¡Esta librería es estupenda!	*This bookstore is great!*
Si esa muchacha se llama Luisa, ese muchacho que está con ella es Alberto.	*If that girl's name is Luisa, that boy (that is) with her is Alberto.*
¿Quiénes son esas personas? Por ejemplo, esos chicos que están con los García...	*Who are those people? For example, those guys who are with the Garcías...*
Aquella joven estudia arquitectura.	*That young woman over there is studying architecture.*
Aquel hombre es ingeniero.	*That man (over there) is an engineer.*

2. Both **ese** and **aquel** correspond to *that* in English. **Ese**, **esa**, **esos**, and **esas** indicate persons or objects located fairly close to the person addressed. **Aquel**, **aquella**, **aquellos**, and **aquellas** indicate persons or objects that are distant from both the speaker and the person spoken to.*

B. Demonstrative pronouns.

1. Demonstrative pronouns in Spanish have the same forms as demonstrative adjectives, except that the pronouns have written accents. They agree in gender and number with the nouns they replace.

¿Éste? Es un libro de alemán.	*This? It's a German book.*
¿Éstos? Son calendarios.	*These? They're calendars.*
¿Ése? Es un estudiante francés.	*That one? He's a French student.*
¿Quiénes son aquellas chicas? —¿Aquéllas? Son amigas de Magdalena.	*Who are those girls? —Those (over there)? They're friends of Magdalena.*

2. There are three neuter demonstrative pronouns in Spanish: **esto** (*this*), **eso** (*that*), and **aquello** (*that* [more distant]). They are used to refer to statements, abstract ideas, or something that has not been identified. There are no plural forms, and they do not have written accents.

Esto no es muy bueno.	*This (situation, idea, etc.) isn't very good.*
¿Qué es eso?	*What's that?*
Todo aquello es de don Sancho.	*All that (over there) is Don Sancho's.*

EJERCICIOS

A. **Chismes profesionales.** (*Professional gossip.*) What's new? To find out, change the subject of each sentence from masculine to feminine and make any other necessary changes.

Modelo Ese profesor es aburrido.
Esa profesora es aburrida también.

1. Esos escritores son malos.
2. Aquel doctor es excelente.

---

* **Aquel** and its forms are used less commonly in the New World than in Spain.

3. Ese estudiante es muy irresponsable.
4. Este ingeniero es muy trabajador.
5. Aquellos comerciantes italianos son muy amables.
6. Estos músicos son famosos y populares.

B. Compañeros de clase. (*Classmates.*) Using adjectives from the **Vocabulario activo** of Chapter 2 or others you know, describe your classmates. Use demonstrative adjectives and pronouns to indicate whom you mean.

Modelos **Esa estudiante es buena y aquéllas son excelentes.**
Estos chicos son trabajadores y ésos también.

C. Respuestas breves. (*Brief responses.*) Answer each question with one word, as in the model, pointing to the object(-s) or person(-s) as you respond.

Modelo ¿Cuál es el lápiz de usted?
Éste.

1. ¿Cuáles son los papeles del profesor (de la profesora)?
2. ¿Cuál es el cuaderno de _____ (un[-a] estudiante de la clase)?
3. ¿Cuál es la silla de usted?
4. ¿Cuáles son los libros de _____ (un[-a] estudiante de la clase)?
5. ¿Cuál es la puerta principal?
6. ¿Cuál es el libro de español?

PREGUNTAS

1. ¿Estudia mucho esa chica (que está al lado de usted)? ¿ésta? ¿aquélla?
2. ¿Cómo se llama este muchacho (que está cerca del profesor o de la profesora)? ¿ése? ¿aquél? **3.** ¿Qué es esto? (Es un libro.) ¿eso? ¿aquello? **4.** ¿Cómo es esta clase? ¿esta universidad? ¿esta ciudad?

Mural por David Alfaro Siqueiros, UNAM

The present indicative of *tener*

BÁRBARA	¿*Tienes* tiempo para estudiar inglés esta tarde?
DORA	No, no *tengo* tiempo. Robert y yo *tenemos* otros planes. Él *tiene* ganas de visitar el Museo Nacional de Antropología.
BÁRBARA	Pero... ¿y el examen de inglés que *tienen* mañana?
DORA	No *tiene* importancia. El inglés es fácil, y con Robert aprendo más.
BÁRBARA	Comprendo. La escuela de la vida, ¿no?

1. ¿Tiene tiempo Dora para estudiar inglés con Bárbara?   2. ¿Qué planes tienen Dora y Robert?   3. ¿Por qué para Dora no tiene importancia el examen de inglés?

A. The verb **tener** is irregular.

tener (*to have*)	
tengo	tenemos
tienes	tenéis
tiene	tienen

Tengo muchos libros sobre medicina.	*I have lots of books about medicine.*
¿Tienes tiempo para comer ahora?	*Do you have time to eat now?*
Tenemos una clase de ingeniería a las dos.	*We have an engineering class at two o'clock.*

B. **Tener que** + infinitive means *to have to* (do something). **Tener ganas de** + infinitive means *to feel like* (doing something).

Tengo que escribir una composición sobre los dioses de los aztecas.	*I have to write a composition about the gods of the Aztecs.*
¿Tienes ganas de visitar a Enrique?	*Do you feel like visiting Enrique?*

C. The verb **tener** is not normally followed by the personal **a: Tengo dos hermanos. Tenemos una amiga chilena.**

BÁRBARA: Do you have time to study English this afternoon? DORA: No, I don't have time. Robert and I have other plans. He feels like visiting the National Museum of Anthropology. BÁRBARA: But...what about the English test that you have tomorrow? DORA: It's not important. English is easy, and with Robert I learn more. BÁRBARA: I understand. The school of life, right?

A. ¿Tienes...?   Ask a classmate whether he or she has the following things.
Then make a sentence telling the class a few of the things your classmate has.

1. una clase de literatura (filosofía, etcétera)
2. un reloj alemán (japonés, francés)
3. ganas de viajar a México (España, etcétera)
4. ganas de estudiar hoy
5. amigos hispanos (franceses, egoístas, sociables, etcétera)
6. ideas interesantes
7. libros de antropología (biología, historia, etcétera)

B. Conversación.   Complete the conversation with the correct forms of **tener**.

DELIA	Ernesto, ¿————₁ (tú) tiempo de visitar al tío Pedro?
ERNESTO	Sí, mamá. ————₂ tiempo. Y Conchita y yo ————₃ un libro para él.
DELIA	Pero Conchita ————₄ un examen hoy, ¿no?
ERNESTO	¡Sí! Y creo que ella ————₅ otros planes. El problema es que necesito unos pesos. ¿————₆ (tú) unos pesos para el taxi?

1. ¿Tiene la universidad una buena biblioteca?   **2.** ¿Tienen programas de español aquí en televisión?   **3.** ¿Tiene usted una clase de francés? ¿de matemáticas? ¿de biología? ¿de literatura? ¿Son fáciles o difíciles?   **4.** ¿Tiene usted ganas de aprender música? ¿arte? ¿Qué tiene ganas de aprender?   **5.** ¿Tiene que estudiar esta noche? ¿Tiene ganas de estudiar?   **6.** ¿Tenemos muchos estudiantes inteligentes en esta clase? ¿Y en esta universidad?   **7.** ¿Tiene usted una familia grande o pequeña? ¿Cuántos hermanos tiene? ¿Cuántos primos?

El Museo Nacional de Antropología, en la Ciudad de México

The verbs *hacer*, *poner*, *salir*, and *venir*

Los policías *salen* de la policía.

Nosotros *hacemos* ejercicios.

El turista *pone* unos regalos en la maleta.

Ellos *vienen* de la biblioteca.

BIBLIOTECA

hacer *(to do; to make)*		**poner** *(to put)*	
hago	hacemos	**pongo**	ponemos
haces	hacéis	pones	ponéis
hace	hacen	pone	ponen

salir (to leave, go out)		**venir** (to come)	
salgo	salimos	**vengo**	venimos
sales	salís	**vi**enes	venís
sale	salen	**vi**ene	**vi**enen

The verbs **hacer**, **poner**, and **salir** have irregular first-person singular forms: **hago**, **pongo**, **salgo**. **Venir** is conjugated like **tener** except for the **nosotros** and **vosotros** forms.

¿Qué hace Miguel? —Hace las maletas.

What is Miguel doing? —He's packing the suitcases.

Pongo el libro de física aquí, ¿está bien?

I'm putting the physics book here, okay?

Salimos este mes para Acapulco.

We're leaving this month for Acapulco.

Fernando siempre viene a las fiestas.

Fernando always comes to parties.

EJERCICIO

Entre amigos. It's Saturday afternoon, and Jorge is trying to find someone to spend the afternoon with. Complete the conversation between Jorge and his friend Pedro using the correct present-tense forms of the verbs in parentheses.

JORGE ¿Qué _____1 (hacer) tú hoy, Pedro?

PEDRO Ahora estudio química, pero esta tarde _____2 (salir) con Luisa. Deseamos ir al teatro.

JORGE ¿Y Roberto? ¿Qué _hace_3 (hacer) él?

PEDRO Él está en el aeropuerto. Debe recibir a unos amigos que _vienen_4 (venir) de Guadalajara.

JORGE ¿Qué _hacen_5 (hacer) Rita y Paco?

PEDRO Ellos _ponen_6 (poner) las maletas en el auto. En unos minutos ellos _salen_7 (salir) de viaje.

JORGE Y entonces (then), ¿qué _hace_8 (hacer) yo?

PEDRO Pues, tienes dos posibilidades: (tú) _vienes_9 (venir) al teatro con nosotros o _pones_10 (poner) también las maletas en el auto y _sales_11 (salir) de viaje con Rita y Paco.

JORGE ¡Buena idea! ¡Ahora _____12 (poner) los pijamas en una maleta y pronto _____13 (salir) para la casa de ustedes!

PREGUNTAS

1. ¿De dónde viene usted ahora? **2.** ¿Hace usted la comida por la noche? ¿Quién pone los platos y la comida en la mesa? ¿Prepara usted comidas deliciosas? ¿O sale con un(-a) amigo(-a) a comer? **3.** ¿A qué hora sale de casa por la mañana? ¿A qué hora viene a la clase de español? **4.** Cuando hace la maleta, ¿siempre pone allí una cámara? ¿un libro? ¿los pijamas?

México: El Museo Nacional de Antropología[1]

La Piedra del Sol, o calendario azteca, en el Museo Nacional de Antropología

Bob, un joven neoyorquino°, estudiante de antropología, y Paco, un amigo mexicano, están en el Museo Nacional de Antropología de la ciudad de México.

PACO   ¿Todavía crees que los buenos museos están todos en Nueva York?

BOB   Bueno... allá tenemos unos treinta y cinco o cuarenta. Pero éste es una maravilla°. Hay arquitectos° que vienen a México sólo° para visitar este museo.

PACO   Sí, eso es verdad y también vienen antropólogos° o estudiantes de antropología como tú. Aquí es posible aprender mucho sobre las civilizaciones indias del pasado.

BOB   ¿Estudian ustedes la historia de las civilizaciones indígenas° mexicanas en la universidad?

PACO   ¡Claro! Mi hermana es profesora de historia y tiene muchos estudiantes en una clase. Ellos hacen excursiones regulares a sitios° históricos. Por ejemplo, hoy visitan las pirámides de Teotihuacán.[2]

BOB	¿Cómo? Más despacio, por favor. ¿Las pirámides de qué?
PACO	De Teotihuacán, una antigua° ciudad azteca que está cerca de aquí. Salen a las tres. ¿Deseas visitar ese sitio?
BOB	Sí, pero no hoy. Creo que no tenemos tiempo.

Entran a otra sala°.

BOB	¡Hombre°! Aquél debe ser el famoso calendario azteca.[3] ¡Es estupendo!
PACO	Y es un calendario bastante exacto. El año azteca tiene dieciocho meses de veinte días... y cinco días extras.
BOB	Ahora que hablas del tiempo, ¿qué hora es?
PACO	Son las doce y media. Es hora de comer, ¿no?
BOB	Sí, y creo que debemos comer tacos[4] en honor de Cinteotl, el dios del maíz°.
PACO	Tú aprendes pronto, Bob.
BOB	Gracias. Todos los neoyorquinos somos inteligentes.
PACO	¡Y modestos°!

---

neoyorquino *New Yorker, from New York*   **maravilla** *marvel, wonder*
arquitectos *architects*   **sólo** *only*   **antropólogos** *anthropologists*
indígenas *native, indigenous*   **sitios** *sites*   **antigua** *ancient, old*
Entran a otra sala. *They go into another room.*   **¡Hombre!** *Wow!*   **maíz** *corn*
modestos *modest*

PREGUNTAS

1. ¿Dónde están los dos amigos?   **2.** ¿Quién cree que los buenos museos están todos en Nueva York?   **3.** ¿Quiénes vienen a México para visitar el Museo Nacional de Antropología? ¿Por qué?   **4.** ¿Qué estudian Paco y los otros estudiantes mexicanos en la universidad?   **5.** ¿Es profesora de arquitectura la hermana de Paco?   **6.** ¿Qué hacen los estudiantes de esa profesora? ¿Qué visitan hoy? ¿A qué hora salen?   **7.** ¿Es bastante exacto el calendario azteca?   **8.** ¿Cuántos meses tiene el calendario azteca?   **9.** ¿Quién es Cinteotl?   **10.** ¿Qué deben comer los dos amigos en honor de Cinteotl?   **11.** ¿Come usted tacos? ¿Dónde?

Notas culturales

1. The National Museum of Anthropology in Mexico City is an immense building with a huge suspended roof that houses exhibits from all over the world. Most of the exhibits, however, are artifacts from the many Indian cultures that have successively inhabited various regions of Mexico.

2. Teotihuacán, which means "city of the gods" or "where men become gods," is a city that dates from the first century A.D. Located thirty-three miles north of Mexico

City, it covers eight square miles and contained dwelling places, plazas, temples, and palaces of priests and nobles. The Pyramid of the Moon, at the north end, and the great Pyramid of the Sun, at the east end, are its most impressive features.

3. The Aztec calendar stone, or **Piedra del Sol**, is a gigantic carved stone from the sixteenth century. The Aztec year consisted of eighteen months, each with twenty days. Five extra days, considered unlucky and dangerous, followed; during this time, the Aztecs stayed close to home and behaved cautiously for fear that an accident would set a bad pattern for the entire year ahead.

4. Tacos are made with **tortillas**, flat corn pancakes that are filled with cheese, beans, or meat and sometimes tomatoes or lettuce. Corn has been a staple of the Mexican diet for as long as history and mythology record.

FUNCIONES Y ACTIVIDADES

In this chapter you have seen examples of the following language functions, or uses. Here is a summary and some additional information about these functions of language.

Telling time

See Section I for time expressions. The use of digital watches is beginning to change the way people tell time: Hispanics are more and more likely to say **Son las tres y cuarenta** rather than **Son las cuatro menos veinte**, for example.

Expressing incomprehension

Even in your native language, you probably find that you frequently have to stop someone who is speaking and ask him or her to clarify or explain something, repeat part of a sentence, slow down, and so on. In a foreign language, it's even more important to learn how to stop a speaker and ask for clarification. Here are some ways to express that you just aren't following and need some help.

¿Cómo? *What?*	¿Perdón? *Pardon me?*
No comprendo. *I don't understand.*	¿Qué? *What?* (very informal)
¿Mande? *What?* (Mexico)	

¿Cómo? is used to ask the speaker to repeat; **¿Qué?** will usually elicit a specific answer to the question *What...?* If you want the speaker to repeat, you can also say:

Otra vez, por favor. *Again, please.*   Repita, por favor. *Repeat, please.*

If you want him or her to slow down, you can say:

Más despacio, por favor.   *Slower, please.*

If you miss part of a statement or question, you can use a question word to ask just for the part you missed (see Chapter 1, Section IV):

¿Pero dónde (cuándo, por qué, etcétera)...?

When you have a general idea of what the speaker is saying but just want to confirm that you understand, you may want to use confirmation tags: **¿(no es) verdad?**, **¿no?**, and so on. (See Chapter 1, Section IV.)

Marisa estudia química, ¿verdad?

A. Un momento, por favor.   You don't understand what someone is saying to you when you hear the following sentences. Interrupt the speaker and ask for clarification.

> **Modelo**   El avión de Caracas llega a las cuatro y cuarto.
> **¿Cómo? ¿A qué hora llega el avión? ¿De dónde viene?**

1. Roberto estudia ciencias sociales y matemáticas en la Universidad de Salamanca.
2. La señora Otavalo vive en Chiquinquirá, pero ahora está en Bucaramanga.
3. El señor Montenegro tiene sesenta y seis años. La señora Montenegro tiene sesenta y dos años. Ellos tienen una fiesta mañana.
4. ¿El número de teléfono del señor Barrios? 62-84-51.
5. AquelestudiantesellamaOsvaldo. Creoqueesmuysimpático. (Said rapidly.)

B. Situación.   Role-play the following situation. You are in the National Museum of Anthropology in Mexico City. Someone comes up to you and asks where the famous Aztec calendar stone is. You don't understand at first and ask for clarification. She explains, but you say you don't know. Then you ask her what time it is. She tells you, but you don't hear at first, so you ask her to say it more slowly. You thank her and say good-bye.

Cognados

azteca	el futuro	el momento	el programa
el calendario	la importancia	práctico	universitario
exacto	maya	la profesión	

Verbos

abrir	*to open*
aprender	*to learn*
comer	*to eat*
comprender	*to understand*
creer	*to believe, think*
deber	*~ should, ought to, must*
decidir	*to decide*
descubrir	*to discover*
escribir	*to write*
hacer	*to do; to make*
hacer ejercicios	*to do exercises*
hacer la maleta	*to pack one's suitcase*
leer	*to read*
poner	*to put*
practicar	*to practice*
recibir	*to receive*
representar	*to represent*
salir	*to leave, go out*
tener	*to have*
tener ganas de + inf.	*to feel like (doing something)*
tener que + inf.	*to have to + inf.*
vender	*to sell*
venir	*to come*
vivir	*to live*

Estudios universitarios

la antropología	*anthropology*
la arquitectura	*architecture*
la biología	*biology*
las ciencias de computación	*computer science*
las ciencias políticas	*political science*
las ciencias sociales	*social science*
la filosofía	*philosophy*
la física	*physics*
la historia	*history*
la ingeniería	*engineering*
la literatura	*literature*
las matemáticas	*mathematics*
la medicina	*medicine*
la psicología	*psychology*
la química	*chemistry*

Profesiones y oficios (Professions and jobs)

el abogado, la abogada	*lawyer*
la camarera	*waitress*
el camarero	*waiter*
el, la comerciante	*~ businessperson*
el escritor, la escritora	*writer*
el ingeniero, la ingeniera	*engineer*
el, la músico	*musician*
el policía, la mujer policía	*police officer*
el secretario, la secretaria	*secretary*
el vendedor, la vendedora	*salesperson*

La hora / el tiempo

el año	year
de la mañana	A.M.
de la tarde (noche)	P.M.
en punto	on the dot
la hora	hour
el mes	month
el pasado	past
por la mañana	in the morning
por la noche	at night
por la tarde	in the afternoon
¿Qué hora es?	What time is it?
el siglo	century
el tiempo	time (in a general sense)*

Otras palabras y frases

alemán (el alemana)	German
bastante	rather; enough
la biblioteca	library
cada	each, every
la carta	letter
¿Cuánto(-s)?	How much? How many?
despacio	slowly
el dios	god
la escuela	school
estupendo	great

la fiesta	party
la librería	bookstore
la maleta	suitcase
la muchacha	girl
el muchacho	boy
por ejemplo	for example
pronto	soon; fast
si	if, whether
siempre	always
todavía	still, yet
todo	all, every, everything
todos	all, every, everyone
la vida	life

Expresiones útiles

¡Claro!	Of course!
Más despacio, por favor.	Slower, please.
Repita, por favor.	Repeat, please.

> **Don't forget:**
> Demonstrative adjectives and pronouns, pages 73–74.

---

* The word **tiempo** normally refers to weather; this use is discussed in Chapter 4.

comerciante
bastante
maleta
todavia

Las estaciones del año son:

la primavera   el verano   el otoño

¿Qué tiempo hace hoy?

Hace (muy) buen tiempo.   Hace (muy) mal tiempo. Llueve. (Hay lluvia.)

Hace (mucho) calor.   Hace (mucho) sol.   Hace (mucho) viento.

Los meses del año son: enero   marzo   mayo   julio   se(p)tiembre   noviembre
febrero   abril   junio   agosto   octubre   diciembre

Las estaciones y el tiempo ____ 4

el invierno

(mucho) frío. Nieva.

Está nublado.

Expressing Obligation
Making Small Talk
Giving a Warning

EJERCICIO

Create questions to which the following would be possible answers.

> **Modelo** Hace mucho calor hoy.
> **¿Qué tiempo hace hoy?**

1. Hace buen tiempo aquí.
2. Hace mucho frío ahora.
3. Hace calor en el verano.
4. Hace viento en las montañas (*mountains*).
5. Donde yo vivo, siempre hace sol.

PREGUNTAS

1. ¿Hace frío hoy? ¿calor? ¿Está nublado? ¿Llueve? **2.** ¿Hace frío o calor en la clase? **3.** ¿Qué tiempo hace aquí en el invierno? ¿en la primavera? **4.** ¿Qué tiempo hace en la región de los Andes? ¿en el trópico? **5.** ¿En qué estación estamos ahora? ¿En qué estación hace mucho sol aquí? ¿mucho viento? **6.** ¿Qué mes es muy lindo?

Hay nubes

The irregular verb *ir*

Un reportero habla con unas personas en una calle de Concepción.

EL REPORTERO ¿*Va a ir* usted de vacaciones este verano, señor?
RAMÓN Por supuesto. *Voy* a Viña del Mar. *Voy* a pasar las vacaciones en la playa.
EL REPORTERO ¿Y usted, señora?
GLORIA *Voy* a Santiago con una amiga. *Vamos a ir* de compras.
EL REPORTERO ¿Y tú, niño? ¿*Vas a ir* de vacaciones este verano?
PEDRITO Sí, señor. *Voy a ir* al paraíso con la familia. *Vamos* a visitar a los ángeles. ¿Verdad, papá?
RAFAEL No, no *vamos* al paraíso, hijo; *vamos* a Valparaíso.

---

1. ¿Adónde va Ramón de vacaciones?   2. ¿Qué va a hacer Gloria?   3. ¿Adónde va la familia de Pedrito?

A. The present-tense forms of the irregular verb **ir** are:

ir	*(to go)*
voy	vamos
vas	vais
va	van

B. Like other verbs of motion, the verb **ir** is usually followed by the preposition **a** when a destination is mentioned.

Según Rafael, en Valparaíso todo el mundo va a la playa.	*According to Rafael, in Valparaíso everyone goes to the beach.*
Todos los días (todas las semanas) vamos al mar.	*Every day (week) we go to the sea.*

A reporter is talking to some people on a street in Concepción. REPORTER: Are you going to go on vacation this summer, sir? RAMÓN: Of course. I'm going to Viña del Mar. I'm going to spend my vacation at the beach. REPORTER: And you, ma'am? GLORIA: I'm going to Santiago with a friend. We're going to go shopping. REPORTER: And you, little boy? Are you going to go on vacation this summer? PEDRITO: Yes, sir. I'm going to Paradise with my family. We're going to visit the angels. Right, Dad? RAFAEL: No, we're not going to Paradise, son; we're going to Valparaíso.

C. The verb **ir** is also followed by the preposition **a** before an infinitive. The construction **ir a** + infinitive is often used in place of the future tense to express an action or event that is going to take place in the near future.

Mañana voy a nadar en el lago Villarrica.	*Tomorrow I'm going to swim in Lake Villarrica.*
Vamos a esquiar en las montañas cerca de Portillo.	*We're going to ski in the mountains near Portillo.*
Van a ser unas vacaciones estupendas.	*It's going to be a great vacation.*

D. **Vamos a** + infinitive can mean *we're going to do something* or *let's do something.*

Vamos al mar.
 { *We're going to the sea.*
 { *Let's go to the sea.*

E. **Ir de compras** means *to go shopping.* **Ir de vacaciones** is *to go on vacation.*

Voy de compras al centro.	*I'm going shopping downtown.*
Mucha gente va de vacaciones a Valparaíso.	*Many people go on vacation to Valparaíso.*

EJERCICIOS

A. ¿Adónde vamos? Everyone is leaving for vacation. Say where everyone is going by completing the sentences with the correct forms of **ir**.

1. Felipe y Manuel _____ a ir a Santiago; _____ a visitar museos y teatros.
2. Elena _____ a las montañas; _____ a esquiar.
3. Yo _____ a visitar a los abuelos y _____ a pasar unos días cerca del lago que hay allí.
4. Rafael y yo _____ a Viña del Mar. Nosotros _____ en auto.
5. Ustedes _____ a Temuco. ¿_____ en avión o en autobús?
6. Tú _____ de vacaciones a Barcelona. _____ a ir a la playa allí, ¿verdad?
7. El profesor _____ a Buenos Aires. Creo que él _____ con un amigo.
8. Usted _____ al mar; _____ a leer muchos libros allí, ¿no?

B. Mañana... Luis is a procrastinator. Answer the questions for him, following the models.

Modelos ¿Trabajas ahora?
 No, pero voy a trabajar mañana.

1. ¿Haces ejercicios ahora?
2. ¿Lees el capítulo 4 ahora?
3. ¿Vas a la biblioteca ahora?
4. ¿Escribes la composición ahora?
5. ¿Llamas a la familia ahora?

C. ¿Qué vamos a hacer?   Complete each of the following sentences with the appropriate form of **ir a** + infinitive and any additional information needed.

> **Modelo**   En julio tú...
> **En julio tú vas a estar de vacaciones (ir a Venezuela, etcétera).**

1. Esta tarde yo...
2. Hoy hace buen tiempo. Mañana...
3. En diciembre todos los estudiantes...
4. Esta noche ustedes...
5. Este fin de semana tú...

D. Una encuesta. (*A survey.*)   Find out how some of your classmates will spend their vacations and report back to the class.

1. ¿Quiénes van a la playa?   **2.** ¿Quiénes van a las montañas? ¿Quiénes van a esquiar?   **3.** ¿Quiénes van a casa de parientes? ¿a visitar a amigos? **4.** ¿Quiénes van a estudiar? ¿trabajar?

PREGUNTAS

1. ¿Qué va a hacer usted esta noche? ¿este fin de semana?   **2.** ¿Va mucho a la biblioteca? ¿al teatro? ¿a los museos? ¿a la playa? ¿a las montañas?   **3.** ¿Va a visitar a unos amigos hoy? ¿a unos parientes?   **4.** ¿Va a comer esta noche en un restaurante o en casa?

Dates

En una calle de Santiago de Chile.

PABLO   Ana, ¿vamos al teatro *el lunes...? ¿o el martes...? ¿o el miércoles...?*
ANA   Bueno, es que...
PABLO   Vamos *el viernes,* ¿de acuerdo? Es *el veintisiete de septiembre.*
ANA   Pues... *el viernes* tengo que estudiar.
PABLO   ¿Y *el veintiocho?* Es *sábado.*
ANA   Ese día tengo que trabajar.
PABLO   ¿Y *el veintinueve...* o *el treinta?*
ANA   Pues, *el treinta y uno* está bien.
PABLO   ¡Qué bien! Gracias, Ana. ¡Hasta *el treinta y uno!*
ANA   ¡Chau, Pablo!
PABLO   (Mira un calendario.) *El treinta de septiembre, el primero de octubre...* Pero, ¡Ana! ¡Un momento!

1. ¿Adónde desea ir Pablo?   2. ¿Qué tiene que hacer Ana el viernes? ¿el sábado?   3. ¿Van a ir al teatro el treinta y uno? ¿Por qué sí o por qué no?

A. The days of the week in Spanish are all masculine and are not capitalized.

lunes	*Monday*	viernes	*Friday*
martes	*Tuesday*	sábado	*Saturday*
miércoles	*Wednesday*	domingo	*Sunday*
jueves	*Thursday*		

B. The definite article is almost always used with the days of the week as the equivalent of *on* when *on* could be used in English. It is not used otherwise.

Hoy es lunes. ¿Es necesario ir a clase?	*Today is Monday. Is it necessary to go to class?*
Ella llega el martes. Es el cumpleaños de José.	*She's arriving (on) Tuesday. It's José's birthday.*
Va a hacer sol el viernes.—¿Está seguro?	*It's going to be sunny (on) Friday.—Are you sure?*

C. The plurals of **sábado** and **domingo** are formed by adding **-s: los sábados, los domingos**. The plurals of the other days are formed simply by adding the plural article **los**.

Siempre estamos en casa los jueves.	*We're always home on Thursdays.*

D. With one exception, *the first* (**el primero**), cardinal numbers are used to express dates.

¿Cuál es la fecha de hoy? Es el primero de diciembre.	*What's the date today? It's December 1st.*
Viajan a España el 10 (diez) de mayo.	*They are traveling to Spain on May 10th.*

Cardinal numbers are used with **siglo** (*century*) in Spanish although with *century* in English, ordinal numbers (first, second, and so on) are used.

¿En qué mundo vives? ¡Estamos en el siglo veinte!	*What world are you living in? We're in the twentieth century!*

On a street in Santiago, Chile. PABLO: Ana, shall we go to the theater on Monday...? Or on Tuesday...? Or on Wednesday...? ANA: Well, it's just that... PABLO: Let's go on Friday, okay? It's the twenty-seventh of September. ANA: Well, on Friday I have to study. PABLO: And the twenty-eighth? It's Saturday. ANA: That day I have to work. PABLO: And the twenty-ninth...or the thirtieth? ANA: Well, the thirty-first is fine. PABLO: Great! Thanks, Ana. See you on the thirty-first! ANA: Good-bye, Pablo! PABLO: (He looks at a calendar.) The thirtieth of September, the first of October...But, Ana! Just a minute!

A. ¿Qué fecha es...?   Test your memory for dates by matching the holidays listed below with their corresponding dates.

Modelos   el Día de la Raza (*Columbus Day*)
Es el 12 de octubre.

el Día de Año Nuevo
Es el 1° (primero) de enero.

1. el Día de "Halloween"
2. la Navidad (*Christmas*)
3. el cumpleaños de Martin Luther King, Jr.
4. el Día de San Valentín
5. la Nochebuena (*Christmas Eve*)
6. el Día de los Reyes Magos (*Epiphany*)
7. el Día de los Trabajadores (*May Day, International Labor Day*)
8. el Día de los Muertos (*All Souls' Day*)
9. el Día de la Independencia de los Estados Unidos
10. el cumpleaños del presidente George Washington

a. 4 de julio
b. 1° de mayo
c. 31 de octubre
d. 2 de noviembre
e. 25 de diciembre
f. 22 de febrero
g. 15 de enero
h. 1° de enero
i. 14 de febrero
j. 24 de diciembre
k. 6 de enero

B. Días de la semana.   Complete the sentences.

1. No tengo muchas clases los...
2. Si hoy es jueves, mañana es...
3. Vamos a la clase de español los...
4. El primer día de la semana es...
5. El día favorito de muchos estudiantes es...

PREGUNTAS

1. ¿Qué día es hoy? ¿Y mañana? ¿Cuál es la fecha de hoy?   **2.** ¿Cuándo es el cumpleaños de Abraham Lincoln? ¿de usted?   **3.** ¿En qué mes(es) hace mucho frío aquí? ¿calor? ¿sol? ¿viento?   **4.** ¿Tiene usted un mes favorito? ¿Cuál? ¿Por qué?   **5.** ¿Tiene también un día favorito? ¿Cuál? ¿Por qué?

Cardinal numbers 100 and above

MOVIMIENTO DE AVIONES

MARTES

AEROPUERTO COMOD. ARTURO MERINO BENITEZ

LLEGAN:

PROCEDENCIAS	VUELO	COMPAÑIAS	LLEGA
AMSTERDAM-RIO-SAO PAULO-BAIRES	791	KLM	04.55
MONTREAL-NUEVA YORK-MIAMI	161	LAN CHILE	08.10
BUENOS AIRES	040	ECUATORIANA	10.15
FRANKFURT-BRUSELAS-MADRID-MIAMI	502	PARAGUAYA	10.20
NUEVA YORK-MIAMI-BUENOS AIRES	027	EASTERN	10.46
MIAMI-CARACAS-MANAOS-SANTA CRUZ-LA PAZ	907	LLOYD	11.30
COPENHAGEN-LISBOA-RIO-BAIRES	957	SAS	11.35
RIO DE JANEIRO-SAO PAULO	920	VARIG	13.15
MIAMI-PANAMA-GUAYAQUIL-LIMA	695	AEROPERU	13.30
BUENOS AIRES-CORDOBA-MENDOZA	226	AEROLINEAS	14.45
CARACAS-LIMA	129	LAN CHILE	14.55
MIAMI-PANAMA	159	LAN CHILE	17.35
BUENOS AIRES	124	LAN CHILE	19.05
BUENOS AIRES	696	AEROPERU	19.35
MADRID-RIO DE JANEIRO-SAO PAULO	171	LAN CHILE	21.00

SALEN:

SALE	COMPAÑIAS	VUELO	DESTINOS
07.50	KLM	792	BAIRES-SAO PAULO-RIO-AMSTERDAM
11.15	ECUATORIANA	040	GUAYAQUIL-QUITO-MEXICO-LOS ANGELES
12.00	PARAGUAYA	503	MIAMI-MEXICO-MADRID-BRUSELAS-FRANKFURT
12.20	SAS	958	BAIRES-RIO-COPENHAGEN
12.30	LLOYD	908	LA PAZ-STA. CRUZ-PANAMA-MIAMI
13.00	LAN CHILE	125	BUENOS AIRES
14.15	VARIG	921	SAO PAULO-RIO DE JANEIRO
14.20	AEROPERU	695	BUENOS AIRES
15.20	AEROLINEAS	227	MENDOZA-CORDOBA-BUENOS AIRES
18.40	EASTERN	010	BUENOS AIRES-MIAMI-NUEVA YORK
20.00	LAN CHILE	140	LIMA-MIAMI-NUEVA YORK
20.25	AEROPERU	696	LIMA-MEXICO (conex.)-MIAMI

procedencias *points of departure*   **destinos** *destinations*

PREGUNTAS

1. ¿A qué hora llega el vuelo (*flight*) de Frankfurt al aeropuerto Arturo Merino Benítez de Santiago? ¿el vuelo de Caracas–Lima?   **2.** ¿Adónde va el avión que sale a la una? ¿y el avión que sale a las ocho?

100	cien(to)	10.000	diez mil
101	ciento uno (un, una)	100.000	cien mil
200	doscientos(-as)	150.000	ciento cincuenta mil
300	trescientos(-as)	500.000	quinientos(-as) mil
400	cuatrocientos(-as)	1.000.000	un millón (de...)
500	quinientos(-as)	1.200.000	un millón doscientos(-as) mil
600	seiscientos(-as)		
700	setecientos(-as)	2.000.000	dos millones (de...)
800	ochocientos(-as)		
900	novecientos(-as)		
1.000	mil		

A. **Cien** is used to mean *one hundred* before nouns and before the number **mil** (*one thousand*). It is also used in counting.

cien años	*100 years*	cien mil dólares	*100,000 dollars*
cien personas	*100 people*	cien mil ciudades	*100,000 cities*

B. **Ciento** is used in all other cases; it does not have a feminine form.

ciento una noches	*101 nights*	ciento un días	*101 days*
ciento cincuenta niñas	*150 girls*	ciento noventa niños	*190 boys*

C. The numbers 200–900 agree with the nouns they modify in gender.

doscientas páginas	*200 pages*
cuatrocientos diez pasajeros	*410 passengers*
quinientas cuatro horas	*504 hours*

D. To express numbers above 1,000, **mil** is always used. With **millón** and exact multiples of **millón** (**dos millones, diez millones**), the preposition **de** is used before a noun. Notice that a decimal point is used in numbers in Spanish where a comma is used in English.

diez mil trescientas (10.300) personas
cien mil quinientos (100.500) años
quinientos mil cien (500.100) alemanes
cinco millones (5.000.000) de dólares

E. **Mil** is used for years over 999. In expressing dates, the day, month, and year are connected by **de**.

(el) trece de enero de mil ochocientos sesenta y tres	*January 13, 1863*
(el) ocho de diciembre de mil novecientos cuarenta y uno	*December 8, 1941*
Hoy no es el veintiocho de febrero de mil novecientos treinta y ocho.	*Today is not February 28, 1938.*

A. Números de suerte. (*Lucky numbers.*)   Mr. Rodríguez is trying to pick up a clue for tomorrow's lottery, so he circled the following numbers in *El Mercurio,* a well-known Chilean newspaper. Read to the class the items he circled.

1. 201 hoteles
2. 999 casas
3. 21.021 estudiantes
4. 867.000 turistas
5. 1.000.000 de dólares
6. 4.880.000 pesos
7. 100 días de mucho calor
8. 11.660.000 personas
9. 555.499 franceses
10. 3.667 profesores

B. Un examen de historia.   Work in pairs. Read the events listed below and match each of them with the corresponding date on the right. Take turns reading the events and giving the date.

Modelo   Estudiante 1: **el descubrimiento** (*discovery*) **de América**
Estudiante 2:   **1492 (mil cuatrocientos noventa y dos)**

1. la exploración de la luna (*moon*)   1492
2. la Guerra (*War*) Civil Española   1605
3. la Declaración de Independencia   1776
4. la publicación del *Quijote,*   1789
   de Miguel de Cervantes   1910
5. la Revolución Cubana   1936
6. la Revolución Mexicana   1959
7. la Revolución Francesa   1969

C. Los vuelos de hoy.   Look at the airline schedule at the beginning of this section and answer these questions.

1. ¿Cuál es el número de vuelo del avión que llega de Montreal? ¿del avión que viene de Santa Cruz–La Paz? ¿A qué hora llegan estos vuelos?   **2.** ¿Cuál es el número de vuelo del avión que llega a las diez y veinte? ¿a las dos cuarenta y cinco?   **3.** ¿Cuál es el número de vuelo del avión que sale para Copenhagen? ¿Qué vuelos salen para Buenos Aires? ¿A qué horas?   **4.** ¿A qué hora sale el vuelo número 908? ¿Adónde va?

D. Agente de viajes.   In pairs, ask and answer questions about the airline schedule. One of you is the **agente de viajes**, and the other is the **pasajero(-a)**. Practice a conversation and perform it for the class.

Modelo   Pasajero: **Necesito ir a Nueva York. ¿A qué hora salen los vuelos para esa ciudad?**
Agente: **Hay un vuelo de Eastern a las seis y cuarenta; es el vuelo número 10. Va primero a Buenos Aires y a Miami. Y hay otro a las ocho, el vuelo número 140 de Lan Chile que pasa por Lima y también por Miami.**
Pasajero: **Pues, el vuelo de las ocho está bien.**
Agente: **¿En qué fecha desea viajar?**
Pasajero: **El tres de noviembre.**
Agente: **Está bien.**

1. Aproximadamente (*Approximately*), ¿cuántos estudiantes hay en esta universidad? **2.** ¿Cuántas personas viven en esta ciudad? ¿en este país? ¿Cuántas mujeres cree usted que hay en los Estados Unidos? ¿Y hombres? ¿Y niños? **3.** ¿Qué precio debe tener un Toyota nuevo? ¿y un Mercedes Benz? ¿y un Rolls Royce? **4.** ¿Qué precio debe tener una casa pequeña en esta ciudad? **5.** ¿Qué años asocia usted con dos libros muy populares: uno de George Orwell y uno de Arthur C. Clarke?

Idiomatic expressions with *tener*; *hay que*

SR. GARCÍA	*¿Hay que* contestar todas las preguntas, señorita?
SEÑORITA	Sí, es necesario poner el nombre, la nacionalidad, la fecha de hoy...

Unos minutos después.

DOCTOR	*¿Cuántos años tiene usted*, señor García?
SR. GARCÍA	Treinta y ocho.
DOCTOR	¿Y por qué está aquí hoy?
SR. GARCÍA	Porque *tengo dolor de cabeza y de estómago*. También *tengo calor y sed*. Y estoy muy cansado.
DOCTOR	*Tiene que tomar* aspirinas y *tener cuidado* con la comida. Pero no *tiene fiebre* y en realidad está en muy buenas condiciones físicas.
SR. GARCÍA	¡Estupendo! Voy a morir sano.

1. Según la señorita, ¿hay que contestar todas las preguntas? 2. ¿Cuántos años tiene el señor García? 3. ¿Tiene dolor de cabeza? ¿Tiene dolor de estómago? 4. ¿Tiene calor? ¿sed? 5. ¿Está cansado? 6. ¿Qué tiene que tomar, según el doctor? 7. ¿Tiene fiebre? 8. ¿Está en buenas condiciones físicas?

MR. GARCÍA: Is it necessary to answer all these questions, miss? RECEPTIONIST: Yes, it is necessary to put your name, nationality, today's date... (*A few minutes later.*) DOCTOR: How old are you, Mr. García? MR. GARCÍA: Thirty-eight. DOCTOR: And why are you here today? MR. GARCÍA: Because I have a headache and a stomachache. Also, I'm hot and thirsty. And I'm very tired. DOCTOR: You must take aspirin and be careful about the food (you eat). But you don't have a fever, and, in reality (actually), you are in very good physical condition. MR. GARCÍA: Wonderful! I'm going to die healthy.

A. In addition to **tener ganas**, which you saw in Chapter 3, many idioms in Spanish contain the verb **tener** (*to have*).

tener (veinte) años
tener dolor de cabeza, de estómago
tener fiebre

to be (twenty) years old
to have a headache, a stomachache
to have a fever

B. Many constructions with **tener** + noun are expressed in English with *to be* + adjective.

tener $\begin{cases} \text{calor} \\ \text{frío} \\ \text{cuidado} \\ \text{razón} \\ \text{hambre} \\ \text{sed} \end{cases}$ to be $\begin{cases} \textit{warm, hot} \\ \textit{cold} \\ \textit{careful} \\ \textit{right} \\ \textit{hungry} \\ \textit{thirsty} \end{cases}$

Note that **no tener razón** means *to be incorrect, wrong*. Also, note that to express the idea of *very* in Spanish, a form of **mucho** agreeing with the noun is used. The nouns **calor**, **frío**, and **cuidado** are masculine; **razón**, **hambre**, and **sed** are feminine.

Tengo mucho frío. Ellos tienen mucha hambre.

I'm very cold. They're very hungry.

C. The impersonal expression **hay que** means *one (we, you, etc.) must, it is necessary to.*

Hay que ir de compras por la tarde.
Hay que estudiar todos los días (todas las semanas).

We must go shopping this afternoon.
It's necessary (you must) study every day (week).

EJERCICIOS

A. **En la clase.** El profesor Galdós feels that his students are doing exactly as they please today. Answer the questions for his students, using an idiom with **tener**.

Modelo ¿Por qué abres las ventanas, Miguel?
Porque tengo calor.

1. ¿Por qué tomas una Coca-Cola, Edgar?
2. ¿Por qué comen ustedes ahora?
3. ¿Por qué tomas aspirinas, Susana?
4. ¿Por qué cree Jorge que Nueva York es la capital de los Estados Unidos?
5. ¿Por qué no estudian ustedes?

Modelo   tomar Alka Seltzer
         tener dolor de estómago

1. tomar una Coca-Cola	a. tener que estudiar más
2. recibir cinco mil pesos	b. tener hambre
3. tomar unas aspirinas	c. tener sed
4. ir a las montañas en el invierno	d. tener (dieciocho) años hoy
5. ir a la playa	e. tener cuidado
6. necesitar una chaqueta (*jacket*)	f. tener calor
7. ir a un restaurante	g. tener frío
8. hacer una fiesta de cumpleaños	h. tener ganas de esquiar
9. esquiar por primera vez (*for the first time*)	i. tener suerte
	j. tener dolor de cabeza
10. recibir una «F» en un examen	k. tener fiebre
	l. tener ganas de nadar

PREGUNTAS

1. ¿Cuántos años tiene usted?   **2.** ¿Tiene hambre ahora?   **3.** ¿Tiene dolor de cabeza?   **4.** ¿Hace calor aquí? ¿frío?   **5.** ¿Tiene usted calor? ¿frío? **6.** «Valparaíso es la capital de Chile.» ¿Tengo razón o no? ¿Cómo se llama la capital de Chile?   **7.** ¿Tiene ganas de viajar? ¿Adónde? Para ir allí, ¿cómo hay que viajar? (¿En avión, tren, bus, auto...?)

Chile: Un país de inmigrantes

Jessica, una estudiante del Canadá, pasa unos meses de vacaciones en Santiago con una familia chilena. Va en auto con los dos hijos de la familia.

JESSICA	¡Huy!° Tengo mucho frío.
ANDREA	Por supuesto, hace frío porque es el primero de julio.[1] ¿Qué tiempo hace ahora en Vancouver?
JESSICA	Hace calor. Los domingos todo el mundo va a la playa.
JORGE	¡Qué gracioso!° En Chile vamos a la playa en diciembre, enero y febrero.
JESSICA	En esos meses tenemos mucha nieve en el Canadá. ¿Y ahora esquían ustedes aquí?
ANDREA	Claro, porque es invierno, Jessica.
JESSICA	¡Dios mío! Aquí hacen todo al revés°.
JORGE	Aquí somos normales; ustedes hacen todo al revés.
ANDREA	¿Van a discutir° toda la tarde? ¿Por qué no vamos de compras? Creo que vamos a tener lluvia.
JESSICA	Bueno, ¿adónde vamos?

La Alameda, en Santiago de Chile

ANDREA A la Alameda, una avenida que está en el centro. En realidad el nombre es Avenida O'Higgins, en honor del héroe° nacional de Chile.[2]

JESSICA O'Higgins... ¿Estás segura? ¿No es de Irlanda?

ANDREA ¡Qué va!° En este país Bernardo O'Higgins es muy famoso; es el líder de la revolución chilena de 1814 a 1818 contra° los españoles.

JORGE Sí, Jessica, Chile es un país de inmigrantes, como el Canadá. Aquí vive gente de origen inglés, español, alemán...

JESSICA Y también es el país de la escritora Isabel Allende.[3] El libro *La casa de los espíritus* es famoso en el Canadá y en los Estados Unidos. Miles de personas tienen esa novela—¡y yo también!

ANDREA Bueno, no es posible ir a esa casa... pero ¿qué tal si vamos a un salón de té° inglés? ¿De acuerdo...? ¡Té caliente para todos!

¡Huy! *Wow!*	**¡Qué gracioso!** *How funny!*	**al revés** *backwards* **discutir** *to argue*
el héroe *hero*	**¡Qué va!** *Oh come on! Not at all!*	**contra** *against*
salón de té *teahouse*		

PREGUNTAS

1. ¿Dónde pasa Jessica unos meses de vacaciones?   **2.** ¿Qué tiempo hace en Chile en el mes de julio? ¿Y en Vancouver?   **3.** ¿En qué meses tienen nieve en Vancouver? ¿Y en Chile?   **4.** ¿Cuándo van a la playa en Chile?   **5.** ¿Qué es la Alameda? ¿Cómo se llama en realidad esa avenida?   **6.** ¿Quién es Bernardo O'Higgins? **7.** ¿Es Chile un país de inmigrantes? ¿Y el Canadá?   **8.** ¿Qué libro tiene Jessica? ¿De quién es?   **9.** ¿Adónde van a llevar Andrea y Jorge a Jessica?

Notas culturales

1. The seasons are reversed in the Northern and Southern hemispheres.
2. Bernardo O'Higgins is the hero of Chile's war of independence against Spain (1814–1818). His mother was Chilean, and his father was an Irish immigrant who began as a traveling peddler in Ireland, moved to Spain, and was later appointed viceroy of Peru by the Spanish government. (This was most unusual in the rigid society of colonial Spanish America.) A brilliant and daring general during the war, O'Higgins served afterward as the first head of government in Chile.
3. Isabel Allende, niece of the deposed president of Chile, Salvador Allende, has written several novels that have been popular worldwide. Her book *La casa de los espíritus* (*The House of the Spirits*) is about the history of modern-day Chile, focusing primarily on the era when the democratic government of Salvador Allende was overthrown by the dictator General Augusto Pinochet.

FUNCIONES Y ACTIVIDADES

In this chapter you have seen examples of the following language functions, or uses. Here is a summary and some additional information about these uses of language.

Expressing obligation

You've seen several ways to express obligation so far in this book:

hay que + infinitive:
  Hay que ir.   *One (you, and so on) must go.*
es necesario + infinitive:
  Es necesario ir.   *It's necessary to go.*
necesitar + infinitive:
  Necesito ir.   *I need (have) to go.*
tener que + infinitive:
  Tengo que ir.   *I have to (must) go.*
deber + infinitive:
  Debo ir.   *I should (ought to) go.*

Es necesario and **hay que** + infinitive express strong impersonal obligation. **Necesitar** + infinitive also expresses strong obligation but of a more personal nature—the person is indicated, and the verb is conjugated. **Tener que** + infinitive also expresses personal obligation, but not as strongly. **Deber** + infinitive expresses the least strong obligation.

Making small talk

Here are some common phrases to open a casual conversation; as in English, weather is a common topic for small talk.

¿Qué piensa(s) del tiempo?	*What do you think about the weather?*
¡Qué calor (frío, viento, etcétera)!	*How hot (cold, windy and so on) it is!*
¡Qué buen tiempo!	*What nice weather!*
¿Cree(s) que vamos a tener lluvia?	*Do you think we're going to have some rain?*
¿Qué hora es? No llevo reloj.	*What time is it? I don't have (am not wearing) a watch.*
¡Qué mundo más pequeño! ¿Usted también va a Santa Ana (estudia biología, es de los Estados Unidos, etcétera)?	*What a small world! You're also going to Santa Ana (studying biology, from the United States, and so on)?*

Giving a warning

The expression **¡Cuidado!** (*Be careful! Watch out!*) is used to give a warning.

A. Obligaciones. Make sentences using these cues and an expression of obligation. More than one answer may be correct.

Modelos   todos / estudiar (*strong*)
Necesitamos estudiar. (Hay que estudiar. Es necesario estudiar.)

Enrique / hacer ejercicios (*fairly strong*)
Enrique tiene que hacer ejercicios.

tú / abrir la ventana (*weak*)
Debes abrir la ventana.

1. Anita / tomar aspirinas (*weak*)
2. todos / tener cuidado (*strong*)
3. Felipe / no tomar café (*weak*)
4. todos / comer para vivir (*strong*)
5. Rosario / llamar al doctor (*strong*)
6. tú / ir a casa ahora (*fairly strong*)

B. Esta semana... In pairs, take turns asking and answering questions in Spanish until you each find out at least two things your partner thinks he or she should or must do this week. The obligations may be related to school, home, work, health, or family. Here are some ideas:

no tomar café	ir a la biblioteca
hacer ejercicios	trabajar
visitar a un(-a) amigo(-a) o pariente en el hospital	tomar un examen
estudiar	leer la lección de español
escribir una carta, una composición	ser cortés

C. El tiempo. Review weather expressions and numbers while making small talk about the accompanying weather map of Chile. Note that Chile is so long and narrow it is often broken into three zones in newspaper maps, with the northern zone on the left. In the north, near the equator, it is almost always hot and dry. In the south, near Antarctica, it gets very cold. It is also very cold in the Andean areas, of course. This map is from the newspaper *El Mercurio*, May 23, or late fall. Temperatures are in degrees Celsius. Take turns asking and answering questions about it.

EL MERCURIO.

Santiago de Chile, Lunes 23 de Mayo

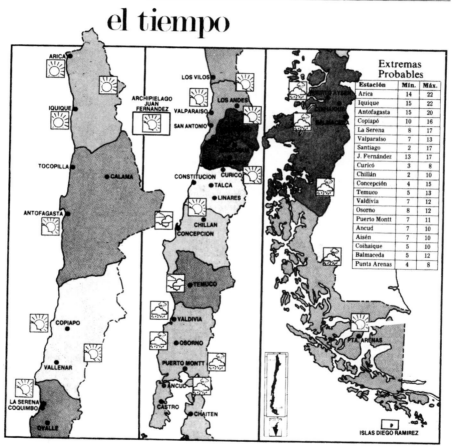

Extremas Probables		
Estación	Mín.	Máx.
Arica	14	22
Iquique	15	22
Antofagasta	15	20
Copiapó	10	16
La Serena	8	17
Valparaíso	7	13
Santiago	2	17
J. Fernández	13	17
Curicó	3	8
Chillán	2	10
Concepción	4	15
Temuco	5	13
Valdivia	7	12
Osorno	8	12
Puerto Montt	7	11
Ancud	7	10
Aisén	7	10
Coihaique	5	10
Balmaceda	5	12
Punta Arenas	4	8

Vocabulario: **la temperatura mínima (máxima); grados** (*degrees*)

Modelo
Estudiante 1: **¿Qué tiempo hace hoy en Concepción?**
Estudiante 2: **Está nublado. ¿Cuál es la temperatura mínima en Temuco?**
Estudiante 1: **Cinco grados.**

Situaciones. Role-play the following situations.

1. You are waiting for a bus. A person your age is also waiting. You both make small talk about the weather. You ask what time it is, and he or she answers. A car comes by close to the curb. "Watch out!" you say, as water splashes onto the curb. You ask where he or she is going, and he or she responds, "The National Museum on the Avenida Matucana." "What a small world!" you say; you are going to the museum also. "The bus is coming," says your new friend, and you both get on.

2. You're at the doctor's office. The doctor asks how old you are. You reply that you are twenty. He asks why you are there, and you reply that you have a stomachache and a headache and that you're also tired and cold. He tells you that you don't have a fever but that you should take two aspirins and call him tomorrow.

VOCABULARIO ACTIVO

Cognados

la aspirina	el, la inmigrante	la nacionalidad	el origen	el té
favorito	la montaña	necesario	el reportero, la reportera	

Verbos

contestar	to answer
esquiar	to ski
hay que (*from* haber)	— it's necessary; one (we, you, and so on) must
ir	to go
ir a + *inf.*	to be going to + inf.
ir de compras	to go shopping
ir de vacaciones	to go on vacation
ir en auto (autobús, avión, tren)	to go by car (bus, plane, train)
nadar	to swim
tener...años	to be . . . years old
tener cuidado	to be careful
tener dolor de cabeza (estómago)	to have a headache (stomachache)
tener fiebre	to have a fever
tener hambre (sed)	to be hungry (thirsty)
tener razón	to be right
tomar	to take; to drink

El tiempo

Está nublado.	It's cloudy.
Hace buen (mal) tiempo.	The weather is nice (bad).
Hace calor (fresco, frío, sol, viento).	The weather is warm (cool, cold, sunny, windy).
Llueve.	— It's raining.
Nieva.	— It's snowing.
¿Qué tiempo hace?	What's the weather like?
tener calor (frío)	to be warm (cold) (a person or animal)

La naturaleza (*Nature*)

el lago	lake
la lluvia	rain
el mar	— sea
la nieve	— snow
la playa	beach

Las estaciones del año

la primavera	*spring*
el verano	*summer*
el otoño	*fall*
el invierno	*winter*

Otras palabras y frases

cansado	*tired*
el centro	*downtown; center*
el cumpleaños	*birthday*
en realidad	*in reality, really*
¿Está usted seguro?	*Are you sure?*
la fecha	*date*
la gente	*people*
el mundo	*world*
el nombre	*name*
por supuesto	*of course, naturally*

primero	*first*
todas las semanas	*every week*
todo el mundo	*everyone*
todos los días	*every day*
el vuelo	*flight*

Expresiones útiles

¡Cuidado!	*Be careful! Watch out!*
¡Qué mundo más pequeño!	*What a small world!*

> **Don't forget:**
> Months of the year, page 86
> Days of the week, page 91
> Cardinal numbers 100 and above, page 94

La gente hispana

Mire° las fotos en las páginas 104 y 105. ¿Cuáles de las personas que allí vemos cree usted que son de origen hispano?... ¿La respuesta°? ¡Todas°! La palabra *hispano* se usa° para una gran variedad° de gentes y razas.° Los estereotipos de amantes° latinos con guitarras (tipo «don Juan»), las mujeres que bailan° flamenco con una rosa entre los dientes° o los «low-riders» de los Estados Unidos son sólo° eso: estereotipos. Después de todo,° mucha gente hispana cree que todos los norteamericanos llevan cámaras y «bermuda shorts», que tienen poco contacto con la familia, que no son religiosos y que están obsesionados por el dinero°... ¡otro estereotipo! Pero vamos ahora a conocer° a algunas° personas hispanas...

Esta chica rubia° es española. Muchos españoles son rubios, especialmente° en el norte. Los gallegos (de Galicia) son de origen céltico, como los irlandeses y escoceses.° En el sur la mayoría de la gente tiene pelo negro y ojos oscuros.°

Look at
answer / All of them
is used / variety / races
lovers / dance /
teeth / only
Después... *After all*

money
meet / some

blond / especially
Irish and Scots
majority / black hair
and dark eyes

Una española de Barcelona

Unos españoles de Barcelona

En muchas partes de Hispanoamérica, la gente es mestiza (parte india y parte europea).

Una niña peruana

En otras partes de Hispanoamérica, como en Bolivia o en el Perú, gran parte de la población° es india.

population

Una puertorriqueña, San Juan

En el Caribe la influencia africana es muy grande. Por ejemplo, la mayoría de la población de la República Dominicana es mulata (parte negra y parte europea). Y muchos puertorriqueños (de Puerto Rico) tienen sangre° india, negra y española.

blood

PREGUNTAS

1. Según (*According to*) los estereotipos populares, ¿cómo son los hispanos típicos? ¿y los norteamericanos típicos? **2.** ¿Cree usted en los estereotipos? **3.** ¿Tiene usted sangre india? ¿europea? ¿africana? **4.** ¿Es usted rubio(-a)? ¿moreno(-a) (*brunette*)? ¿pelirrojo(-a) (*redhead*)? **5.** ¿Tiene usted ojos oscuros? ¿azules (*blue*)? ¿castaños (*chestnut*)? **6.** ¿Tiene pelo negro? ¿castaño? ¿rubio?

Problemas de hoy

la inflación

el desempleo

la basura

la pobreza, el hambre

el crimen, el robo

la discriminación
(contra las mujeres, las minorías)

el tráfico

La ciudad y sus problemas

5

Expressing Sympathy
Expressing Lack of Sympathy

SIDA (AIDS)

contaminación
aire, del agua)

las huelgas

EJERCICIO

Match the persons listed with the political or social issue you think they would be likely to consider most important. Then create sentences following the model.

Modelo **Un policía cree que el crimen es un problema urgente.**

1. una madre de seis hijos
2. una secretaria
3. un joven que no tiene trabajo
4. un ecólogo (*ecologist*)
5. un señor que tiene mucho dinero (*money*)
6. una persona que vive lejos del empleo
7. un doctor

a. el desempleo
b. la contaminación del aire
c. la discriminación contra (*against*) las mujeres
d. el robo
e. el SIDA
f. el crimen
g. el uso de drogas en las escuelas
h. el tráfico

PREGUNTAS

1. ¿Vive usted en una ciudad grande o pequeña? ¿en una casa o en un apartamento? **2.** ¿En qué calle vive usted? **3.** ¿Qué problemas tienen en el barrio (*neighborhood*) donde usted vive? ¿en Harlem? ¿en Beverly Hills? **4.** Para usted, ¿cuál es el problema número uno de muchas ciudades de los Estados Unidos?

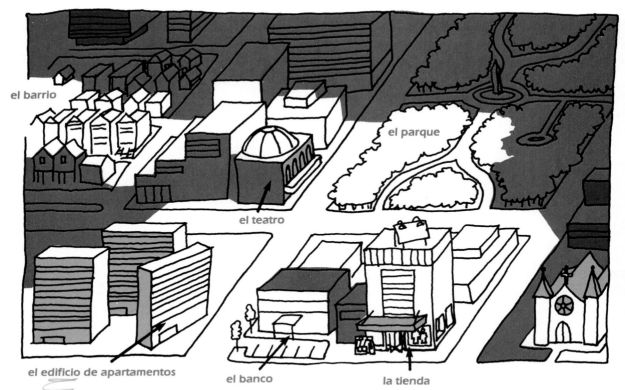

el barrio

el parque

el teatro

el edificio de apartamentos

el banco

la tienda

EJERCICIO

Match each word on the left with a word on the right that you associate with it.

Modelo plaza
plaza—parque

1. calle (*street*)
2. plaza
3. dinero
4. casa
5. pobreza
6. crimen

a. banco
b. apartamento
c. desempleo
d. robo
e. avenida
f. parque

Possessive adjectives

En un parque, cerca de una escuela.

SR. MORALES ¿Cuándo va a terminar la huelga, profesor?

PROFESOR Mañana..., pero *nuestros* problemas no terminan: mucho trabajo, poco salario, clases de 40 a 50 niños, etcétera.

SR. MORALES ¡Qué barbaridad! Pues..., ¿y cómo van *mis* hijos en *sus* estudios?

PROFESOR En realidad, no muy bien. Ricardo...

SR. MORALES Pero, ¿qué pasa con Ricardo? ¿No hace *sus* deberes?

PROFESOR *Su* hijo no estudia mucho. Por ejemplo, *su* última composición, sobre la lucha entre los conquistadores y los aztecas, no tiene mucha información.

SR. MORALES Comprendo, pero es *mi* culpa. En *nuestra* casa hablamos poco de básquetbol.

---

1. Según el profesor, ¿cuándo termina la huelga?   2. ¿Qué problemas tienen los profesores?   3. ¿Cómo van los hijos del Sr. Morales en sus estudios?   4. ¿Estudia sus lecciones Ricardo?   5. ¿Está bien su última composición?   6. ¿Por qué cree el Sr. Morales que es su culpa?   7. Según su opinión, ¿cómo va usted en sus estudios? ¿Va a recibir buenas notas (*grades*) en sus exámenes finales?

A. Possessive adjectives agree with the nouns they modify (the items possessed) in gender and number. They do not agree with the possessor.

mi(-s) amigo(-s) }
       amiga(-s) } *my friend(-s)*

nuestro(-s) amigo(-s) }
nuestra(-s) amiga(-s) } *our friend(-s)*

tu(-s) amigo(-s) } *your friend(-s)*
      amiga(-s) } (familiar)

vuestro(-s) amigo(-s) }
vuestra(-s) amiga(-s) } *your friend(-s)*

su(-s) amigo(-s) } *his (her, your (formal), their)*
      amiga(-s) } *friend(-s)*

In a park near a school. MR. MORALES: When is the strike going to end, professor? PROFESSOR: Tomorrow..., but our problems are not ending: lots of work, low pay, classes of 40 to 50 children, etc. MR. MORALES: Good grief! Well..., and how are my children doing in their studies? PROFESSOR: In reality, not too well. Ricardo... MR. MORALES: But what's the matter with Ricardo? Doesn't he do his homework? PROFESSOR: Your son doesn't study much. For example, his last composition, about the struggle (competition) between the conquistadors and the Aztecs, doesn't have much information (in it). MR. MORALES: I understand, but it's my fault. In our house we don't talk much about basketball.

nuestro primo, nuestra prima, nuestros
primos, nuestras primas
tu hijo, tu hija, tus hijos, tus hijas

our cousin (m.), *our cousin* (f.), *our cousins*
(m. or m. and f.), *our cousins* (f.)
*your son, your daughter, your sons (sons and
daughters), your daughters*

B. **Su** and **sus** have several possible meanings: *his, her, its, your, their.*

¿Cuántos niños hay en su familia?

*How many children are there in his (her,
your, their) family?*

Es su propia culpa.

It's his (her, your, their) own fault.

For this reason, it is often necessary to use **de** + a subject for clarity:

su hermano: el hermano de él (de ella, de usted, de ellos, de ellas, de ustedes)
sus hermanos: los hermanos de él (de ella, de usted, de ellos, de ellas, de ustedes)

¿Cuántos niños hay en la familia de él?

EJERCICIOS

A. ¿De quién es? (¿De quiénes son?)   From the list of items, identify those that
go with the key word, as shown in the model.

> **Modelo**   mis: libro, cuadernos, pluma, deberes, clases, mamá
> **mis cuadernos, mis deberes, mis clases**

1. nuestras: lección, amigas, edificio, papel, clases, problemas
2. su: estudios, auto, casa, amigos, padre, abuelos
3. tus: padre, hermanos, lecciones, abuela, prima, crimen
4. mi: tío, calle, papeles, hija, familia, dinero
5. nuestro: lección, lucha, edificio, verano, fecha, vacaciones

B. ¿Nosotros?   In pairs, respond to the following questions. Use **nuestro (-a,
-os, -as)**.

1. ¿Cómo son sus padres? ¿sus hermanos?
2. ¿Cómo es su clase de español? ¿Cómo son sus amigos en esta clase?
3. ¿Cómo es su universidad o escuela? ¿su ciudad?

C. ¿De quién es?   Make sentences using names of your classmates and the
following items or others that you think of.

> **Modelos**   **Es el dinero de María. Es su dinero.**
> **Son los cuadernos de Pablo. Son sus cuadernos.**

1. libro   5. mochila (*backpack*)
2. escritorio   6. calendario
3. carta   7. lápiz
4. reloj   8. examen

D. Entrevista. Interview a classmate to find the answers to the following questions.

1. ¿Cuál es tu ciudad favorita? ¿Por que? ¿Tiene problemas tu ciudad favorita?
2. ¿Cuántas personas hay en tu familia?
3. ¿Cómo se llaman tus hermanos?
4. ¿Dónde trabaja tu padre?, ¿tu madre?
5. ¿Cuál es tu estación favorita?
6. ¿Cómo se llama tu amigo(-a) favorito(-a)?

Stem-changing verbs: *e* to *ie*

En la Avenida Broadway de Nueva York.

ANA	¡Qué suerte vivir cerca de un lugar donde hay películas en español! Margarita, *¿quieres* una Coca-Cola, un café o...?
MARGARITA	Una Coca-Cola, por favor. ¿Y tú?
ANA	Yo *prefiero* café. *¿Quieres* esperar aquí?
MARGARITA	*Prefiero* entrar.

Ellas entran.

MARGARITA	Ana, *empieza* la película. Pero estas señoras hablan y hablan.
ANA	Perdón, señora. ¡Es imposible *entender!*
LA SEÑORA	¿Cómo? ¿No *entiende* usted? ¡Pero, caramba, esta es una conversación privada, señorita!

1. ¿Qué quiere Margarita, un café o una Coca-Cola?   2. ¿Qué prefiere Ana?
3. ¿Por qué no entienden la película Ana y Margarita?   4. ¿Cómo es la conversación de las señoras?   5. ¿Qué clase de películas prefiere usted: las cómicas, las dramáticas o las de ciencia ficción (*science fiction*)?

On Broadway Avenue in New York. ANA: How lucky to live near a place where there are films in Spanish! Margarita, do you want a Coca-Cola, coffee, or... MARGARITA: A Coca-Cola, please. And you? ANA: I prefer coffee. Do you want to wait here? MARGARITA: I prefer to go in. (*They go in.*) MARGARITA: Ana, the film is beginning. But these ladies are talking and talking. ANA: Excuse me, ma'am. It's impossible to hear (understand)! THE WOMAN: What? You can't hear? But good grief! This is a private conversation, miss!

A. Certain groups of Spanish verbs are known as stem-changing verbs. These verbs have regular endings but show a change in the stem when it is stressed. In the following verbs, the **e** of the stem is changed to **ie** in all but the **nosotros** and **vosotros** forms. In vocabulary lists, these verbs are followed by (**ie**).

pensar (to think; to plan; to intend)		**entender** (to understand)		**preferir** (to prefer)	
pienso	pensamos	entiendo	entendemos	prefiero	preferimos
piensas	pensáis	entiendes	entendéis	prefieres	preferís
piensa	piensan	entiende	entienden	prefiere	prefieren

B. Other **e** to **ie** stem-changing verbs are

cerrar	to close
empezar	to begin
nevar	to snow
perder	to lose; to miss (a train, boat, etc.); to waste (time)
querer	to want; to love

Cierran dos tiendas en la Avenida Lexington.	They're closing two stores on Lexington Avenue.
No entiendo el problema.	I don't understand the problem.
¿Entiende usted el formulario?	¿Do you understand the form?
Empiezas mañana.	You begin tomorrow.
Juan no quiere trabajar en ese lugar.	Juan doesn't want to work in that place.
Quiero a Paco.	I love Paco.
Pensamos ir a Guadalajara.	We are planning to go to Guadalajara.
A veces pienso en ella.	Sometimes I think of her.
¿Qué piensas de la huelga?	What do you think about the strike?
Preferimos regresar temprano.	We prefer to return early.
Prefiero trabajar en la oficina, no en casa.	I prefer to work at the office, not at home.
Ellos siempre pierden dinero. Además, pierden el tiempo.	They always lose money. Besides, they waste time.
¡Caramba! Es tarde. ¡Voy a perder el avión!	Good grief! It's late. I'm going to miss the plane!

Notice that **pensar** takes the preposition **en** when it means *to think of* or *about* (someone or something); it takes **de** when it means *to think of* in the sense of *to have an opinion* (of someone or something).

A. Pues, nosotros no. Take the role of Rodolfo's co-workers, Raúl and Blanca, and react negatively to his complaints.

Modelo   Pienso mucho en los problemas que tengo.
          Pues, nosotros no pensamos mucho en los problemas que tenemos.

1. Empiezo a tener problemas aquí.
2. Vengo tarde al trabajo por el tráfico.
3. Prefiero vivir en Puerto Rico.
4. Quiero vivir en San Juan.
5. Pierdo la paciencia con los precios de aquí.
6. Pienso mucho en los problemas que tengo.

B. En Puerto Rico. Complete the following conversation with the correct forms of the verbs in parentheses.

RAFAEL: La tía Rosita y yo _____₁ (querer) regresar a Puerto Rico. Nosotros _____₂ (pensar) viajar en noviembre.
MIGUELITO: Pero... ¡qué lástima! Mamá _____₃ (venir) de allí en diciembre. Ella _____₄ (pensar) pasar aquí las fiestas (*holidays*). ¿No _____₅ (preferir) ustedes esperar?
RAFAEL: No, Miguelito, nosotros _____₆ (cerrar) la tienda el primero. _____₇ (Empezar) a hacer las maletas.
MIGUELITO: Pero, tío, yo no _____₈ (entender). ¿Por qué no _____₉ (cerrar) ustedes la tienda después de Año Nuevo?
RAFAEL: Es que hace mucho frío aquí en el invierno. _____₁₀ (Preferir) pasar diciembre y enero en Puerto Rico.

C. ¿Pensar de... o pensar en...? Complete the sentences using **de** or **en** as appropriate.

1. Papá siempre piensa _____ los problemas de la oficina.
2. ¿Qué piensas _____ la esposa de Bernardo?
3. ¿Piensas a veces _____ el pasado?
4. Ustedes no piensan eso _____ la abogada, ¿verdad?

D. Entrevista. Ask a classmate questions using the following cues and ideas of your own. Make a general statement to the class telling some of your classmate's answers.

Modelo   preferir vivir aquí o en Nueva York
          Estudiante 1: **¿Prefieres vivir aquí o en Nueva York?**
          Estudiante 2: **Prefiero vivir aquí.**

1. preferir vivir en una ciudad grande o en una región rural (¿Por qué?)
2. querer vivir en San Francisco (¿Los Ángeles? ¿Madrid? ¿Tokio? ¿París?)
3. preferir vivir en un apartamento moderno o en una casa
4. pensar que la contaminación es un problema urgente (¿la pobreza? ¿la inflación? ¿el SIDA?)

5. pensar que hay mucha discriminación contra las mujeres (¿contra las minorías? ¿contra los jóvenes?)
6. preferir ir a la universidad en autobús, tren, auto o bicicleta
7. perder mucho tiempo en el tráfico

PREGUNTAS

1. ¿Entiende usted español? ¿francés? ¿italiano? ¿alemán? **2.** ¿Tiene muchas oportunidades de hablar español? ¿de escuchar español? ¿Dónde? **3.** ¿Piensa tomar otra clase de español? **4.** ¿Quiere mirar películas en español en esta clase? **5.** ¿Estudia mucho? ¿A qué hora empieza usted a estudiar? **6.** ¿Qué piensa hacer esta noche? ¿mañana? ¿el domingo? ¿en las vacaciones?

Direct object pronouns

TERESA	En esta ciudad hay mucha gente que vive en la calle. ¡Qué problema!
ROSA	Pues es de esperar. Muchos quieren vivir así. No quieren trabajar, ¿*me* entiendes?
TERESA	Sí, *te* entiendo, pero... ¿realmente *lo* crees? Pienso que debemos ayudar*los* con comida y otras cosas. Por ejemplo, hay una mujer que vive en la calle, cerca de mi casa. Creo que tiene problemas mentales. Deben poner*la* en una institución. En la calle tiene hambre y frío y...
ROSA	¿Y qué? En una institución la gente pierde la libertad.

1. ¿Cómo es Teresa? ¿Qué piensa ella? 2. ¿Cómo es Rosa? ¿Qué cree ella?
3. ¿Con quién está usted de acuerdo? ¿Por qué?

TERESA: In this city there are a lot of people who live on the street. What a problem! ROSA: Well, it's to be expected. Many people want to live like that. They don't want to work—do you understand me? TERESA: Yes, I understand you, but...do you really believe that (it)? I think we should help them with food and other things. For example, there's a woman who lives in the street near my house. I think she has mental problems. They should put her in an institution. In the street she's hungry and cold and ... ROSA: And so what? In an institution people lose their freedom.

A. Direct object pronouns replace the direct object of a sentence (either a person or a thing) and receive the direct action of the verb. For instance, in the sentence *I see it* (*the book*), the direct object pronoun is *it*.

Direct Object Pronouns			
Singular		**Plural**	
me	*me*	nos	*us*
te	*you* (tú)	os	*you* (vosotros)
lo*	*him, it, you* (usted)	los	*them, you* (ustedes)
la	*her, it, you* (usted)	las	*them, you* (ustedes)

B. **Lo** and **la** are the direct object pronouns that correspond to the subject pronouns **él**, **ella**, and **usted**. **Lo** is used to refer to a person or thing of masculine gender, and **la** is used to refer to a person or thing of feminine gender. **Lo** is also used to refer to actions or situations.

¿La carta? No la tengo.	*The letter? I don't have it.*
No lo entiendo a usted, señor.	*I don't understand you, sir.*
¡No lo creo!	*I don't believe it!*

C. **Los** and **las** are the direct object pronouns that correspond to the subject pronouns **ellos**, **ellas**, and **ustedes**. **Los** is used to refer to people or things of masculine gender, and **las** is used to refer to people or things of feminine gender. **Los** is also used to refer to groups in which the genders are mixed.

¿Esos lugares? Los voy a visitar pronto.	*Those places? I'm going to visit them soon.*
¿Las bicicletas? Si no las usan mucho, ¿me las venden?	*The bicycles? If you don't use them a lot, will you sell them to me?*
¿Los libros? No los veo.**	*The books? I don't see them.*

D. Use **te** when speaking to someone you address as **tú**. Use **lo** when speaking to a man and **la** when speaking to a woman whom you address as **usted**.

Te llamo mañana, Carlota.	*I'll call you tomorrow, Carlota.*
Adiós, señorita. La llamo mañana.	*Good-bye, miss. I'll call you tomorrow.*

E. Direct object pronouns can be placed directly before a conjugated verb (a verb with an ending that tells the tense, person, and number).

¿Me esperas?	*Will you wait for me?*
Nos miran ahora.	*They are looking at us now.*

---

* In Spain it is common to use **le (les)** instead of **lo (los)** as the masculine direct object pronoun to refer to a man (men) and to use **lo (los)** to refer to things or ideas. However, this distinction is not normally observed in Latin America. Depending on one's background, one may say **Le veo** or **Lo veo**; both mean *I see him.*

** The first-person singular of **ver** (*to see*) is **veo**. The other forms of the present tense are regular.

F. Direct object pronouns can also be placed after an infinitive and attached to it.

Vamos a visitarla mañana.	*We are going to visit her tomorrow.*
No tengo que hacerlo ahora. Es temprano.	*I don't have to do it now. It's early.*

However, if the infinitive is part of a larger verb construction, the direct object pronoun can be attached to the infinitive, as above, or it can be placed in front of the entire verb construction. In spoken Spanish, the latter position is more common.

¿Mi programa favorito?	*My favorite program?*
Lo voy a mirar ahora.⎫	
Voy a mirarlo ahora. ⎭	*I'm going to watch it now.*

EJERCICIOS

A. Al revés. (*Backwards.*)   Change the position of the pronouns in italics.

> **Modelo**   ¿Cuándo *lo* vamos a visitar?
> **¿Cuándo vamos a visitarlo?**

RAFA	Ese café es muy bueno. ¿*Lo* vas a comprar?
HUGO	Sí, creo que Susana *nos* va a visitar.
RAFA	¿Quién *la* va a invitar (*invite*)?
HUGO	Yo. *La* voy a llamar ahora.
RAFA	¿Tienes su número de teléfono?
HUGO	*Lo* voy a buscar.
RAFA	¿Cuándo vas a hacer la comida?
HUGO	¿Yo...? ¿hacer la comida? No, amigo. ¡Tú *la* vas a hacer!

B. ¿No lo ves...?   Ignacio is having trouble seeing the things his friend Mario is pointing out. Answer Mario's questions in the negative, as Ignacio would. Use direct object pronouns.

> **Modelo**   ¿Ves ese edificio?
> **No, no lo veo.**

1. ¿Ves aquella bicicleta?
2. ¿Ves esa calle?
3. ¿Ves al hermano de Pepe?
4. ¿Ves el parque?
5. ¿Ves a esos muchachos?
6. ¿Ves las oficinas?
7. ¿Ves aquellos autos?
8. ¿Ves esas librerías?

Now ask questions of a classmate, using names of classroom objects.

> **Modelos**   **¿Ves la pizarra?**
> **Sí, la veo.**
> **¿Ves el cuaderno de Scott?**
> **No, no lo veo.**

C. Otro día. Tell the following people good-bye and that you'll call or see them another day.

Modelos tu mamá / llamar el jueves
Adiós, mamá. Te llamo el jueves.

unos profesores de la universidad / ver el lunes
Adiós, señores. Los veo el lunes.

1. tu amiga Laura / llamar mañana
2. el doctor Ramírez / llamar el miércoles
3. tus amigas Ana y Carolina / ver el sábado
4. la secretaria del departamento de español / ver el viernes
5. los señores Blanco / ver el domingo
6. tu amigo Felipe / llamar el lunes

D. Conversación. Complete the conversation with appropriate direct object pronouns.

RAFAEL: Cecilia, ¿vas a apoyar (*support*) a Ramón García en las elecciones?
CECILIA: No, no _____1 voy a apoyar, Rafael. Prefiero a Josephine Smith.
RAFAEL: ¿Prefieres a una mujer? ¿Y _____2 vas a apoyar? Pero García es puertorriqueño. Entiende los problemas del barrio.
CECILIA: Nosotras, las mujeres, preferimos a Smith. _____3 necesitamos.
RAFAEL: ¿Realmente _____4 crees? Pues yo tengo mis dudas (*doubts*).

E. Entrevista. Ask someone the following questions. The other person should answer using a direct object pronoun. (Fibs are permitted!)

Modelo ¿Deseas mirar el programa "¡Salud!" ("Cheers!")?
Sí, lo deseo mirar. (No, no lo deseo mirar.)

1. ¿Tomas el café de la cafetería?
2. ¿Visitas a la doctora mañana?
3. ¿Compras los libros en la librería de la universidad?
4. ¿Te llama el profesor (la profesora) en la casa?
5. ¿Contestas las preguntas del profesor (de la profesora)?

PREGUNTAS

1. ¿Necesita usted un auto? ¿Por qué lo necesita? **2.** ¿Tiene una bicicleta? ¿La usa mucho? ¿Adónde la lleva? **3.** ¿Mira televisión? ¿Cuáles son sus programas favoritos? ¿Cuándo los mira? **4.** ¿Estudia usted las lecciones de español de noche? ¿de tarde? ¿de día? **5.** ¿Llama usted a sus amigos por teléfono? ¿Los llama de noche o prefiere llamarlos de tarde? ¿Prefiere llamarlos o visitarlos? ¿Por qué?

The present tense of *saber* and *conocer*

CRISTINA	Rosa, ¿*conoces* a Ramón?
ROSA	¿Ese chico dominicano que vive con Jesús y Marta? Sí, lo *conozco*.
CRISTINA	Va a perder el trabajo, pobrecito.
ROSA	¡Qué mala suerte!
CRISTINA	Además, *sé* que no está muy contento aquí. En el barrio donde vive hay crímenes, robos, personas adictas a las drogas, basura por todas partes...
ROSA	Sí, lo *sé*. ¡Qué lástima!
CRISTINA	El problema es que Ramón no *conoce* bien la ciudad y no *sabe* buscar apartamento en otro barrio.
ROSA	Pues si tú lo llevas a buscar apartamento, yo voy a ayudarlo con el empleo, ¿de acuerdo? *Conozco* a un ingeniero y *sé* que ahora necesitan ayuda en la compañia de construcción donde trabaja.

1. ¿Quién es Ramón? ¿Lo conoce Rosa?   2. ¿Por qué no está contento?
3. ¿Conoce bien la ciudad?   4. ¿Qué va a hacer Cristina?   5. ¿A quién conoce Rosa? ¿Qué va a hacer ella?

A. The verbs **saber** and **conocer** are irregular in the first-person singular.

saber *(to know, know how to)*		**conocer** *(to know, be acquainted with)*	
sé	sabemos	**conozco**	conocemos
sabes	sabéis	conoces	conocéis
sabe	saben	conoce	conocen

CRISTINA: Rosa, do you know Ramón? ROSA: That Dominican guy (guy from the Dominican Republic) who lives with Jesús and Marta? Yes, I know him. CRISTINA: He's going to lose his job, poor thing. ROSA: What bad luck! CRISTINA: What's more, I know he's not very happy here. In the neighborhood where he lives there are crimes, robberies, drug addicts, garbage everywhere... ROSA: Yes, I know. What a shame! CRISTINA: The problem is that Ramón doesn't know the city well and doesn't know how to look for an apartment in another neighborhood. ROSA: Well, if you take him to look for an apartment, I'll help him with work, okay? I know an engineer, and I know that they need help in the construction company where he works.

B. **Saber** and **conocer** both mean *to know*, but they are not interchangeable. **Saber** means *to have knowledge of facts or information about something or someone*; with an infinitive, it means *to know how to do something*. **Conocer** means *to know* or *to be acquainted with a person, place, or thing*. Before a direct object that refers to a person or persons, **conocer** takes a personal **a** (see Chapter 2, section V).

Conozco a Conchita pero no sé dónde está.	*I know* (am acquainted with) *Conchita but I don't know* (have information about) *where she is.*
¿Conoces el barrio?	*Do you know the neighborhood?*
Saben hablar italiano.	*They know how to speak Italian.*

EJERCICIOS

A. **Conversaciones.**   With a classmate, complete the conversations using appropriate forms of **saber** or **conocer**.

JOSÉ ¿Tus padres _____₁ hablar francés?
EVA   No, pero _____₂ bien París.

JUAN ¿_____₃ (tú) a Mercedes Sosa?
EVA   No, pero _____₄ quién es.

FELIPE ¿_____₅ ustedes cómo llegar al centro?
TERESA No, no lo _____₆.

B. **Breves encuentros.** (*Brief encounters.*)   Working with a partner, act out these brief conversations.

1. A: Ask if this bus goes to the Museo del Oro.
   B: Say that you don't know because you don't know the city very well.
2. A: Ask if your partner knows Felipe Restrepo.
   B: Say yes, you know him. Add that you know he's in one of your classes.

PREGUNTAS

1. ¿Sabe usted cómo se llama la capital de Chile? ¿de Argentina?   **2.** ¿Conoce la ciudad de Nueva York? ¿Conoce Los Ángeles? ¿Qué problemas tienen estas dos ciudades? ¿Sabe por qué?   **3.** ¿Quién sabe más (*the most*) sobre el problema del desempleo: el sociólogo (*sociologist*) o la persona que no tiene trabajo?   **4.** ¿Sabe usted qué estados de los Estados Unidos tienen nombres españoles?

Nueva York: Los puertorriqueños

Un barrio hispano, en Nueva York

Dos amigos puertorriqueños están en la oficina de empleos del edificio municipal de Nueva York. Uno de ellos lleva en la mano° un formulario de empleo.

RAFAEL ¡Carlos! ¿Qué haces aquí?

CARLOS Hola, Rafa. Yo trabajo en esta oficina. ¿Y tú?

RAFAEL Busco empleo. Pero este formulario es difícil...

CARLOS ¿No lo entiendes? Te ayudo. Primero tienes que escribir tu nombre y apellido°.

RAFAEL Bueno. Los escribo en esta línea°. Escribo mi nombre completo... Rafael Álvarez Balboa.[1]

CARLOS ¡No, hombre! ¿No sabes que aquí prefieren los nombres fáciles? ¿Por qué no escribes simplemente° Ralph Álvarez?

RAFAEL Pero ése no es mi nombre. Todos me conocen como Rafael... Bueno, Ralph está bien... Sé que los americanos tienen todos los buenos empleos.

CARLOS Pero ¡nosotros también somos americanos! Por lo menos° no tenemos problemas legales como toda la gente que viene aquí por razones políticas°.[2]

El Condado, en San Juan, Puerto Rico

RAFAEL	Eso sí es verdad, y no tenemos problemas en regresar a la Isla.[3] Estoy cansado de esta ciudad, de los crímenes, de la basura por todas partes, de la gente adicta a las drogas...
CARLOS	¿Qué esperas? Todas las grandes ciudades tienen problemas similares. San Juan también, ¿no?
RAFAEL	Sí, lo sé, pero en San Juan no hace frío en el invierno. Allí conozco a mucha gente y entiendo las costumbres°..., ¿me comprendes?
CARLOS	Sí, te entiendo, pero en San Juan no hay empleos. Yo prefiero vivir aquí. Pero... ¿qué tipo de trabajo buscas, Rafa?
RAFAEL	Pues, un trabajo de guardia de seguridad°, por ejemplo.
CARLOS	Un momento... (*Pasan unos minutos.*) Hay un puesto° en Brooklyn y otro en una tienda en Manhattan. ¿Cuál prefieres?
RAFAEL	No lo sé. ¿Qué piensas?
CARLOS	¿Por qué no llamas a los dos lugares? Aquí están las direcciones y los números de teléfono.
RAFAEL	Buena idea. Gracias, Carlos.
CARLOS	¡Buena suerte!

---

mano *hand*   **apellido** *surname*   **línea** *line*   **simplemente** *simply*
por lo menos *at least*   **por razones políticas** *for political reasons*   **costumbres** *customs*
guardia de seguridad *security guard*   **puesto** *position*

1. ¿Qué lleva uno de los puertorriqueños en la mano? ¿Qué hace él allí? ¿y Carlos?   **2.** ¿Entiende Rafael el formulario?   **3.** ¿Qué nombre quiere poner Carlos en el formulario? ¿Por qué?   **4.** ¿Hay gente hispana que tiene problemas en regresar a sus países? ¿Por qué? ¿Tienen ese problema los puertorriqueños? ¿Por qué sí o por qué no?   **5.** ¿Dónde prefiere vivir Rafael: en Nueva York o en Puerto Rico? ¿Y Carlos? ¿Y usted?

Notas culturales

1. Most people of Spanish descent use both their father's and mother's surnames (**apellidos**), sometimes separating them with **y**. The father's name is customarily put first. Thus, Rafael's father's surname is Álvarez, and his mother's, Balboa.

2. In New York about a fourth of the population is composed of immigrants, and about a fifth of all New Yorkers are of Hispanic background. Besides the large Puerto Rican community, there are many Dominicans, Ecuadorians, and Colombians, as well as people from all other Spanish-speaking countries. (Three-fourths of all Dominicans, half of all Ecuadorians, and a third of all Colombians who live in the United States are in New York.) Many come seeking political refuge, legally or illegally. However, since Puerto Rico is a United States commonwealth, its inhabitants are U.S. citizens, and no visa is required for entry into the U.S. mainland.

3. Many Puerto Ricans refer to their homeland as **la Isla del Encanto** (*the Isle of Enchantment*) or simply as **la Isla**. Because of its natural beauty, agreeable climate, and Hispanic atmosphere, most Puerto Ricans who leave to find work long to return.

FUNCIONES Y ACTIVIDADES

In this chapter, you have seen examples of the following language functions, or uses. Here is a summary and some additional information about these functions of language.

Expressing sympathy

Here are some expressions to show that you feel sympathy for someone, understand what he or she is going through:

¡Qué lástima!   *What a shame (pity)!*

¡Qué mala suerte!   *What bad luck!*

¡Qué barbaridad!   *Good grief!*
 (literally, *What barbarity!*)

¡Qué horror!   *How horrible!*

¡Pobrecito(-a)!   *Poor thing!*

Eso debe ser terrible.   *That must be terrible.*

¡Ay, Dios mío!   *Oh, my goodness!*

¡Caramba!   *Good grief!*

Expressing lack of sympathy

Here are some expressions to use when you think someone is creating his or her own bad fortune or "has it coming":

¡Buena lección!   *That's a good lesson for you!*

Es de esperar.   *It's to be expected.*

¿Qué espera(-s)?   *What do you expect?*

¿Qué importancia tiene?   *What's so important (about that)?*

¿Y qué?   *So what?*

Es su (tu) propia culpa.   *It's your own fault.*

A. **¿Compasión o falta de compasión?** (*Sympathy or lack of sympathy?*)   Your friend Pedro is always getting into trouble and having problems. Sometimes it's just bad luck, but sometimes he brings trouble on himself. Express sympathy or lack of sympathy for him when you find out each of the following things.

Modelos   Su mamá está en el hospital.
   ¡Qué mala suerte!

   Va en su Fiat a cien kilómetros por hora cuando un policía lo ve.
   Es tu propia culpa.

1. Busca empleo, pero siempre llega tarde a las entrevistas (*interviews*).
2. Hay un robo en el edificio donde vive y pierde su bicicleta.
3. Recibe una «F» en un examen porque no estudia mucho.
4. No está en buenas condiciones físicas porque no come bien y no hace ejercicios.
5. Llega tarde al aeropuerto porque hay mucho tráfico; pierde el avión.
6. Tiene un accidente de auto que no es por su culpa.
7. Compra un auto nuevo pero no anda bien (*it doesn't run well*).
8. Va a la playa y pierde su cámara.

B. Problemas. Everyone has problems. In small groups, find out at least one problem—large or small—that someone in the group has. If necessary, ask your teacher for help in stating it. Then take turns expressing sympathy (or lack of sympathy) for the person with the problem.

VOCABULARIO ACTIVO

Cognados

el apartamento	contento	favorito	la oportunidad
el banco	el crimen	la inflación	el parque
el básquetbol	la discriminación	la minoría	puertorriqueño
la bicicleta	la droga	la oficina	urgente
la composición			

Verbos

ayudar	to help
cerrar (ie)	to close
conocer	to be familiar with, to know
empezar (ie)	to begin, start
entender (ie)	to understand; to hear
esperar	to wait for; to hope; to expect
nevar (ie)	to snow
pasar	to happen
pensar (ie)	to think; to plan; to intend
pensar de	to think about, have an opinion of
pensar en	to think about, reflect on
perder (ie)	to lose; to miss (train, plane, etc.); to waste (time)
preferir (ie)	to prefer
querer (ie)	to want; to love
regresar	to return, go back
saber	to know, know how to
terminar	to finish, end
usar	to use
ver	to see

La ciudad y sus problemas

el barrio	neighborhood, community
la basura	garbage
la calle	street
la contaminación del aire (del agua)	air (water) pollution
el desempleo	unemployment
el dinero	money
el edificio	building
el empleo	employment
el hambre (f.)	hunger
la pobreza	poverty
el robo	theft, robbery
el SIDA	AIDS
la tienda	shop, store
el trabajo	work

Otras palabras y frases

a veces	sometimes
además	moreover, besides
así	like that
la ayuda	help
el café	coffee; café
contra	against
corto	brief, short (not used in reference to people)

la culpa	— guilt
los deberes	homework
la huelga	— strike
la lucha	fight, struggle
el lugar	place; room (space)
la mano	hand
la película	film
poco	little
pocos	few
por todas partes	— everywhere
tarde	— late
temprano	early
último	— most recent, latest

Expresiones útiles

¡Buena lección!	That's a good lesson for you!
¡Caramba!	Good grief!
Es de esperar.	— It's to be expected.
Es su (tu) propia culpa.	It's your own fault.
¡Pobrecito!	Poor thing!
¡Qué barbaridad!	Good grief! (literally, What barbarity!)
¿Qué espera(-s)?	What do you expect?
¡Qué horror!	How horrible!
¿Qué importancia tiene?	— What's so important (about that)?
¡Qué mala suerte!	What bad luck!
¿Realmente lo cree?	Do you really believe it?
¿Y qué?	— So what?

> **Don't forget:**
> Possessive adjectives, page 109
> Direct object pronouns, page 115

ir al cine a ver una película

bailar, ir al baile

sacar foto

cantar canciones folklóricas

programa

ir al teatro a ver una obra o a escuchar un concierto

jugar a los naipes

tocar la guitarra, el piano, el violín

escuchar mús

Diversiones y pasatiempos 6

Making Requests
Offering Assistance
Expressing Gratitude

EJERCICIO

Choose the correct word to complete each sentence.

1. José (toca/juega) la guitarra.
2. Vamos al (cine/teatro) a ver una película.
3. El tango es (un baile/una canción).
4. Pedro y Julia (tocan/juegan) a los naipes.
5. Queremos escuchar un concierto en el (Cine/Teatro) Nacional.
6. Luis Buñuel es un director español de muchas (obras de teatro/películas) famosas.

computadora

PREGUNTAS

1. ¿Qué hace usted los fines de semana? ¿Va al cine? ¿Escucha música? ¿Tiene muchos discos? ¿cintas? ¿Mira televisión?   **2.** ¿Qué va a hacer el fin de semana que viene?   **3.** ¿Prefiere usted bailar o escuchar música? ¿Por qué?   **4.** ¿Sabe usted tocar la guitarra? ¿el piano? ¿el violín?   **5.** ¿Sabe usted programar una computadora? ¿Qué tipo de computadora tiene?   **6.** ¿Va usted mucho al cine? ¿Cuál es el título (*title*) de su película favorita?   **7.** ¿Qué diversiones prefiere usted cuando está con amigos? Y cuando no está con amigos, ¿cuál es su pasatiempo (*pastime*) favorito?

discos, cintas

Indirect object pronouns

TOMÁS	Pedro, ¿*me* haces un favor? Silvia y yo queremos ir a una presentación en el teatro Herbst hoy. ¿*Nos* prestas el auto?
PEDRO	¡Cómo no! ¿Qué van a ver?
TOMÁS	Una presentación de una compañía de danza española. ¿Quieres ir con nosotros? *Te* compro la entrada.
PEDRO	¡Gracias, amigo! ¿A qué hora vamos?

---

1. ¿Adónde quieren ir Silvia y Tomás? ¿Qué van a ver?   2. ¿Quién les va a prestar el auto?   3. ¿Qué le va a comprar Tomás a Pedro?

A. The indirect object in a sentence indicates the person or thing that receives the action of the verb. In the sentence *I told Carmen the truth*, *Carmen* is the person who benefits or is affected by the truth being told; she is the indirect object. (*The truth* is what gets told; it is the direct object.) In English, indirect objects are often replaced by prepositional phrases: *I told Carmen the truth (I told the truth to Carmen). I bought Carmen the book (I bought the book for Carmen).* An indirect object pronoun is a pronoun that replaces an indirect object noun: *I bought* her *the book*.

B. Except for the third-person forms, **le** and **les**, the indirect object pronouns are the same as direct object pronouns.

<table>
<tr><td colspan="4">Indirect Object Pronouns</td></tr>
<tr><td colspan="2">Singular</td><td colspan="2">Plural</td></tr>
<tr><td>me</td><td>(to, for) me</td><td>nos</td><td>(to, for) us</td></tr>
<tr><td>te</td><td>(to, for) you</td><td>os</td><td>(to, for) you</td></tr>
<tr><td>le</td><td>(to, for) you, him, her, it</td><td>les</td><td>(to, for) you, them</td></tr>
</table>

TOMÁS: Pedro, will you do me a favor? Silvia and I want to go to a show at the Herbst theater today. Will you loan us the car? PEDRO: Of course! What are you going to see? TOMÁS: A show by a Spanish dance company. Do you want to go with us? I'll buy you the ticket. PEDRO: Thanks, my friend! What time shall we go?

C. Like direct object pronouns, indirect object pronouns immediately precede a conjugated verb.

Le hablo.

I'm speaking to him (her, you).

No les escribo una carta hoy.

I'm not writing a letter to them (you, pl.) today.

Te compro un regalo después del almuerzo.

I'm buying you a present after lunch.

¿Me preparas la cena? —Sí, y luego te hago un café.

Are you preparing (Will you prepare) dinner for me? —Yes, and then I'll make coffee for you.

D. When used with an infinitive, indirect object pronouns follow the same rules as direct object pronouns: either they precede the entire verb construction, or they follow the infinitive and are attached to it.

Mis papás me prometen comprar un piano.

Mis papás prometen comprarme un piano.

My parents promise to buy me a piano.

E. For clarity, a prepositional phrase is often used in addition to the indirect object pronoun in the third person.

Le hablo {a él. / a ella. / a usted.}

Les hablo {a ellos. / a ellas. / a ustedes.}

Since these expressions function as objects of the preposition **a**, they are called prepositional object pronouns. They are the same as the regular subject pronouns, except for the first- and second-person singular: **mí** and **ti**.

¿Me hablas a mí? —Sí, a ti te hablo.

Are you talking to me? —Yes, I'm talking to you.

F. The indirect object pronoun is often used even when the noun to which it refers is also expressed. This is considered good style.

Le escribo a mi abuelo antes del almuerzo.

I'm writing to my grandfather before lunch.

Felipe les lee un poema a sus amigos.

Felipe is reading a poem to his friends.

A. El cumpleaños de Miguel. What presents do Miguel's parents and friends buy him for his birthday?

Modelo **Su abuelo le compra unos discos.**

su tío Pablo

su amiga
Rosa

su abuelo

su
hermano
Jaime

Miguel

su hermana
Ana

B. ¡Mil gracias, Gastón! Gastón is very popular and well liked by everyone. To find out why, do the following exercises, using indirect object pronouns as in the models.

Modelos a Martín / muestra sus libros
Le muestra sus libros.

a ti y a mí / hacer favores
Nos hace favores.

1. a nosotros / cantar canciones
2. a su hermana / leer poemas
3. a los niños / comprar chocolates
4. a mí / escribir cartas
5. a Raquel y a ti / tocar la guitarra
6. a ti / preparar el almuerzo
7. a Roberto / prestar el auto
8. a sus padres / comprar entradas para el teatro
9. a Paquito / prometer llevar al cine
10. a sus tíos / prestar la computadora

C. ¿Cuál es la pregunta? Provide questions to which the following are possible answers.

1. Sí, a ti te hablo.
2. Sí, a Manuel le prestamos las cintas.

3. No, no les escribo a mis padres.
4. Sí, a ti te voy a comprar este violín.
5. No, a mí no me prestan dinero.

D. Entrevista. Interview a classmate using the following questions. Possible answers using direct and indirect object pronouns are shown. The person answering should keep the textbook closed.

1. ¿Les escribes a tus padres?   Sí, les escribo.
2. ¿Escribes tus ideas importantes?   No, no las escribo.
3. ¿Les hablas mucho a tus amigos?   Sí, les hablo mucho.
4. ¿Hablas alemán?   No, no lo hablo.
5. ¿Practicas español en el laboratorio? Sí, lo practico allí.
6. ¿Vendes tus libros?   Sí, los vendo.
7. ¿Siempre haces preguntas difíciles?   Sí, siempre las hago.
8. ¿Te escriben tus amigos?   No, no me escriben.
9. ¿Quieres mucho a tus hermanos?   Sí, los quiero mucho.
10. ¿Ayudas mucho a tus padres?   No, no los ayudo mucho.

Stem-changing verbs: *e* to *i*; the verb *dar*

En casa de una familia méxico-americana en Denver, Colorado.

JOSÉ	Papá, necesito dinero para ir al cine.
SR. ORTEGA	¿Qué *dices*? Te *doy* dinero todas las semanas. ¿Por qué no le preguntas a tu mamá dónde está su bolso?
JOSÉ	Mamá no está en casa.
SR. ORTEGA	¡Caramba! ¿Cuánto dinero crees que tengo? Los niños de hoy no saben el valor de un dólar.
JOSÉ	Sí, papá, sé muy bien el valor de un dólar. Por eso te *pido* diez.

1. ¿Qué quiere el niño?   2. El señor Ortega le da dinero a José todos los días, ¿no?   3. ¿Qué debe preguntarle el niño a su mamá?   4. ¿Por qué no lo hace el niño?   5. ¿Qué dice el papá sobre los niños de hoy?   6. ¿Cuántos dólares le pide el niño?

A. Certain **-ir** verbs show a stem change from **e** to **i** when the stem syllable is stressed. This change does not occur in the **nosotros** and **vosotros** forms because the stress does not fall on the stem.

pedir (to ask for, order)		**repetir** (to repeat)	
pido	pedimos	repito	repetimos
pides	pedís	repites	repetís
pide	piden	repite	repiten

seguir (to continue; to follow)		**servir** (to serve)	
sigo	seguimos	sirvo	servimos
sigues	seguís	sirves	servís
sigue	siguen	sirve	sirven

¿Pides un café?	Are you ordering (asking for) coffee?
Seguimos los consejos de Ana.	We're following Ana's advice.
El camarero nos sirve el desayuno.	The waiter is serving us breakfast.
Rafael sigue cuatro cursos y trabaja al mismo tiempo.*	Rafael is taking four courses and working at the same time.
Repiten su promesa.	They repeat their promise.

B. **Pedir** means *to ask* (for something), *to order*, or *to request* ([someone] to do something). **Preguntar** means *to ask* (a question), *to query*.

Pedimos la cena.	We're ordering (asking for) dinner.
Me piden un favor.	They're asking me for a favor.
Entonces, ¿por qué no le preguntas al policía?	Then why don't you ask the policeman?

C. The verb **decir** is also an **e** to **i** stem-changing verb; in addition, the first-person singular of the present tense is irregular.

decir (to say, tell)	
digo	decimos
dices	decís
dice	dicen

---

* **Seguir un curso** means *to take a course.*

Te digo la verdad. —Muy agradecido.

I'm telling you the truth. —I'm very grateful.

¿Qué dice el doctor?

What does the doctor say?

¿Qué quiere decir eso?*

What does that mean?

D. The verb **dar** is irregular in the first-person singular only.

dar	*(to give)*
doy	damos
das	dais
da	dan

Le doy los mismos consejos a Mario.

I give Mario the same advice.

Les doy las gracias por las entradas y las otras cosas.

I am thanking them for the tickets and other things.

Damos un paseo todos los días. Es nuestro pasatiempo favorito.

We take a walk every day. It's our favorite pastime.

EJERCICIOS

A. **Ellos no, pero nosotros sí.** Agree with each statement, following the models.

Modelo El profesor no sigue un curso de español.
Él no, pero nosotros sí seguimos un curso de español.

1. El profesor no repite los modelos.
2. Ese estudiante no le da las gracias al profesor.
3. Los malos estudiantes no le piden favores al profesor.
4. Los malos estudiantes no dicen que van a estudiar.
5. Los malos estudiantes no le piden consejos al profesor.

B. **¿Cuál es la pregunta?** The following are possible answers. For each of them, give a reasonable question, as in the model.

Modelo Seguimos dos cursos.
¿Cuántos cursos siguen ustedes?

1. Pido un café.
2. Mi hermano sirve la cena hoy.
3. No, yo no te doy dinero para el cine.
4. Sí, repetimos mucho en esta clase.
5. Sigo cursos de italiano y francés.
6. *To ask for* quiere decir «pedir».

*****Querer decir**—literally, "to want to say"—is translated *to mean.*

C. **¿Pedir o preguntar?**   Complete the paragraph with the appropriate forms of **pedir** or **preguntar**.

Ana quiere ir al teatro. Llama a una amiga y le _____₁ si quiere ver *Romeo y Julieta* con ella. Su amiga le dice que sí. Entonces Ana les _____₂ dinero para las entradas a sus padres. Llama al teatro para _____₃ a qué hora empieza la obra. También le _____₄ a la recepcionista si la obra es muy larga (*long*). Después le dice a su madre: «Mamá, te _____₅ un gran favor. ¿Me prestas el auto?» La señora le _____₆ a su esposo si él no va a necesitar el auto. Él responde que no y le dice a la hija: «Te presto el auto pero te _____₇ una cosa: la promesa de que vas a regresar antes de medianoche (*midnight*).» Ana le dice: «Sí, papá, te prometo regresar antes de las doce.» Ella le _____₈ las llaves (*keys*) del auto y va a buscar a su amiga.

PREGUNTAS

1. ¿Cuál es su restaurante favorito? ¿Sirven el desayuno allí?, ¿el almuerzo?, ¿la cena? ¿Qué platos sirven?   **2.** ¿Les pide muchos favores a sus amigos?, ¿a sus profesores? **3.** ¿Les pide dinero a sus padres? Generalmente, ¿le dan dinero ellos a usted? ¿Qué dicen cuando les pide dinero?   **4.** ¿Qué cursos sigue ahora? ¿Qué cursos piensa seguir?   **5.** ¿Qué dice cuando quiere expresar compasión por una persona? ¿Qué dice cuando no entiende una palabra?   **6.** ¿Da usted un paseo todos los días?

El Paseo del Río, en San Antonio, Tejas

Stem-changing verbs: *o* to *ue*, *u* to *ue*

En el Hotel Dolores de San Antonio, Tejas.

SEÑOR Buenas tardes. ¿En qué *puedo* servirle?

JUAN ¿Me *puede* decir cuánto *cuesta* un cuarto para dos en este hotel?

SEÑOR Treinta dólares.

JUAN Está bien. ¿Me *puede* reservar uno?

SEÑOR Sí, con mucho gusto. ¿Por cuántas noches?

JUAN Solamente por una. Mañana temprano mi esposa y yo *volvemos* a Los Ángeles.

SEÑOR *Vuelven* mañana temprano, ¿eh? Si quieren, la recepcionista *puede* despertarlos.

JUAN No es necesario. *Duermo* como un gato. Todos los días abro los ojos a las seis y media en punto.

SEÑOR En ese caso, ¿*puede* usted despertar a la recepcionista, por favor?

---

1. ¿Cuánto cuesta un cuarto para dos personas en el hotel?   2. ¿Puede el señor reservarle uno a Juan?   3. ¿Cuántas noches van a estar allí?   4. ¿Adónde vuelven mañana?   5. ¿Quién puede despertarlos, si quieren?   6. ¿Cómo duerme Juan?

A. Certain Spanish verbs show a stem change from **o** to **ue** when the stem is stressed. This change does not occur in the **nosotros** and **vosotros** forms, because the stress does not fall on the stem.

dormir (to sleep)		**recordar** (to remember)		**volver** (to return)	
d**ue**rmo	dormimos	rec**ue**rdo	recordamos	v**ue**lvo	volvemos
d**ue**rmes	dormís	rec**ue**rdas	recordáis	v**ue**lves	volvéis
d**ue**rme	d**ue**rmen	rec**ue**rda	rec**ue**rdan	v**ue**lve	v**ue**lven

Verbs of this type are shown in vocabulary lists with the marker **ue**.

At the Dolores Hotel in San Antonio, Texas. GENTLEMAN: Good afternoon. How can I help you? JUAN: Can you tell me how much a room for two costs in this hotel? GENTLEMAN: Thirty dollars. JUAN: Fine. Can you reserve one for me? GENTLEMAN: Yes, gladly. For how many nights? JUAN: Only one. Early tomorrow morning my wife and I are returning to Los Angeles. GENTLEMAN: You're returning early tomorrow? If you want, the desk clerk can wake you. JUAN: That's not necessary. I sleep like a cat. Every morning (day) I open my eyes at 6:30 on the dot. GENTLEMAN: In that case, can you wake the desk clerk, please?

B. Other **o** to **ue** stem-changing verbs are

almorzar *to have lunch*	**mostrar** *to show*
costar *to cost*	**poder** *to be able, can*
encontrar *to find*	**soñar (con)** *to dream (about)*
llover *to rain*	

Recuerdo tu promesa.	*I remember your promise.*
¿No encuentras las entradas para el concierto de mañana?	*You don't find the tickets to tomorrow's concert?*
¿Con quién almuerza usted hoy?	*Who are you having lunch with today?*
Podemos ir al cine mañana mientras ellos trabajan.	*We can go to the movies tomorrow while they work.*
Vuelven a Tejas el jueves.	*They are returning to Texas on Thursday.*
Sueño con Enrique.	*I dream about Enrique.*

C. The verb **jugar** is a **u** to **ue** stem-changing verb.

jugar (*to play*)	
j**ue**go	jugamos
j**ue**gas	jugáis
j**ue**ga	j**ue**gan

Jugar means *to play* (a game or sport); **tocar** means *to play* (music or a musical instrument). Before the name of a sport or game, **jugar** is usually followed by the preposition **a**.

Juego a los naipes todos los viernes.	*I play cards every Friday.*
Jugamos al tenis mañana mientras ellos programan la computadora.	*We're playing tennis tomorrow while they program the computer.*
Y luego Juan toca el violín.	*And then Juan is playing the violin.*

EJERCICIOS

A. **¡Ah, buena idea!** These people have some good ideas about how to spend a lazy Sunday. Make sentences stating that you and a friend are doing the same things they are.

Modelo Los muchachos duermen hasta las diez de la mañana.
Nosotros también dormimos hasta las diez de la mañana.

1. Pablo juega a los naipes con sus amigos.
2. Anita sueña con programar la computadora.
3. La familia almuerza en un restaurante italiano.
4. Pablo y sus amigos pueden jugar al tenis esta tarde.
5. Anita y Jorge vuelven del cine tarde.
6. Los García encuentran un programa interesante en la televisión.

B. Conversaciones. Complete the conversations by filling in each blank with the correct form of the stem-changing verb from the list at the right.

MAMÁ   Rosario, ¿por qué no _____1 a la cama (*bed*)?

ROSARIO   Porque _____2 mucho. No _____3 dormir.

MANUEL   Toño y yo vamos al Restaurante Santa Fe. _____4 con María y Cristina.

PAPÁ   ¿Cuanto _____5 la comida en ese restaurante?

MANUEL   (Yo) no _____6 los precios. (Nosotros) _____7 a las tres.

ALICIA   ¿Qué buscas, tío?

CÉSAR   (Yo) _____8 con el señor Portilla a la una y no _____9 el paraguas (*umbrella*).

ALICIA   En este momento no _____10. Susana y yo _____11 llevarte al restaurante. ¿Dónde _____12 ustedes?

CÉSAR   (Nosotros) _____13 en la calle Olvera. ¿_____14 tú el restaurante donde hacen esas enchiladas deliciosas?

ALICIA   No, no lo _____15. Pero (yo) lo _____16 encontrar si tú me _____17 el camino (*way*).

1. volver
2. llover
3. poder
4. almorzar
5. costar
6. recordar
7. volver
8. almorzar
9. encontrar
10. llover
11. poder
12. almorzar
13. almorzar
14. recordar
15. recordar
16. poder
17. mostrar

PREGUNTAS

1. En general, ¿dónde almuerza usted? Y hoy, ¿dónde piensa almorzar? 2. Cuando usted tiene clases, ¿vuelve a casa tarde o temprano? 3. ¿A qué hora vuelve? 4. ¿Duerme usted bien, en general? Si toma mucho té o café, ¿puede dormir? ¿Duerme en la clase de español? 5. ¿Cuánto cuesta un violín? ¿un texto de español? ¿una radio? ¿una guitarra? ¿un piano? 6. ¿Juega usted a los naipes? ¿al tenis? 7. ¿Con qué o con quién sueña usted mucho? 8. ¿Llueve mucho aquí? ¿Dónde llueve mucho?

Direct and indirect object pronouns in the same sentence

Fernando está de visita en San Francisco, California.

FERNANDO ¿Conoces el Museo de Arte México-Americano, Francisca?
FRANCISCA Sí, y *te lo* quiero mostrar.
FERNANDO ¿Está cerca de aquí?
FRANCISCA No muy cerca. Creo que hay un autobús que va allí pero no recuerdo el número. Podemos preguntár*selo* al policía... ¿Tienes tu cámara?
FERNANDO Sí.
FRANCISCA Si *me la* das por un momento, te saco una foto aquí enfrente de la Misión Dolores.

1. ¿Qué quiere mostrarle Francisca a su amigo Fernando? 2. ¿Está cerca?
3. ¿Cómo van a ir allí? 4. ¿Cuándo van a ir? 5. ¿Qué quiere hacer Francisca?
6. ¿Saca usted muchas fotos cuando está de vacaciones?

A. When an indirect and a direct object pronoun are used in the same sentence, the indirect always precedes the direct object pronoun. They are not separated by any other words. Both pronouns precede a conjugated verb.

Te doy cinco entradas para la obra de teatro.	*I am giving you five tickets for the play.*
Te las doy.	*I am giving them to you.*
Nos muestran el baile.	*They show us the dance.*
Nos lo muestran.	*They show it to us.*
Me toca la guitarra.	*He's playing the guitar for me.*
Me la toca.	*He's playing it for me.*

Fernando is visiting San Francisco, California. FERNANDO: Are you familiar with the Museum of Mexican-American Art, Francisca? FRANCISCA: Yes, and I want to show it to you. FERNANDO: Is it near here? FRANCISCA: Not very near. I think there's a bus that goes there, but I don't remember its number. We can ask a policeman . . . . Do you have your camera? FERNANDO: Yes. FRANCISCA: If you give it to me for a moment, I'll take a picture of you in front of Dolores Mission.

B. When used with an infinitive, the object pronouns (indirect–direct) may be attached to the infinitive or may precede the conjugated verb. Note that when two object pronouns are attached to the infinitive, an accent is required over the last syllable of the infinitive.

Voy a comprarte una entrada. *I'm going to buy you a ticket.*

Te la voy a comprar.⎫
Voy a comprártela.⎭ *I'm going to buy it for you.*

C. Two object pronouns beginning with **l** do not occur in a row. If a third-person indirect object pronoun (**le**, **les**) is used with a third-person direct object pronoun (**lo**, **la**, **los**, **las**), the indirect object pronoun is replaced by **se**. The various meanings of **se** may be clarified by adding to the sentence: **a él**, **a ella**, **a usted**, **a ellos**, **a ellas**, **a ustedes**.

Elena les canta una canción (a ellos). *Elena is singing them a song.*
Elena se la canta (a ellos). *Elena is singing it to them.*

El camarero le sirve el té (a ella). *The waiter is serving her the tea.*
El camarero se lo sirve (a ella). *The waiter is serving it to her.*

EJERCICIOS

A. Rosa la generosa. Tell what Rosa is giving to various people, as suggested by the cues. Then shorten your statement by using direct and indirect object pronouns, as in the model.

Modelo   una cinta / al chico
Rosa le da una cinta al chico. Se la da.

1. una guitarra / a Miguel
2. dinero / a sus hermanas
3. las cartas / a usted
4. consejos / a ustedes
5. un gato / a esas muchachas
6. los discos / a los profesores
7. una bicicleta / a la niña
8. las gracias / al señor Díaz

B. Preguntas. Answer the questions using combined object pronouns.

Modelo   Hace calor. ¿Me vas a abrir la ventana?
Sí, voy a abrírtela ahora.

1. Sé que tienes un libro de Alurista*. ¿Cuándo me lo vas a prestar?
2. Todavía tengo tu guitarra. ¿Cuándo te la puedo llevar?
3. Señora Díaz, sus cintas están aquí. ¿Puedo dárselas el lunes?
4. Veo que tienes un disco de Mercedes Sosa. ¿Vas a tocármelo ahora?
5. Tía, ¿dónde está la carta de mamá? ¿Me la puedes mostrar?

* Alurista is a Mexican-American poet.

C. Traducción. Work with a partner to translate these short conversations.

PEPE	I want to buy you a present.
PEPA	Great! And when are you going to buy it for me?
PEPE	Well, I can't tell you that.
PEPA	Will you give it to me before (**antes del**) Saturday?
PEPE	No, I can't give it to you before February 14.

LUIS	Why don't you give me the tickets for the play?
LUISA	I can't give them to you because I don't have them. Those tickets cost a lot, Luis. You and I can go to the movies and have lunch for the price (**el valor**) of one ticket!
LUIS	Good idea! Can you reserve a table for us at a good restaurant?
LUISA	Pepe is going to reserve it for us this afternoon.

PREGUNTAS

1. ¿Baila usted el cha-cha-chá? ¿la salsa? ¿el tango? ¿el rock? ¿Qué baila usted? ¿Nos lo (la, los) quiere mostrar?   **2.** ¿Toca usted un instrumento musical? ¿el piano? ¿la guitarra? ¿el violín? ¿Cuándo y dónde los (las) toca?   **3.** ¿Escucha usted canciones en español? ¿Las puede entender?   **4.** ¿Tiene usted cincuenta dólares? ¿Me los quiere prestar? ¿Por qué?   **5.** ¿Les pide usted a veces dinero a sus amigos? ¿Se lo dan? ¿Les pide consejos? ¿Se los dan?

LOS ÁNGELES: En la Plaza Olvera

Dos jóvenes están en la Plaza Olvera de Los Ángeles para las celebraciones del cinco de mayo.[1]

ANA	Bueno, ¿qué vamos a hacer? El grupo Tierra° va a tocar ahora. ¿Lo escuchamos? Quisiera° bailar.
TOMÁS	¿Recuerdas a qué hora habla César Chávez[2]?
ANA	No habla hoy—habla mañana, pero no recuerdo a qué hora.
TOMÁS	¡Qué bien! Entonces hoy podemos ver esta plaza y mañana vamos a escuchar a César Chávez.
ANA	Tengo hambre. Si no quieres bailar, ¿almorzamos? El restaurante «La luz° del día» está aquí cerca. Dicen que sirven comida muy buena y que no cuesta mucho.
TOMÁS	De acuerdo. Podemos comer y escuchar la música.

La Calle Olvera, en Los Ángeles

Una hora después, salen del restaurante.

TOMÁS Bueno, esta noche podemos ir al teatro. El Teatro Campesino° presenta *Los pelados°*.³

ANA «Pelados» vamos a estar, Tomás, sin° dinero. ¿Por qué no vamos esta noche al baile del Parque Lincoln? ¡Es gratis°!

TOMÁS ¡Oh, mira! ¡La casa Ávila! ¿Dónde está tu cámara? ¿Me la das por un momento?

ANA Sí, te la presto, si me llevas a bailar.

TOMÁS De acuerdo. ¿Sabes que la casa Ávila es un edificio muy viejo? Muestra la influencia de los españoles en esta región... Si piensas en los nombres de las ciudades de California, es obvio° que aquí la influencia española es muy importante.⁴

ANA ¿Ah... sí?

TOMÁS ¡Sí, claro! Lo puedes ver en nombres como Sacramento, Fresno°, Salinas° y... ¡Los Ángeles!

ANA ¡Tú y tus lecciones de historia, Tomás...! ¿Por qué no vamos a divertirnos°? Hoy es cinco de mayo. ¿O ya no° lo recuerdas?

TOMÁS Sí. ¡Es un día para celebrar y recordar nuestra historia!

Tierra *Earth*   **Quisiera...** *I would like . . .*   **luz** *light*
Teatro Campesino *Rural Theater*   **Los pelados** *The Have-Nots*   **sin** *without*
gratis *free*   **obvio** *obvious*   **Fresno** *ash tree*   **Salinas** *salt pits or marshes*
divertirnos *enjoy ourselves*   **ya no** *any longer*

1. ¿Dónde están Ana y Tomás?   2. ¿Qué día es?   3. ¿Qué quiere hacer Ana?
4. ¿Quién va a hablar al otro día (*the next day*)?   5. ¿Adónde van los jóvenes a
almorzar?   6. ¿Qué quiere hacer Tomás esta noche? ¿Qué prefiere hacer Ana?
7. ¿Qué es la casa Ávila? ¿Qué influencia muestra?   8. Según Ana, ¿qué deben
hacer el cinco de mayo? Y según Tomás, ¿qué hay que hacer ese día?

Notas culturales

1. **El cinco de mayo** is celebrated by Mexican-Americans as well as by Mexicans.
It marks the day that the populist army led by Benito Juárez laid siege to the French
troops in Mexico—May 5, 1862—which was the beginning of the end of French
intervention in Mexico and the downfall of Maximilian of Hapsburg (whom Napo-
leon III had appointed Emperor of Mexico). Benito Juárez is much revered by the
Mexican people; not only did he lead the country to create an independent democratic republic, but he was the first Mexican president of Indian origin.

2. César Chávez has long represented the United Farm Workers Union and has
spoken out vigorously for the rights of its members and for Hispanics in general. In
1989 he went on a 36-day "Fast for Life" to protest the use of pesticides, which he
claims are causing damage not only to farm workers but to consumers and to the
environment in general.

3. Mexican-American theater is very popular in the southwestern United States.
It grew out of the farm workers' strikes in California in the 1960s; people would
improvise plays on such topics as the injustice of the big companies and the plight of
the worker. The plays were written down only after they had been performed many
times, and even today most of the scripts change with each performance.

4. In 1542 the explorer Juan Cabrillo was the first European to explore California,
although Hernán Cortés had explored Baja California and parts of the southwestern
United States in the 1530s. In general, Spanish place names in the United States are
usually descriptive, dramatic, or commemorative. Examples of descriptive names
include: **Sierra Nevada** (snow-covered mountain chain), **Las Vegas** (the plains),
Colorado (red), **Los Álamos** (poplar trees), **Laguna Seca** (dry lake), **Agua
Dulce** (fresh water). Dramatic names include those behind which there was a story,
such as **Calaveras** (skulls), where the skeletons of Indians were found; **Oso Flaco**
(thin bear), where the explorers managed to kill and eat a bear; or **Las Pulgas**
(fleas), where explorers were set upon by fleas. The majority of names, however, are
commemorative, named mainly after saints or religious concepts. For instance,
Punto Reyes (kings' point) was so named because the explorers landed there on
Epiphany, the day of the Three Kings, or Magi. The name Los Angeles comes from
El Río de Nuestra Señora, **Reina de los Ángeles** (The River of Our Lady, Queen
of the Angels), a river near present-day Los Angeles that was discovered on the feast
day of the Virgin Mary.

FUNCIONES Y ACTIVIDADES

In this chapter, you have seen examples of the following language functions, or uses. Here is a summary and some additional information about these functions of language.

Making requests

Here are some expressions that you can use when you need or want to ask for something:

¿Me hace el favor de + *inf*....?	*Will you do me the favor of ...?*
¿Me puede + *inf*....?	*Can you ...(for me)?*
¿Me podría* dar (pasar, prestar, etc.)..., por favor?	*Could you give (pass, loan, etc.) me ..., please?*

In a shop, you should first greet the shopkeeper before making a request—it's considered rude not to: **Buenos días. Busco... Necesito...**

The words **quiero** and **deseo** are rarely used in requests; these words are very direct and can sound rude or childish. After all, you wouldn't normally phrase a polite request in English with *I want . . .*, but rather, *I would like . . .* or *Please give me . . . .* *I would like* in Spanish is **Quisiera**.

Offering assistance

Here are some ways to offer assistance:

¿En qué puedo servirlo(-la)?	*How can I help you?* (Shopkeepers and others use this quite often.)
Si quiere, podría...	*If you like, I could ...*
Hago... con mucho gusto.	*I'll do ... with pleasure (gladly).*
¿Le (Te) puedo + *inf.* ...?	*May I do ... to (for) you?*

Expressing gratitude

Here are some ways to express gratitude:

Gracias. Muchas gracias.	*Thank you. Thank you very much.*
Mil gracias.	*Thank you very much.* (Literally, "A thousand thanks.")
Muy agradecido(-a).	*(I'm) Very grateful.*
Usted es (Tú eres) muy amable.	*You're very kind.*

---

* **Podría** is a conditional form of **poder**, meaning *could*. It is used for **yo**, **usted**, **él**, and **ella**. (You will see other conditional forms in Chapter 15.)

A. ¿Qué dicen? Tell what the people in the drawings might be saying as they make requests.

1.

2.

3.

4.

5.

6.

B. Conversación. Arrange the following conversation in order. Write numbers in the blanks. Then tell who is talking.

_____ Buenos días, señorita. Busco un nuevo bolso.

_____ Sí, tiene razón. ¿Cuánto cuesta?

_____ Tenemos muchos. ¿Qué tipo de bolso quisiera?

___1.___ Buenos días. ¿En qué puedo servirla, señora?

_____ A ver (*Let's see*). Éste es muy bonito.

_____ No, gracias. Pero, ¿me podría envolver (*wrap*) éste, por favor?

_____ Está bien. Lo llevo.

_____ Necesito un bolso grande.

_____ ¿Necesita alguna otra cosa (*anything else*)? Le podría mostrar un bolso de otro color.

_____ Solamente veinte dólares.

_____ Por supuesto... y con mucho gusto, señora.

C. Situación. Role-play this situation: A friend of yours is having a luncheon. After the meal, you ask if you can help her with the dishes. She says no but asks if you would prepare the coffee. Of course, you say, you'd be glad to do it. You ask if you should also serve it. She thanks you and says she's very grateful for your help.

D. ¿Qué pasa en la fiesta? Use your imagination to describe in Spanish with as many details as possible what is happening at the party.

VOCABULARIO ACTIVO

Cognados

la computadora	el favor	el pasatiempo	el, la recepcionista
el concierto	la foto(grafía)	el piano	el tenis
el curso	la guitarra	el poema	el tipo
la diversión	importante	la promesa	el violín
el dólar	la música		

Verbos

almorzar (ue)	to have lunch
bailar	to dance
cantar	to sing
comprar	to buy
costar (ue)	to cost
dar	to give
dar las gracias	to thank
dar un paseo	to take a walk
decir (i)	to say, tell
querer decir	to mean
despertar (ie)	to awaken (someone)
dormir (ue)	to sleep
encontrar (ue)	to find; to meet
jugar (ue)	to play (sport or game)
llover (ue)	to rain
mostrar (ue)	to show
pedir (i)	to ask, ask for; to order (in a restaurant)
poder (ue)	to be able, can
prestar	to loan
programar	to program
prometer	to promise
recordar (ue)	to remember
repetir (i)	to repeat
reservar	to reserve
sacar fotos	to take pictures
seguir (i)	to continue, to follow
seguir un curso	to take a course
servir (i)	to serve
soñar (ue) con	to dream about, to dream of
tocar	to play (music or a musical instrument)
volver (ue)	to return, come back, go back

Diversiones y pasatiempos

el baile	dance
la canción	song
el cine	movie theater, movies
la cinta	tape
el disco	record
la entrada	ticket
el gusto	pleasure
el naipe	card
la obra de teatro	play

Otras palabras y frases

el almuerzo	lunch
antes	first
antes de	before
el bolso	purse, pocketbook
la cena	dinner
con mucho gusto	gladly
el consejo	advice, piece of advice
la cosa	thing
el cuarto	room
el desayuno	breakfast
después	afterward
después de	after
entonces	then
el gato	cat
luego	then, next
mientras	while
mismo	same
al mismo tiempo	at the same time
solamente	only
el valor	value, price

¿En qué puedo servirlo(-la)?   *How can I help you?*

Hago... con mucho gusto.   *I'll do . . . with pleasure.*

Le (Te) puedo + *inf.* **...?**   *May I . . . to (for) you?*

¿Me podría dar (pasar, prestar, etc.)..., por favor?   *Could you give (pass, loan, etc.) me . . . , please?*

Mil gracias.   *Thank you very much. (Literally, "a thousand thanks.")*

Muchas gracias.   *Thank you. Thank you very much.*

Muy agradecido(-a).   *(I'm) very grateful.*

Quisiera...   *I would like . . .*

Si quiere, (yo) podría...   *If you like, I could . . .*

Usted es (Tú eres) muy amable.   *You're very kind.*

> **Don't forget:**
> Indirect object pronouns, page 128

Los hispanos de los Estados Unidos

¿Por qué encontramos letreros° como estos en Nueva York, Miami, Dallas, Chicago, Los Ángeles o San Francisco? La respuesta° está en los dieciocho millones de hispanos que viven en los Estados Unidos (el número es mucho mayor° si incluimos a los millones de inmigrantes indocumentados). Hay tres grupos principales: los chicanos o méxico-americanos (el 60 por ciento del total), los puertorriqueños y los cubanos. Gran° parte de la población de Miami es de origen cubano, y en Nueva York viven más puertorriqueños que en San Juan, la capital de Puerto Rico. A esto hay que agregar° los miles de refugiados° políticos (chilenos, argentinos, salvadoreños, nicaragüenses, guatemaltecos, etcétera) que han venido y siguen viniendo° a este país.

signs
answer
greater

A great

add/refugees
han... *have come and continue to come*

Un restaurante cubano, en la «Pequeña Habana» de Miami

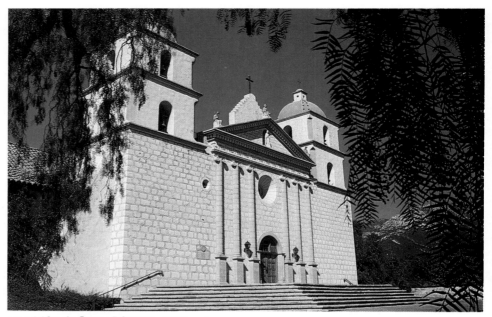

La misión de Santa Bárbara, California

En el suroeste° de los Estados Unidos, la presencia hispana es muy anterior a° la presencia anglosajona. Por ejemplo, hay muchos estados (Colorado, Nevada, Tejas) y ciudades (San Francisco, Las Vegas, Amarillo) que tienen nombres españoles. La Misión de Santa Bárbara (que vemos en la fotografía) fue fundada° por padres españoles en 1786. Con la victoria militar de 1848, los Estados Unidos reciben de México el territorio que hoy forma el suroeste norteamericano. Muchos habitantes° de esta región son descendientes de los colonizadores españoles; otros son trabajadores mexicanos que vienen a este país para buscar trabajo.

Southwest / **muy...** much earlier than

fue... was founded

inhabitants

Una familia hispana en los Estados Unidos

La historia de los puertorriqueños en los Estados Unidos empieza con la victoria norteamericana en la guerra° de 1898 contra España; desde° entonces, Puerto Rico es territorio de los Estados Unidos. Hoy, los puertorriqueños son ciudadanos° de este país.

La mayor° parte de los cubanos están aquí como exiliados° políticos del régimen de Fidel Castro. Hay cubanos en todos los estados, pero la gran mayoría vive en Miami. Allí tienen un barrio muy próspero con teatros, cines, tiendas y restaurantes típicos. La primera gran ola° de inmigrantes cubanos viene en 1959, y la segunda° en 1980.

war/since

citizens

greater/exiles

wave/second

PREGUNTAS

1. ¿Cuántos millones de hispanos viven en los Estados Unidos? **2.** ¿Cuáles son los tres grupos principales? **3.** ¿Dónde viven más puertorriqueños: en San Juan o en Nueva York? **4.** En el suroeste de los Estados Unidos, ¿es la presencia hispana anterior o posterior a la anglosajona? **5.** ¿Qué estados y ciudades con nombres españoles recuerda usted? **6.** En 1848, ¿qué reciben de México los Estados Unidos? **7.** ¿De quiénes son descendientes muchos habitantes de esos estados? **8.** ¿Desde cuándo es Puerto Rico parte del territorio de los Estados Unidos? **9.** ¿Dónde viven muchos cubano-americanos?

La Primera Compañía de Danza Española del Area de la Bahía
Tonadas 1989 Temporada de Casa
Estrenos Mundiales por Miguel Santos
Reestreno de "Regionalismos" de Santos y Adela Clara
Música por Joaquín Nin-Culmell
¡Sólo tres presentaciones!
Viernes y Sábado, 18 y 19 de Agosto 8pm Domingo 20 de Agosto 3pm
Herbst Theatre
401 Van Ness Avenue, San Francisco

Boletos: $10, $13, & $16 en STBS Union Square y Bass. Patrocinadores $26 Noche de Estreno el 18 de agosto con derecho a butacas exclusivas y a la recepción después de la función en Harry's Bar.
CARGUELO POR TELEFONO 552-3656

I. THE PRESENT TENSE

Complete the following sentences with the present tense of the verb in parentheses.

1. Yo _____ (conocer) a una abogada, pero no _____ (saber) dónde vive.
2. Los señores García _____ (buscar) a su prima Isabel.
3. Ahora nosotros _____ (poder) comer.
4. Yo _____ (poner) las maletas en el auto.
5. Yo _____ (salir) ahora para ir al cine. ¿_____ (venir) tú conmigo?
6. ¿Qué _____ (creer) tú? ¿Que yo _____ (ser) idiota?
7. Nosotros _____ (deber) llegar temprano.
8. Los agentes _____ (querer) los pasaportes.
9. Yo _____ (tener) dos semanas de vacaciones. ¿Cuántas _____ (tener) tú?
10. Él _____ (ir) a Venezuela este verano.
11. ¿Qué _____ (tener) que hacer nosotros?
12. Adela _____ (vivir) ahora en Buenos Aires.
13. Pues, yo te _____ (decir) la verdad. Todo el mundo _____ (decir) que Enrique tiene mucho dinero.
14. Él _____ (dormir) como un gato.
15. Marisa y Eduardo _____ (volver) del concierto a las once.
16. Yo no los _____ (ver).

II. SER VS. ESTAR

Complete the following narration with an appropriate form of **ser** or **estar**. In each case, state the reason for your choice.

Tengo un amigo, Felipe, que _____ argentino. Felipe no _____ de Buenos Aires; _____ de Córdoba, otra ciudad importante. Córdoba _____ en el interior de la Argentina. Felipe _____ un chico muy inteligente y amable. Esta noche debemos ir a una cena que _____ en casa de una de nuestras amigas, pero Felipe no _____ bien. Si _____ enfermo (*sick*) esta noche, no va a ir.

III. ADJECTIVES

Complete the sentences with the appropriate possessive or demonstrative adjective, as indicated by the cue in parentheses.

A. 1. ¿Dónde está _____ pasaporte? (*my*)
   2. _____ ideas son brillantes. (*your*, familiar)
   3. ¿Cuándo empiezan _____ vacaciones? (*their*)

4. _____ agente de viajes es Fernando Olivera. (*our*)

5. ¿_____ familia está en Puerto Rico? (*your*, formal)

B. 1. ¿Hay muchos teatros en _____ ciudad? (*this*)

2. ¿Son amables _____ señores? (*those, over there*)

3. _____ libro es de Manuel. (*this*)

4. No entiendo _____ formularios. (*those, by you*)

5. _____ chica es chilena. (*that, by you*)

IV. OBJECT PRONOUNS

Answer the following questions in the affirmative, replacing the words in italics with the appropriate direct or indirect object pronoun.

Modelo   ¿*Me* puedes dar *la entrada*?
        Sí, te la puedo dar. (*or* **Sí**, **puedo dártela.**)

1. ¿Tú llevas *la guitarra*?

2. ¿*Me* puedes esperar unos minutos?

3. ¿*Les* habla usted *a ellos*?

4. ¿Quieres preguntar*les eso a estos pasajeros*?

5. ¿*Me* quieres?

6. ¿Puede decir*nos el nombre del restaurante*?

7. ¿Quiere usted dar*le los naipes*?

8. ¿*Les* escribe Anita mucho *a ustedes*?

9. ¿*Te* puedo visitar mañana?

10. ¿*Le* vas a dar *tu número de teléfono*?

V. VERB PAIRS

Choose the appropriate verb in each pair to complete the following sentences. Use the appropriate form of the present tense or the infinitive.

1. (saber/conocer) ¿_____ usted la ciudad? Yo quiero _____ cómo llegar al teatro.

2. (hablar/decir) ¿Qué _____ Enrique? ¿_____ de los Fernández?

3. (pedir/preguntar) Yo le _____ dinero. Y él me _____ para qué lo quiero.

4. (ser/estar) ¿Dónde _____ Manuel y Silvia? _____ las cinco.

VI. USEFUL EXPRESSIONS

Give the Spanish equivalent of the following expressions.

1. Glad to meet you.   **2.** Good morning.   **3.** Thank you.   **4.** Please. **5.** What time is it?   **6.** What day is today?   **7.** I'm hungry.   **8.** Good afternoon.   **9.** Can I reserve a room for two in this hotel?   **10.** How much does this watch cost?   **11.** I'll take it.   **12.** The weather is warm. **13.** Are you warm?   **14.** Really?   **15.** Of course!   **16.** Can you tell me where the restaurant "La Cazuela" is?   **17.** See you tomorrow.   **18.** What a shame!   **19.** Be careful!

La ropa
¿Qué lleva Carmen?

el vestido

el pijama

la combinación

el sostén

las medias

la blusa

la falda

el sombrero

el traje de baño

las sandalias

¿Qué lleva José?

el traje

la corbata

el abrigo

los guantes

los pantalones

los zapatos

la camisa

el sombrero
una gorra

el impermeable

la ropa interior

el paraguas

la camiseta

los calzoncillos

los calcetines

el suéter

el cinturón

los jeans

las botas

rojo

blanc

negr

viole

claro

anaranjado

amarillo

azul

verde

marrón

gris

oscuro

La ropa, los colores y la rutina diaria — 7

Expressing Hesitation
Making Descriptions (2)

EJERCICIO

Describe what Carmen or José wears in the following situations. Complete the sentences, eliminating the inappropriate words.

1. Cuando llueve, Carmen lleva... (un impermeable, un pijama, calcetines, un vestido, un paraguas)
2. Cuando va a la playa, José lleva... (un sombrero, sandalias, un abrigo, un traje de baño)
3. Cuando viaja a otro país, Carmen lleva... (sandalias, ropa interior, pantalones, un vestido, una camisa)
4. Cuando trabaja en la oficina, Carmen lleva... (medias, calcetines, un traje, una corbata, un traje de baño, zapatos de tenis)
5. Cuando nieva, Carmen lleva... (un suéter, botas, guantes, sandalias, jeans)
6. Cuando duerme, José lleva... (una falda, jeans, un pijama, una corbata)

PREGUNTAS

1. ¿Qué lleva usted hoy? ¿Lleva calcetines blancos? ¿pantalones amarillos? ¿zapatos de tenis? ¿una falda?   **2.** ¿De qué color es la camisa o la blusa de usted? ¿verde o azul claro? ¿Y los pantalones o la falda? ¿azul oscuro o gris claro?   **3.** ¿Cuál es su color favorito?   **4.** ¿Cuánto cuesta un paraguas? ¿y una corbata?   **5.** ¿Qué ropa lleva usted en el otoño? ¿y en el invierno?   **6.** ¿Qué ropa lleva usted cuando va a las montañas? ¿a la playa? ¿a un restaurante elegante? ¿a un centro comercial?   **7.** ¿Qué ropa es solamente para mujeres? ¿solamente para hombres?

 The reflexive

En Barranquilla, Colombia.

ALDO ¡José! ¿Vas a llevar esa camisa a la fiesta? ¿Cómo vas a conocer chicas si *te vistes* así?

JOSÉ No voy a la fiesta; voy a *quedarme* en casa. No *me divierto* en las fiestas.

ALDO Pero, José, ¿por qué no vienes con nosotros? Puedes bailar, hablar con la gente... y estoy seguro que *te vas a divertir.*

JOSÉ No sé bailar y tengo mucho trabajo. *Voy a acostarme* temprano y mañana *me voy a levantar* a las siete.

ALDO ¿*Te levantas* a las siete los domingos? ¡A esa hora yo *me acuesto*!

---

1. ¿Va a la fiesta José o se queda en casa? ¿Por qué?   2. ¿Qué hacen Aldo y sus amigos en las fiestas?   3. ¿Qué va a hacer José?   4. ¿A qué hora se levanta José los domingos?   5. En general, ¿qué hace usted los domingos a las siete de la mañana? ¿Se levanta o se acuesta?

A. In a reflexive construction, the action of the verb "reflects" back to the subject of the sentence, as in the sentences *I enjoy myself* or *The child dresses herself*. In Spanish, reflexive constructions require the reflexive pronouns **me**, **te**, **se**, **nos**, **os**, and **se**. Except for the third-person **se** (singular and plural), these forms are the same as the direct and indirect object pronouns. The pronoun **se** attached to an infinitive indicates that the verb is reflexive.

levantarse *(to get up)*	
me levanto	nos levantamos
te levantas	os levantáis
se levanta	se levantan

Notice that some Spanish reflexive forms, such as **levantarse**, are not translated as reflexive constructions in English. The reflexive is used much more frequently in Spanish than in English.

B. The following verbs are reflexive, with stem changes indicated in parentheses.

acostarse (ue)   *to go to bed*
acostumbrarse   *to get used to*
despertarse (ie)   *to wake up*
divertirse (ie)   *to enjoy oneself; to have fun*
irse   *to leave, go away*
lavarse   *to wash (oneself)*
llamarse   *to be named*
mudarse   *to move* (change residence)
ponerse   *to put on*
quedarse   *to remain, to stay*
quitarse   *to take off*
sentarse (ie)   *to sit down*
vestirse (i)*   *to get dressed*

C. Like object pronouns, reflexive pronouns precede a conjugated verb or follow and are attached to an infinitive.

¿Nos sentamos aquí?	*Shall we sit here?*
Me divierto mucho en las fiestas.	*I enjoy myself a lot at parties.*
¿Te acuestas ahora?	*Are you going to bed now?*
¿No vas a quedarte?	*Aren't you going to stay?*
No queremos mudarnos.	*We don't want to move.*
Raúl se va, pero yo me quedo.	*Raul is leaving, but I am staying.*
Hace calor; voy a quitarme el suéter.	*It's hot; I'm going to take off my sweater.*
Felipe se pone el abrigo.**	*Felipe is putting on his coat.*

D. Reflexive pronouns precede direct object pronouns: **Se lava las manos. Se las lava.**

E. Most verbs that are used reflexively are also used nonreflexively. In some cases, the use of the reflexive pronoun changes the meaning of the verb.

Se llama Carmen.	*Her name is Carmen.*
José llama a Carmen, su novia, todos los días.	*José calls Carmen, his girlfriend, every day.*
Me lavo todos los días.	*I wash (myself) every day.*
Lavo el auto todas las semanas.	*I wash the car every week.*
Nos acostamos a las diez.	*We go to bed at ten o'clock.*
Acostamos a los niños entre las ocho y las nueve.	*We put the children to bed between eight and nine o'clock.*
Elena viste a la niña.	*Elena is dressing the child.*
Elena se viste a la moda (de moda).	*Elena dresses fashionably.*

---

*Conjugated like **servir** (p. 132).
Notice that when **ponerse or **quitarse** is used with articles of clothing, the definite article is used rather than the possessive as in English. This will be practiced in Chapter 14.

F. The reflexive pronouns **nos** and **se** may be used with a first- or third-person plural verb form, respectively, in order to express a reciprocal reflexive action. This construction corresponds to the English *each other* or *one another*.

Todos se miran.   *They all look at one another.*
No nos vemos mucho.   *We don't see each other often.*

A. La rutina diaria de Jorge.   Make sentences about Jorge's daily routine using the cues under each picture and words of your own.

Modelo   llamarse
Me llamo Jorge.

1. 7:15 / despertarse

2. 7:30 / levantarse

3. 7:45 / lavarse

4. 8:00 / vestirse

5. 8:15 / ir a la universidad

6. 12:00 / almorzar

7. después de las 3:00 / quedarse en casa

8. 11:00 / acostarse

B. La rutina diaria de usted.   In pairs, describe your own daily routines. Then change partners and tell your second partner about your first partner's daily routine.

C. Completar las frases... Complete each sentence with the correct form of the more appropriate verb in parentheses.

Modelo   Nosotros ___*vamos*___ (ir/irse) de compras los sábados.

1. En general, yo _____ (acostar/acostarse) a mi hijo temprano.
2. ¿A qué hora _____ (levantar/levantarse) tú?
3. Ustedes _____ (divertir/divertirse) en las fiestas, ¿no?
4. Jorge prefiere _____ (quedar/quedarse) en casa esta noche.
5. Nosotros _____ (lavar/lavarse) el auto todos los viernes.
6. ¿Cuándo vas a _____ (llamar/llamarse) a Susana?
7. Ricardo _____ (poner/ponerse) el abrigo y los guantes.
8. Marta _____ (mudar/mudarse) a otro apartamento.

D. Traducción. Give the Spanish equivalent of the following sentences.

1. They're leaving, but we're staying.
2. Are you putting on your sweater?—Yes, I'm putting it on.
3. He calls her every day.
4. We are going to enjoy ourselves at the concert tomorrow.
5. She puts them to bed at eight.
6. We are used to this house.
7. When are you moving?

E. Los novios. To follow Juan and Juanita's love story, complete the puzzle below using the reciprocal reflexive as a model. The ending of the story will appear in the column marked **Final**. (Allow for a blank between words.)

Modelo   (querer) **Juan y Juanita** | s | e | | q | u | i | e | r | e | n | **mucho.**

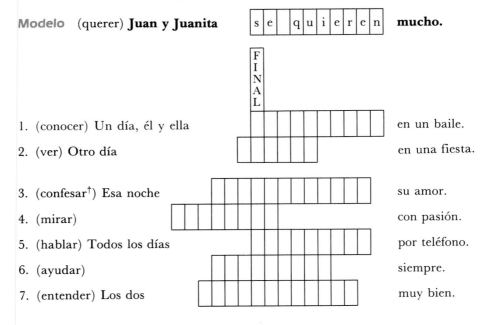

1. (conocer) Un día, él y ella   en un baile.
2. (ver) Otro día   en una fiesta.
3. (confesar†) Esa noche   su amor.
4. (mirar)   con pasión.
5. (hablar) Todos los días   por teléfono.
6. (ayudar)   siempre.
7. (entender) Los dos   muy bien.

---

† **Confesar** (*to confess*) is an **e** to **ie** stem-changing verb.

F. Juan (Juanita) y yo. Rewrite the story above, changing "Juan y Juanita" to "Juan (Juanita) y yo." Include the ending.

Modelo   (querer) **Juan (Juanita) y yo** | n | o | s | | q | u | e | r | e | m | o | s | **mucho.**

1. ¿A qué hora se levanta usted los lunes?, ¿los sábados? ¿A qué hora se acuesta?
2. ¿Va a quedarse en casa esta noche? ¿Va a salir? En general, ¿adónde va para divertirse?   **3.** ¿Nos vemos aquí los domingos?, ¿los lunes?, ¿los jueves?   **4.** ¿Se ayudan usted y sus amigos? ¿Se dicen sus problemas? ¿Se hablan mucho por teléfono? ¿Se hablan en español usted y sus amigo cuando no están en clase?   **5.** ¿Tiene usted novio(-a)? ¿Se entienden usted y su novio(-a)? ¿Se necesitan? ¿Se ven todos los días?
6. ¿Se pone usted ropa diferente para cada día de la semana?   **7.** ¿Qué hay que ponerse para ir a un restaurante en los Estados Unidos?   **8.** ¿Es importante vestirse a la moda?   **9.** ¿Qué ropa lleva usted cuando se queda en casa?

Adjectives used as nouns

RECEPCIONISTA	Buenos días.
SEÑORA	Buenos días. Habla la señora Vega. Tengo unas preguntas sobre este formulario de empleo. ¿Qué copia les mando—*la azul* o *la amarilla*? ¿Y quién recibe *la verde*?
RECEPCIONISTA	¿Cómo? No la entiendo.
SEÑORA	¿No hablo con la tienda «La Elegancia»?
RECEPCIONISTA	No, esto es una oficina de abogados: Díaz, Blasco, Bosco y Villacrés.
SEÑORA	¡Oh! Pues, perdón, perdón, perdón, perdón...

1. ¿Por qué llama la señora?   2. ¿Con quién cree que habla?   3. ¿Con quien habla, en realidad?

RECEPTIONIST: Good morning. WOMAN: Good morning. This is Mrs. Vega. I have some questions about this employment form. Which copy do I send you—the blue one or the yellow one? And who gets the green one? RECEPTIONIST: What? I don't understand (you). WOMAN: Am I not speaking with "The Elegance" shop? RECEPTIONIST: No, this is a law office: Díaz, Blasco, Bosco, and Villacrés. WOMAN: Oh! Excuse me, excuse me, excuse me, excuse me, . . .

In Spanish, a noun that is modified by an adjective may be deleted unless its absence will cause confusion. The adjective that remains then functions as a noun; it keeps the same ending as if the original noun were still expressed. In English, the noun is not just dropped but is replaced, usually by *one* or *ones*.

¿Prefieres esta camisa azul o aquella camisa gris? — Prefiero la azul.	*Do you prefer this blue shirt or that gray shirt? — I prefer the blue one.*
¿Tienes mi suéter? — ¿Cuál? ¿el violeta o el anaranjado?	*Do you have my sweater? — Which one? The purple one or the orange one?*
El niño tiene un zapato, pero no puede encontrar el otro.	*The child has one shoe, but he can't find the other one.*
¿Cómo se llama esa española? Es muy guapa.	*What is that Spanish woman's name? She's very beautiful.*
¿Vas a comprar los pantalones largos o los cortos?	*Are you going to buy the long pants or the short ones?*

Notice that the adjective used as a noun is usually preceded by an article or a demonstrative adjective.

EJERCICIO

¿El uno o el otro?   Anita and Jorge are going shopping. Following the model, answer Anita's questions to Jorge.

> **Modelo**   Anita: ¿Prefieres los pantalones marrones o los pantalones verdes?
> Jorge: **Prefiero los verdes.**

1. ¿Prefieres la camisa azul o la camisa blanca?
2. ¿Vas a comprar el cinturón rojo o el cinturón negro?
3. ¿Quieres los zapatos italianos o los zapatos argentinos?
4. ¿Necesitas el suéter marrón o el suéter rojo?
5. ¿Prefieres ir al restaurante francés o al restaurante alemán?

PREGUNTAS

1. ¿Prefiere usted los colores vivos, como el rojo y el anaranjado, o prefiere los colores neutros, como el blanco o el gris?   **2.** ¿Qué tipo de música prefiere usted: la clásica, la popular o la folklórica? ¿Por qué?   **3.** ¿Con qué mano escribe usted: con la derecha o con la izquierda?   **4.** ¿Prefiere usted los autos grandes o los pequeños? ¿Por qué?

Affirmative and negative words

Affirmative words

alguien   *someone, anyone*
algo   *something*
algún, alguno(-s), alguna(-s)   *some, any*

también   *also*
siempre   *always*
o...o   *either ... or*

Negative words

nadie   *no one, not anyone*
nada   *nothing, not anything*
ningún, ninguno, ninguna   *none, not any, no, neither (of them)*

tampoco   *not either, neither*
nunca, jamás   *never, not ever*
ni... ni   *neither ... nor*

A. The negative words **nadie**, **nada**, **ninguno**, **tampoco**, and **nunca** can be placed either before or after a verb.

No se va nadie ahora.
Nadie se va ahora. } *No one is leaving now.*

No tienen trajes tampoco.
Tampoco tienen trajes. } *They don't have suits either.*

No llevo corbata nunca.
Nunca llevo corbata. } *I never wear a tie.*

Notice that **no** precedes the verb when a negative word follows the verb. **No** is omitted when a negative word precedes the verb.

B. **Alguno** and **ninguno** can refer either to people or to things, while **alguien** and **nadie** refer only to people. **Alguno** and **ninguno** usually refer to certain members or elements of a group the speaker or writer has in mind. Before a masculine singular noun, **alguno** becomes **algún**, and **ninguno** becomes **ningún**. **Ningún**, **ninguno**, and **ninguna** are generally used in the singular.

Aquí nadie se levanta antes de las ocho.	*No one here gets up before eight o'clock.*
Ninguno de ellos se muda.	*Neither (none) of them is moving.*
¿Alguien tiene paraguas?	*Does anyone have an umbrella?*
¿Hay algunos colombianos aquí?	*Are there some (any) Colombians here?*
—Sólo uno.	*— Only one.*
¿Hay algún problema?	*Is there some (any) problem?*

The personal **a** is used with the pronouns **alguien** and **nadie**, and with **alguno** and **ninguno** when they refer to people, in the same way that it is used with nouns or other pronouns.

¿Busca usted a algunos amigos de Enrique?	*Are you looking for some of Enrique's friends?*
No se lo voy a decir a nadie.	*I'm not going to tell it to anyone.*

C. Several negatives can be used in the same sentence.

¡No da nada a nadie nunca!	*He never gives anything to anyone, ever!*

D. **Ni... ni** expresses *not either ... or* or *neither ... nor.*

No son caras ni las botas marrones ni las rojas.	*Neither the brown boots nor the red ones are expensive.*
Aquí no venden ni faldas ni vestidos.	*They don't sell either skirts or dresses here.*

EJERCICIOS

A. **Construcciones sinónimas.** Change the negative constructions in these sentences, following the model.

Modelo   Yo nunca me despierto antes de las ocho.
Yo no me despierto nunca antes de las ocho.

1. ¿Nadie almuerza con ustedes?
2. Ella nunca pide té.
3. ¿Tampoco van ustedes?
4. Ninguno de los chicos se queda aquí.
5. ¿Nunca vas al centro?
6. Nada compro en esa tienda.
7. Nadie se divierte allí.
8. ¿Ningún estudiante vino a clase hoy?

B. Dos amigos. Felipe and Guillermo are friends who are very different. Complete the sentences in the negative, following the model.

Modelo   Felipe siempre quiere estar con alguien, pero Guillermo...
          Guillermo nunca quiere estar con nadie.

1. Felipe siempre quiere hacer algo, pero Guillermo...
2. Felipe siempre se levanta temprano, pero Guillermo...
3. Felipe va o al cine o al teatro los viernes, pero Guillermo...
4. Felipe sale los domingos también, pero Guillermo...
5. Felipe va a algún lugar interesante mañana, pero Guillermo...

C. Diferencias entre amigos. Using affirmative and negative words, make at least three sentences contrasting you and a good friend.

Modelos   **Mi amigo Jack nunca se levanta temprano, pero yo siempre me levanto a las siete.**

          Mi amiga Cristina tiene algunos sombreros interesantes, pero yo no tengo ningún sombrero.

D. Traducción. Give the Spanish equivalent of the following sentences.

1. She can't find anything in this store.
2. I'm going to get up at either six or seven tomorrow.
3. Do you need something?
4. No one is wearing an overcoat.
5. Are any of your friends going to the movies tonight?
6. Rogelio never finishes anything.

PREGUNTAS

1. ¿Conoce usted alguna tienda linda o interesante? ¿Cómo se llama? Cuando va allí de compras, ¿va con algún amigo (alguna amiga)? En general, ¿compra algo allí o sólo va a mirar? ¿Son caras las cosas que tienen?   **2.** ¿Alguien le da consejos sobre la ropa que lleva? ¿Quién? ¿Su mamá o su papá?, ¿un(-a) amigo(-a)? ¿Qué le dice? **3.** Cuando quiere llevar algo elegante, ¿qué lleva, en general?

De compras en una boutique

 Common uses of *por* and *para*

En Cartagena, Colombia, Manuel y Rosita se hablan por teléfono.

MANUEL	¿Por qué no viajamos a Bogotá *por* avión, Rosita?
ROSITA	Es que yo prefiero ir *por* auto, Manuel. El viaje *por* los Andes es muy lindo, sabes.
MANUEL	Pero sólo vamos *por* una semana y tenemos que estar allí *para* el jueves. ¿Recuerdas que nos esperan *para* la fiesta de Rosario ese día?
ROSITA	¡Tienes razón! Pues, entonces vamos *por* avión. Debemos llevarle un regalo a Rosario, ¿no?
MANUEL	Bueno, eso depende de ti.
ROSITA	Entonces, voy al centro *para* buscarle un suéter elegante. Después podemos encontrarnos en casa de mamá *para* cenar juntos, ¿de acuerdo?
MANUEL	De acuerdo. Prometo estar allí *para* la hora de la cena.

---

1. ¿Cómo prefiere ir a Bogotá Rosita? ¿Por qué?   2. ¿Por cuánto tiempo van Manuel y Rosita a Bogotá? ¿Para cuándo tienen que estar allí? ¿Por qué?   3. ¿Qué quiere comprar Rosita para Rosario?   4. ¿Dónde se van a encontrar después Manuel y Rosita? ¿Para qué?   5. ¿Qué promete Manuel?

Por and **para** have many uses in Spanish. While both prepositions are often translated by "for" in English, there is a great difference in usage between them. Here are some of the most common uses of **por** and **para**; you will see others in Chapter 17.

Por is generally used to express:

1.   Cause or motive (*because of, on account of*).

No van a venir por la lluvia.   *They're not going to come because of (on account of) the rain.*

Estos zapatos son muy hermosos y no son caros. Por eso (Por esas razones) los voy a comprar.	*These shoes are very lovely and aren't expensive. Because of that (For those reasons) I'm going to buy them.*

2. Duration or length of time, including parts of the day.

Los García se quedan con nosotros por dos semanas.	*The Garcías are staying with us for two weeks.*
Trabajo por la mañana y estudio por la tarde.	*I work in the morning and study in the afternoon.*

3. The equivalent of *through* or *along*.

Voy por el parque todos los días.	*I go through the park every day.*
Hay muchas tiendas interesantes por la calle Balboa.	*There are a lot of interesting shops along Balboa Street.*

4. *By* or *on* with means of transportation or communication.

Hablan por teléfono todas las semanas.	*They talk on the telephone (by telephone) every week.*
Tomás piensa viajar por avión.	*Tomás plans to travel by plane.*
Lo ven por televisión.	*They see it on television.*

Para is used to express:

1. An intended recipient (*for someone or something*).

Este vestido es para Evita.	*This dress is for Evita.*
Trabajo para el señor Calderón.	*I work for Mr. Calderón.*

2. Purpose (*in order to*).

Van a la biblioteca para estudiar juntos.	*They're going to the library (in order) to study together.*
Voy allí para comprar unas sandalias.	*I'm going there to buy some sandals.*

3. A specific point in time.

Tenemos que leer la lección para el lunes.	*We have to read the lesson by Monday.*

4. Direction or destination.

Salieron para México el jueves.	*They left for Mexico Thursday.*
Voy para la universidad.	*I'm going to (toward) the university.*

Here are some common expressions with **por**, some of which you have seen in previous chapters:

por ejemplo *for example*	**por fin** *finally*
por esas razones *for those reasons*	**¿por qué?** *why?*
por eso *for that reason*	**por suerte** *luckily*
por favor *please*	**por supuesto** *of course*

A. Por... para todos. (***Por*** . . . *for everyone.*)   Complete each phrase on the left with an appropriate ending on the right. Use each phrase on the left twice.

Modelo   **No queremos irnos por el frío.**
No queremos irnos por razones económicas.

siempre hablamos   por el frío
no vienen   por tres meses
no queremos irnos   por el parque
quieren ir   por la noche
siempre veo cosas interesantes   por tren
se van a San Francisco   por razones económicas
viajamos a España   por la calle Colón
se mudan a un apartamento   por teléfono
se queda en Madrid   por avión

B. Para... para practicar. (***Para*** . . . *for practice.*)   Complete each phrase on the left with an appropriate ending on the right. Use each phrase on the left twice.

Modelo   **Carlos viene para cenar con ustedes.**
Carlos viene para las once y media.

mi hermana trabaja   para las once y media
Carlos viene   para Toledo
esos estudiantes van   para comprar ropa de invierno
los Muñoz se mudan   para ir al baile con Susana
prometo estar allí   para la clase de español
tengo un regalo   para cenar con ustedes
ese dinero es   para la doctora Díaz
no necesito corbata   para el sur *(south)*
tenemos que hacer los ejercicios   para la señora Solé

C. Memorándum.   Here is a list of things Marisa wants to accomplish before she goes to bed tonight. Complete her phrases with **por** or **para**, as appropriate.

Modelos   estudiar / la mañana
estudiar por la mañana

leer la lección de física / las once
leer la lección de física para las once

1. llamar a Susana / teléfono
2. escribir la composición / la clase de francés
3. ir de compras / la tarde
4. ir al centro / autobús
5. comprar una corbata / David
6. buscar una falda / llevar a una fiesta
7. volver a casa / las nueve y media
8. mirar «Noches colombianas» / televisión

D. En acción. Describe the following drawings, using **por** or **para**, as appropriate. Make more than one sentence if possible.

Modelo

Prefiero un suéter de otro color.

No va a comprar el suéter por el color.

1.

CARTAGENA

2.

PARQUE CENTRAL

3.

4.

No voy a salir. Llueve mucho.

5.

Miércoles, 5 de diciembre: Leer Capítulos 6 y 7

6.

Tengo dolor de cabeza. Necesito comprar aspirinas.

FARMACIA

BOGOTÁ: De compras

En Bogotá, Colombia, dos amigas van de compras.

KATHY Gloria, necesito comprar algo para mi mamá. Quizás un suéter...

GLORIA ¿Pues por qué no entramos aquí? Tienen cosas muy elegantes y mi primo José trabaja en esta tienda.

Entran en la tienda.

GLORIA Ese suéter es muy bonito. ¿O prefieres el verde?

KATHY No, este azul es el color perfecto para mamá.

JOSÉ Hola, Gloria. ¿No me vas a presentar° a tu amiga?

GLORIA Por supuesto, José. Ésta es Kathy. Es de los Estados Unidos.

JOSÉ Mucho gusto, Kathy. Ese suéter va muy bien con tus ojos°... azul claro como el cielo°, como el mar en un día de sol, como...

GLORIA Kathy, José siempre dice piropos.¹ Tienes que acostumbrarte. Pero es inofensivo°.

KATHY ¡No sé si me puedo acostumbrar!

JOSÉ Pero, guapa, soy inofensivo como un bebé°. ¿Qué hacen ustedes hoy por la tarde? Van a Monserrate, ¿no?² Y yo voy con ustedes. Debes llevar el suéter, Kathy. Allí hace frío...por la altitud.

KATHY	El suéter no es para mí. Es para mi mamá. Además, hoy quiero ver algunos de los museos.
JOSÉ	En un museo de arte debes estar tú, hermosa.
GLORIA	José es incurable.... Podemos visitar el Museo del Oro, Kathy, o el Museo de Arte Moderno, o...[3]
JOSÉ	¡Qué aburrido! Si no quieren ir a Monserrate, ¿por qué no vamos a la Quinta de Bolívar?[4] Y esta noche, Kathy, te llevamos al club Noches de Colombia. Allí tocan música muy buena y nos podemos divertir.
GLORIA	Bogotá es una ciudad maravillosa° para los turistas.
KATHY	¿Conocen ustedes todos esos lugares?
GLORIA	Claro que no. ¡Vivimos aquí!

presentar *to introduce*   **ojos** *eyes*   **el cielo** *sky*   **inofensivo** *harmless, inoffensive*
bebé *baby*   **maravillosa** *wonderful*

PREGUNTAS

1. ¿Dónde están las dos amigas?   **2.** ¿Por qué entran en una tienda? ¿Quién trabaja allí?   **3.** ¿Cómo es José? ¿Adónde quiere ir él con ellas?   **4.** ¿Qué quiere hacer Kathy?   **5.** ¿Qué piensa José de los museos?   **6.** ¿Qué lugares quiere mostrarle José a Kathy?   **7.** ¿Conocen Gloria y José todos los lugares que mencionan?   **8.** ¿Conoce usted todos los lugares turísticos de su ciudad?

Notas culturales

1. **Piropos** are compliments made by men to women, often to women passing by on the street. Some Hispanics consider it an art to be able to instantly devise a **piropo** appropriate to a particular occasion. This is a time-honored custom and is usually not taken as harmful or offensive.

2. At the top of Monserrate is a world-famous church and shrine, which can be reached by funicular railroad, cable car, or on foot. There is a magnificent view of the capital, Bogotá, which is at 8,600 feet.

3. One of the world's greatest collections of Indian jewelry is housed in the **Museo del Oro**. The collection traces its beginnings back to two early Indian tribes: the Chibcha and the Quimbay.

4. Simón Bolívar was born in Caracas, Venezuela, in 1783. He led Venezuela's fight for freedom from Spain. In 1817 he captured Caracas, earning the name **El Libertador**. He was also responsible for freeing Ecuador, Colombia, Panamá, and Perú, and for founding Bolivia, which bears his name. The widely visited villa (**quinta**) of Simón Bolívar, near Bogotá, is now a museum of the colonial era. He lived there from 1826 to 1828.

FUNCIONES Y ACTIVIDADES

In this chapter, you have seen examples of the following language functions, or uses. Here is a summary and some additional information about these functions of language:

Expressing hesitation

There will often be times when you don't have a ready answer for something someone has asked. This happens even in your native language, but it can happen even more frequently when you are speaking a foreign language. Here are some expressions you can use to fill in those moments of conversational hesitation.

A ver. *Let's see.*
Es que... *The thing is that . . . (Literally, "It's that . . .")*
Buena pregunta. *Good question.*
Pues... *Well . . .*
Bueno... *Well . . .*
Depende de... *It depends on . . .*

Making descriptions (2)

There will be many times when you have to describe something in Spanish, whether you are in a shop and trying to describe what you want or whether you are just trying to explain to someone what something is—especially if you don't know the word for it in Spanish. Here are some ways to ask for a description and to describe something.

¿De qué color es? —Es rojo (blanco, etcétera).

What color is it? —It's red (white, etc.).

¿De qué tamaño es? — Es grande (pequeño, del tamaño de un libro, etcétera).

What size is it? —It's big (little, the size of a book, etc.).

¿De qué es? —Es de madera (plástico, metal, etcétera).

What is it made of? —It's made of wood (plastic, metal, etc.).

¿Para qué sirve? —Sirve para tocar (leer, escribir, etcétera).

What do you use it for? — You use it for playing (reading, writing, etc.).

A. **Pues...** Ask a classmate the following questions. Your classmate should express hesitation before answering them, using one of the expressions from this chapter.

1. ¿Qué tipo de ropa te pones cuando quieres darle una buena impresión a la gente? ¿De qué color? ¿Te pones ropa elegante, informal, extraña (*strange*)?
2. ¿Cuál es tu color favorito? ¿Por qué?
3. ¿Qué color asocias tú con el otoño?, ¿con la primavera?, ¿con la alegría (*happiness*)?
4. ¿Cuántas horas duermes cada noche? ¿Duermes bien, en general?

B. ¿Qué es esto?   In small groups, one person will think of the name of an object that he or she can say in Spanish (something that has been presented in this book or in class). The others will take turns asking questions about the object; these must be yes/no questions. The person who guesses the object then takes a turn.

C. En «La Elegancia».   The clerk in the shop "La Elegancia" is trying to encourage customers to buy some clothing. With the names of the appropriate items, complete the sentences he might say.

1. ¿Se queda usted en casa por la lluvia? ¿Por qué no se compra un _____ y un _____?
2. Para ir a un restaurante elegante, señor, debe usar _____ y corbata.
3. Para el frío del invierno usted necesita este _____.
4. Para una fiesta, señorita, puede comprarse una _____ larga o un _____ elegante.
5. No, señor, esas son blusas para señoras; pero aquí hay _____ para usted.

D.   Imagine you are in a Spanish-speaking country and you need the following items but don't know the Spanish words. Describe each item using the hints below and, if necessary, gestures. (The Spanish words are given at the bottom of the page.)

1. hotel or restaurant bill
2. glass
3. blanket
4. tablespoon
5. clothes hanger
6. credit card

E.   With one of your classmates, role-play the following situations in Spanish. Be sure to express hesitation before answering the questions.

1. Your friend wants to know what sort of clothing to wear to a party.
2. A prospective freshman asks you about various aspects of campus and college life at your school.
3. Your friend asks you to recommend a good movie or a good restaurant.
4. Your friend is going out on a blind date and would like some suggestions for topics of conversation or places to go.

1. la cuenta   2. el vaso   3. la manta   4. la cuchara   5. la percha
6. la tarjeta de crédito

VOCABULARIO ACTIVO

Cognados

el arte	la elegancia	el pijama	la sandalia
la blusa	el grupo	la rutina	el suéter
económico	los jeans		

Verbos

acostar (ue)	to put to bed
acostarse	to go to bed
acostumbrarse	to get used to
cenar	to have dinner
depender (de)	to depend (on)
despertar (ie)	to awaken (someone)
despertarse	to awaken, wake up
divertir (ie)	to amuse, entertain
divertirse	to enjoy oneself, have a good time
entrar (en)	to enter, go into
irse	to go away; leave
lavar	to wash
lavarse	to wash oneself
levantar	to raise
levantarse	to get up, stand up
llamarse	to be called, to be named
llevar	to wear; to take
mudarse	to move, change residence
ponerse	to put on (clothing)
quedar	to be left, remain
quedarse	to stay
quitarse	to take off (clothing)
sentarse (ie)	to sit down, be seated
vestir (i)	to dress
vestirse	to get dressed

La ropa

el abrigo	coat (winter coat)
la bota	boot
el calcetín	sock
la camisa	shirt
el cinturón	belt
la corbata	tie
la falda	skirt
el guante	glove
el impermeable	raincoat
las medias	stockings
la moda	fashion, style
el pantalón	pair of pants
los pantalones	pants

el paraguas	umbrella
la ropa	clothing
el sombrero	hat
el traje	suit; outfit
el traje de baño	swimming suit
el vestido	dress
el zapato	shoe

Otras palabras y frases

a la moda (de moda)	in style, fashionable
caro	expensive
claro	clear, light
diario	daily
entre	between, among
guapo	handsome, good-looking
hermoso	beautiful
juntos	together
largo	long
la novia	girlfriend
el novio	boyfriend
oscuro	dark
por esas razones	for those reasons
por fin	finally
por suerte	luckily
sólo (= solamente)	only
el tamaño	size

Expresiones útiles

A ver.	Let's see.
Bueno...	Well...
¿De qué color es?	What color is it?
¿De qué es?	What is it made of?
¿De qué tamaño es?	What size is it?
Es que...	The thing is that...
¿Para qué sirve?	What do you use it for?
Pues...	Well...

> **Don't forget:**
> Names of colors, pages 152–153
> Affirmative and negative words, page 160

el vólibol

el béisbol

el esquiador

los esquíes

el esquí

la pelota
(el balón)

el jugador de fútbol
(el futbolista)

el fútbol

el jugador de tenis
(el tenista)

la raqueta

los espectadores

los corredores

los aficionados

el torero

el toro

la corrida de toros

la carrera, el trote

la esquiadora

la raqueta

la jugadora de tenis

el tenis

fútbol americano

Deportes y deportistas

8

Expressing Disbelief
Using *para* in Comparisons

EJERCICIO

Choose the word that does not belong and tell why.

1. pelota, raqueta, esquí, espectador
2. aficionado, jugador, torero, toro
3. llevar, jugar, nadar, esquiar
4. básquetbol, vólibol, pelota, fútbol
5. violento, pequeño, interesante, popular

PREGUNTAS

1. En un equipo de béisbol hay nueve jugadores. ¿Cuántos jugadores hay en un equipo de fútbol americano? ¿de fútbol? ¿de tenis? ¿de básquetbol?   **2.** ¿Juega usted al fútbol? ¿al tenis? ¿Qué deportes practica usted?   **3.** ¿Es usted aficionado(-a) al básquetbol? ¿al béisbol? ¿al fútbol?   **4.** ¿Con qué deporte(-s) asocia usted a José Canseco? ¿a Gabriela Sabatini? ¿a Doug Flutie? ¿a Michael Jordan?

The preterit of regular and stem-changing verbs

En Galicia, España.

EVA	Te *llamé* anoche, Alfonso, pero no *contestaste*.
ALFONSO	*Asistí* a un partido de jai alai* con Elena.
EVA	¿Te *divertiste*?
ALFONSO	Sí, mucho. Pedro Ramos y Paco González *jugaron* muy bien.
EVA	¿*Ganaste* dinero?
ALFONSO	No, *perdí* tres mil pesetas, pero Elena *ganó* cuatro mil. Así que *ganamos* mil.

1. ¿A quién llamó Eva?   2. ¿Contestó él el teléfono?   3. ¿A qué asistieron Elena y Alfonso?   4. ¿Quiénes jugaron bien?   5. ¿Ganó dinero Alfonso? ¿y Elena? 6. ¿Se divirtieron?   7. ¿Asistió usted a un partido de jai alai alguna vez (*ever*)?

A. The preterit tense is used to relate actions or events that occurred and were completed at a specific time or within a definite period in the past. The preterit tense of regular **-ar** verbs is formed by adding the endings **-é, -aste, -ó, -amos, -asteis, -aron** to the stem.

comprar

compr**é**	compr**amos**
compr**aste**	compr**asteis**
compr**ó**	compr**aron**

Tres jugadores importantes no participaron en el partido de ayer.	*Three important players did not participate in yesterday's game.*

---

* See **Nota cultural 3** of this chapter.

In Galicia, Spain. EVA: I called you last night, Alfonso, but you didn't answer. ALFONSO: I went to a jai alai game with Elena. EVA: Did you have a good time? ALFONSO: Yes, very good. Pedro Ramos and Paco González played very well. EVA: Did you win money? ALFONSO: No, I lost three thousand pesetas, but Elena won four thousand. So we won a thousand.

B. The preterit tense of regular **-er** and **-ir** verbs is formed by adding the endings **-í**, **-iste**, **-ió**, **-imos**, **isteis**, **-ieron** to the stem.

correr (to run)		**volver**		**escribir**	
corrí	corrimos	volví	volvimos	escribí	escribimos
corriste	corristeis	volviste	volvisteis	escribiste	escribisteis
corrió	corrieron	volvió	volvieron	escribió	escribieron

Aprendí a jugar al básquetbol. Es un deporte muy emocionante.

Escribieron un artículo sobre el equipo.

Corrieron casi dos kilómetros.

I learned how to play basketball. It's a very exciting sport.

They wrote an article about the team.

They ran almost two kilometers.

Notice that regular preterit forms are stressed on the endings rather than on the stems: **Llego temprano.** (*I arrive early.*) **Llegó temprano.** (*He [she, you] arrived early.*) Notice also that the **nosotros** forms of **-ar** and **-ir** verbs are the same in the preterit as in the present tense.

	Present	**Preterit**
-ar *verbs*	compramos	compramos
-er *verbs*	corremos	corrimos
-ir *verbs*	escribimos	escribimos

C. While the preterit forms of stem-changing **-ar** and **-er** verbs are all regular (**pensé, volví**), stem-changing **-ir** verbs show a change in the third-persons singular and plural of the preterit tense. The stem change is from **e** to **i** or **o** to **u**.

pedir		**dormir**	
pedí	pedimos	dormí	dormimos
pediste	pedisteis	dormiste	dormisteis
pidió	pidieron	durmió	durmieron

Other verbs that are conjugated like **pedir** in the preterit are **divertirse**, **seguir**, **servir**, and **preferir**. **Morir** (*to die*) is conjugated like **dormir**.

Alfredo siguió tres cursos el semestre pasado.

Murieron tres toreros el año pasado en las corridas de toros.

Alfredo took three courses last semester.

Three bullfighters died last year in the bullfights.

D. A number of verbs have a spelling change in the first-person singular of the preterit tense. Verbs ending in **-gar**, **-car**, and **-zar** have the following spelling changes, respectively: **g** to **gu**, **c** to **qu**, and **z** to **c**. These changes are required to preserve the sound of the last syllable of the infinitive.

llegar		tocar		empezar	
lle**gué**	lle**gamos**	to**qué**	to**camos**	empe**cé**	empe**zamos**
lle**gaste**	lle**gasteis**	to**caste**	to**casteis**	empe**zaste**	empe**zasteis**
lle**gó**	lle**garon**	to**có**	to**caron**	empe**zó**	empe**zaron**

Jugué al tenis ayer.	*I played tennis yesterday.*
Te busqué anoche en el partido de fútbol.	*I looked for you last night at the soccer game.*
Le explicó* la situación a su esposa.	*He explained the situation to his wife.*

E. Verbs such as **creer** and **leer** show a spelling change in the third-persons singular and plural: **creyó**, **creyeron**; **leyó**, **leyeron**. The other forms are regular. This change is made because an **i** between two vowels becomes a **y**.

Felipe leyó que el béisbol es un deporte muy popular en Centroamérica y México.	*Felipe read that baseball is a very popular sport in Central America and Mexico.*
Creyeron su historia — ¿De veras?	*They believed his story. — Really?*

F. The verb **nacer** (*to be born*) is used almost exclusively in the preterit.

¿Dónde naciste? — Nací en Galicia, España.	*Where were you born? — I was born in Galicia, Spain.*

EJERCICIOS

A. **¿Otra vez?** Mrs. Fernández is talking to her son Nicolás. Respond as Nicolás would, saying that the same things happened yesterday.

Modelos   Hoy practicas piano.
¡Pero ayer practiqué piano también!

Hoy tu papá llega tarde.
¡Pero ayer llegó tarde también!

Hoy nos quedamos aquí.
¡Pero ayer nos quedamos aquí también!

1. Hoy tu hermano asiste a un partido de fútbol.
2. Hoy Ana y yo jugamos al tenis.
3. Hoy le escribo a tu abuela.
4. Hoy te acuestas temprano.

---

* The infinitive is **explicar**.

5. Hoy tu hermana juega al vólibol.
6. Hoy tu papá sale con sus amigos.
7. Hoy empiezas tus deberes antes de la cena.
8. Hoy comemos después del partido de fútbol.
9. Hoy tú y Ana me ayudáis a lavar los platos.

B. Traducción. Give the Spanish equivalent.

1. They watched a program about basketball.
2. He called Juanita, but she didn't answer.
3. The soccer players returned from Asunción yesterday.
4. Did you (**tú**) have a good time at the movies?
5. The team played well.
6. The game began at eight o'clock.

C. El sábado pasado. Look at the pictures and describe what the people did last Saturday. Use your imagination. (Several infinitives are listed by each picture to give you ideas.) Give at least two sentences for each picture.

Modelo

Roberto: quedarse, mirar, jugar

El sábado pasado Roberto no salió con sus amigos. Él se quedó en casa y miró un partido de fútbol por televisión. Según él, los dos equipos jugaron muy bien.

1.

El señor Díaz: llamar, hablar, explicar

2.

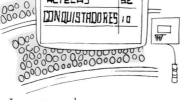

Los aztecas y los conquistadores: jugar, perder, ganar

3.

Ramón y Ana Luisa: bailar, hablar, divertirse

4.

Juan y Jaime: jugar, correr mucho

5.

Susana y Jesús: asistir, divertirse, escuchar música

6.

Los estudiantes: leer, escribir, buscar

D. Y ayer, ¿qué? Ask a classmate questions to find out what he or she did yesterday, then report the information to the class. You might want to use some of the following verbs: **levantarse, tomar el desayuno, asistir, ir, participar, jugar, hablar, leer, almorzar, escribir, volver, mirar, acostarse.**

PREGUNTAS

1. ¿Dónde nació usted? ¿Cuánto tiempo vivió allí? ¿Se mudó a otro lugar? ¿En qué año se mudó? **2.** ¿Visitó a algunos amigos ayer? ¿Asistió a algún concierto o partido de fútbol (tenis, etcétera)? ¿Jugó a algún deporte? ¿Salió por la noche (la tarde)? ¿Fue a algún lugar interesante? ¿Se divirtió? ¿Miró la televisión? **3.** ¿Leyó algún libro interesante el mes pasado? ¿Qué libro? **4.** ¿A qué hora se acostó usted anoche? ¿Durmió bien? ¿Con qué o con quién soñó? **5.** ¿A qué hora llegó a clase hoy?

Adverbs ending in *-mente;* comparisons of equality

En el apartamento de Bárbara, cerca de la Plaza Mayor, de Madrid.

TERESA	Hola, Bárbara. ¿Qué hay de nuevo? ¿Todavía haces ejercicios *diariamente*?
BÁRBARA	No, no tengo tiempo. Busco otro apartamento.
TERESA	¿Por qué? ¿*Realmente* quieres mudarte?
BÁRBARA	Sí, no quiero pagar *tanto como* pago ahora, *especialmente* porque este apartamento es muy pequeño. Tú sabes que cuando Rita viene a hacer ejercicios aquí, ¡una de nosotras tiene que hacerlos en el corredor!
TERESA	¡No puede ser! Pero, ¿sabes?... este lugar no es *tan pequeño como* mi cuarto. Allí, cuando entra el sol, ¡tengo que irme yo!

1. ¿Hace ejercicios diariamente Bárbara? ¿Por qué? 2. ¿Está contenta Bárbara con el apartamento que tiene? 3. ¿Por qué quiere mudarse Bárbara? 4. ¿Es grande o pequeño el apartamento de Bárbara?, ¿tan grande (pequeño) como el apartamento de Teresa?

A. Most adverbs in Spanish are derived from the feminine form of an adjective plus the suffix **-mente**.

rápido(-a)	*rapid, fast*	rápidamente	*rapidly, fast*
lento(-a)	*slow*	lentamente	*slowly*
reciente	*recent*	recientemente	*recently*
fácil	*easy*	fácilmente	*easily*

El profesor explica la lección claramente.

The professor explains the lesson clearly.

Es un deporte verdaderamente peligroso.

It's a truly dangerous sport.

Los aficionados hablan alegremente.

The fans are talking happily.

B. Comparisons of equality are formed by using **tan** + adjective or adverb + **como**.

Juana toca la guitarra tan bien como Marisol.

Juana plays the guitar as well as Marisol.

Elvira es tan alta y tan fuerte como José.

Elvira is as tall and as strong as José.

Paco nada tan rápidamente como Pablo.

Paco swims as fast as Pablo does.

Yo no contesto las cartas tan pronto como Eva.

I don't answer letters as soon as Eva does.

C. **Tan** can also mean *so*: **¡Eres tan vanidoso!** (*You are so vain!*)

D. **Tanto(-a, -os, -as)** is used before a noun. **Tanto como** after a verb means *as much as*. **Tanto** by itself means *so much*.

Él tiene tantas oportunidades como yo.

He has as many opportunities as I do.

Ellos hacen tantos ejercicios como yo.

They do as many exercises as I do.

Tomás come tanto como yo.

Tomás eats as much as I do.

¡Pobre Luis! ¿Por qué trabaja tanto?

Poor Luis! Why does he work so much?

In Bárbara's apartment, near the Plaza Mayor, in Madrid. TERESA: Hi, Bárbara. What's new? Are you still doing exercises daily? BÁRBARA: No, I don't have time. I'm looking for another apartment. TERESA: Why? Do you really want to move? BÁRBARA: Yes, I don't want to pay as much as I'm paying now, especially because this apartment is very small. You know that when Rita comes to do exercises here, one of us has to do them in the hallway! TERESA: It can't be! But, you know what?... this place is not as small as my room. There, when the sun comes in, I have to go out!

A. Tan... Based on the drawings, make as many sentences as possible using **tan** plus the following adjectives or others of your own. Use the appropriate form of the adjectives.

alto	elegante	joven
bonito	fuerte	peligroso
cansado	grande	viejo
contento		

Modelos   **Las tenistas no están tan contentas como la esquiadora.**

El futbolista es casi tan alto como los jugadores de básquetbol.

B. De adjetivos a adverbios.   Make adverbs from the following adjectives.

1. posible
2. amable
3. claro
4. lento
5. general
6. completo
7. rápido
8. simple

C. **¡Ganamos!**   Your school football team has just won a very important game. As a member of that team, answer the questions a journalist is asking you.

Modelos   ¿Practicaron mucho? (diario)
Sí, practicamos diariamente.

¿Jugó bien el otro equipo? (horrible)
No, ¡jugó horriblemente!

1. ¿Jugaron bien ustedes? (estupendo)
2. ¿Ganaron con dificultad (*difficulty*)? (fácil)
3. ¿Jugaron también en Michigan? (reciente)
4. ¿Piensan jugar en otros estados? (regular)
5. ¿Necesita practicar el otro equipo? (probable)
6. ¿Durmieron bien anoche? (terrible)
7. ¿Volvieron contentos? (alegre)

D. **¿Cómo me comparo con mis parientes o con otra gente?** (*How do I compare to my relatives or to other people?*)   It's a hard question, but ... Form affirmative or negative sentences comparing yourself to your relatives or friends in terms of what you are like, what you have, and what you do. Follow the models.

Modelos   fuerte
No soy tan fuerte como mis hermanos.

amigas
Tengo tantas amigas como mi hermana.

estudiar
No estudio tanto como José.

1. alto(-a)	6. problemas	11. correr
2. trabajador(-a)	7. dinero	12. divertirse
3. joven	8. ropa	13. dormir
4. vanidoso(-a)	9. clases	14. comer
5. optimista	10. paciencia	15. leer

E. **Entrevista.**   In pairs, ask and answer questions about exercise habits using adverbs from the following list or others of your own.

Modelos   ¿Qué deporte practicas regularmente?
Ninguno. Pero hago ejercicios diariamente.

¿Corres frecuentemente?
No, raramente. Pero practico yoga regularmente.

bien	lentamente	raramente
diariamente	nunca	regularmente
frecuentemente	rápidamente	terriblemente

Comparisons of inequality and the superlative

ADELA	Eduardo, soy *la mejor jugadora del equipo,* ¿verdad?
EDUARDO	Claro, Adela, *la mejor.*
ADELA	¿Y soy *la muchacha más inteligente* que conoces?
EDUARDO	*Inteligentísima.*
ADELA	¿Y *la más sensible* y *la menos vanidosa?*
EDUARDO	¡Por supuesto!
ADELA	¿Y no hablas en broma...?
EDUARDO	Claro que no, mi amor.
ADELA	Ah, Eduardo, ¡sólo tú puedes decir cosas tan lindas!

---

1. Según Eduardo, ¿quién es la mejor jugadora del equipo?   2. ¿Quién es la chica más inteligente y menos vanidosa que Eduardo conoce?   3. ¿Qué dice Adela de Eduardo?

A. Comparisons of inequality.

1. In Spanish, comparisons of inequality are expressed with **más** (*more*)**... que** or **menos** (*less*)**... que**. *More than* is **más que**, and *less than* is **menos que.**

Es un deporte más emocionante que el fútbol. —¡Qué va!	*It's a more exciting sport than soccer. —Oh, come on!*
Juan corre más rápidamente que los otros jugadores.	*Juan runs faster than the other players.*
Siempre tengo menos dinero que él.	*I always have less money than he does.*
Esta raqueta de tenis es menos cara que la otra.	*This tennis racket is less expensive than the other one.*
Solamente Luis ganó más que nosotros.	*Only Luis won more than we did.*
Juan practica menos que yo.	*Juan is practicing less than I am.*

ADELA: Eduardo, I'm the best player on the team, right? EDUARDO: Of course, Adela, the best. ADELA: And am I the most intelligent girl whom you know? EDUARDO: Extremely intelligent. ADELA: And the most sensitive and least vain? EDUARDO: Of course! ADELA: And you're not joking . . .? EDUARDO: Of course not, dear (my love). ADELA: Oh, Eduardo, only you can say such beautiful things!

2. Before a number, **de** is used instead of **que** to mean *than*.*

Esperamos más de diez minutos.	*We waited more than ten minutes.*
Asistieron menos de cincuenta aficionados.	*Fewer than fifty fans attended.*

B. The **superlative**.

The superlative forms of adjectives and adverbs (which express *the most, the least,* etc.) are the same as the comparative forms.

Ana es la jugadora más (menos) importante del grupo.	*Ana is the most (least) important player of the group.*
Esteban es el más (menos) trabajador de la familia.	*Esteban is the most (least) hard-working in the family.*
Yo soy la más (menos) atlética de la clase. — ¡Es increíble!	*I am the most (least) athletic (one) in the class. — It's incredible!*

Notice that **de** is used after a superlative to express the English *in* or *of.*

C. Irregular comparative and superlative forms.

Adjective	Comparative	Superlative
bueno *good*	mejor *better*	el mejor *the best*
malo *bad*	peor *worse*	el peor *the worst*
pequeño *small*	menor (más pequeño) *younger (smaller)*	el menor (el más pequeño) *the youngest (smallest)*
grande *big*	mayor (más grande) *older (bigger)*	el mayor (el más grande) *the oldest (biggest)*

Adverb	Comparative	Superlative
bien *well*	mejor *better*	mejor *best*
mal *badly*	peor *worse*	peor *worst*

The comparative adjectives **mejor**, **peor**, **menor**, and **mayor** have the same forms in the feminine as in the masculine; the plurals are formed by adding **-es.**

Josefina es la mejor jugadora de vólibol de su equipo, pero es la peor estudiante de su clase de historia.	*Josefina is the best volleyball player on her team, but she's the worst student in her history class.*

---

*However, in a negative sentence, **más que** can be used to mean *only*: **No tengo más que diez centavos.** (*I have only ten cents.*)

¿Cómo se llama el chico que nadó mejor?	*What is the name of the boy who swam the best?*
¿Dónde están las mejores playas?	*Where are the best beaches?*

Note that **menor** and **mayor**, which usually follow the nouns they modify, are often used with people to refer to age (*younger, older*). When referring to physical size, *bigger* is usually expressed by **más grande(-s)** and *smaller* is expressed by **más pequeño(-a, -os, -as)**.

Paco y Pancho son menores que Felipe, pero Felipe es más pequeño.	*Paco and Pancho are younger than Felipe, but Felipe is smaller.*
Adriana es mi hermana mayor; Silvia y Marta son mis hermanas menores.	*Adriana is my older sister; Silvia and Marta are my younger sisters.*

D. The absolute superlative.

1. One way to express the superlative quality of an adjective is to use **muy** (*very*): **La casa es muy grande**. A second way is to add **-ísimo** (**-ísima, -ísimos, -ísimas**) to the adjective. The **-ísimo** ending is the absolute superlative, much stronger than **muy** + the adjective. If the adjective ends in a vowel, drop the final vowel before adding the **-ísimo** ending.

Como futbolista, él es malísimo. —¿En serio?	*As a soccer player, he is extremely bad. —Really?*
El uso de drogas entre los atletas es un problema grandísimo.	*The use of drugs among athletes is a very big problem.*
Estas entradas son carísimas.	*These tickets are extremely expensive.*
Ese atleta es altísimo.	*That athlete is extremely tall.*
¿La corrida de toros? Es un drama simbólico, lindísimo.	*The bullfight? It's a symbolic drama, extremely beautiful.*

2. The **-ísimo** ending can also be added to an adverb.

Luis llegó tardísimo.	*Luis arrived extremely late.*
Hoy practicaron poquísimo.*	*Today they practiced extremely little.*
Pagaron muchísimo.	*They paid quite a lot.*

EJERCICIOS

A. ¿Cuál es la palabra apropiada?   Complete the sentences by choosing the correct word or phrase in parentheses.

1. Babe Ruth es (más / menos) famoso que Juan Pérez.
2. Un equipo de béisbol tiene (más de / más que) tres jugadores.
3. Luis perdió cincuenta pesetas. Mi padre perdió diez pesetas. Luis perdió (más de / más que) mi papá.
4. El Océano Pacífico es el océano (mayor / más grande) del mundo.
5. El béisbol es el deporte más popular (en / de) este país.

---

* The **c** of **poco** is changed to **qu** to preserve the **k** sound.

B. ¡Laura no anda con rodeos! (*Laura doesn't beat around the bush!*)   React to her boyfriend's comments as she would, following the model.

Modelo   Estas raquetas son caras.
         ¡Son carísimas, hombre!

1. Esos equipos son buenos.
2. Aquella atleta es alta.
3. Ayer practicamos poco.
4. Anoche nos divertimos mucho.
5. Ese jugador español es famoso.

6. Estos ejercicios son fáciles.
7. El jai alai es un deporte peligroso.
8. Las películas de Clint Eastwood son violentas.

C. ¿Más... o menos...?   Following the example, create sentences by adding the appropriate comparative.

Modelo   Millard Fillmore / ser / famoso / Abraham Lincoln
         Millard Fillmore es menos famoso que Abraham Lincoln.

1. un equipo de fútbol / tener / 70 jugadores
2. Argentina / ser / grande / Nicaragua
3. un día / tener / 25 horas
4. un auto / ser / caro / bicicleta
5. febrero / tener / días / diciembre

D. Traducción.   Give the Spanish equivalent of the following sentences.

1. This is the most important game of the year.   *Este es el mas importante*
2. Tomás is a good player, but he is not the best.
3. She is the best friend I have.
4. Paco is less vain than Pedro.   *Paco es menos vanidoso que Pedro*
5. Adela is our youngest sister, but she is the tallest.
6. Mexico is bigger than Guatemala. *Mex es mas grande que Guat*
7. He's the worst athlete in the world.
8. Alicia is the girl who sings the best.

E. Los deportes.   Make several sentences with comparative and superlatives about the sports events shown. You might want to use some of the following adjectives: **aburrido, caro, emocionante, peligroso, violento.**

1.   2.   3.
4.   5.   6.

1. ¿Quién cree usted que es el mejor jugador de fútbol de los Estados Unidos? ¿de béisbol? ¿de tenis? ¿de básquetbol?   **2.** ¿Cuál es el deporte más popular de los Estados Unidos? ¿de América del Sur? ¿del mundo?   **3.** ¿Cuál es el deporte más violento que usted conoce? ¿el más aburrido?   **4.** ¿Cuál es el país más grande de América del Sur? ¿el más pequeño?   **5.** ¿Tiene usted un hermano o una hermana mayor? ¿menor?   **6.** ¿Es usted el (la) más pequeño(-a) de su familia? ¿el (la) menor?   **7.** ¿Vive usted en un apartamento grandísimo? ¿pequeñísimo? ¿carísimo?   **8.** ¿Tiene usted muchísimo que estudiar esta noche? ¿este fin de semana?

Omission of the indefinite article after *ser*

Un partido de vólibol

El chico con la pelota es atleta.
Es español.

Following the verb **ser**, the indefinite article is omitted before an unmodified noun that indicates profession, religion, nationality, or political affiliation.

Juan es
- atleta.
- católico.
- colombiano.
- socialista.

Juan is
- *an athlete.*
- *a Catholic.*
- *a Colombian.*
- *a socialist.*

Es un
- buen atleta.
- católico devoto.
- colombiano patriótico.
- socialista rico.

He's a
- *good athlete.*
- *devout Catholic.*
- *patriotic Colombian.*
- *rich socialist.*

EJERCICIOS

A. Asociaciones.   List whatever professions, political interests, religious beliefs, and nationalities you associate with the following people.

Modelos   Julio Iglesias
Julio Iglesias es cantante (*singer*), español y católico.

Ronald Reagan
Ronald Reagan es político, actor, protestante y norteamericano.*

1. Pancho González
2. Fidel Castro
3. Gabriel García Márquez
4. Edward James Olmos
5. Carlos Fuentes
6. Fernando Valenzuela
7. Margaret Thatcher
8. Michael Jackson
9. Dan Marino
10. Carl Sagan

B. Cualidades y características.   Now give one outstanding quality or characteristic of each of the people listed in Exercise A.

Modelo   Pancho González
Pancho González es un atleta famoso. Es tenista.

PREGUNTAS

1. ¿Qué profesión tiene su padre? ¿su madre?   **2.** ¿Es usted demócrata? ¿republicano(-a)? ¿independiente?   **3.** ¿Puede nombrar (*name*) a un(-a) famoso(-a) atleta latinoamericano(-a)? ¿a un(-a) atleta muy rico(-a)? ¿De qué nacionalidad es?

---

* The feminine form of **el político** (*politician*) is **la político**.

SANTANDER: Los deportes

Unos jugadores de jai alai

Los señores Moreno y los señores Blanco, con su hija Adriana, están en un café de Santander a las siete de la tarde.

SR. BLANCO	Buenas tardes. ¿Ya° pedisteis?[1]
SR. MORENO	Sí, pedimos jerez[2] para todos.
SR. BLANCO	¿De veras? ¿No recordasteis que mi señora no toma bebidas° tan fuertes como el jerez? ¿Verdad, María?
SRA. BLANCO	Pues, yo... solamente...
SR. BLANCO	¡Camarero! Un vino° blanco para la señora, por favor.
CAMARERO	Se lo sirvo inmediatamente, señor.
SR. MORENO	Bueno, ¿y qué hay de nuevo?
SR. BLANCO	Anoche asistimos a un partido de jai alai.[3]
SRA. BLANCO	Participaron los equipos más populares de España.
SR. BLANCO	El mejor jugador es Pardo. Empezó muy bien. Ganó doce puntos seguidos°.
SR. MORENO	¡Qué bien!... pero..., ¿no lo dices en broma?
SR. BLANCO	No, pero no siguió así... Después jugó muy mal.
SR. MORENO	¡Ah! Triunfó° el otro equipo. Y tú, ¿perdiste dinero?

SR. BLANCO	Perdí ochenta pesetas°, pero me divertí.
SRA. MORENO	¿Y tú, María? ¿Te divertiste también?
SRA. BLANCO	Pues yo... verdaderamente...
SR. BLANCO	¡Claro que se divirtió!
SRA. MORENO	Francamente°, yo prefiero la corrida de toros. Es más emocionante que el jai alai o el fútbol.
SR. MORENO	Y menos violento.
SR. BLANCO	¡Pero no hablas en serio! Hay mucha violencia en las corridas de toros.
SR. MORENO	No tanta... y casi nunca muere el torero; sólo muere el toro.
SRA. MORENO	Y después les dan la carne° a los pobres. Pero, ¿por qué no escuchamos la voz° de la futura generación? ¿Qué piensas, Adriana, de la corrida de toros?
SR. BLANCO	Es un espectáculo° violentísimo, ¿verdad?
ADRIANA	No, papá. Realmente creo que es un drama simbólico, lindísimo.[4]
SR. MORENO	Ah, los jóvenes de hoy, ¡son tan inteligentes!
SR. BLANCO	¡Bah! ¡Un grupo de rebeldes° y desconformes°!

Una corrida de toros

Ya *Already*   **bedidas** *drinks*   **vino** *wine*   **seguidos** *in a row*   **Triunfó** *won*
pesetas *monetary unit of Spain*   **Francamente** *Frankly*   **carne** *meat*   **voz** *voice*
espectáculo *spectacle*   **rebeldes** *rebels*   **desconformes** *nonconformists*

1. ¿Dónde están los señores Moreno y los Blanco?   **2.** Según el señor Blanco, ¿toma su señora bebidas tan fuertes como el jerez?   **3.** ¿Asistieron los señores Blanco a un partido de fútbol anoche?   **4.** ¿Quiénes participaron en el partido?   **5.** ¿Quién ganó doce puntos seguidos?   **6.** ¿Ganó dinero el señor Blanco?   **7.** ¿Se divirtió él? ¿y su señora?   **8.** ¿Cuál es el deporte favorito de la señora Moreno?   **9.** ¿Cree la señora Moreno que la corrida de toros es más violenta que el fútbol? ¿Qué dice Adriana? ¿Qué cree usted?

Notas culturales

1. Between the hours of about 6:00 and 8:00 P.M., it is customary in Spain to go out to bars and restaurants for snacks (**tapas**) to help tide one over until the 9:00 or 10:00 P.M. supper hour. A few simple **tapas**, such as olives or sausage, usually come free when you buy a drink; many places also feature a varied and elaborate selection for a price.

2. **El jerez** (*sherry*) comes from the south of Spain and takes its name from the city of Jerez de la Frontera. (*Sherry* is an English corruption of the word **jerez**.) Its production and exportation have been largely in the hands of several families of English descent.

3. Jai alai, or **la pelota vasca** (*Basque ball*), is a fast and strenuous game originated by the Basque people and now popular in Spain, Mexico, Cuba, and, to a lesser extent, in some other Hispanic countries and in certain parts of the United States. It is usually played in a rectangular court called a **frontón**, with spectators seated on one side, which has a protective screen, and with walls on the other three sides. The ball is thrown against the other three walls with the aid of curved baskets attached to the players' hands. One or two players are on each team. The extremely high velocity often attained by the ball makes the game somewhat dangerous. It is common to bet money on jai alai games.

4. For many Hispanic people, bullfighting is more than a sport; it is a symbolic drama of life against death. The bullfighter, confronting death in the bullring, represents all human beings. There is a great deal of pageantry and spectacle associated with the traditional **fiesta brava**, or bullfight, including the brightly colored costumes and ritualistic steps of the **toreros**.

FUNCIONES Y ACTIVIDADES

In this chapter, you have seen examples of the following language functions, or uses. Here is a summary and some additional information about these functions of language.

Expressing disbelief

Here are some ways to express that you can't quite believe what you've heard.

¿De veras? *Really?*
¿Habla(-s) en broma? *Are you joking?*
¡Pero lo dice(-s) en broma! *But you're saying it in jest!*
¡Pero no habla(-s) en serio! *But you're not serious!*
No lo creo. *I don't believe it.*

No lo puedo creer. *I can't believe it.*
¡Qué ridículo! *How ridiculous!*
¡Qué va! *Oh, come on!*
Increíble. *Incredible.*
Imposible. *Impossible.*
No puede ser. *It can't be.*

Using *para* in comparisons

In addition to the expressions you've learned in this chapter for making comparisons, there is one other expression you might need. The word **para** is used in comparisons to mean *for*.

Es muy alto para su edad.
Para norteamericana, ella habla muy bien el español.

He's very tall for his age.
For an American, she speaks Spanish very well.

A. ¡No lo creo!   Give a reaction of disbelief to each of the following statements.

1. El jugador de tenis John McEnroe es un hombre que siempre está contento.
2. El jugador de béisbol Fernando Valenzuela vino a los Estados Unidos de Francia.
3. Joe Montana no sabe mucho sobre el fútbol americano.
4. Martina Navratilova ganó un partido de golf muy importante en Pebble Beach el año pasado.
5. Dan Marino es un famoso jugador de tenis.

B. ¿Lo crees?   Working with a partner, make at least three statements about yourself, some of them true and some of them false. Your partner should respond with either **Sí, te creo** or an expression of disbelief.

Modelos   Yo tengo diecinueve años.
   Sí, te creo.

   Gané un partido de tenis con Chris Evert ayer.
   ¡Qué va! Eso es imposible.

C. Para... Make statements with **para**, following the model.

> Modelo Felipe es atleta. Come muy poco. (Los otros atletas comen mucho más.)
> **Para atleta, Felipe come muy poco.**

1. Jane es de Florida. Habla muy bien el francés. (Los otros norteamericanos no hablan tan bien el francés.)
2. David es policía. No conoce bien la ciudad. (Los otros policías conocen muy bien la ciudad.)
3. Raúl es agente de viajes. No viaja mucho. (Los otros agentes de viajes viajan mucho más.)
4. Carmen es músico. Canta muy mal. (Los otros músicos cantan mejor.)
5. Manuelito tiene dos años. Habla muy bien. (Los otros niños de dos años no hablan tan bien.)

VOCABULARIO ACTIVO

Cognados

el, la atleta	el espectador, la	probablemente	regularmente
el béisbol	espectadora	rápidamente	ridículo
católico	el jai alai	la raqueta	terriblemente
completamente	el jogging	raramente	violento
especialmente	el, la político	realmente	el vólibol
	posiblemente	recientemente	

Verbos

asistir a	to attend
correr	to run
explicar	to explain
ganar	to win; to earn
morir (ue)	to die
nacer (zc)	— to be born
pagar	to pay (for)
participar	to participate

Los deportes

el aficionado, la aficionada	fan
el corredor, la corredora	runner
la corrida de toros	bullfight
el deporte	sport

el equipo	team
el esquí	skiing; ski
el esquiador, la esquiadora	skier
el fútbol	soccer
el fútbol americano	football
el jugador, la jugadora	player
el partido	match, game
la pelota	— ball
el punto	point
el, la torero	bullfighter
el toro	bull

Otras palabras y frases

alegremente	happily
alto	tall

anoche	*last night*
ayer	*yesterday*
casi	*almost*
claramente	*clearly*
diariamente	*daily*
emocionante	*exciting*
fácilmente	*easily*
fuerte	*strong*
lentamente	*slowly*
lento	*slow*
mayor	*older*
el, la mayor	*oldest, eldest*
mejor	*better*
el, la mejor	*best*
menor	*younger*
el, la menor	*youngest*
peligroso	*dangerous*
peor	*worse*
el, la peor	*worst*
pobre	*poor*
rico	*rich*
tan, tanto (como)	*so much, so many (as)*
vanidoso	*vain*
verdaderamente	*truly*

Expresiones útiles

¿De veras?	*Really?*
¿Habla(-s) en broma?	*Are you joking?*
Imposible.	*Impossible.*
Increíble.	*Incredible.*
No lo creo.	*I don't believe it.*
No lo puedo creer.	*I can't believe it.*
No puede ser.	*It can't be.*
¡Pero lo dice(-s) en broma!	*But you're saying it in jest!*
¡Pero no habla(-s) en serio!	*But you're not serious!*
¿Qué hay de nuevo?	*What's new?*
¡Qué ridículo!	*How ridiculous!*
¡Qué va!	*Oh, come on!*

> **Don't forget:**
> Comparisons of equality, page 179
> Comparisons of inequality and the
>   superlative, pages 182–183

Los deportes

En general, los deportes—y muy especialmente el fútbol—son muy populares en el mundo hispano. Otros deportes también populares son el tenis, el jai alai y el básquetbol. El béisbol es un deporte favorito en América Central, México, Venezuela y en las islas del Caribe.

Hoy día hay equipos femeninos en casi todos los deportes. El vólibol es probablemente el deporte más popular entre las mujeres.

En muchos países hispanos hay playas lindas donde la gente va a nadar o a tomar sol.

Las montañas invitan a la gente a dejar° la ciudad para gozar° de la natu- leave / enjoy
raleza. El esquí es muy popular en las regiones montañosas de España y Latino-
américa.

PREGUNTAS

1. ¿Qué deportes practica usted? ¿Qué deportes mira por televisión? **2.** ¿Va usted
a la playa o a las montañas para gozar de la naturaleza? ¿Prefiere la vida del campo
(*country*) a la vida urbana? ¿Por qué sí o por qué no? **3.** ¿Piensa usted que debemos
proteger (*protect*) la naturaleza? ¿Cómo? ¿Necesitamos más parques nacionales? ¿Para
qué? ¿Qué podemos hacer para proteger la ecología?

Carnes para platos principales

el bistec, la carne de vaca
el jamón
el pollo

Postres

el helado
el queso
la torta

Platos comunes

el pan

el arroz
los frijoles
la ensalada
la hamburguesa

Frutas y verduras

la manzana
las papas
las bananas
la naranja
el maíz
la lechuga

Bebidas

el café
la cerveza
el té
el vino
el jugo

Ingredientes comunes

el azúcar
la sal
la pimienta

bocadillo – sandwich

cado

os fritos

te   la piña

el agua mineral

Comidas y bebidas

9

Expressing Likes
Expressing Dislikes
Ordering a Meal in a Restaurant

EJERCICIO

Match the dishes (foods or drinks) on the left with the ingredients they contain on the right.

1. una tortilla (*omelet*)
2. una ensalada
3. una sopa (*soup*)
4. un sandwich
5. la sangría

a. frutas y vino
b. huevos, queso, sal, pimienta
c. pollo o carne de vaca, verduras, frijoles
d. lechuga, tomate
e. pan, lechuga, jamón, queso

PREGUNTAS

1. ¿Qué toma usted de desayuno generalmente? ¿Come huevos fritos con jamón o solamente toma café negro? ¿Prefiere café o té?   **2.** ¿A qué hora almuerza usted? ¿Qué almuerza? ¿Prefiere un almuerzo abundante o sólo un sandwich?   **3.** ¿Come usted carne?, ¿pescado? ¿Prefiere frutas y verduras?   **4.** ¿Cuáles son sus frutas y verduras favoritas?   **5.** ¿Toma usted mucho café?, ¿vino?, ¿mucha cerveza?, ¿leche? **6.** ¿Está usted a dieta? ¿Come muchas papas fritas (*french fries*)?, ¿mucho arroz?, ¿maíz?, ¿muchos frijoles?   **7.** ¿Cena usted temprano o tarde? ¿A qué hora? ¿Qué cena generalmente?

The present tense of *encantar*, *faltar*, *gustar*, *importar*, *interesar*; the verbs *oír* and *traer*

CAMARERO	¿Qué le *gustaría* comer, señor?
SR. GUTIÉRREZ	Dos platos de chiles rellenos—me *gustan* mucho los chiles rellenos. Y picantes—¡a mí me *encanta* la comida picante!
CAMARERO	Sí, señor. (*Unos minutos más tarde.*) Aquí lo tiene. ¿Le *falta* algo?
SR. GUTIÉRREZ	Perdón, pero pedí dos platos. Siempre pido un plato de chiles rellenos para mí y otro para mi mejor amigo. Trabajamos juntos por muchos años, y luego él se mudó a Guatemala. Como a los dos nos *encantan* los platos picantes, especialmente los chiles rellenos, yo siempre pido un plato extra para él y él siempre pide un plato extra para mí. Lo hacemos como un acto simbólico, como recuerdo.
CAMARERO	¡Oh! Sí, señor, entiendo. Ahorita le *traigo* otro plato.

Pasan unas semanas. Otra vez entra el señor Gutiérrez en el restaurante.

CAMARERO	Buenas tardes, señor.
SR. GUTIÉRREZ	Buenas tardes. Un plato de chiles rellenos, por favor.
CAMARERO	¿Un plato? ¿Es que... es que se murió su amigo?
SR. GUTIÉRREZ	No, pero mi doctor me dice que ya no debo comer platos picantes.*

---

1. ¿Qué pide el señor Gutiérrez?   2. ¿Al señor Gutiérrez le gusta la comida picante?   3. ¿Qué le trae el camarero?   4. ¿Por qué pidió dos platos de chiles rellenos el señor Gutiérrez?   5. ¿Qué pasa unas semanas después?   6. ¿Murió el amigo del señor Gutiérrez?

---

* **Ya** *generally means* already: **Ya están allí**. They're already there. **Ya no** *means* no longer, not any longer.

WAITER: What would you like to eat, sir? MR. GUTIÉRREZ: Two plates of *chiles rellenos*—I like *chiles rellenos* very much. And hot (spicy)—I love spicy food! WAITER: Yes, sir. (*A few minutes later.*) Here you are. Do you need anything? ("Is anything missing?") MR. GUTIÉRREZ: Excuse me, but I ordered two plates. I always ask for one plate of *chiles rellenos* for myself and one for my best friend. We worked together for many years, and then he moved to Guatemala. Since both of us love hot food, especially *chiles rellenos*, I always order an extra plate for him, and he always orders an extra plate for me. We do it as a symbolic act, as a remembrance. WAITER: Oh! Okay sir, I understand. I'll bring you another plate right away. (*Several weeks go by. Mr. Gutiérrez comes into the restaurant again.*) WAITER: Good afternoon, sir. MR. GUTIÉRREZ: Good afternoon. One plate of *chiles rellenos*, please. WAITER: One plate? Did ... did your friend die? MR. GUTIÉRREZ: No, but my doctor says I shouldn't eat hot foods (dishes) anymore.

A. **Gustar** means *to please* or *to be pleasing*. **Gustar** can be used to express the equivalent of the English term *to like* (or *not like*). However, in Spanish the person, thing, or idea that is pleasing (pleases) is the subject of the sentence. **Gustar** is usually used in the third-person singular or plural, depending on whether the subject is singular or plural. The person who is pleased is the indirect object. (In English, the verb *to disgust* functions the same way: *Your attitude disgusts us.* = *We don't like your attitude.*) An indirect object pronoun is normally used with the verb **gustar**.

Me gusta esta bebida.	*I like this beverage.* ("This beverage pleases me.")
¿Te gustan las verduras?	*Do you like vegetables?*
Nos gustan mucho los postres.	*We like desserts a lot.*

B. The prepositional phrase **a** + noun or pronoun is often used with **gustar**. It is frequently necessary for emphasis or clarity. It is usually placed at the beginning of the sentence.

A Fernando le gusta el helado de chocolate.	*Fernando likes chocolate ice cream.*
En general, a los hispanos les gusta el café con leche.	*In general, Hispanic people like coffee with milk.*
A usted le gustan los vinos buenos, ¿no?	*You like good wines, don't you?*

C. If what is liked (or what is pleasing) is an infinitive, the third-person singular of **gustar** is used.

No me gusta estar a dieta, pero aumenté algunos kilos el mes pasado.	*I don't like to be on a diet, but I gained a few kilos last month.*
A José le gusta cocinar.	*José likes to cook.*

D. The form **gustaría** + an infinitive means *would like to*. (This form will be covered further in Chapter 15.)

¿Qué les gustaría tomar?	*What would you like to drink?*
Me gustaría ir a ese restaurante italiano.	*I'd like to go to that Italian restaurant.*

E. **Encantar** (*to delight*), **faltar** (*to be lacking or missing*), **importar** (*to be important, to matter*), and **interesar** (*to interest*) function like **gustar**. **Encantar** is often used to express the equivalent of *to love* (things, ideas, and so forth, but not people).

No nos importa el dinero.	*Money doesn't matter to us.*
Me falta azúcar para hacer una torta.	*I need ("lack") sugar to make a cake.*
Me encantan las papas fritas.	*I love french fries (fried potatoes).* (Literally, "They delight me.")
¿Te interesa el arte?	*Are you interested in art?*

F. The verb **oír** (*to hear*) is irregular:

oír	
o**ig**o	o**í**mos
o**y**es	o**í**s
o**y**e	o**y**en

¿Oyes música?   *Do you hear music?*

G. The verb **traer** (*to bring, carry*) is irregular in the first-person singular: **traigo**. The other forms are regular.

EJERCICIOS

A. Y entonces, ¿qué te gusta?   Eduardo is a very fussy eater. Every time his mother asks him why he's not eating something, he answers that he doesn't like it. Give Eduardo's answers, following the model.

Modelo   ¿Por qué no comes la hamburguesa?
         ¡Es que no me gusta la hamburguesa!

1. ¿Por qué no comes el pollo?
2. ¿Por qué no comes las papas?
3. ¿Por qué no comes la manzana?
4. ¿Por qué no comes las bananas?
5. ¿Por qué no comes el queso?
6. ¿Por qué no comes la ensalada?

B. ¿Te gusta...?   Ask a classmate whether he or she likes the following.

Modelo   el pescado
         ¿Te gusta el pescado?

1. el jamón   4. las naranjas
2. los frijoles   5. cocinar
3. viajar   6. los chiles rellenos

Now ask your instructor the same questions.

Modelo   **¿Le gusta el pescado?**

C. ¿Qué nos falta...? Everybody I know is going out to dinner tonight. Why? Because we are all lacking something we need to prepare a meal at home! Form sentences according to the models, and you'll find out what ingredients each of us is missing.

Modelos   a Rubén / sal / comida
Le falta sal para la comida.

a nosotros / frutas para la ensalada de frutas
Nos faltan frutas para la ensalada de frutas.

1. a Eduardo / lechuga / ensalada verde
2. a mí / huevos / tortilla
3. a ustedes / papas / papas fritas
4. a ti / arroz / paella
5. a nosotros / verduras / sopa
6. a los Ruiz / carne / hamburguesas

D. «Sobre gustos y colores no hay nada escrito.» (*"There's nothing written [i.e., no laws] about tastes and colors."*) Complete the following sentences as shown in the example.

Modelos   A mí me gusta(-n) mucho...
A mí me gusta mucho viajar.
A mí me gustan mucho las motocicletas.

1. A mí me gusta(-n) mucho...
2. A mí no me gusta(-n)...
3. A mí no me importa(-n) mucho...
4. A mí me importa(-n) muchísimo...
5. A las mujeres no les gusta(-n) mucho...
6. A los hombres les importa(-n) mucho...
7. A los jóvenes de hoy les encanta(-n)...
8. A mis padres les encanta(-n)...

E. Traducción. Give the Spanish equivalent of the following sentences.

1. Do you (**tú**) hear music?
2. He likes meat, and she likes vegetables.
3. I'll bring you (**tú**) the salt.
4. We need bread and eggs.
5. They are bringing a cake.
6. Are you (**usted**) interested in history?

PREGUNTAS

1. ¿Qué tipo de comida le gusta más: la mexicana o la italiana? ¿la china o la japonesa? ¿Por qué? **2.** En su casa, ¿quién compra la comida? ¿Quién cocina? ¿Quién lava los platos? ¿A usted le gusta cocinar o prefiere lavar los platos? **3.** ¿A usted le gusta comer carne de vaca? ¿pollo? ¿jamón? ¿O prefiere el pescado? ¿Le gustan las frutas? ¿y las verduras?

The preterit of irregular verbs

En clase en la Universidad de Salamanca.

FRED ¿Qué *hiciste* anoche, Hilda?

HILDA *Fui* al restaurante «La Cazuela». Fernando *quiso* ir también, pero no *pudo*.

FRED Y ¿con quién *fuiste*?

HILDA *Fui* con Ramona. También *fueron* unos amigos de ella. Y pedí paella. Es un plato que tiene arroz, pescado y mariscos.

FRED Y Ramona... ¿qué pidió?

HILDA Primero*, gazpacho andaluz, que es una sopa fría de tomates y pepinos. Después pidió un bistec, y el camarero se lo *trajo* con una ensalada.

FRED ¿Y el postre? ¿Cómo *estuvo*?

HILDA Muy rico. Nos *dieron* flan.

FRED *Tuviste* que abandonar la dieta, entonces.

HILDA No totalmente—*supe* cuidarme. No le *puse* azúcar al café.

---

1. ¿Qué hizo Hilda anoche?   2. ¿Quién quiso ir pero no pudo?   3. ¿Qué es la paella?   4. ¿Qué pidió Ramona?   5. ¿Cómo estuvo el postre que les dieron? 6. ¿Tuvo que abandonar la dieta Hilda?

***Primero** is an adverb meaning *first*. It is also an adjective; as an adjective, it becomes **primer** before a masculine singular noun: **el primer tren** (*the first train*), **la primera vez** (*the first time*), **los primeros invitados** (*the first guests*). You may remember from Chapter 4 that **el primero** is used in dates.

FRED: What did you do last night, Hilda? HILDA: I went to the restaurant "La Cazuela." Fernando wanted to go, too, but couldn't. FRED: And whom did you go with? HILDA: I went with Ramona. Some friends of hers went, too. And I ordered paella. It's a dish that has rice, fish, and shellfish. FRED: And Ramona ..., what did she order? HILDA: First, *gazpacho andaluz*, which is a cold soup of tomatoes and cucumbers. Afterwards, she ordered a steak, and the waiter brought it to her with a salad. FRED: And the dessert? How was it? HILDA: Very delicious. They gave us flan. FRED: You had to give up (abandon) your diet, then. HILDA: Not completely—I knew how to be careful. I didn't put sugar in my coffee.

A. There are a number of verbs in Spanish that have irregular preterit-tense forms, both stems and endings. These forms do not have written accents.

Infinitive	Preterit Stem	Preterit Endings	
hacer	hic-	-e	-imos
querer	quis-	-iste	-isteis
venir	vin-	-o	-ieron
poder	pud-		
poner	pus-		
saber	sup-		
estar	estuv-		
tener	tuv-		

The endings in the chart are attached to the stems shown to form the preterit of all of the verbs listed. There is only one spelling change: the third-person singular of **hacer** is **hizo**, which involves a change from **c** to **z** to retain the sound of the infinitive. Note that the preterit of **saber** usually means *to find out*. The preterit of **querer** in the affirmative means *to try*; in the negative, it means *to refuse*.

Paco hizo una tortilla con tres huevos, queso y un poco de sal.	Paco made an omelet with three eggs, cheese, and a little salt.
Supimos que Fernando está a dieta.	We found out that Fernando is on a diet.
Los niños quisieron hacer una torta.	The children tried to make a cake.
Luisa no quiso ir sola a la fiesta.	Luisa refused to go to the party alone.
Vinieron invitados a cenar la semana pasada.	Guests came for dinner last week.
Felipe tuvo la oportunidad de oír al jefe anoche.	Felipe had the chance to hear the leader last night.
¿Estuviste en casa ya?	Were you at home already?
Puse la mesa.*	I set the table.
¿Pudieron preparar el postre? —No, no pudimos encontrar el azúcar.	Did you manage to prepare dessert? —No, we couldn't find the sugar.

B. **Traer** and **decir** have irregular preterits; note that the third-person plural ending is **-jeron** rather than **-ieron**.

decir		traer	
dije	dijimos	traje	trajimos
dijiste	dijisteis	trajiste	trajisteis
dijo	di**jeron**	trajo	tra**jeron**

Luz dijo que trajeron vino.	Luz said that they brought wine.

---

* Notice that **poner la mesa** means *to set the table.*

C. **Ir** and **ser** have the same forms in the preterit tense.

ir, ser	
fui	fuimos
fuiste	fuisteis
fue	fueron

La fiesta fue en tu casa, ¿no?
Fuimos allí anoche y comimos arroz
   con pollo. ¡Qué sabroso!

The party was at your house, right?
We went there last night and ate rice with
   chicken. How delicious!

D. **Dar** is considered irregular in the preterit because it requires the preterit endings
   for regular **-er** and **-ir** verbs rather than the endings for **-ar** verbs.

dar	
di	dimos
diste	disteis
dio	dieron

Le di el dinero para la piña.

I gave him the money for the pineapple.

E. **Hubo** is the preterit form of **hay**; the infinitive is **haber**.

Hubo un accidente en la calle Quinta
   ayer.

There was an accident on Fifth Street
   yesterday.

EJERCICIOS

A. **¿Qué hay de nuevo?** (*What's new?*) Complete the sentences with appropriate
   information. In each case, use the preterit form of the verb in parentheses.

   Modelo   (decir) La semana pasada Felipe...
            La semana pasada Felipe me dijo que trabaja en un restaurante.

   1. (hacer)   Anoche mis amigos...
   2. (traer)   Ayer ustedes...
   3. (dar)   Paco y Susana...
   4. (ir)   En 1985 mi familia...
   5. (poner)   Después de cocinar, mamá...
   6. (poder)   Anoche tú...
   7. (saber)   Antes de cenar, yo...
   8. (venir)   El año pasado nosotros...

B. Un viaje a Sevilla. Restate the following paragraph, changing the verbs from the present tense to the preterit.

Esta semana voy (1) a Sevilla. Salgo (2) el miércoles a las dos de la tarde y llego (3) dos horas después. En el aeropuerto me esperan (4) unos amigos y paso (5) la noche en casa de ellos. El jueves vamos (6) a visitar las ruinas de Itálica, una antigua (*ancient*) ciudad romana. Allí tengo (7) la oportunidad de aprender muchas cosas interesantes sobre la historia española. Volvemos (8) a Sevilla a las diez de la noche y cenamos (9). Al otro día (*The next day*), viernes, doy (10) un paseo por la ciudad y esa misma noche vuelvo (11) a casa. ¡Es (12) un viaje estupendo!

C. Traducción. Give the Spanish equivalent of the following sentences.

1. Ana brought me some eggs.
2. We came here last week.
3. Yesterday we had to eat late.
4. Catalina was at the airport at six o'clock.
5. They told her the truth.
6. Did you (**tú**) do this?

PREGUNTAS

1. ¿Fue usted a un partido de fútbol ayer? ¿de béisbol? ¿A otra parte (*somewhere else*)? ¿Fue solo(-a) o con amigos?   **2.** ¿Dónde estuvo ayer a las dos de la tarde? ¿a las nueve de la noche?   **3.** ¿Comió usted en un restaurante la semana pasada? ¿Dónde? ¿Qué pidió?   **4.** ¿Fue usted a un restaurante donde sirven comida española o latinoamericana? ¿Pudo usted pedir en español?   **5.** ¿Qué hizo usted el fin de semana pasado?

The relative pronouns *que* and *quien*

A las nueve de la mañana, en un restaurante de Sevilla.

CAMARERO	¿Qué desean pedir?
ELLEN	Para mí, huevos fritos con jamón, por favor.
RAFAEL	Sólo café con leche.
ELLEN	Rafael, en mi país la gente dice *que* es necesario tomar un buen desayuno. ¿No quieres comer algo?
RAFAEL	Pues, yo soy uno de esos hispanos típicos a *quienes* no les interesa el desayuno, Ellen. Nosotros creemos *que* el almuerzo es más importante.
CAMARERO	(*Algunos minutos más tarde.*) Aquí tienen el desayuno. ¡Buen provecho! ¿Desean algo más?
RAFAEL	No, esto es todo, gracias. ¡Ah! La cuenta, por favor.
CAMARERO	Muy bien, señor.
ELLEN	Sabes, Rafael, pienso *que* voy a aumentar algunos kilos aquí en España, pero «estómago lleno, corazón contento», ¿no?

1. ¿Qué pide Ellen? ¿Por qué desayuna bien ella?   2. ¿Come mucho Rafael en el desayuno? ¿Qué pide él?   3. ¿Por qué nunca desayuna mucho Rafael?
4. ¿Quién va a aumentar algunos kilos? ¿Por qué?

A. **Que** is the most commonly used equivalent for *that, which, who,* and *whom,* used to refer to both people and things.

¿Son esos los platos que nos recomendó el camarero?	*Are those the dishes the waiter recommended to us?*
Esta es la catedral de que hablo.	*This is the cathedral* (that) *I'm talking about.*
¿Quién es esa mujer que pone la mesa?	*Who is that woman who is setting the table?*

In a restaurant in Seville at nine o'clock in the morning. WAITER: What would you like to order? ELLEN: For me, fried eggs with ham, please. RAFAEL: Just coffee with milk. ELLEN: Rafael, in my country people say that it's necessary to have a good breakfast. Don't you want to eat something? RAFAEL: Well, I'm one of those typical Hispanics, for whom breakfast is of no interest, Ellen. We think lunch is more important. WAITER: (*A few minutes later.*) Here is your breakfast. Enjoy your meal! Would you like anything else (something more)? RAFAEL: No, this is all, thank you. Oh! The check, please. WAITER: Very well, sir. ELLEN: You know, Rafael, I think I'm going to gain a few kilos here, but . . . "Full stomach, happy heart," right?

Ella es la mujer que cuida a los niños.   *She's the woman who takes care of the children.*

Relative pronouns are often omitted in English, but they are always used in Spanish. **Que** is used after prepositions (**a, con, de, en, para**) when referring to things.

B. **Quien** (**quienes** in the plural) refers only to people. It is usually used as the object of a preposition (**a, con, de, en, para,** etc.). When used as an indirect object, **quien** (**quienes**) must be preceded by the preposition **a**.

Ésa es la chica a quien le pedí la cuenta.   *That's the girl from whom I asked for the check.*

Ésos son los amigos con quienes cenamos la semana pasada.   *Those are the friends with whom we had dinner last week.*

¿Adolfo es el músico de quien hablas?   *Is Adolfo the musician you are talking about?*

La mujer para quien trabajo siempre está a dieta.   *The woman for whom I work is always on a diet.*

EJERCICIOS

A. **En el supermercado.**   Blanca and Víctor are talking at the supermarket. Complete each of the following sentences with either **que** or **quien(es)**.

Modelos   ¿Dónde está ese pan ___**que**___ a ti te gusta?

Los señores con ___**quienes**___ cenamos esta noche son vegetarianos.

1. La gente _____ trabaja aquí es muy cortés.
2. ¿Ésos son los helados de _____ hablas?
3. Allí veo a dos chicas con _____ trabajo.
4. ¿Quién es esa mujer _____ compra carne? Creo que la conocemos.
5. Aquí está un vino _____ podemos llevar a la cena en casa de los Suárez.
6. Las frutas y verduras _____ tienen aquí son muy frescas.
7. ¿Cómo se llama la amiga a _____ le vas a preparar el almuerzo mañana?
8. Bueno... Creo que no tienen el queso _____ busco.

B. **Opiniones.**   Complete the first blank in each sentence with an appropriate noun that expresses your opinion and the second blank with **que** or **quien(es)**.

1. _____ es una persona _____ respeto mucho.
2. _____ es una bebida _____ me gusta mucho.
3. _____ son personas de _____ prefiero no hablar.
4. _____ son dos películas _____ pienso ver.
5. _____ es el (la) profesor(-a) con _____ sigo un curso muy interesante.
6. _____ son ciudades _____ quiero visitar.
7. _____ son dos estudiantes _____ siempre están en clase.
8. _____ es una universidad _____ tiene muy buena reputación.

Sevilla: en la Giralda

La Giralda de Sevilla · **Una casa en el barrio judío de Sevilla**

Claudio, un joven de Sevilla, lleva a unos amigos a visitar la Giralda, que es la torre° de la catedral.[1]

ESTEBAN	¡Qué subida° más larga!
CLAUDIO	No hay ninguna vista de Sevilla como ésta. ¿Qué dicen? ¿Les gusta?
LUISA	¡A mí me encanta! Veo el Barrio de Santa Cruz.[2] Anoche fuimos allí a ver baile flamenco.
ESTEBAN	Y comimos una paella que nos gustó muchísimo..., un postre muy rico...
LUISA	¿Por qué no hablamos del postre más tarde? Claudio, ¿sabes quién hizo esta torre?
CLAUDIO	La empezó un jefe árabe en el siglo doce y la terminó Almanzor, su sucesor.
ESTEBAN	¿Por qué no vamos a almorzar y venimos otra vez por la tarde? Tengo un hambre terrible.
LUISA	Esteban, ¡por favor! Claudio, esta torre probablemente fue un lugar ideal para esperar el ataque° del enemigo, ¿no?
CLAUDIO	Sí, y el enemigo vino. Fue Fernando III, a quien llamaron «el Santo».[3] Tuve la oportunidad de verlo el año pasado.
ESTEBAN	¿Oigo bien? ¿No vivió en el siglo trece?

CLAUDIO	Oyes bien. Dije que lo vi el año pasado. Estuve en la catedral el día de su fiesta, cuando abren la tumba. Su cadáver se mantiene° muy bien. Es un milagro.°
LUISA	Sí, alguien me dijo eso y no lo quise creer.
ESTEBAN	Y ustedes no quieren creer que en el hotel no me dieron el desayuno. ¡Ni siquiera° café negro!
CLAUDIO	Creo que Esteban sólo tiene ganas de ver una vista de platos variados°...
ESTEBAN	¡Sí!... montañas de carne de vaca, ríos° de vino y océanos de helado de chocolate.
LUISA	Mejor vamos a comer.
ESTEBAN	¡Bueno, éste es el milagro! Y mañana no voy a salir antes de tomar un buen desayuno.

torre *tower*   **subida** *climb*   **ataque** *attack*   **se mantiene** *is maintained, preserved*
milagro *miracle*   **Ni siquiera** *Not even*   **variados** *various, varied*   **ríos** *rivers*

PREGUNTAS

1. ¿Qué es la Giralda?   **2.** ¿A quién le encanta la vista desde (*from*) allí?   **3.** ¿Para qué fueron los estudiantes al Barrio de Santa Cruz?   **4.** ¿Qué comieron allí? ¿Les gustó?   **5.** ¿Quiénes hicieron la torre? ¿Cuándo?   **6.** ¿Quién vino a atacar a los árabes?   **7.** ¿Qué milagro vio Claudio el año pasado?   **8.** En el hotel, ¿le dieron a Esteban algo para el desayuno?   **9.** ¿Cuál es la «vista» que Esteban quiere ver?   **10.** ¿Cree usted en los milagros? ¿Puede dar un ejemplo de un milagro?

Notas culturales

1. **La Giralda**, the exquisite tower of Seville's cathedral, can be seen from almost any part of the city. The bottom section was the minaret of the sumptuous mosque built by the Moslem rulers of southern Spain in the 1100s and later demolished by the Christians. The top section, called the Triumph of Faith, was added by the Christian rulers during the Renaissance. The pinnacle turns around in the wind and so has given rise to the popular name of the tower, **la Giralda** (*the Weather Vane*). The cathedral itself, third largest in the world, is a treasure house of art and artifacts.

2. The Santa Cruz district, the old Jewish section of the city (**la judería**), has narrow streets, flower-filled patios, and quaint and colorful houses. Several places there feature flamenco dancing and guitar music.

3. King Ferdinand III of Castile and Leon, called **el Santo** (*the Saint*) because he was later canonized by the Catholic church, captured Seville from the Moslems in 1248.

FUNCIONES Y ACTIVIDADES

In this chapter, you have seen examples of the following language functions, or uses. Here is a summary and some additional information about these uses of language.

Expressing likes

Me gusta(-n)...	*I like . . .*
Me gustaría (+ *infinitive*)...	*I would like . . .*
Me interesa(-n)...	*I am interested in . . .*
Me encanta(-n)...	*I love . . .*
...es lindo (interesante, etcétera).	*. . . is beautiful (interesting, etc.).*
...está bueno (rico, sabroso, etcétera).	*. . . is good (delicious, etc.;* used for foods).

Expressing dislikes

No me gusta(-n)...	*I don't like . . .*
No me gustaría (+ *infinitive*)...	*I wouldn't like . . .*
No me interesa(-n)...	*I am not interested in . . .*
...es horrible (aburrido, etcétera).	*. . . is horrible (boring, etc.).*
...está frío (muy picante, etcétera).	*. . . is cold (too hot, etc.;* used for foods*).*

Ordering a meal in a restaurant

Here are some useful expressions for ordering in a restaurant:

¿Qué nos recomienda?	*What do you recommend (to us)?*
¿Nos puede traer...?	*Can you bring us . . .?*
A mí me gustaría tomar (comer)...	*I would like . . . to drink (eat).*
Nos falta(-n)...	*We need . . .*
Quisiera...	*I'd like . . .*
...estuvo muy rico (bueno, sabroso).	*. . . was very delicious (good, tasty).*
La cuenta, por favor.	*The check, please.*

These are some expressions a waiter might use:

¿Qué desea(-n) pedir?	*What do you wish (would you like) to order?*
¿Qué le(-s) gustaría comer (tomar)?	*What would you like to eat (drink)?*
¡Buen provecho!	*Enjoy the meal!*

A. Gustos. Working with a classmate, find out five things that he or she likes and five things that he or she dislikes. You might want to start by asking about the following things:

Modelos   ¿Te gusta jugar a los naipes?
No, para mí eso es muy aburrido.

¿A ti te interesan las películas de los hermanos Marx?
Sí, me interesan mucho.

el chocolate	las películas de los	el fútbol
los pepinos	hermanos Marx	americano
el pescado	la música de Sting	el esquí
vestirse a la moda	la música «punk rock»	ir a la playa
llevar ropa elegante	jugar a los naipes	ir de compras
ir al doctor o al dentista	jugar al tenis	la lluvia
las películas de horror	el fútbol	la nieve

B. **En el restaurante «La Cazuela».** Arrange the following dialog in the proper order. Write the numbers in the blanks.

Restaurante La Cazuela
Menú Bilingüe

Entradas	Hors d'oeuvres	Postres	Desserts
Gazpacho	Gazpacho (cold soup)	Flan	Custard with
Sopa de verduras	Vegetable soup		caramel sauce
		Torta	Cake
		Fruta fresca	Fresh fruit
		Helado	Ice cream

RESTAURANTE 3ª categoria

Platos del día	Today's specialties
Paella	Paella (rice, seafood, vegetables)
Arroz con pollo	Chicken with rice
Tortilla de huevos	Omelet
Bistec	Steak
Mariscos	Shellfish

Bebidas	Beverages
Vino	Wine
Sangría	Sangría (chilled red wine with fruit)
Cerveza	Beer
Gaseosas	Soft drinks
Leche	Milk
Agua mineral	Mineral water
Café/té	Coffee/tea

¡Buen provecho!

_____ —Nuestra especialidad es la paella, pero el arroz con pollo y el bistec también están muy ricos.

_____ —No, gracias. Pero necesitamos la cuenta, por favor.

__1.__ —Buenas noches, señores. ¿Qué desean pedir?

_____ —Estuvo riquísima.

_____ —¿Algún postre? ¿Café?

_____ —Pues, es la primera vez que estamos aquí. ¿Qué nos recomienda?

_____ —Para mí la paella, entonces.

_____ (*Algunos minutos después.*) —¿Cómo estuvo la comida?

_____ —Y para mí el bistec... y una ensalada, por favor.

_____ —Es un plato con arroz, pescado y mariscos.

_____ —Y la paella, ¿qué es?

C. **Conversación.** Now, in small groups, invent your own conversation, based on the menu.

D. **Entrevista.** Ask a classmate the following questions. Then report the information to the class.

1. ¿Qué comidas o bebidas te gustan más cuando hace calor?, ¿cuando hace frío?, ¿cuando no tienes tiempo de cocinar?, ¿cuando estás a dieta?, ¿cuando estás en un restaurante elegante?
2. ¿Qué comiste anoche? ¿Estuviste en algún restaurante? ¿En cuál?
3. ¿Comiste comida española alguna vez? ¿Te gustó?
4. ¿Fuiste a comer a la casa de alguien la semana pasada? ¿Qué te dieron de postre? ¿Llevaste algo a la cena?
5. En una semana típica, ¿cuánto cuesta la comida que compras? ¿Compras mucha carne? ¿Qué compras?
6. ¿Cocinas todas las noches? ¿Qué cocinas cuando tienes invitados?

VOCABULARIO ACTIVO

Cognados

árabe	la dieta	extra	el minuto
la banana	estar a dieta	la fruta	la sal
la catedral	el enemigo, la	la hamburguesa	el sandwich
común	enemiga	mineral	el tomate
el chocolate	la ensalada		

Verbos

abandonar	to abandon
aumentar	to gain, increase
cocinar	to cook
cuidar	to take care of
cuidarse	to take care of oneself
encantar	to delight
Me encanta(-n)...	I love ...
faltar	to be missing or lacking
Me falta(-n)...	I need ...
gustar	to please, be pleasing
Me gusta(-n)...	I like ...
interesar	to interest
Me interesa(-n)...	I am interested in ...
oír	to hear
recomendar (ie)	to recommend
traer	to bring, carry

Comidas y bebidas

el arroz	rice
el azúcar	sugar
la bebida	beverage, drink
el bistec	beef (steak)
la carne	meat
la carne de vaca	beef
la cerveza	beer
el flan	caramel custard
los frijoles	beans
el gazpacho	cold soup made of tomatoes, cucumbers, onions
el helado	ice cream
el huevo	egg
el jamón	ham
el jugo	juice

la leche	milk
la lechuga	lettuce
el maíz	corn
la manzana	apple
el marisco	shellfish
la naranja	orange
la paella	dish with rice, shellfish, chicken, and vegetables
el pan	bread
la papa	potato
el pepino	cucumber
el pescado	fish
la pimienta	(black) pepper
la piña	pineapple
el pollo	chicken
el postre	dessert
el queso	cheese
la sangría	drink made with fruit and wine
la sopa	soup
la torta	cake
la tortilla	omelet
la verdura	vegetable
el vino	wine

Adjetivos

frito	fried
picante	hot, spicy (said of foods)
rico	delicious
sabroso	delicious
solo	alone

Otras palabras y frases

como	as, since
el corazón	heart
la cuenta	bill, check
el invitado, la invitada	guest
el jefe	leader; boss
poner la mesa	to set the table
tener la oportunidad de	to have the opportunity to
la vista	view
ya	already
ya no	no longer, not any longer

Expresiones útiles

A mí me gustaría tomar (comer)...	I would like . . . to drink (eat).
¡Buen provecho!	Enjoy the meal!
...estuvo muy rico (bueno, delicioso, sabroso).	. . . was very delicious (good, tasty).
La cuenta, por favor.	The check, please.
¿Nos puede traer...?	Can you bring us . . . ?
¿Qué nos recomienda?	What do you recommend (to us)?

besarse, el beso

tener celos (de)

quererse (amarse), enamorarse (de), el amor

tener una cita

casarse (con), la bo

acompañar,
el compañero
(la compañera)
de clase

llevarse bien

Novios y amigos

10

Telling a Story
Giving the Speaker Encouragement
Using Polite Expressions

la iglesia

EJERCICIO

Complete the sentences with an appropriate word or words.

1. A Pedro no le gusta ver a su novia con esos muchachos; Pedro _____ de ellos.
2. En junio mi hermana _____ con su novio Javier.
3. A Paco y a Silvia les gusta hacer las mismas cosas; ellos _____ bien.
4. En el mundo hispano, cuando dos amigos o amigas se encuentran, generalmente se _____.
5. ¿Dónde es la _____? —En la iglesia de San Francisco.
6. Hoy no puedo ir, Marta, porque tengo una _____ con Federico.
7. Quiero ver esa película pero no me gusta ir sola al cine. ¿Me _____, Alicia?

zarse, el abrazo

PREGUNTAS

1. ¿Tiene usted muchos amigos? ¿un(-a) amigo(-a) favorito(-a)? ¿Dónde y cuándo se conocieron? **2.** En general, ¿cómo se lleva usted con sus amigos? ¿Se ven mucho? ¿Se ayudan? ¿Cómo? **3.** ¿Se enamoró usted alguna vez de algún actor (alguna actriz) de cine o de televisión? ¿De quién? ¿Vio muchas películas o muchos programas de ese actor (esa actriz)? **4.** ¿Tiene usted novio(-a) ahora? ¿Se llevan bien? ¿mal? ¿más o menos bien? ¿Tiene usted celos de los amigos de su novia (las amigas de su novio)? ¿Piensa casarse con él (ella)? ¿Por qué sí o por qué no? **5.** ¿Cree usted que puede existir una amistad (*friendship*) profunda y sincera (sin implicaciones románticas) entre un hombre y una mujer?

The imperfect of regular and irregular verbs
(*ir, ser, ver*)

ANA	*¿Sabías* que antes José *trabajaba* y *estudiaba* al mismo tiempo?
ELENA	¿En serio? Entonces, ¿cómo *sacaba* tan buenas notas?
ANA	*Sabía* organizarse: *trabajaba* por la mañana, *asistía* a clases por la tarde y *estudiaba* por la noche.
ELENA	¿Y qué *hacía* los fines de semana?
ANA	*Practicaba* deportes, *veía* televisión y *salía* con sus amigos.
ELENA	¡Qué muchacho más admirable! Pero entonces, ¿por qué rompiste con él?
ANA	¡Porque no le *quedaba* tiempo para tener novia!

1. ¿Qué hacía José antes?   2. ¿Sacaba buenas o malas notas?   3. ¿Cuándo estudiaba? ¿Cuándo trabajaba?   4. ¿Qué hacía los fines de semana?   5. ¿Por qué rompió Ana con José?   6. ¿Cree usted que es posible trabajar, salir con amigos y también sacar buenas notas? ¿Cómo?

A. The imperfect tense of regular **-ar** verbs is formed by adding the endings **-aba**, **-abas**, **-aba**, **-ábamos**, **-abais**, and **-aban** to the stem of the infinitive.

hablar	
habl**aba**	habl**ábamos**
habl**abas**	habl**abais**
habl**aba**	habl**aban**

ANA: Did you know that before, José was working and studying at the same time? ELENA: Seriously? Then, how did he get such good grades? ANA: He knew how to organize himself: He worked in the morning, attended classes in the afternoon, and studied at night. ELENA: And what did he do on weekends? ANA: He played sports, watched television, and went out with his friends. ELENA: What a great guy! But then, why did you break up with him? ANA: Because he had no time left to have a girlfriend!

B. To form the imperfect of regular **-er** and **-ir** verbs, the endings **-ía**, **-ías**, **-ía**, **-íamos**, **-íais**, and **-ían** are added to the stem.

comer		vivir	
comía	comíamos	vivía	vivíamos
comías	comíais	vivías	vivíais
comía	comían	vivía	vivían

Note that the stress is on the endings, not the stems, so stem-changing verbs do not change their stems in the imperfect: **recordaba**, **volvía**, **pedía**.

C. There are only three verbs that are irregular in the imperfect: **ir**, **ser**, and **ver**.

ir		ser		ver	
iba	íbamos	era	éramos	veía	veíamos
ibas	ibais	eras	erais	veías	veíais
iba	iban	era	eran	veía	veían

D. The imperfect is a past tense used in the following ways.

1. To express customary or repeated past actions:

Pedro siempre sacaba buenas notas. — *Pedro always got (used to get) good grades.*

Ellos me visitaban todos los veranos. — *They visited (used to visit) me every summer.*

Acompañábamos a mi tía al mercado todos los viernes. — *We went (used to go) to the market with my aunt every Friday.*

Siempre se insultaban en público. —¡Qué escándalo! — *They always used to insult each other in public. — What a scandal!*

2. To express actions that were occurring or in progress at a certain time in the past:

Hablábamos con el maestro de Toñito. — *We were talking with Toñito's teacher.*

Él leía mientras ella estudiaba.* — *He was reading while she was studying.*

Íbamos a la boda. — *We were going to the wedding.*

¿Qué hacían los novios? —Se besaban. — *What were the sweethearts (boyfriend and girlfriend) doing? — They were kissing.*

---

*Notice that subject pronouns are often used with first and third-person forms for clarity.

3. To describe situations or conditions that existed for an indefinite period of time:*

Mi compañera de cuarto trabajaba más el semestre pasado.	*My roommate was working more last semester.*
Pablo siempre llevaba a clase un anillo de oro muy caro.	*Pablo always wore to class a very expensive gold ring.*
En la época del rey Alfonso, había una escuela de traductores en Toledo.** Allí trabajaban juntos los maestros árabes, cristianos y judíos.	*In the era of King Alfonso, there was a school of translators in Toledo: There Arab, Christian, and Jewish masters (scholars) worked together.*

4. To express the time of day in the past or the age of people or things:

Eran las ocho de la mañana.	*It was eight o'clock in the morning.*
El rey Juan Carlos de España tenía cuarenta años en 1978.	*King Juan Carlos of Spain was forty years old in 1978.*

5. In addition, the imperfect is generally used to describe mental or emotional states in the past:

Jorge quería mucho a Lisa; parecían muy felices y querían casarse.***	*Jorge loved Lisa very much; they seemed very happy and wanted to get married.*
Yo pensaba que Ana era más cariñosa.	*I thought that Ana was more affectionate.*
Cuando eras soltero, Enrique, ¿eras más feliz?	*When you were single, Enrique, were you happier?*
Adela tenía celos de su hermana.	*Adela was jealous of her sister.*

E. There are several possible translations of the imperfect in English.

Ellos estudiaban juntos.
- *They used to study together.*
- *They were studying together.*
- *They studied together (often, from time to time).*
- *They would study together (often).*

EJERCICIOS

A. **¿Qué hacían?**   Tell what the following people were doing when the blackout occurred in your neighborhood yesterday.

Modelo   Felipe / estudiar para un examen
Felipe estudiaba para un examen.

1. mamá / preparar la cena
2. Federico / hacer unos ejercicios de matemáticas
3. Susana y Guillermo / poner la mesa
4. tú / leer la carta de tu novio
5. Luisa y yo / mirar televisión

---

* If a specific period of time is viewed as completed, the preterit is generally used: **Viví allí por (durante) diez años.**
** **Había** is the imperfect form of **hay.**
*** The verb **parecer** (*to seem, appear*) has an irregularity in the first-person, present tense: **parezco.**

6. Anita / hablar por teléfono con una amiga
7. papá / dormir en el sofá
8. los Herrera / cenar en casa de los Balbuena

B. Cuando tú eras joven...   Blanca tells her mother about her daughter Susana. Blanca's mother says Blanca was the same when she was young.

Modelo   Es muy generosa.
   Tú también eras muy generosa cuando eras joven.

1. Casi siempre está contenta.
2. Juega mucho al béisbol.
3. Tiene muchas amigas.
4. Duerme hasta tarde todos los días.
5. Dice que no tiene problemas.

C. Buenos amigos.   Complete the story about a friendship, using appropriate imperfect-tense forms of the verbs in parentheses.

Cuando yo (1)_____ (ser) menor, (yo) (2)_____ (jugar) con mis hermanos. (Yo) (3)_____ (tener) una amiga que (4)_____ (llamarse) Amalia y que (5)_____ (vivir) cerca de nosotros. Ella (6)_____ (asistir) a otra escuela y (ella y yo) no (7)_____ (verse) durante la semana. (Ella y yo) (8)_____ (ir) a jugar al parque todos los fines de semana.

D. Cuando todos éramos más jóvenes.   Your mother is telling you about people and things in the past, when she was younger. Using the verbs **ser**, **ir**, and **ver**, tell what she says, as suggested by the cues.

Modelo   el señor García / rico / teatro / amigos
   El señor García era rico. Siempre iba al teatro. Allí veía a sus amigos.

1. mis padres / profesores / universidad / colegas
2. yo / aficionado al fútbol / los partidos / equipo favorito
3. tío Juan / soltero / playa / novia
4. tú / muy pequeño / parque / primos
5. mis abuelos / pobres / iglesia / parientes
6. nosotros / más jóvenes / cine / amigos

PREGUNTAS

1. ¿Dónde vivía cuando era niño(-a)?   **2.** ¿Cómo era su casa?   **3.** ¿Vivía cerca o lejos de sus abuelos?   **4.** ¿Cómo eran ellos?   **5.** ¿A qué escuela asistía cuando tenía ocho años?   **6.** ¿Trabajaba su mamá? ¿Dónde se quedaba cuando ella trabajaba?   **7.** ¿Qué quería ser cuando era niño(-a)?   **8.** ¿Qué le gustaba hacer de niño(-a)?   **9.** ¿Dónde y con quién jugaba?   **10.** ¿Jugaba al béisbol?, ¿al fútbol?, ¿al tenis?, ¿a otros deportes?   **11.** ¿Adónde iba su familia de vacaciones?   **12.** ¿Qué le gustaba de la escuela? ¿Qué no le gustaba?   **13.** ¿Salía con otros(-as) chicos(-as) cuando tenía catorce años?   **14.** ¿Veía mucha televisión? ¿Cuáles eran sus programas favoritos?   **15.** ¿Qué hacía durante sus vacaciones?   **16.** ¿Era más feliz antes que ahora? ¿Por qué sí o por qué no?

The imperfect versus the preterit

Una celebración de una boda

EMA	¡Hola, Olga! ¡Hola, Bob! No *sabía* que ustedes se *conocían*.
OLGA	Nos *conocimos* anoche en la boda de Amparo y Domingo. Y *bailamos* toda la noche.
EMA	¿Así que tú *eras* la «misteriosa» muchacha que *bailó* con Bob? Lo *supe* esta mañana por Antonio. Me *dijo* que hacen una linda pareja. ¡Oh!... y esta noche vienen a mi fiesta, ¿no?
BOB	¡Otro baile! ¿Pero cuándo duermen ustedes los latinos?

1. ¿Sabía Ema que Olga y Bob se conocían?   2. ¿Cuándo se conocieron ellos?   3. ¿Bailaron mucho o poco en la boda? ¿Cómo lo supo Ema?   4. ¿Qué más le dijo Antonio a Ema?   5. ¿Adónde van Olga y Bob esta noche?   6. ¿Cree Bob que los latinos duermen mucho? ¿Qué pregunta él?

EMA: Hi, Olga! Hi, Bob! I didn't know that you knew each other. OLGA: We met last night at Amparo and Domingo's wedding. And we danced all night. EMA: So, you were the "mysterious" young lady who danced with Bob? I found (it) out this morning from Antonio. He told me that you make a nice couple. Oh, and tonight you are coming to my party, right? BOB: Another dance! But when do you Latins sleep?

A. The imperfect emphasizes an indefinite duration of time, whereas the preterit reports a past completed action or event, or limits an action or event in the past by indicating when it began or when it ended or by stating its specific duration.

Todos los días Pedro besaba a su mujer antes de ir a la oficina.	*Every day Pedro kissed his wife before going to the office.*
Pedro besó a su mujer y se fue.	*Pedro kissed his wife and left.*
Marina siempre iba al cine los fines de semana.	*Marina always went to the movies on weekends.*
Marina fue al cine diez veces el mes pasado.	*Marina went to the movies ten times last month.*
Antes yo estudiaba tres horas por día.	*Before (in the past), I studied (used to study) three hours a day.*
Empecé a estudiar a las ocho. Terminé a las once.	*I began to study at eight o'clock. I finished at eleven.*

Whenever a time limit, however long or short, is specified for the past action or condition, the preterit is used. Time expressions like **ayer**, **anoche**, **el domingo** (**mes**, **año**, **etc.**) **pasado**, or **diez** (**cien**, **muchas**) **veces** often reinforce the notion introduced by the preterit that the event or series of events is completed. With the imperfect, time expressions like **siempre**, (**todos**) **los domingos**, **todos los días** (**meses**, **años**, **etc.**), or **mientras** are often used. Patterns of habitual action, mental states, descriptions of the way things looked or sounded, the time of day, and other background conditions in the past are typically reported with verbs in the imperfect; the speaker's interest is not in their start or end but in the fact of their existence.

B. Often the preterit and imperfect are used in the same sentence to report that an action or situation that was in progress in the past (expressed with the imperfect) was interrupted by another action or event (expressed with the preterit).

Paco miraba televisión cuando Teresa lo llamó.	*Paco was watching television when Teresa called him.*
Encontré las joyas que buscaba.	*I found the jewelry I was looking for.*
Mirabel tenía treinta años cuando se enamoró de Pablo.	*Mirabel was thirty years old when she fell in love with Pablo.*
Paseábamos por la plaza cuando vimos a Enrique.	*We were walking around (through) the plaza when we saw Enrique.*
Tomábamos champaña cuando Felipe entró, se sentó a la mesa y dijo «¡Salud!»	*We were drinking champagne when Felipe came in, sat down at the table, and said "Cheers!"*
¿Por qué había tanta gente en ese lugar? —Porque hubo un accidente y murieron dos personas.	*Why were there so many people at that place? —Because there was an accident (an accident happened) and two people died.*

C. The imperfect of **conocer** means *to know, to be acquainted with,* whereas the preterit means *to meet, to make the acquaintance of.* The imperfect expresses ongoing acquaintance, whereas the preterit emphasizes meeting for the first time. The imperfect of **saber** means *to know,* whereas the preterit means *to find out.* Again, the imperfect emphasizes indefinite duration of time in the past, whereas the preterit indicates a completed action.

Mamá sabía que Eduardo conocía a mi hermano.	*Mom knew that Eduardo knew (was acquainted with) my brother.*
Esta mañana supe que usted conocía a mi hermano. ¿Dónde lo conoció?	*This morning I found out that you knew my brother. Where did you meet him?*

EJERCICIOS

A. ¿Pretérito o imperfecto? Restate the following sentences in the past. Use the preterit or the imperfect, as appropriate. In some cases, either is possible, depending on the meaning.

1. Esta tarde veo a mi novia.
2. Siempre vas al cine con Pablo, ¿no?
3. ¿Cuántos años tiene su hermana?
4. Son las seis en punto.
5. Alicia y Rodolfo se casan en julio.
6. En general, nosotros salimos todos los domingos.
7. Hoy llego tarde a clase.
8. ¿A quién le das esa carta?
9. Pasean por la plaza cuando ven a Marisa.
10. ¿Parecemos felices?

B. ¿Qué pasaba cuando...? Choose the correct form of the verbs.

1. Ayer cuando (llamaste, llamabas), nosotros (celebramos, celebrábamos) el cumpleaños de papá.
2. Nosotros (llegamos, llegábamos) tarde a la boda porque no (supimos, sabíamos) cómo llegar a la iglesia y (tuvimos, teníamos) que preguntar.
3. Hoy cuando (salí, salía) para el trabajo (llovió, llovía); por eso (volví, volvía) a casa y (me puse, me ponía) el impermeable.
4. Anoche (fui, iba) a una fiesta y (bailé, bailaba) toda la noche. (Hubo, Había) mucha gente en un apartamento muy pequeño, pero mis amigos y yo (nos divertimos, nos divertíamos) muchísimo.
5. Lucía (conoció, conocía) a Juan en una fiesta, pero no (supo, sabía) que vivía cerca de aquí.

C. El misterioso robo de los regalos de boda. Change the numbered verbs in the following story to the appropriate past-tense forms.

(1) **Es** una noche de verano. Susana y su esposo Jaime (2) **duermen** después de su boda. En la sala (*living room*) (3) **están** todos los regalos. (4) **Hay** cosas muy lindas. A las doce en punto un hombre (5) **entra** en la casa. (6) **Es** el hombre a quien la policía (7) **busca** desde el sábado. (8) **Va** a la sala, (9) **abre** la puerta y (10) **ve** los regalos allí. Jaime y Susana no lo (11) **escuchan** cuando (12) **entra** y no lo (13) **ven** cuando (14) **se va**. Cuando ellos (15) **se despiertan**, los regalos

ya no (16) **están** allí. Susana (17) **llama** a la policía. Los dos (18) **están** tristes, pero no muy tristes, porque los regalos más importantes, los anillos, todavía los (19) **tienen**.

Now answer the following questions.

1. ¿Qué estación del año era cuando pasó esto? **2.** ¿Qué hacían Susana y su esposo? **3.** ¿Qué había en la sala? ¿Eran regalos de poco o de mucho valor? **4.** ¿Qué pasó a las doce? **5.** ¿Qué descubrieron Jaime y Susana cuando se despertaron? **6.** ¿Qué hizo Susana? **7.** ¿Estaban muy tristes los esposos? ¿Por qué sí o por qué no?

D. **En el pasado...** Complete the following sentences with appropriate information, using verbs in past tenses.

Modelo La semana pasada mi mejor amigo(-a)...
   La semana pasada mi mejor amiga rompió con su novio.

1. En 1985 mis padres...
2. El mes pasado mi profesor(-a) favorito(-a)...
3. Anoche yo... cuando...
4. Esta mañana mi compañero(-a) de cuarto...
5. Eran más de las ocho cuando...
6. El semestre (trimestre) pasado yo... porque...

PREGUNTAS

1. ¿Trabajaba o estudiaba usted el año pasado? **2.** Y anoche, ¿trabajó o estudió? **3.** Cuando era niño(-a), ¿qué hacía los fines de semana? **4.** ¿Qué hizo el fin de semana pasado? **5.** ¿Veía usted muchas películas cuando era un poco menor? ¿Le gustaba ir al cine con amigos o prefería ir solo(-a)? ¿Por qué? **6.** ¿Qué película(-s) vio el mes pasado? ¿Vio alguna película interesante? ¿Cuál? **7.** ¿Qué hora era cuando se acostó anoche? ¿Qué hizo después de cenar y antes de acostarse? (¿Estudió? ¿Habló con un(-a) amigo(-a)? ¿Salió con su novio(-a)?...)

Un baile

Hacer with expressions of time

JANE	¡Por fin llegas!
FERNANDO	¿«Por fin»? *¿Cuánto tiempo hace* que me esperas?
JANE	*Hace una hora* que estoy aquí. ¿Dónde estabas?
FERNANDO	En casa, hasta que salí *hace media hora.* ¿Por qué?
JANE	¿No teníamos que encontrarnos a las cinco? *Hacía media hora* que estaba aquí cuando tú saliste.
FERNANDO	Tú y tu puntualidad yanqui. Estás en América Latina, Jane, ¿recuerdas?
JANE	Pero Fernando, si tienes una cita a las cinco, ¿a qué hora llegas generalmente?
FERNANDO	Un poco más tarde, por supuesto. A las cinco y media, o a las seis, o...

---

1. ¿Cuánto tiempo hace que Jane espera a Fernando?   2. ¿Cuándo salió Fernando de su casa?   3. ¿A qué hora tenían que encontrarse?   4. ¿Cuánto tiempo hacía que Jane estaba allí cuando Fernando salió?   5. Generalmente, ¿llega Fernando tarde, a tiempo o temprano a una cita? ¿Y Jane?

A. Hace + time period + **que** + verb in the present tense expresses an action or event that began in the past and continues into the present.

Hace tres años que vivo aquí.	*I have been living (have lived) here for three years* (and still do).
Hace seis meses que trabajo en Toledo.	*I've been working in Toledo for six months.*

The verb in the main clause is in the present tense, since the action is still in progress. If the action is no longer in progress, the preterit is used.

Viví aquí tres años.	*I lived here three years* (but no longer do).
Trabajé en Toledo por seis meses.	*I worked in Toledo for six months.*

JANE: So you got here at last! FERNANDO: "At last"? How long have you been waiting for me? JANE: I've been here for an hour. Where were you? FERNANDO: At home, until I left a half hour ago. Why? JANE: Weren't we supposed to meet at five o'clock? I had been here half an hour when you left. FERNANDO: You and your Yankee punctuality. You're in Latin America, Jane, remember? JANE: But Fernando, if you have an appointment at five o'clock, when do you generally arrive? FERNANDO: A little later, of course. At five-thirty or six o'clock, or . . .

B. **Hacía** + time period + **que** + verb in the imperfect tense can be used to express an action or event that began at some point in the past and continued up to some other point in the past.

Hacía tres años que vivía allí cuando te conocí.	*I had been living (had lived) there for three years when I met you.*
Hacía seis meses que trabajaba en Toledo.	*I had been working in Toledo for six months (and was still there at the moment I'm thinking of).*

C. The clause in the present or imperfect can occur at the beginning of the construction; in this case, **que** is omitted.

Vivo aquí hace tres años. (Hace tres años que vivo aquí.)*	*I have been living here for three years.*
Vivía aquí hacía tres años. (Hacía tres años que vivía aquí.)	*I had been living here for three years.*

D. **Hace** can also mean *ago*; in this case the verb is in the preterit or imperfect.

Hablé con Juan hace varios** meses.	*I spoke with Juan several months ago.*
Vi a ese actor en el Teatro Nacional hace una semana.	*I saw that actor at the National Theater a week ago.*
Éramos compañeros de clase hace diez años.	*We were classmates ten years ago.*
Supe que ganaste la lotería hace diez minutos. ¡Felicitaciones!	*I found out you won the lottery ten minutes ago. Congratulations!*

EJERCICIOS

A. **Una entrevista.**   Felipe Torres is being interviewed for a job as a bilingual secretary for a big company in New York City. Here are some of the questions he is being asked. Answer them in the affirmative, using **hace** + a time expression, as he would.

Modelo   Usted busca trabajo como secretario bilingüe, ¿no? (diez días)
Sí, hace diez días que busco trabajo como secretario bilingüe.

1. Su familia vive en Nueva York, ¿no? (cinco años)
2. Uno de sus amigos trabaja aquí, ¿no? (cuatro meses)
3. Usted da clases de español por la noche, ¿no? (mucho tiempo)
4. Su hija y mi hijo se ven todos los días, ¿no? (varios meses)
5. Nuestros hijos piensan casarse, ¿no? (unas tres semanas)
6. Usted quiere trabajar aquí, ¿no? (varios días)
   ¡Pues hace varios años que necesito una persona como usted!

---

* The word **desde** (which normally means *from* or *since*) often occurs in this construction: **Vivo aquí desde hace tres años.**
** **Varios** (**varias**) is always used in the plural and means *some* or *several.*

B. Lo hice hace tiempo. Silvia is all ready for her trip to Toledo. Take Silvia's part and answer her mother's questions using **hace** + a time expression. Follow the model and use object pronouns wherever possible.

Modelo La mamá: ¿Ya reservaste un cuarto en el hotel? (un mes)
Silvia: **Sí, lo reservé hace un mes.**

1. ¿Ya le hablaste a Roberto? (diez minutos)
2. ¿Fuiste al banco? (dos días)
3. ¿Compraste los regalos para los Sanabria? (mucho tiempo)
4. ¿Hiciste las maletas? (una hora)
5. ¿Ya llevaste las cartas a la oficina? (una semana)
6. ¿Llamaste un taxi? (media hora)

C. Al corriente. (*Up to date.*) Felipe is visiting his cousin Jaime. Take the part of Felipe and let Jaime know where things stand with the family, using time expressions with **hace**. Follow the models.

Modelo Jaime: Anoche viste a abuela Victoria, ¿verdad? (un mes)
Felipe: **Sí, pero hacía un mes que no la veía.**

1. a. Anoche le escribiste a Ernesto, ¿verdad? (tres semanas)
   b. Anoche cenaste con tío Rafael, ¿verdad? (mucho tiempo)
   c. Anoche fuiste a casa de tus padres, ¿verdad? (dos meses)
   d. Anoche te encontraste con los primos, ¿verdad? (varios días)

Modelo Jaime: ¿Cuándo se casó Rosita? (dos semanas)
Felipe: **Hace dos semanas que ella se casó.**

2. a. ¿Cuándo rompiste con Isabel? (una semana)
   b. ¿Cuándo viajaron tus padres? (tres días)
   c. ¿Cuándo te escribió Amparo? (unos tres meses)
   d. ¿Cuándo se mudaron Pepe y Beatriz? (un año)

Modelo Jaime: ¿Ves a tía Carmen todos los días? (cuatro días)
Felipe: **No, hace cuatro días que no la veo.**

3. a. ¿Sales con Marisa todos los días? (mucho tiempo)
   b. ¿Llamas a Ester todos los días? (dos días)
   c. ¿Recibes cartas de tu hermano todos los días? (varias semanas)
   d. ¿Comes con abuelo José todos los días? (cinco meses)

D. Traducción. Give the Spanish equivalent.

1. We saw the actor three weeks ago. Nos, vimos al actor hace 3 semanas
2. She started to work here seven months ago, right?
3. Rosita had been in Toledo for eight days when she met Pablo.
4. My brother has not played the guitar for several years.
5. I had been living here for a week when my parents visited me.

Hace 3 semanas que nos vimos a la actriz

1. ¿Cuántas semanas hace que comenzó el semestre (trimestre)? ¿Y cuánto tiempo hace que comenzó la clase de hoy?　**2.** ¿Cuánto hace que usted es estudiante universitario(-a)? ¿Y cuánto hace que estudia español?　**3.** ¿Cuánto tiempo hace que usted conoció a su profesor(-a) de español?　**4.** ¿Cuánto hace que se casaron sus padres? ¿Dónde y cuándo se conocieron ellos?　**5.** ¿Hace mucho que ellos viven en la misma casa? ¿Dónde vivían hace diez años?　**6.** ¿A qué hora llegó usted a la universidad hoy? ¿Cuántas horas o minutos hace que está aquí?　**7** ¿Dónde estaba hace dos horas? (¿cinco horas? ¿doce horas...?)

Prepositions

A. The preposition **con** combines with **mí** to form **conmigo** and with **ti** to form **contigo**.

¿Quién fue contigo?—Tu hermano fue
　conmigo.

*Who went with you?— Your brother went
　with me.*

B. In Spanish, infinitives are often used after **antes de**, **después de**, **sin**, and **para**, although in English the -*ing* form of the verb may be used.

Antes de almorzar, fuimos de compras.	*Before having lunch, we went shopping.*
Después de almorzar, fuimos a ver una película.	*After having lunch, we went to see a movie.*
Sin decir nada, José salió.	*Without saying anything, José left.*
Dentro de una hora, voy a la biblioteca para estudiar.	*In (Within) an hour, I'm going to the library to study.*

EJERCICIOS

A. ¡Claro que sí!   Lola and Héctor have a rather stormy relationship. Take Lola's part and contradict Héctor's statements.

> Modelo   No puedo hablar contigo ahora.
> **Claro que puedes hablar conmigo ahora.**

1. Hoy no almuerzo contigo.
2. No necesito estar cerca de ti.
3. No pienso en ti.
4. No salgo contigo este fin de semana.
5. No quiero jugar al tenis contigo.
6. No voy al cine contigo esta noche.

B. La vida de Jorge.   Include the information suggested by the English cues in these sentences about Jorge's activities.

> Modelo   Jorge siempre va a la playa... (with me)
> **Jorge siempre va a la playa conmigo.**

1. Jorge y sus padres no se llevan bien. Él quiere vivir... (far from them)
2. Jorge habla mucho... (about you—**tú**)
3. Jorge tiene un regalo... (for us)
4. En la clase de español, Jorge se sienta... (behind me)
5. Cuando está solo, Jorge siempre piensa... (of you—**tú**)
6. Jorge te quiere mucho... Él quiere casarse... (with you)

C. Completar lógicamente...   Complete the following phrases with appropriate infinitive phrases, as in the models.

> Modelos   Lo hicimos después de...
> **Lo hicimos después de tener los ingredientes.**
>
> Susana fue a España para...
> **Susana fue a España para visitar a sus abuelos.**

1. Ellos pusieron la mesa antes de...
2. ¿Pudiste hacerlo sin...?
3. Teresa y Ramón fueron al cine después de...
4. Queremos ir allí para...
5. José Luis se casó con Inés sin...
6. ¿Por qué no llamaron antes de...?

Toledo: Un importante centro cultural

El Greco, *Vista de Toledo*. The Metropolitan Museum of Art. Bequest of
Mrs. H. D. Havemeyer, 1929. The H. O. Havemeyer Collection.

En un autobús de turismo° que entra en la ciudad de Toledo.

GUÍA	Hace mucho tiempo, en la época del rey Alfonso el Sabio,[1] Toledo era un importante centro cultural. Aquí el rey estableció° la famosa Escuela de Traductores°, donde trabajaban juntos los maestros árabes, cristianos y judíos y...
SR. BLANCO	¡Cómo habla el tipo°! ¡Hace dos horas que habla de Toledo!
SOFÍA	Pero dice cosas que yo no sabía. Es interesante.
SRA. VEGA	Para usted, quizás. Yo venía con la idea de comprar joyas.[2]
SOFÍA	Probablemente me interesa porque soy judía y...

DAVID	¡Ah!, tú eres judía también. Me llamo David Blum. Soy argentino.
SOFÍA	Mucho gusto. Sofía Marcus. Conocí a un Blum en Bogotá cuando era niña y...
GUÍA	...iban y venían los sabios de Europa por estas calles. Bueno, alguien me preguntó algo hace unos minutos. ¿Fue usted, señor Blanco?
SR. BLANCO	Sí. ¿Cuántos años tenía El Greco³ cuando pintó° *Vista de Toledo*?
GUÍA	Bueno... El Greco tenía... Pues lo sabía, pero ahora realmente no lo recuerdo. En fin, ustedes tienen dos horas para visitar la ciudad. Salimos a las once en punto. Y ahora, con permiso...
DAVID	¿Tú también pensabas ir a comprar joyas, Sofía?
SOFÍA	No, quiero visitar la Sinagoga del Tránsito⁴ y el Museo Sefardí que está dentro de ella.
DAVID	No está lejos, creo. ¿Puedo acompañarte? Yo viajo solo... Soy soltero... ¿Y tú?

El barrio gótico de Toledo

Dos horas más tarde.

GUÍA	¡Hora de salir! Señora, aquí está su cámara. La encontré en el autobús.
SRA. VEGA	¡Oh!, ¡muchas gracias!
GUÍA	No hay de qué°. Bueno, ¿estamos todos?

SRA. VEGA	¿Dónde están los dos jóvenes, Sofía y David? Hace unos veinte minutos los vi en la plaza. Iban del brazo° y parecían muy felices.
SR. BLANCO	¡Qué escándalo! Esos jóvenes se conocieron esta mañana y ahora parece que se besan y se abrazan en público. ¿No podían esperar?
SRA. VEGA	¿Y no hacíamos lo mismo° nosotros, cuando éramos jóvenes?
SR. BLANCO	Posiblemente lo hacía usted, señora. Pero yo... nunca fui tan joven.
SRA. VEGA	Pues... con esas ideas, ¡ya lo creo!

autobús de turismo *tour bus*   **estableció** *established*   **Traductores** *Translators*
tipo *guy*   **pintó** *he painted*   **No hay de qué.** *You're welcome.*
Iban del brazo *They were walking arm in arm*   **lo mismo** *the same thing*

PREGUNTAS

1. ¿Dónde estableció el rey Alfonso el Sabio la Escuela de Traductores?
2. ¿Quiénes trabajaban en esa escuela? 3. ¿Con qué idea venía la señora Vega?
4. ¿Qué le preguntó el señor Blanco al guía? 5. ¿Supo contestar la pregunta el guía? 6. ¿Adónde quería ir Sofía? ¿Quién la acompañó? 7. ¿Iban del brazo o de la mano Sofía y David? 8. ¿Cuál fue la reacción del señor Blanco? ¿Qué piensa usted de su reacción?

Notas culturales

1. King Alfonso X of Castile (1221–1284) was known as **el Sabio** (*the learned*) because he devoted most of his energies to scholarly projects such as poetry, law codes, and the writing of a history of the world. Many ancient manuscripts (including those of Aristotle, Euclid, Ptolemy, Hippocrates, and Averroës) would have been lost had it not been for the School of Translators, which employed Arab, Jewish, and Christian scholars to translate ancient texts into Latin and Spanish.

2. The jewelry and metalwork of Toledo have been distinctive and famous for centuries. During the Middle Ages, Toledo was also famous for the production of swords, which are still made for decorative use.

3. Domenikos Theotokopoulos (1541–1614) was known as **El Greco** (*The Greek*). He lived in Spain most of his life and is considered one of the world's greatest painters.

4. The synagogue called **El Tránsito**, located in the Jewish Quarter (**la judería**) of Toledo, is considered one of the most beautiful in the world. The building is a fine example of the **mudéjar** style of architecture, the style perfected by Arab craftsmen living under Christian rule. Attached to the synagogue is a small museum containing relics from the history of the Sephardic Jews (**los sefardíes**)—the Jews who lived in Spain until they were expelled at the end of the fifteenth century.

FUNCIONES Y ACTIVIDADES

In this chapter, you have seen examples of some important language functions, or uses. Here is a summary and some additional information about these functions of language.

Telling a story

Here are some expressions that are often used in telling a story.

¿Sabe(-s) qué le pasó a Julio (me pasó a mí) ayer?	*Do you know what happened to Julio (to me) yesterday?*
¿Sabía(-s) que...?	*Did you know that . . . ?*
Eso me recuerda...	*That reminds me of . . .*
Siempre recuerdo...	*I'll always remember . . .*
Después (Entonces)...	*Then . . .*
¿Y sabe(-s) qué?	*And do you know what?*
En fin...	*Finally . . . (Well . . .)*

Giving the speaker encouragement

When someone is telling a story, it's important to give the speaker some sort of response to show you are listening and want him or her to continue. Here are some ways to do this in Spanish.

¿Y después?	*And then what?*
¿Y qué pasó después?	*And then what happened?*
¿Y qué hacía(-s) mientras pasaba eso?	*And what were you doing while that was happening?*
¿Y qué hizo (hiciste) después?	*And then what did you do?*
¿Hace cuánto tiempo pasó eso?	*How long ago did that happen?*
Sí, entiendo.	*Yes, I understand.*
Sí, claro.	*Yes, sure.*
Sí, cómo no.	*Yes, of course.*
¿En serio? (¿De veras?)	*Really?*

Using polite expressions

Con permiso means *Excuse me* (literally, "With your permission"). It is used when you are about to pass in front of someone, eat something in front of someone, etc. **Perdón** means *Excuse me* when you have done something for which you are apologizing (like stepping on someone's toe, spilling something on someone, etc.).

¡Salud! (literally, "Health!") is used when making toasts to mean *Cheers!* and also when someone sneezes to mean *Gesundheit!* **¡Felicitaciones!** means *Congratulations!*

There are two ways to say *You're welcome*: **De nada** and **No hay de qué**, both of which mean basically *It's nothing.*

A. **¿Es usted una persona cortés?** Referring to the cartoons, use the polite expression that best fits each of the situations described below and at the top of page 234. To evaluate your results, see page 239.

¿Qué dice usted...?

1. si alguien le da un regalo
2. si alguien le da las gracias por un favor
3. si quiere pasar delante de (*in front of*) alguien
4. si usted no conoce a alguien, pero quiere, por alguna razón, decirle su nombre
5. antes de tomar vino o champaña

6. a unas personas que empiezan a comer
7. si alguien estornuda (*sneezes*)
8. si alguien viene a visitarlo(-la); ustedes están en el aeropuerto
9. si su mejor amigo(-a) anuncia su boda
10. si alguien a quien usted no conoce le dice: «Hola, me llamo Julio Rendón.»
11. si usted está en un ascensor (*elevator*) lleno de gente y quiere salir

B. Historia de amor. Tell a story based on the following pictures. Use the expressions you've learned in this chapter.

C. ¿Y sabes qué...? With a partner, tell a story about something that happened to you or someone you know. Your partner will ask questions and give encouragement; use words and expressions from this chapter. Then change roles, and have your partner tell a story.

D. Compañero(-a) de cuarto. Tell a story about a roommate you've had, or invent one. Include the answers to these questions:

1. ¿Cómo era su compañero(-a)? ¿Qué estudiaba? ¿Estudiaban juntos(-as)?
2. ¿Qué diferencias había entre su compañero(-a) y usted? Por ejemplo, ¿estudiaban a las mismas horas? ¿Se levantaban más o menos a la misma hora? ¿Les gustaba el mismo tipo de música?, ¿de comida?, ¿de ropa?
3. En general, ¿se llevaban bien o no muy bien...?

VOCABULARIO ACTIVO

Cognados

el actor
la actriz
la época

generoso
misterioso

el público
el semestre

el sofá
el trimestre

Verbos

abrazar	to hug, embrace
acompañar	to accompany, go with
amar	to love
besar	to kiss
casarse (con)	to get married (to)
enamorarse (de)	to fall in love (with)
llevarse (bien, mal) con	to get along (well, poorly) with
organizar	to organize
parecer (zc)	to seem
pasear	to stroll, walk
respetar	to respect, esteem
romper	to break
romper con	to break up with
sacar	to take (out)
sacar una nota	to get a grade

Novios y amigos

el abrazo	hug, embrace
el amor	love
el anillo	ring
el beso	kiss
la boda	wedding
los celos	jealousy
tener celos de	to be jealous of
la cita	date, appointment
tener una cita	to have a date or an appointment
el compañero (la compañera) de clase	classmate
el compañero (la compañera) de cuarto	roommate
la joya	jewel
las joyas	jewelry
la iglesia	church
la pareja	pair, couple

Adjetivos

cariñoso	tender, affectionate
cristiano	Christian
feliz	happy
judío	Jewish
medio	half
soltero	single, unmarried
varios	several, some

Otras palabras y frases

dentro (de)	inside, within
desde	from, since
el maestro (la maestra)	teacher, master, scholar
la nota	grade
¡Qué escándalo!	What a scandal!
el rey	king
el tipo	type, (slang) guy

Expresiones útiles

Cómo no.	Of course.
Con permiso.	Excuse me. (With your permission.)
De nada.	You're welcome.
En fin...	Finally...; Well... (as an expletive)
¿En serio?	Really?
¡Felicitaciones!	Congratulations!
No hay de qué.	You're welcome. (It's nothing.)
Perdón	Excuse me.
¿Sabías que...?	Did you know that...?
¡Salud!	Cheers! Gesundheit! (literally, "Health!")

> **Don't forget:**
> **Hacer** with expressions of time, pages 224–225

La España del pasado

El acueducto de Segovia

La historia de España es una historia de muchas razas y culturas. Los primeros habitantes históricamente conocidos° de España fueron los iberos°, gente de origen europeo. Después vinieron los fenicios°, los griegos° y, también, los cartagineses° del norte de África. Una guerra° terrible y larga entre° los cartagineses y los romanos terminó en el año 218 a. C. con el triunfo de los romanos. Es fácil ver la influencia cultural de Roma en la lengua° española (el latín que en aquella época hablaba la gente formó la base del español moderno), en el sistema de leyes y en la religión católica, proclamada° como religión oficial por Teodosio, emperador romano nacido° en España. Los romanos construyeron° puentes°, caminos° y acueductos por todo el país. En la foto vemos parte del famoso acueducto de Segovia.

known / Iberians
Phoenicians / Greeks /
Carthaginians /
war / between

language

proclaimed / born
constructed / bridges /
roads

La mezquita de Córdoba

En el año 711 los moros (musulmanes del norte de África) invadieron la Península Ibérica. Les tomó tres años conquistarla°, pero establecieron allí una cultura que durante mucho tiempo fue la más espléndida del mundo occidental. Los sabios de toda Europa viajaban a las ciudades de Córdoba, Granada, Sevilla y a otras más para aprender de los moros nuevos conocimientos° en las ciencias en general, la arquitectura, la agricultura y el arte. En la foto vemos la mezquita° de Córdoba: sus arcos y columnas que simbolizan el poder° infinito de Alá.

Desde el norte de España los reinos° cristianos empezaron la Reconquista°, guerra que duró° casi ocho siglos. En 1492 las fuerzas° militares de Isabel de Castilla y Fernando de Aragón conquistaron Granada, último reino de los moros. Ese mismo año Cristóbal Colón descubrió un nuevo mundo en nombre de España. Ahora los españoles podían utilizar la disciplina militar de la Reconquista para la colonización del Nuevo Mundo. En la foto de la página 238 vemos la tumba de Isabel y Fernando en Granada.

Les... It took them three years to conquer it

knowledge
mosque
power
kingdoms
Reconquest / lasted / forces

1. ¿Quiénes fueron los primeros habitantes de España? ¿Qué otros grupos llegaron después? **2.** ¿Fue larga o corta la guerra entre los cartagineses y los romanos? ¿En qué año terminó? ¿Quiénes triunfaron? **3.** ¿Qué ejemplos puede dar usted de la influencia romana sobre la cultura española? **4.** ¿Quiénes invadieron la Península Ibérica en el año 711? ¿En cuántos años la conquistaron? **5.** ¿Cómo fue la cultura que establecieron los moros en España? **6.** En el siglo X, ¿para qué viajaban a ciudades como Córdoba, Granada y Sevilla los sabios de toda Europa? **7.** ¿Desde qué parte de España empezaron los cristianos la Reconquista? ¿Cuánto tiempo duró? **8.** ¿Por qué podemos decir que el año 1492 tiene doble importancia en España?

La tumba de los Reyes Católicos

Evaluación: ¿Es usted una persona cortés?, páginas 233–234.

Respuestas:

1. Gracias.   **2.** De nada. (No hay de qué.)   **3.** Con permiso.   **4.** ¡Hola! Me llamo...   **5.** ¡Salud!   **6.** ¡Buen provecho!   **7.** ¡Salud!   **8.** Bienvenido(-a).   **9.** ¡Felicitaciones!   **10.** Mucho gusto.   **11.** Con permiso.

Respuestas correctas:

10–12 Usted es muy cortés; es una persona bien educada (*well brought up*).

 6–9 Usted es bastante cortés, pero...

 0–5 ¡Qué horror! Usted todavía tiene mucho que aprender...

la catedral

el museo de arte

el barco

el mercado

el correo

el parque zoológico

oficina de aduana

Bienvenidos a México

el puerto

Hoy: México vs. Perú

el estadio

el banco

un mapa de la ciudad con sitios de interés turístico

Acapulco/Veracruz

Oaxaca

equipaje

la estación de trenes (del ferrocarril)

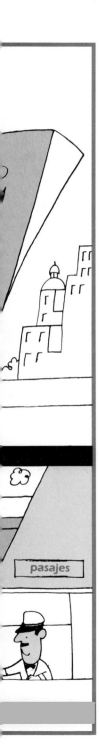

Viajes y paseos

11

Asking for Directions
Understanding Directions
Getting Someone's Attention

EJERCICIO

Match the words on the left with the definitions or descriptions on the right.

1. la catedral	a. las maletas
2. el barco	b. sitio (lugar) donde se puede comprar frutas, verduras, etcétera
3. el banco	
4. el equipaje	c. oficina pública relacionada (*related*) con la inmigración o emigración
5. el estadio	
6. la aduana	d. medio (*means*) de transporte acuático
7. el mercado	e. edificio relacionado con créditos, dinero, etcétera
8. el correo	f. sitio para competiciones deportivas
9. el puerto	g. iglesia grande
10. el pasaje	h. algo que uno recibe después de pagar por el derecho (*right*) de viajar de un lugar a otro
	i. lugar donde generalmente hay barcos
	j. lugar donde uno compra estampillas (*stamps*)

PREGUNTAS

1. ¿A usted le gusta viajar? ¿Qué ciudad(-es) o sitio(-s) visitó durante su último viaje?   **2.** ¿Piensa hacer algún viaje este año? ¿Adónde? ¿Cuándo?   **3.** Uno de los paseos favoritos de muchos niños es ir al zoológico o al parque. ¿Cuál es su paseo favorito?   **4.** ¿Piensa hacer algún paseo este fin de semana? ¿Adónde?   **5.** ¿Pasea usted mucho a pie (*on foot*) o prefiere pasear en auto? ¿Por qué? Cuando usted viaja, ¿le gusta más viajar por avión? ¿por autobús? ¿por barco? ¿Por qué?

Formal *usted* and *ustedes* commands

En la ciudad de México, cerca del Museo de Historia Natural.

SR. SMITH   *Oiga*, señor, ¿sabe usted si hay algún banco por aquí cerca? Necesitamos cambiar dinero.

OTRO SEÑOR   Pues, el Banco de México está a siete cuadras de aquí. *Vayan* derecho por esta calle hasta la Avenida Juárez. *Doblen* a la izquierda y *caminen* dos cuadras. El banco está en la esquina de las avenidas Juárez y San Juan de Letrán.

SR. SMITH   Señor, *espere* un momento, por favor. A ver... Vamos derecho por esta calle hasta la Avenida Juárez. Allí doblamos a la izquierda y caminamos dos cuadras, ¿no?

OTRO SEÑOR   Exacto..., ¡pero son las cuatro menos cuarto! Aquí los bancos cierran a las cuatro. ¡*Tomen* un taxi o no llegan a tiempo!

SR. SMITH   Muchas gracias, señor. ¡Taxi!... ¡Taxi!

---

1. ¿Adónde quieren ir los señores Smith? ¿Para qué?   2. ¿Qué banco está a siete cuadras de allí?   3. ¿Cuántas cuadras deben caminar por la Avenida Juárez? 4. ¿A qué hora cierran los bancos en esa ciudad?   5. ¿Qué deben hacer los señores Smith para no llegar tarde?

A. To form the singular formal (**usted**) command of regular verbs, drop the **-o** ending from the first-person singular (**yo**) form of the present tense and add **-e** for **-ar** verbs and **-a** for **-er** and **-ir** verbs. The **ustedes** command is formed by adding an **-n** to the singular command forms.

-ar   Compro esa maleta. {
Compr**e** (usted) esa maleta.
Compr**en** (ustedes) esa maleta.

-er   Como algo. {
Com**a** (usted) algo.
Com**an** (ustedes) algo.

In Mexico City, near the Museum of Natural History.   MR. SMITH: Excuse me, sir, do you know if there is a bank around here? We need to exchange some money. ANOTHER GENTLEMAN: Well, the Bank of Mexico is seven blocks from here. Go straight on this street to Juárez Avenue. Turn left and walk two blocks. The bank is on the corner of Juárez Avenue and San Juan de Letrán Avenue. MR. SMITH: Sir, wait a minute, please. Let's see . . . We go straight on this street to Juárez Avenue. There, we turn left and walk two blocks, right? ANOTHER GENTLEMAN: Right . . ., but it's a quarter to four! Here the banks close at four. Take a taxi or you won't make it on time (literally, "you won't arrive on time")! MR. SMITH: Thanks very much, sir. Taxi! . . . Taxi!

-ir | Escribo la carta. $\begin{cases} \text{Escriba (usted) la carta.} \\ \text{Escriban (ustedes) la carta.} \end{cases}$

The pronouns **usted** and **ustedes** are usually omitted, but they are sometimes used to soften a command, to make it more polite. To make a command negative, place **no** before the verb.

No compre un pasaje de ida y vuelta. | *Don't buy a round-trip ticket.*
No hablen ustedes ahora; escriban la carta... | *Don't talk now; write the letter ...*

B. If a verb has an irregularity or a stem change in the first-person singular of the present tense, this irregularity or stem change is carried over into the command forms.

No salga todavía. | *Don't leave yet.*
Recuerde el número de la casa. | *Remember the house number.*
Duerman un poco. | *Sleep a little (while).*
Vuelvan en seguida. | *Come back right away.*
No pierdan los cheques de viajero. | *Don't lose the traveler's checks.*

C. Infinitives that end in **-zar**, **-car**, and **-gar** have a spelling change in the **usted** and **ustedes** command forms to preserve the sound of the infinitive ending.

c to **qu** | buscar | yo busco | bus**que**(n)
g to **gu** | llegar | yo llego | lle**gue**(n)
z to **c** | empezar | yo empiezo | empie**c**e(n)

Saquen unas fotos (fotografías) aquí. | *Take some photos (photographs) here.*
Busque la maleta. | *Look for the suitcase.*

D. Some irregular formal (**usted** and **ustedes**) commands are:

ir | **vaya(n)**
ser | **sea(n)**
saber | **sepa(n)**
estar | **esté(n)**
dar | **dé,* den**

Vayan primero a la estación de trenes. | *First go to the train station.*
Sean puntuales. | *Be punctual.*
Sepa el precio del boleto antes de llegar al aeropuerto. | *Know the price of the ticket before arriving at the airport.*
No esté triste. | *Don't be sad.*
Den un paseo con los niños. | *Take a walk with the children.*

---

* The accent on **dé** distinguishes the word from the preposition **de**.

A. Vuelva en seguida, por favor. Mr. Roa has to leave on a business trip. Tell his secretary to do some last-minute errands, as he would, following the models.

Modelos   ir al banco.
Vaya al banco.

no llegar tarde
No llegue tarde.

1. llamar a la agencia de viajes
2. hablar con Luisa
3. reservar los pasajes
4. no perder el tiempo
5. salir para el banco
6. no ir en autobús
7. tomar un taxi
8. sacar diez mil pesos del banco
9. pagar por los pasajes y...
10. ¡... volver inmediatamente!

B. ¡Recuerden mis consejos! Some friends of yours will soon be going to Mexico City for two weeks. Having been to Mexico before, you give them some advice. Follow the models.

Modelos   llevar cheques de viajero
Lleven cheques de viajero.

no perder sus pasaportes
No pierdan sus pasaportes.

1. hacer las maletas hoy o mañana
2. no llegar tarde al aeropuerto
3. asistir a una corrida de toros
4. no olvidar la cámara
5. sacar muchas fotografías
6. ir al Museo Nacional de Antropología
7. dar un paseo por el Zócalo y...
8. ¡...comer comidas típicas!

C. Preguntas... It is the first day of a tour, and the tourists are asking their guide many questions. Answer their questions, as the guide would, with an affirmative **usted** or **ustedes** command.

Modelos   ¿Puedo ir al banco ahora?
Sí, vaya al banco ahora.

¿Podemos buscar el equipaje?
Sí, busquen el equipaje.

1. ¿Puedo cambiar dinero aquí?
2. ¿Puedo usar el teléfono?
3. ¿Podemos salir de la aduana ya?
4. ¿Puedo comprar algunos regalos ahora?
5. ¿Podemos hacer una excursión en barco?
6. ¿Podemos sacar unas fotografías?

D. ...y más preguntas. Now answer the tourists' questions from Exercise C with a negative **usted** or **ustedes** command, as appropriate.

Modelos   ¿Puedo ir al banco ahora?
No, no vaya al banco ahora.

¿Podemos buscar el equipaje?
No, no busquen el equipaje.

E. Traducción. Give the Spanish equivalent.

Doble

1. Don't open the window, sir.   *No abra la ventana, ~~por~~ Sr.*
2. Turn right on Florida Street, ma'am. *~~Vaya~~ ¹ª derecha en Calle Florida Sra.*
3. Eat, children. *Coman chicos*
4. Wait a minute, gentlemen. *Esperen un momento Srs*
5. Don't go tomorrow, miss; go today. *No vaya mañana, Sra, vaya voy*

PREGUNTAS

Imagine you are asking the following questions of three different people: a professor, your doctor, and your advisor. How would each one of them answer? Use **usted** commands for their answers.

1. **a un(-a) profesor(-a):** ¿Cómo voy de aquí a la biblioteca? ¿de aquí a la cafetería? ¿de aquí a la oficina del presidente?
2. **a su doctor(-a):** ¿Qué debo hacer para perder peso (*weight*)? ¿para aumentar de peso?
3. **a su consejero(-a):** ¿Qué puedo hacer para sacar mejores notas? ¿para hablar español correctamente?

¿Cómo elegir una Agencia de viajes?

Evidentemente una buena forma de evaluar una agencia de viajes es considerar el volumen de los servicios ofrecidos, reconocer los productos que ofrece, apreciar la atención personal y esmerada de la misma y, también, consultando a amigos y parientes que lo hubieran requerido con anterioridad.

Se debe tener siempre presente que la agencia de viajes debe estar autorizada por la Secretaría de Turismo pero también es fundamental que la misma se encuentre asociada a la Asociación Mexicana de Agencias de Viajes, A.C. —AMAV—. Esta es la garantía real que le asegura calidad, profesionalidad y seguridad en los servicios prestados.

 Tú **commands**

Cerca del puerto de Veracruz.

FERMÍN *Oye*, Tito, ¿me puedes decir cómo llegar al puerto?
TITO *Toma* el autobús aquí y *baja* en la estación de autobuses; allí, *dobla* a la derecha. Después *ve* hasta el hotel El Viajero, pero ¡cuidado!, no *dobles* a la izquierda. *Sigue* derecho hasta el edificio de la aduana.
FERMÍN ¿Crees que llego a tiempo para reservar los pasajes?
TITO No hay problema. Los niños te acompañan. (*Llama a los niños.*) ¡Toño! ¡Lisa! Vayan con el tío Fermín adonde están los barcos, ¿eh?
TOÑO ¿Los barcos? ¡Oh, ya sé! ¡Lisa! ¡*Ven* aquí! ¡Corre! ¡Vamos a la juguetería con el tío Fermín!

---

1. ¿Adónde quiere ir Fermín?   2. Según las instrucciones de Tito, ¿dónde debe doblar Fermín?   3. ¿Para qué quiere llegar Fermín al puerto?   4. ¿Quiénes lo van a acompañar?   5. ¿Adónde cree Toño que van a ir?   6. En general, ¿prefiere usted viajar en autobús, en barco o en avión? ¿Por qué?

A. Informal singular (**tú**) affirmative commands for regular verbs are the same as the third-person singular, present-tense form. The pronoun **tú** is not used, except very rarely for emphasis.

Gloria toma el tren.	*Gloria is taking the train.*
Toma (tú) el tren.	*Take the train.*
Juan lee el mapa.	*Juan is reading the map.*
Lee el mapa.	*Read the map.*
Julia sube al autobús.*	*Julia gets on the bus.*
Sube al autobús.	*Get on the bus.*

---

* **Subir a** with a means of transportation means *to get on*. **Subir** without the preposition **a** means *to climb* or *to go up*: **Subimos una montaña. Los precios suben.**

Near the port of Veracruz. FERMÍN: Listen, Tito, can you tell me how to get to (arrive at) the harbor? TITO: Take the bus here and get off at the bus station; there, turn right. Then go as far as the hotel El Viajero (*The Traveler*), but careful! Don't turn left. Continue straight on to the customs building. FERMÍN: Do you think I'll arrive in time to reserve the tickets? TITO: There's no problem. The children will accompany you. (*He calls the children.*) Toño! Lisa! Go with Uncle Fermín to where the boats are, okay? TOÑO: The boats? Oh, I get it! (literally, "now I know!") Lisa! Come here! Run! We're going to the toy store with Uncle Fermín!

Felipe cruza la calle.   *Felipe is crossing the street*
Cruza la calle.   *Cross the street.*

B. Some irregular affirmative **tú** commands are:

di	(decir)	**sal**	(salir)
haz	(hacer)	**sé**	(ser)
ve	(ir)	**ten**	(tener)
pon	(poner)	**ven**	(venir)

Irene, di "gracias".   *Irene, say "thank you."*
Haz la maleta.   *Pack your suitcase.*
Ve a la aduana, Jorge.   *Go to the customs office, Jorge.*
Pon el equipaje aquí.   *Put the luggage here.*
Sal ahora o no llegas a tiempo. *Leave now or you won't arrive on time.*
Sé simpático, Mateo.   *Be nice, Mateo.*
¡Ten cuidado, José!   *Be careful, José!*
Ven acá, María.   *Come here, María.*

C. Negative **tú** commands are formed by adding an **s** to the **usted** commands.

No doble (usted) aquí. }
No dobles (tú) aquí.   } *Don't turn here.*

No vuelva (usted) tarde. }
No vuelvas (tú) tarde.   } *Don't come back late.*

No salga (usted) ahora. }
No salgas (tú) ahora.   } *Don't leave now.*

No vaya (usted) a ninguna parte ahora. }
No vayas (tú) a ninguna parte ahora.   } *Don't go anywhere now.*

EJERCICIOS

A. **¡No salgas muy tarde!**   Eliana has invited Lelia to come to her house at 8:00 P.M. Using the phrases below, form affirmative **tú** commands to give Lelia directions to her friend's house, as Eliana would.

Modelo   salir antes de las siete.
         Sal antes de las siete.

1. tomar la calle Colonia
2. caminar tres cuadras
3. doblar a la izquierda
4. ir a la estación de autobuses
5. subir al autobús número 85
6. pagar el pasaje
7. leer los nombres de las calles
8. bajar del autobús en la calle Colón
9. seguir por Colón hasta el número 121, que es donde vivo
10. ¡ser puntual!

B. ¡Feliz viaje! Rubén is planning a trip to Buenos Aires, but he's very confused after talking to Marisa and Arturo. While Marisa, his girlfriend, tells him to do one thing, Arturo advises him to do just the opposite! Play the roles of both Marisa and Arturo, following the model.

Modelo   buscar un hotel en el centro
           Marisa: **Busca un hotel en el centro.**
           Arturo: **No busques un hotel en el centro.**

1. visitar el zoológico
2. ir al teatro los fines de semana
3. asistir a algún concierto en el Teatro Colón
4. ver películas argentinas
5. comer mucha carne y tomar mucho vino
6. usar el transporte público; no andar en taxi
7. hacer un viaje a Montevideo y...
8. ¡sacar fotos de todos los sitios de interés!

C. Conversación. Complete the conversation between Carlos and his mother with **tú** commands. Pay attention to Carlos' reactions in order to guess what his mother is suggesting.

CARLOS	Ay, mamá, estoy aburrido.
SRA. GIL	Pues, _____₁ algo.
CARLOS	¿Qué hago?
SRA. GIL	_____₂, hijo.
CARLOS	Pienso estudiar esta noche para las clases de mañana.
SRA. GIL	Pues _____₃ unos poemas de Octavio Paz.
CARLOS	No me gustan sus poemas, mamá...
SRA. GIL	_____₄ televisión...
CARLOS	No hay ningún programa interesante ahora.
SRA. GIL	Entonces _____₅ una carta a tu tía Julia.
CARLOS	¡Pero, mamá!, sabes que no me gusta escribir cartas...
SRA. GIL	¡Ay!, pues entonces _____₆ de la casa por unos minutos... Puedes dar un paseo por La Alameda o correr por el parque...
CARLOS	¡Buena idea! Voy a correr por el parque y después vengo a ayudarte con la cena, ¿de acuerdo...?

PREGUNTAS

Ask these questions of a fellow student. **Tú** commands should be used in all the answers.

1. ¿Cómo puedo ir de aquí al correo? ¿a la librería universitaria? ¿a la estación del ferrocarril? ¿al aeropuerto? ¿al centro?   **2.** ¿Qué debo hacer para tener más amigos? ¿para divertirme los fines de semana? ¿para no ponerme nervioso(-a) en los exámenes?

Position of object pronouns with commands

En la ciudad de México, donde los señores Castellón
viajan en auto con sus tres hijos.

PEPE	Papá, tengo hambre. ¿Cuándo vamos a llegar al Parque de Chapultepec?
SR. CASTELLÓN	*Déjanos* en paz, Pepe. Y *siéntense*, niños, porque vamos a parar. (*Para el coche.*) Silvia, *dame* el mapa.
SRA. CASTELLÓN	¿Otra vez estamos perdidos? Mejor salgo a preguntar.
PAQUITA	¡Qué bien! ¡Qué bien! ¡Llegamos!
SRA. CASTELLÓN	No, niños. *Quédense* en el coche. (*Sale del coche y regresa en unos minutos.*) Dice el señor que hay que regresar a la Plaza de las Tres Culturas, doblar a la izquierda en Paseo de la Reforma y después...
SR. CASTELLÓN	¡Pero no puede ser! Ya estuvimos en Paseo de la Reforma y nos dijeron que debíamos buscar Insurgentes.
SRA. CASTELLÓN	*Cálmate*, Mario. Ten paciencia.

Media hora más tarde.

SRA. CASTELLÓN	Niños, ¡estamos aquí! Pero, ¿qué les pasa? *¡Despiértense!*
LOS NIÑOS	Zzzzzzz.

---

1. ¿Dónde está la familia Castellón?   2. ¿Qué quieren saber los niños?   3. ¿Por qué para el coche el señor Castellón?   4. ¿Qué hace la señora Castellón?   5. Según el señor, ¿qué hay que hacer?   6. Cuando llegan al parque, ¿qué hacen los niños?

In Mexico City, where Mr. and Mrs. Castellón are traveling by car with their three children. PEPE: Daddy, I'm hungry. When are we going to get to Chapultepec Park? MR. CASTELLÓN: Leave us in peace, Pepe. And sit down, children, because we're going to stop. (*He stops the car.*) Silvia, give me the map. MRS. CASTELLÓN: We're lost again? I'd better get out and ask. PAQUITA: Oh, boy! Oh, boy! We're here! MRS. CASTELLÓN: No, kids. Stay in the car. (*She gets out of the car and returns in a few minutes.*) The man says that we have to go back to the Plaza of the Three Cultures, turn left on Paseo de la Reforma, and then ... MR. CASTELLÓN: But it can't be! We were already on Paseo de la Reforma, and they told us we should take Insurgentes (Avenue). MRS. CASTELLÓN: Calm down, Mario. Have patience. (*A half hour later.*) MRS. CASTELLÓN: Children, we're here! But what's wrong with you? Wake up! THE CHILDREN: Zzzzzzz.

A. Object and reflexive pronouns are attached to affirmative commands, familiar and formal. The stressed vowel of the command form is still stressed when pronouns are attached, which usually means that an accent mark must be written on the stressed vowel to maintain the stress.

Compra los cheques de viajero. Cómpralos (tú).	*Buy the traveler's checks. Buy them.*
Léeme la dirección. Léemela (tú).	*Read me the address. Read it to me.*
Cuéntenos (usted) algo del viaje de negocios.*	*Tell us something about the business trip.*
Denle (ustedes) la bienvenida a tía Carmen.	*Welcome* (literally, "Give welcome to") *Aunt Carmen.*
Perdónenme (ustedes)	*Pardon (Excuse) me.*

B. Object pronouns precede negative commands, familiar and formal.

No cierres la puerta. No la cierres (tú).	*Don't close the door. Don't close it.*
No te preocupes.	*Don't worry.*
No saque la foto aquí. No la saque (usted) aquí.	*Don't take the photo here. Don't take it here.*
No les digan (ustedes) eso.	*Don't tell them that.*

C. When both a direct object pronoun and an indirect object pronoun are used, the indirect object pronoun precedes the direct object pronoun, just as with statements or questions.

Dímelo. No me lo digas (tú).	*Tell me (it). Don't tell me (it).*
Déjenselos (los cheques de viajero).** No se los dejen (ustedes).	*Leave them (the traveler's checks) for them (her, him). Don't leave them for them (her, him).*

EJERCICIOS

A. Búscalos aquí, por favor. You have just arrived home from a long trip and are telling your brother to please look for certain things for you. Follow the model.

Modelo los regalos / la maleta grande
Búscalos en la maleta grande, por favor.

1. las maletas / el auto
2. el pasaporte / la mesa
3. los mapas / el equipaje
4. la carta de José / aquí
5. las fotos / la maleta pequeña

---

* The verb **contar** (*to tell, relate*) is an **o** to **ue** stem-changing verb.
** Here **dejar** means *to leave* in the sense of *to leave behind, not take* and requires a direct object. (**Dejar**, of course, also means *to allow, permit,* or *let.*) **Salir** means *to leave* in the sense of *to depart;* it does not take a direct object.

B. No lo compre, señora. You are a tourist guide in an open-air market and realize that one of the ladies in your group is about to make some bad purchases. Advise her not to buy these items because the prices are too high. Follow the model.

Modelo   un reloj de oro
          No lo compre, señora.

1. unos sombreros
2. un vestido
3. una blusa típica
4. varias joyas
5. un mapa turístico
6. libros y cuadernos
7. una guitarra grande
8. unas sandalias

C. ¡Háganlo ahora! Replace the nouns with object pronouns.

Modelo   Escribe la carta, Susana.
          Escríbela, Susana.

1. Lee tu lección, Pablo.
2. Compra frutas, Carmela.
3. Abre tu maleta, Marcelo.
4. Lleva esta camisa, Miguel.
5. Cuente su dinero, señora.
6. Deje los cheques aquí, señor.
7. Pidan la dirección, chicos.
8. Pongan los sombreros aquí, señores.

D. ¡No lo hagan! Replace the nouns with object pronouns.

Modelo   No busques los pasajes allí, Teresa.
          No los busques allí, Teresa.

1. No traigas a los niños, Mónica.
2. No hagas esas cosas, Antonio.
3. No ponga el reloj en la mesa, señorita.
4. No comas estos sandwiches, Paco.
5. No lleve ese pasaporte, señor.
6. No cuenten sus secretos, chicas.
7. No hagan ese viaje, muchachos.
8. No crucen la calle, niños.

E. Órdenes (*Orders*) **de papá.** Roberto and Carolina's father leaves them a note telling them some things they should or shouldn't do while he's away on business. Write the suggestions or orders he leaves, following the model.

Modelo   acostarse temprano todas las noches
          Acuéstense temprano todas las noches.

1. levantarse a las siete todos los días
2. no irse a la escuela sin desayunar
3. ponerse los pijamas antes de acostarse
4. vestirse bien para la fiesta de Pedrito
5. divertirse en la fiesta de cumpleaños
6. no acostarse después de las diez
7. no preocuparse por la cena el domingo
8. quedarse en casa a esperarme... Esa noche todos vamos a cenar... ¡en "McDonald's" o en "Pollo Frito Kentucky"!

F. Órdenes y consejos.   Work with a classmate to answer the following questions.

1. ¿Qué órdenes oye mucho un niño? Dé cuatro o cinco ejemplos de esas órdenes.
2. ¿Qué consejos quiere darle usted a un(-a) amigo(-a)?
   Dé cuatro o cinco ejemplos de esos consejos.
3. ¿Qué órdenes (que a usted no le gustan) le dan sus padres? Dé cuatro o cinco ejemplos de esas órdenes.
4. ¿Qué clase de órdenes o consejos sí le gustan a usted? Dé cuatro o cinco ejemplos de ese tipo de órdenes o consejos.

Ciudad de México: En la antigua capital azteca

El Zócalo

En una oficina del Zócalo, México, D. F.[1] *Dos agentes de la Compañía Turismo Mundial° le dan la bienvenida a Amalia Mercado, una agente uruguaya en viaje de negocios.*

HÉCTOR   ¡Bienvenida, señorita Mercado! ¿Qué tal el viaje?
AMALIA   Bastante bueno, gracias. Pero ¡no me llame «señorita»! Llámeme Amalia, por favor. ¿Y usted es...?

HÉCTOR	¡Oh, perdóneme! Yo soy Héctor Peralta, y este es Alonso Rodríguez. Él está a cargo de° las excursiones al Caribe...
AMALIA	¡Alonso! ¡Pero ya nos conocemos! Fue en Montevideo que nos conocimos. ¿Recuerdas...?
ALONSO	¡Claro! Me llevaste a pasear por la playa.
AMALIA	No sabía que ahora vivías en México.
ALONSO	Vine aquí hace dos años.
HÉCTOR	Cuéntenos algo de usted, Amalia. ¿Es éste su primer viaje a México?
AMALIA	Sí. Vine por invitación de la Compañía Mexicana de Aviación. ¡Y vean mi suerte! La invitación incluye° pasaje de ida y vuelta y seis días en el mejor hotel de esta ciudad, que me parece extraña y fascinante.
HÉCTOR	Es verdad. La ciudad está construida° sobre las ruinas de la antigua capital azteca...
ALONSO	...que estaba en medio de un lago,[2] algo así como una antigua Venecia mexicana, ¿no?
HÉCTOR	Exacto. Dicen que los aztecas tenían su gran templo° aquí cerca, en el sitio donde ahora está la catedral.
AMALIA	¿Realmente? ¡Qué interesante!... ¿Y qué les parece si ahora me llevan a conocer el centro? ¡Recuerden que sólo tengo seis días!
ALONSO	Tus deseos° son órdenes, Amalia. Vengan. Síganme. Los invito a tomar una copa° en el bar de la Torre Latinoamericana.[3]
HÉCTOR	Desde allí usted va a poder admirar la belleza° de esta ciudad. ¡La vista es hermosa!
AMALIA	¡Qué suerte!... Pero por favor, espérenme unos minutos. Quiero comprar película para mi cámara. Vuelvo en seguida. ¡No me dejen!
ALONSO	Tú no cambias, Amalia. Nunca vas a ninguna parte sin tu famosa cámara. Pero no te preocupes, aquí te esperamos.

Mundial *World*   **a cargo de** *in charge of*   **incluye** *includes*
construida *built, constructed*   **templo** *temple*   **deseos** *wishes*
tomar una copa *to have a drink*   **belleza** *beauty*

PREGUNTAS

1. ¿Dónde están los tres agentes? **2.** ¿Se conocían ya Amalia y Alonso? ¿Dónde se conocieron? **3.** ¿Cuánto tiempo hace que Alonso está en México? **4.** ¿Es este el primer viaje de Amalia a México? ¿Qué incluye la invitación de la Compañía Mexicana de Aviación? **5.** ¿Dónde está construida la ciudad de México? **6.** ¿Qué tenían los aztecas en el sitio donde ahora está la catedral? **7.** ¿Para qué piensan ir a la Torre Latinoamericana? **8.** ¿Qué quiere hacer Amalia antes de ir allí? **9.** ¿Le gusta a ella sacar fotos? ¿Cómo sabemos que la fotografía es una de sus diversiones favoritas? **10.** ¿Le gusta a usted sacar muchas fotos cuando viaja o prefiere comprar postales (*postcards*) en los lugares que visita? ¿Por qué?

Notas culturales

1. El Zócalo (officially called **Plaza de la Constitución**), one of the biggest squares in the world, is located in the center of Mexico City (**México, Distrito Federal**). One side is occupied by the cathedral, one of the largest in America, built on the site of a former Aztec temple. Another side is occupied by the **Palacio Nacional**, which contains the offices of the president and other government officials. It was built over the site of Moctezuma's palace. Moctezuma was the emperor of the Aztecs, who had conquered most of the other Indians of Mexico by the time the Spanish arrived.

2. The subsoil of Mexico City is like a giant sponge; about 85 percent of it is water, much of which is extracted from time to time for use in the growing city. For this reason, many of the older public buildings have been thrust upward and must be entered by stairways added later to the original structure, while others have sunk and must now be reached by descending a stairway.

3. The **Torre Latinoamericana** is a forty-four–story skyscraper, one of the tallest in Latin America. It literally floats on its foundation, which consists of piers sunk deep into the clay beneath Mexico City. The observatory on top is popular with tourists.

MEXICO, D.F.
HOTEL
PLAZA
REFORMA

A unos pasos del Paseo de la Reforma, en el corazón del área comercial y turística más importante de la Ciudad de México, se yergue majestuosamente el HOTEL PLAZA REFORMA "El Hotel con sabor Europeo"

"El Hotel cuenta con 102 habitaciones y suites, todas orientadas hacia el Paseo de la Reforma.

Salones para banquetes y convenciones con capacidad hasta 400 personas; agencia de viajes, tabaquería, alberca y televisión a color.

También podrá disfrutar en nuestro Restaurant de la exquisita comida mexicana e internacional o descansar mientras toma una copa en nuestro Bar.

Venga a visitarnos y haga del HOTEL PLAZA REFORMA "su casa en la Ciudad de México"

FUNCIONES Y ACTIVIDADES

In this chapter, you have seen examples of some important language functions, or uses. Here is a summary and some additional information about these functions of language.

Asking for directions

The ability to ask for and understand directions is one of the most important language functions you will need when traveling in a Spanish-speaking country. Here are some ways to ask for directions.

¿Dónde está...?	*Where is . . . ?*
Busco la calle...	*I'm looking for . . . Street.*
¿Hay un correo (una estación de autobuses) cerca de aquí?	*Is there a post office (a bus station) near here?*
Por favor, señor(-a), ¿está lejos (está cerca) el mercado?	*Please, sir (ma'am), is the marketplace far away (nearby)?*
¿Cuál es la dirección de...?	*What's the address of . . . ?*
¿Me puede decir cómo llegar a...?	*Can you tell me how to get to . . . ?*
¿Por dónde va uno a...?	*How do you get to . . . ?*

Understanding directions

Here are some responses you may hear when you ask for directions.

Siga por la calle...	*Follow . . . Street.*
Doble a la izquierda (derecha).	*Turn left (right).*
Siga adelante (derecho).	*Keep going straight.*
Vaya derecho hasta llegar a...	*Go straight until you get to . . .*
Sígame hasta llegar a...	*Follow me until you get to . . .*
Camine dos cuadras hasta llegar a...	*Walk two blocks until you arrive at . . .*
Cruce la calle y...	*Cross the street and . . .*
Está al lado de...	*It's next to . . .*
Está al norte (sur, este, oeste) de...	*It's north (south, east, west) of . . .*
Está en la esquina de...	*It's on the corner of . . .*
Está en el centro.	*It's downtown.*
Después de pasar por..., está...	*After you pass . . . , it's . . .*

Getting someone's attention

One way to get attention is to simply say. **¡Oiga, señor (señora, señorita)! Oiga** is a word that never fails to get people to lend an ear. **Perdón, perdóneme,** or **discúlpeme** are also often used and are more polite.

A. ¿Por dónde va uno para llegar a...? In pairs, ask and tell each other how to get from class to each of the following places:

1. un buen restaurante
2. un parque o un lugar bonito para dar un paseo
3. un sitio de interés que a usted le gusta visitar

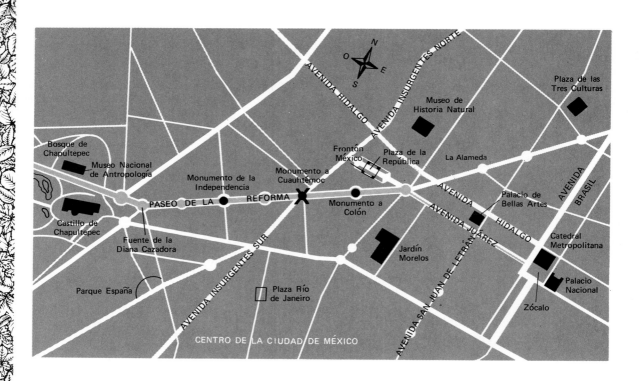

B. En la ciudad de México. You are in Mexico City, at the intersection of Avenida Insurgentes and Paseo de la Reforma. If you followed these directions, where would you be? (Begin each time from Insurgentes and Paseo de la Reforma.) The answers are on page 259.

Modelo Tome la Avenida Insurgentes Norte hasta llegar a la Avenida Hidalgo. Doble a la derecha. Siga derecho hasta la Avenida San Juan De Letrán y doble a la derecha. Camine media cuadra y lo va a ver a su derecha.
el Palacio de Bellas Artes

1. Vaya derecho por Paseo de la Reforma hasta llegar a la Fuente de la Diana Cazadora. Allí no vaya derecho. Usted va a entrar al Parque de Chapultepec, pero siga por Paseo de la Reforma hasta llegar a un gran edificio a su derecha.

2. Tome Paseo de la Reforma hacia el Monumento a Colón y vaya hasta la Avenida Juárez. Doble a la derecha. Cruce las Avenidas San Juan De Letrán y Brasil. Siga adelante. Es una gran plaza que va a ver enfrente de usted.

3. Tome Paseo de la Reforma hasta llegar a la Avenida Juárez. Doble a la izquierda. Está en la Plaza de la República.

4. Tome Insurgentes Norte hasta la Avenida Hidalgo. Doble a la derecha. Cruce las Avenidas San Juan De Letrán y Brasil. Está en la esquina de Hidalgo y Brasil.

C. **¿Qué hace el (la) turista experimentado(-a)** (*experienced*)? Eduardo has not traveled very much and asks his friend Ana, an experienced traveler, about the most important rules for traveling. Formulate six rules (using the **tú** command form, negative and affirmative) that Ana might give to Eduardo.

Modelo   **No dejes las cosas para último momento. Compra los boletos temprano.**

El (la) turista experimentado(-a)

1. Hace la maleta varios días antes de viajar. Nunca lleva mucho equipaje; prefiere llevar una sola maleta.

2. Llega temprano al aeropuerto, al puerto o a la estación de trenes. No llega tarde nunca.

3. Lee varios libros sobre el país donde va a viajar. También consulta mapas de las diferentes ciudades y regiones.

4. Siempre recuerda las tres cosas más importantes: los boletos (pasajes), el dinero (o cheques de viajero) y el pasaporte.

5. Pide información sobre los precios de los cuartos antes de quedarse en un hotel.

D. Un viaje imaginario. One student should begin by saying the following phrase: **Mañana me voy de viaje. Llevo... mi pasaporte.** The next student should repeat the phrase and add another object; for example: **Mañana me voy de viaje. Llevo mi pasaporte y una raqueta de tenis.** The game continues until someone can't remember all the objects or makes a grammar mistake. Then the game begins again.

VOCABULARIO ACTIVO

Cognados

la compañía	el estadio	la parte	el taxi
el cheque	fascinante	puntual	uruguayo
la estación	el mapa	la ruina	

Verbos

calmar	to calm
calmarse	to calm down, be calm
cambiar	to change, exchange
caminar	to walk
contar (ue)	to tell; to count
cruzar	to cross
doblar	to turn
insistir (en)	to insist (on)
parar	to stop
perdonar	to forgive, pardon
preocuparse (de)	to worry (about)
subir	to climb, go up
subir a	to get on

Viajes y paseos

adelante	straight, straight ahead
la aduana	customs; customs house
a tiempo	on time
el barco	ship, boat
la bienvenida	welcome
darle la bienvenida a alguien	to welcome someone
el boleto	ticket
de ida y vuelta	round-trip
el correo	post office; mail
la cuadra	(city) block
el cheque de viajero	traveler's check
derecho (adv.)	straight, straight ahead
el equipaje	luggage
la esquina	corner
el mercado	market
el negocio	business
el viaje de negocios	business trip
alguna parte (ninguna parte)	somewhere (nowhere)
el pasaje	ticket; fare
el paseo	outing
el puerto	port
el sitio	place
sitio de interés	point (site) of interest
el viajero (la viajera)	traveler
el zoológico	zoo

Otras palabras y frases

antiguo	ancient; (before a noun) former
en medio de	in the middle of
en seguida	at once, immediately
extraño	strange
la juguetería	toy store
la suerte	luck

Expresiones útiles

Camine dos cuadras... — *Walk two blocks . . .*

¿Cuál es la dirección de...? — *What's the address of . . . ?*

Doble a la izquierda (derecha). — *Turn left (right).*

Está al norte (sur, este, oeste) de... — *It's north (south, east, west) of . . .*

Oiga, señor(-a)... — *Excuse me, sir (madam) . . . (literally, "Listen, sir (madam) . . .")*

¿Por dónde va uno a...? — *How do you get to . . . ?*

Siga adelante (derecho). — *Keep going straight.*

Vaya derecho hasta llegar a... — *Go straight until you get to . . .*

Respuestas, Ejercicio B, página 256.

1. el Museo Nacional de Antropología
2. el Zócalo
3. el Frontón México
4. la Catedral Metropolitana

No a la
censura

Paz,
pan y
libertad

Preferencias y opiniones

12

Expressing Agreement
Expressing Disagreement

EJERCICIO

Choose the word that does not belong.

1. escritor, autora, pintor, escuela
2. cuento, cuadro, pintura, retrato
3. revista, teatro, periódico, novela
4. pintar, escribir, leer, dormir
5. censura (*censorship*), literatura, cine, pan

PREGUNTAS

1. ¿Adónde quiere ir hoy Eduardo?   **2.** ¿Qué prefiere hacer Blanca?   **3.** ¿A usted le gusta ir al teatro? ¿Le gusta leer obras de teatro?   **4.** ¿Prefiere usted leer cuentos o novelas?   **5.** ¿Cuál es su autor(-a) favorito(-a)?, ¿su novela o cuento favorito? **6.** ¿Lee usted el periódico todos los días? ¿Lee revistas? ¿Cuáles? **7.** ¿Le gusta escribir? ¿Le gusta pintar? ¿Qué le gusta hacer en sus ratos libres (*free time*)?   **8.** ¿Le gustan los cuadros realistas o prefiere el arte abstracto? ¿Cuál es su pintor(-a) favorito(-a)?   **9.** ¿A usted le interesa la política (*politics*)? ¿Va a manifestaciones políticas? ¿Por qué sí o por qué no?

The impersonal *se* and passive *se*

En un pueblo de Guatemala.

CINDY ¿Es verdad que en este país no *se abren* los negocios entre el mediodía y las tres?

MARTA Pues, eso depende... En general, en los pueblos todavía *se cierran* los negocios durante esas horas, pero en las ciudades más grandes ya prácticamente *se perdió* esa costumbre.

CINDY ¿Y cómo *se explica* ese cambio? Yo pienso que *se trabaja* mejor después de una buena siesta, ¿no lo crees?

MARTA Por supuesto que sí, pero *se dice* que con el horario de nueve a cinco *se puede* conservar energía, especialmente en el invierno.

CINDY ¿Y tú estás de acuerdo con eso?

MARTA Teóricamente sí, pero en la práctica, de ninguna manera. Si a mí no me permiten dormir la siesta, ¡creo que me muero!

CINDY ¿En serio? Entonces, ¡hoy te mueres!... porque vi que en la Librería Báez *se venden* libros en inglés. ¿Me acompañas a comprar dos o tres?

MARTA Sí, claro, pero después de las tres. Es que allí todavía *se respeta* la siesta hispana. ¡Esa librería es de mis padres, Cindy!

---

1. En general, ¿se cierran los negocios a la hora de la siesta en el pueblo donde vive Marta?   2. ¿Cree Cindy que es mejor olvidar (*to forget*) la siesta y trabajar de nueve a cinco? ¿Por qué?   3. Según Marta, ¿cómo se explica este cambio de horario? ¿Está ella de acuerdo con ese nuevo horario? ¿Por qué?   4. ¿En qué librería se venden libros en inglés? ¿Por qué no se puede comprar nada allí antes de las tres? ¿De quién es la Librería Báez?   5. ¿Qué piensa usted de la costumbre de dormir la siesta? ¿Cree, como Cindy, que se trabaja mejor después de una buena siesta? ¿Por qué sí o por qué no?

In a town in Guatemala. CINDY: Is it true that in this country businesses aren't open between noon and three? MARTA: Well, that depends ... In general, in the towns businesses are still closed during those hours, but in the bigger cities that custom is practically lost by now. CINDY: And how can that change be explained? I think that one works better after a good siesta, don't you? MARTA: Of course I do, but they say that with the nine-to-five schedule it is possible to conserve energy, especially in the winter. CINDY: And you agree with that? MARTA: In theory yes, but in practice, by no means (no way). If I am not allowed to have my siesta, I believe I'll die! CINDY: Really? Then you're dying today! ... because I saw that at the Báez Bookstore they sell books in English. Will you come with me to buy two or three? MARTA: Yes, of course, but after three. There they still honor the Hispanic siesta. That bookstore belongs to my parents, Cindy!

A. The pronoun **se** followed by a verb in the third-person singular is a construction frequently used when it is not important to express or identify the agent or doer of an action. This use of **se** is often translated in English with *one, people, we, you, they,* or a passive construction. It is known as the impersonal **se**.

Se cree que el estilo de escultura de Picasso era único.	*It's believed (People believe) that Picasso's style of sculpture was unique.*
Se dice que la obra más importante de García Márquez es su novela *Cien años de soledad*.	*People say that García Márquez's most important work is his novel* One Hundred Years of Solitude.
¿Cómo se vive allí? —Se vive bien: se come mucho y se trabaja poco.	*How does one live there? —One (Everybody) lives well: you (people) eat a lot and don't work much (work little).*

B. When there is a grammatical subject, **se** is followed by a verb that agrees with the subject—either third-person singular or plural. This construction is called the passive **se**, since it is often used instead of the true passive when the agent is not expressed.

¿Se vende ese retrato?	*Is that portrait being sold?*
¿Se venden esos retratos?	*Are those portraits being sold?*
Se necesita maestro(-a) bilingüe.	*A bilingual teacher is needed.*
Se necesitan maestros y escritores bilingües.	*Bilingual teachers and writers are needed.*
Se trajo el cuadro aquí ayer.	*The painting was brought here yesterday.*
Se trajeron los cuadros aquí ayer.	*The paintings were brought here yesterday.*
Aquí se estudia francés en la escuela secundaria.	*French is studied in high school here.*
Aquí se estudian lenguas en la escuela secundaria.	*Languages are studied in high school here.*

EJERCICIOS

A. **¿Qué se hace aquí?** Susan Johnson is spending a few months in Guatemala as an exchange student. After a month there, she still has many questions for Gloria, her Guatemalan "sister." Using an expression with **se**, answer Susan's questions in the affirmative or negative, as Gloria would.

Modelos ¿Estudian aquí lenguas en la escuela secundaria? (sí)
Sí, aquí se estudian lenguas en la escuela secundaria.

¿Enseñan arte en la universidad? (no)
No, aquí no se enseña arte en la universidad.

1. ¿Van aquí mucho a las montañas en las vacaciones? (sí)
2. ¿Pagan aquí para asistir a la universidad? (no)
3. ¿Ven aquí películas norteamericanas? (sí)
4. ¿Practican aquí tantos deportes como en los Estados Unidos? (no)
5. ¿Juegan aquí mucho al fútbol? (sí)
6. ¿Leen aquí literatura inglesa en la escuela secundaria? (sí)

7. ¿Siguen aquí el sistema de semestres? (no)
8. ¿Presentan aquí muchas obras de teatro en la universidad? (sí)
9. ¿Traen aquí mucho café de los Estados Unidos? (no)

B. Otra época, otro mundo. Imagine that you live in a completely different time and/or world where things are done in an unusual way. Using the impersonal **se**, mention some things that are done differently.

Modelos **Se come sólo una vez cada 24 horas.**
Se cree que es malo comer más.
No se toman bebidas alcohólicas.
Se duerme de día y se trabaja de noche.

C. Traducción. Give the Spanish equivalent of the following sentences.

1. Spanish is spoken here.
2. They don't sell novels in that store.
3. Wine is not served there.
4. Spanish writers needed.
5. They say that German is very difficult.
6. It is believed that *Don Quixote* is the first modern novel.
7. One learns a lot in this class.
8. People drink good coffee and eat very well here.

[handwritten margin notes: No se venden novelas en esa tienda / No se sirva / Se recisitan escritores español]

PREGUNTAS

1. ¿Sabe usted cómo se dice «Good-bye» en español? ¿en francés? ¿en japonés? ¿en alemán?   **2.** ¿Qué lenguas se enseñan en esta universidad?   **3.** ¿Se venden novelas o cuentos en español en la librería universitaria? ¿Y en otras librerías? ¿Dónde? **4.** ¿Qué se necesita, además de tiempo y dinero, para viajar a otro país? ¿Cree usted que se necesita hablar la lengua del país que se visita? ¿Por qué?   **5.** ¿Se traen películas españolas o hispanoamericanas aquí? ¿En qué cine se las puede ver? **6.** ¿Se presentan obras de teatro en español en esta universidad? ¿en algún teatro de esta ciudad?   **7.** ¿Se puede ver algún programa de televisión en español aquí? ¿Qué programa(-s)?

The past participle used as an adjective

La biblioteca está *abierta* ahora.

Los bancos están *cerrados*.

En esta librería se venden libros *usados*.

En esta casa de música se venden guitarras *hechas* en México.

A. To form the past participle of regular **-ar** verbs, add **-ado** to the stem of the infinitive. For **-er** and **-ir** verbs, add **-ido**.

hablado	*spoken*
comido	*eaten*
vivido	*lived*

If the stem of an **-er** or **-ir** verb ends in **a**, **e**, or **o**, the **-ido** ending takes an accent.

traído	*brought*
creído	*believed*
oído	*heard*

B. Some irregular past participles are:

abrir	**abierto**	*open, opened*
cubrir*	**cubierto**	*covered*
describir	**descrito**	*described*
descubrir	**descubierto**	*discovered*
decir	**dicho**	*said*
escribir	**escrito**	*written*
hacer	**hecho**	*made, done*
morir	**muerto**	*died, dead*
poner	**puesto**	*put*
resolver	**resuelto**	*solved*
romper	**roto**	*broken*
ver	**visto**	*seen*
volver	**vuelto**	*returned*

C. The past participle is often used as an adjective, in which case it agrees in number and gender with the noun it modifies. It is often used with **estar**, frequently to describe a condition or state that results from an action.

¿El poema está escrito en español? —Correcto.	*The poem is written in Spanish? —Right.*
Los cuadros pintados en México y las tazas hechas en el Japón son de la señora Ordóñez.	*The pictures painted in Mexico and the cups made in Japan are Mrs. Ordóñez's.*
El problema está resuelto.	*The problem is solved.*
En el invierno las montañas están cubiertas de nieve.	*In the winter the mountains are covered with snow.*
Estamos muy ocupados ahora; en cambio, ellos no tienen mucho que hacer.	*We're very busy now; on the other hand, they don't have much to do.*

EJERCICIOS

A. La casa de los Botero. The Boteros like to travel and bring many things back with them to Guatemala. Using the elements given, describe what they have brought back, following the models. (Pay close attention to the forms of the past participles.)

Modelos tazas / comprar / en Colombia
tazas compradas en Colombia

una guitarra / hacer / en España
una guitarra hecha en España

1. dos sombreros / traer / de Panamá
2. un bolso / hacer / en Argentina

*** Cubrir** (*to cover*) is conjugated like **descubrir**.

3. varias maletas / comprar / en Chile
4. una foto de Pancho Villa / sacar / hace mucho tiempo
5. libros / escribir / en inglés, francés y alemán
6. un cuadro de Picasso / pintar / en 1924
7. zapatos / hacer / en Italia
8. joyas / traer / de Toledo
9. una escultura antigua / encontrar / en México

B. Sí, ya está hecho. Mrs. Ibáñez is asking her husband, Ricardo, if he has done certain things. Answer her questions in the affirmative, as Ricardo would.

Modelo ¿Abriste las ventanas?
  Sí, las ventanas ya están abiertas.

1. ¿Lavaste el auto?   4. ¿Resolviste el problema?
2. ¿Pusiste la mesa?   5. ¿Hiciste los ejercicios?
3. ¿Escribiste las cartas?   6. ¿Pagaste la cuenta?

C. ¡Un crimen en la casa de los Solís! A murder has just been discovered at the home of Mr. and Mrs. Solís. After examining the house, detective Rocha solves the crime. Discover who the murderer is by filling in the blanks with the appropriate past participle forms of the verbs in parentheses.

Modelo El detective Rocha vio muchas cosas ___*rotas*___ (romper) en el cuarto.

La mesa ya estaba (1) _____ (poner) y allí había cosas muy caras, (2) _____ (comprar) en Francia. Rocha vio que los Solís eran gente rica. Tenían obras de arte (3) _____ (pintar) por Picasso, varias cosas bonitas (4) _____ (traer) de Europa y unos libros (5) _____ (escribir) en el siglo XVI. Pero... allí también había una persona (6) _____ (morir). Era el señor Solís y tenía las manos muy (7) _____ (cerrar). En la mano derecha tenía un papel. Era una carta (8) _____ (escribir) por una mujer (9) _____ (llamar) Carolina. La carta decía: «(10) _____ (querer) amor: Tu esposa lo sabe todo. Hay que tener mucho cuidado... Te besa, Carolina.» Rocha descubrió que en la mano izquierda, también (11) _____ (cerrar), el señor Solís tenía un botón verde y observó que su camisa estaba (12) _____ (cubrir) de sangre (*blood*). Después Rocha fue a la sala y allí encontró a la señora Solís, (13) _____ (vestir) de verde y (14) _____ (sentar) en el sofá. Parecía (15) _____ (dormir) pero estaba (16) _____ (morir). Rocha dijo: «El misterio está (17) _____ (resolver).» ¿Qué vio el detective en la sala? Había un bolso (18) _____ (abrir) al lado de la señora Solís. También en el sofá había una botella (*bottle*) de píldoras (*pills*) para dormir, totalmente vacía (*empty*). En la mano derecha de la señora había un cuchillo (19) _____ (cubrir) de sangre.

Now answer the following questions.

1. ¿Cómo estaba la mesa? **2.** ¿Qué clase de obras de arte tenían los Solís? **3.** ¿Qué tenía en la mano derecha el señor Solís? ¿Y en la izquierda? ¿Cómo estaban sus manos? **4.** ¿Cómo estaba la camisa del señor Solís? **5.** ¿De qué color estaba vestida la señora Solís? **6.** ¿Dormía o descansaba la señora Solís? ¿Cómo estaba ella? **7.** ¿En qué condición estaba el cuchillo? **8.** ¿Quién fue el asesino (*murderer*)?

PREGUNTAS

1. ¿Está usted inspirado(-a) en este momento? ¿cansado(-a) ¿preocupado(-a)? ¿Por qué? **2.** ¿Está usted sentado(-a) cerca de la ventana? ¿de la puerta? ¿del (de la) profesor(-a)? **3.** ¿Tiene usted el libro de español abierto o cerrado ahora? **4.** ¿Vio usted alguna vez un cuadro pintado por Picasso? ¿por Velázquez? ¿por El Greco? ¿por algún otro pintor español conocido (famoso)? ¿Qué cuadro(-s)? **5.** ¿Leyó cuentos escritos por Edgar Allan Poe? ¿Leyó alguna novela escrita por Ernest Hemingway? ¿William Faulkner? ¿Emily Brontë? ¿H. G. Wells? ¿Virginia Woolf? ¿Ray Bradbury? ¿Isaac Asimov? ¿Anne Tyler? ¿Cuál(-es)? ¿Qué piensa de esas obras?

The present and past perfect tenses

PRIMER SEÑOR	Perdone, señor. ¿*Ha visto* usted a algún policía por esta calle?
SEGUNDO SEÑOR	Por aquí, no, pero me *he encontrado* con unos policías enfrente del Teatro de Comedias.
PRIMER SEÑOR	¿No *ha visto* a nadie por aquí?
SEGUNDO SEÑOR	No, antes de encontrarme con usted, no *había visto* a nadie.
PRIMER SEÑOR	Entonces, ¡arriba las manos!

1. ¿Ha visto el señor a algún policía por la calle?   2. ¿Y enfrente del Teatro de Comedias?   3. ¿Se ha encontrado con alguien?   4. ¿Qué le dice el bandido después de todas las preguntas?

FIRST GENTLEMAN: Excuse me, sir. Have you seen a policeman on this street? SECOND GENTLEMAN: Not around here, but I came across (met) a few policemen in front of the Comedy Theater. FIRST GENTLEMAN: You haven't seen anyone around here? SECOND GENTLEMAN: No, before meeting you I hadn't seen anyone. FIRST GENTLEMAN: Then, hands up!

A. The present perfect tense is formed with the present tense of the auxiliary verb **haber** + a past participle.

haber *(to have)*		
he	hemos	
has	habéis	} + past participle
ha	han	

It is used to report an action or event that has recently taken place or been completed and still has a bearing upon the present. It is generally used without reference to any specific time in the past (that is, without words such as **ayer**, **la semana pasada**, etc.), since it implies a reference to the present day, week, month, etc.

La obra de ese pintor ha sido muy admirada recientemente.

That painter's work has been much admired recently.

¿Carlos e Inés ya han hablado contigo?* —Al contrario, no me han dicho nada.

Carlos and Inés have already spoken with you? —On the contrary, they haven't said anything to me.

A pesar de que Julio escribe poesía constantemente, no ha escrito un solo poema bueno.

In spite of the fact that Julio writes poetry constantly, he hasn't written a single good poem.

¿Te ha gustado la comida? —Sí, ¡por supuesto!

Have you enjoyed the food? —Yes, of course!

Felipe dice que la censura de los periódicos aquí ha sido una cosa buena. —¡Qué tontería!

Felipe says that censorship of the newspapers here has been a good thing. —What nonsense!

The past participle always ends in **-o** when used to form a perfect tense; it does *not* agree with the subject in gender or number.

B. The past perfect tense is formed with the imperfect of **haber** + a past participle.

haber		
había	habíamos	
habías	habíais	} + past participle
había	habían	

It is used to indicate that an action or event had taken place at some time in the past prior to another past event, stated or implied. If the other past event is stated, it is usually in the preterit or imperfect.

---

*The conjunction **y** becomes **e** before **i** or **hi**: **francés e inglés, Roberto e Hilda.**

| Leí que un escritor peruano había ganado el primer premio. | I read that a Peruvian writer had won first prize. |
| Ya había salido para la manifestación cuando yo llegué. —¿Quién? ¿José u Olga?* | He (She) had already left for the demonstration when I arrived. —Who? José or Olga? |

C. The auxiliary form of **haber** and the past participle are seldom separated by another word. Negative words and pronouns normally precede the auxiliary verb.

No he recibido el retrato.	I haven't received the portrait.
¿Ya me has enviado el cuento?	Have you already sent me the story?
No, no te lo he enviado todavía.	No, I haven't sent it to you yet.

EJERCICIOS

A. ¡Hemos tenido mucha suerte! Mrs. Díaz is telling her husband how happy she is because of the many good things that have happened to them recently. Complete the sentences with the present perfect forms of the verbs in parentheses, and you'll see why she is so happy.

Modelo (encontrar) Sonia __*ha encontrado*__ un buen trabajo.

1. (sacar) Los niños _____ muy buenas notas.
2. (ganar) Tú _____ más dinero que nunca (*than ever*).
3. (escribir) Yo _____ una novela muy leída.
4. (pintar) Nuestra hija _____ sus mejores cuadros.
5. (hacer) Tú y yo _____ muchos viajes.
6. (casarse) Pedro _____ con una muchacha muy simpática. *[se ha casado]*
7. (resolver) Carlos y Marisa _____ muchos de sus problemas.
8. (pedir) ¡Y nadie nos _____ dinero!

B. Completar las frases. Complete the sentences with the past perfect forms of the verbs in parentheses.

Modelo (leer) Conocía el cuento porque lo __*había leído*__ en una antología.

1. (cenar) Ellos ya _____ cuando llegué.
2. (llamar) Roberto me dijo que tú _____.
3. (romper) Carlitos confesó que fue él quien _____ esa puerta.
4. (vender) No sabía que tus padres _____ su casa.
5. (ser) Tina me contó que tú y ella _____ novios antes.
6. (levantarse) Tú ya _____ cuando Rita te llamó, ¿no? *[te habías levantado]*
7. (acostarse) ¿Creías que yo _____ tan temprano? *[me había levantado]*
8. (traer) Susana me contó que usted _____ un postre muy rico.

* The conjunction **o** becomes **u** before **o** or **ho**: José u Olga, mujer u hombre.

C. **En acción.** What have these people been doing recently? Describe each one of the following drawings

Modelo

Los novios se han casado.

1.

2.

Juan ha dormido

3.

4.

El se ha bañado

5.

Ellas Han comido

6.

Se Ha lavados su coche

7.

8.

D. **¿Alguna vez...?**   In pairs, ask and answer questions about things you have done. Use the cues below and ideas of your own.

> Modelo   **ir a España**
> Estudiante 1:   **¿Has ido a España alguna vez?**
> Estudiante 2:   **Sí, fui a Madrid en 1985 y pienso pasar allí mis próximas vacaciones.** (or: **No, nunca he ido a España pero tengo ganas de estudiar allí el próximo semestre.**)

1. conducir (manejar) un Porsche
2. viajar en barco (helicóptero, tren, motocicleta)
3. comer caracoles (*snails*)
4. quedarse en un hotel muy elegante (primitivo)
5. hacer auto-stop (*hitch-hike*)
6. vivir en otro país
7. nadar en el Pacífico (Atlántico)
8. ver a un(-a) autor(-a) (actor, actriz, persona) famoso(-a), etc.

E. **Antes de Año Nuevo...**   In pairs, try to find out at least three things your partner had done or accomplishments he or she had made by December 31 of last year.

> Modelo   Estudiante 1:   **¿Habías leído algún cuento en español antes de fin de año?**
> Estudiante 2:   **Sí, había leído dos cuentos de Juan Rulfo, un escritor mexicano.**
> Estudiante 1:   **¿Y habías hecho algún viaje interesante o visitado algún lugar exótico...?**
> Estudiante 2:   **Sí, en julio del año pasado había viajado a Guatemala y había estado en varios pueblos indígenas. No sé si se los puede llamar «exóticos» pero sí sé que son ¡interesantísimos! Y tú, ¿qué tres cosas habías hecho (visto, visitado, etc.) antes del primero de enero de este año...?**
> Estudiante 1:   **Pues..., yo había...**

PREGUNTAS

1. ¿Qué ha hecho usted esta mañana? ¿Ha hecho algo interesante? ¿bueno? ¿malo? ¿original?   **2.** ¿Ha ido al cine recientemente? ¿Qué película(-s) ha visto? ¿Le ha(-n) gustado? ¿Por qué?   **3.** ¿Ha visitado algún museo en los últimos dos meses? ¿Cuál? ¿Había estado allí antes? ¿Cuándo?   **4.** ¿Ha ido a Europa este verano? ¿Había estado allí antes? ¿Cuándo?   **5.** ¿Ha perdido algo importante recientemente? ¿Qué ha perdido?   **6.** ¿Ha encontrado algo de mucho valor? ¿trabajo? ¿amor? ¿dinero en la calle?   **7.** ¿Ha sacado una buena nota en su último examen de español? ¿Había sacado una nota peor o mejor antes?

Guatemala: Ideas en transición

Arquitectura colonial, en la Ciudad de Guatemala

Don Pepe, un guatemalteco° que vive en la capital,[1] *recibe en su casa a unos amigos de los Estados Unidos: Lesley, fotógrafa y su esposo Alan, profesor de historia en St. Anselm College.*

DON PEPE Siéntense, por favor. ¿Tienen hambre?

ALAN No, ya hemos comido, gracias.

DON PEPE Así que han estado en Tikal.[2] ¿Qué tal el viaje?

LESLEY ¡Estupendo! ¡Las pirámides° son magníficas! Saqué unas fotos estupendas...

ALAN ...que probablemente las voy a usar en mi libro sobre esas pirámides. Dicen que los mayas las abandonaron. ¿Sabe usted por qué?

DON PEPE No, eso es un misterio.° No lo sabe nadie.

LESLEY Pasamos la Semana Santa° en un pueblo pequeño y allí vimos las ceremonias° del Maximón.[3] Yo había estado allí antes, pero en agosto. Es una costumbre realmente fascinante.

ALAN Es cierto. Una extraña combinación de elementos paganos° y cristianos.

DON PEPE	Exacto. Los indios creen en el Dios cristiano y en los ídolos° antiguos al mismo tiempo. Pero eso no significa para ellos ninguna contradicción.
ALAN	Son muy supersticiosos, ¿no? En el mundo moderno la religión casi ya no es necesaria...
DON PEPE	Eso depende de la cultura. Los indios siempre han encontrado un gran consuelo° en la religión.
LESLEY	¿Y los ladinos?[4]
DON PEPE	La Iglesia Católica es muy importante para ellos, sobre todo en la educación moral de los hijos.
LESLEY	Pero la Iglesia prohíbe el divorcio, el aborto°, el control de la natalidad°... Personalmente, creo que ha hecho mal° en prohibir todo eso.
DON PEPE	En cambio, yo creo que ha hecho bien... Pero sé que en estas cuestiones no vamos a ponernos de acuerdo. Tengo amigos que piensan como ustedes.
ALAN	Y nosotros tenemos muchos amigos que piensan como usted.
DON PEPE	¡Qué bien! ¡Viva la democracia°! Y ahora vamos a brindar° por la libertad de expresión con una taza de café guatemalteco, ¡el mejor del mundo!
LESLEY	Pues..., ¡en eso sí todos estamos de acuerdo!

guatemalteco *de Guatemala*   **pirámides** *pyramids*   **misterio** *mystery*
Semana Santa *Holy Week*   **ceremonias** *ceremonies*   **paganos** *pagans*
ídolos *idols*   **consuelo** *consolation*   **aborto** *abortion*
natalidad *birth*   **ha hecho mal** *has been* (literally, ''done'') *wrong*
¡Viva la democracia! *Long live (hurray for) democracy!*   **brindar** *to make a toast*

PREGUNTAS

1. ¿Han estado en Tikal Alan y Lesley? ¿Les gustó?   **2.** ¿Quién sacó fotos estupendas de las pirámides? ¿Cómo piensa usar esas fotos Alan?   **3.** ¿Por qué abandonaron Tikal los mayas?   **4.** ¿Qué vieron Alan y Lesley en un pueblo pequeño durante la Semana Santa?   **5.** ¿En qué creen los indios?   **6.** Según su opinión, ¿es importante la religión para Alan y Lesley?   **7.** Según don Pepe, qué encuentran los indios en la religión?   **8.** ¿Están de acuerdo don Pepe y sus amigos Alan y Lesley con respecto al divorcio y al aborto?   **9.** ¿Piensa usted como don Pepe o como Alan y Lesley?   **10.** ¿Por qué quiere brindar don Pepe? ¿Con qué?

Notas culturales

1. Founded in 1775, Guatemala City is the largest city in Central America and the political, cultural, and economic heart of Guatemala. Destroyed by earthquakes in 1917 and 1918, it was largely rebuilt. There was another serious earthquake in 1976.

2. Tikal is a partially restored ancient Maya city in the Petén, the northern jungle area of Guatemala. It flourished until around A.D. 900, when, like other great Maya cities, it was abandoned for unknown reasons. Archeologists have mapped over 3,000 structures there, plus 10,000 earlier foundations beneath the structures that survived. They have also discovered over 250 stone monuments and countless art treasures. At its peak, Tikal may have covered 25 square miles, with houses of stone and plaster surrounding the ceremonial center, which contained pyramids, palaces, plazas, and shrines.

3. The **Maximón** is an idol honored during Holy Week by the Mayas of the village of Santiago Atitlán. It is composed of many layers of clothing bundled around a mysterious core, which may be a Maya statue; its face in public is a wooden mask that always appears with a large cigar in its mouth. A special brotherhood is responsible for keeping the **Maximón**, dressing it, and officiating at various ceremonies to honor it. Though prayers and gifts are offered to it, **Maximón** is publicly hanged at the height of the celebration. Later it is brought down and hidden until the next year. Some think there may be a connection between the **Maximón** and the effigies of Judas, Christ's betrayer, that are hung in many towns of Guatemala during Holy Week, except that the **Maximón** is the object of devotion, not derision. Only the members of the Indian brotherhood know the true contents and significance of the draped figure, but it is thought to have derived from ancient Maya religious practices.

4. **Ladino** is the term used to designate those Guatemalans who are European in culture and usually of mixed Spanish-Indian ancestry, as opposed to the pure-blood Indians who speak Quiché or other Indian languages. The distinction is much more cultural than racial, for an Indian becomes a **ladino** by learning to speak Spanish and adopting European dress and customs.

FUNCIONES Y ACTIVIDADES

In this chapter, you have seen examples of some important language functions, or uses. Here is a summary and some additional information about these functions of language.

Expressing agreement

Here are some ways to indicate agreement.

Exacto.	*Exactly.*
Claro. (Seguro. Por supuesto. Naturalmente.)	*Certainly. (Sure. Of course. Naturally.)*
Eso es.	*That's it.*
Sí, ¡cómo no!	*Yes, of course!*
Sí, tiene(-s) razón.	*Yes, you're right.*
Sí, así es.	*Yes, that's so.*
Estoy de acuerdo.	*I agree.*
Sí, es verdad.	*Yes, it's (that's) true.*
Así pienso.	*That's how I think.*
¡Ya lo creo!	*I believe it!*
Probablemente sí. (Es probable que sí.)	*Probably. (Probably so.)*
Correcto.	*Right. (Correct.)*

Expressing disagreement

Here are some ways to indicate disagreement.

No, no es verdad.	*No, it's (that's) not true.*
No, no estoy de acuerdo.	*No, I don't agree.*
No, no es así.	*No, it's not so.*
Probablemente no. (Es probable que no.)	*Probably not.*
Pero en cambio...	*But on the other hand . . .*
¡Qué tontería!	*What nonsense!*
¡Qué absurdo (ridículo)!	*How absurd (ridiculous)!*
Al contrario...	*On the contrary . . .*
No, no tienes razón.	*No, you're not right.*
¡Qué va!	*Oh, come on!*

You can use the following expressions to disagree with a suggestion that you or someone else do something.

¡Ni por todo el dinero del mundo!	*Not for all the money in the world!*
¡Ni hablar!	*Don't even mention it!*
¡De ninguna manera!	*No way!*

A. ¿Qué piensas?   Working with a partner, take turns reading and responding to each of the following statements. One of you reads the statement, and the other reacts with an expression of agreement or disagreement.

Modelo   Estudiante 1:   **Hoy día el arte está muy comercializado.**
         Estudiante 2:   **Estoy totalmente de acuerdo contigo.**

1. El escritor más importante de la historia fue Edgar Guest.
2. Gabriel García Márquez es un famoso escritor colombiano.
3. La música clásica es muy aburrida.
4. La música de Mozart es muy hermosa.
5. En esta ciudad siempre hace muy buen tiempo en enero.
6. La primavera es la estación más linda del año.
7. El sistema de notas de esta universidad es perfecto.
8. Es mejor vivir solo(-a) que en una residencia estudiantil (*dorm*).
9. Como ahora existe la fotografía, el realismo en el arte ya no es importante.
10. El aborto (*abortion*) debe ser ilegal.

B. Al contrario...   Work with a partner. One of you makes at least five statements of opinion. The other plays "devil's advocate" and disagrees, making a contradictory statement. Try to use as many expressions of disagreement as possible.

Modelo   Estudiante 1:   **La comida de la cafetería de la universidad es excelente.**
         Estudiante 2:   **Al contrario, ¡es horrible!**

You may choose your own topics or choose from among the following.

1. los exámenes de la clase de español
2. el control de los revólveres y de las pistolas
3. el arte surrealista
4. el equipo de fútbol de la universidad
5. las clases de matemáticas (de historia, etcétera)
6. los lunes por la mañana / los sábados por la noche
7. el verano / las vacaciones
8. el uso de drogas como la marijuana o la cocaína
9. las leyes sobre la edad de tomar bebidas alcohólicas / votar
10. el transporte público en su área
11. las novelas de... (su escritor favorito)
12. la película... (nombre de una película), que es realmente artística

VOCABULARIO ACTIVO

Cognados

abstracto	el autor, la autora	el fotógrafo, la fotógrafa	la novela
la antología	la escultura		el pintor, la pintora
el, la artista	el estilo	magnífico	secundario

Verbos

cubrir	to cover
describir	to describe
enviar	to send
olvidar	to forget
pintar	to paint
ponerse de acuerdo	to agree
significar	to mean

Arte y literatura

la censura	censorship
el cuadro	painting
el cuento	story
la lengua	language
la libertad	freedom
el periódico	newspaper
la pintura	painting
la poesía	poetry
el premio	prize
el retrato	portrait
la revista	magazine

Otras palabras y frases

a pesar de	in spite of
el cambio	change

la cuestión	issue, question
despierto	awake, alert
En cambio...	On the other hand . . .
la escuela secundaria	high school
el horario	schedule
la manifestación	demonstration
el mediodía	noon
ocupado	busy
el pueblo	town; people
la taza	cup
único	unique; only

Expresiones útiles

Al contrario...	On the contrary . . .
Claro.	Certainly.
Correcto.	Right. (Correct.)
¡Ni hablar!	Don't even mention it!
¡Ni por todo el dinero del mundo!	Not for all the money in the world!
Probablemente no. (Es probable que no.)	Probably not.
Probablemente sí. (Es probable que sí.)	Probably. (Probably so.)
¡Qué tontería!	What nonsense!

Hispanoamérica: Antes y después de la conquista

La Pirámide del Sol, Teotihuacán (construida aprox. en el año 500 a.C.)

Antes del siglo XVI, cuando los españoles llegaron al Nuevo Mundo, ya existían allí varias civilizaciones indígenas°. Una civilización muy avanzada° fue la de los mayas. Los mayas sabían mucho sobre matemáticas, astronomía y arte. También tenían su propio° sistema de escritura° a base de símbolos jeroglíficos°.

    Otra civilización bastante avanzada fue la de los toltecas°, quienes construyeron° ciudades imponentes° y sabían mucho de agricultura. Cuando llegaron a Teotihuacán (en el centro de México), encontraron allí pirámides enormes como la Pirámide del Sol que se ve en la foto. Cuando en 1519 el conquistador español Hernán Cortés llegó a México, Teotihuacán estaba en manos de los aztecas. Era una ciudad magnífica, con templos, palacios, mercados y escuelas. Los aztecas tenían un gran imperio°, pero también tenían muchos enemigos. Con la ayuda de las otras tribus indígenas de la región, Cortés conquistó° fácilmente a los aztecas.

    Otra gran cultura indígena de Hispanoamérica fue la de los incas. Los incas vivían en la región de los Andes (hoy Perú, Ecuador, Bolivia y Chile) y tenían una

native / advanced

*own / writing
hieroglyphic
Toltecs / built
impressive*

*empire
conquered*

estructura social piramidal, con un jefe supremo (el Inca) y varias clases sociales. La muchacha de la foto es descendiente de los incas. La gente común trabajaba en tierras colectivas y solamente recibía la comida necesaria para vivir. Los nobles eran muy ricos. Los viejos y enfermos° recibían ayuda del estado, un sistema bastante «socialista». Los incas sabían mucho sobre medicina. Por ejemplo, usaban anestesia y hacían operaciones delicadas. Construyeron, entre otras cosas, excelentes caminos°, puentes°, acueductos y ciudades.

the ill

roads
bridges

Un mercado indio en Huancayo, Perú

Durante los tres siglos de la Colonia—desde el siglo XVI hasta el XIX—la estructura social en Hispanoamérica fue básicamente feudal. Los indios trabajaban para los españoles y para los criollos°, que eran los blancos nacidos en América. Poco a poco°, los mestizos formaron un puente social entre los otros grupos. Los españoles (nacidos en España) tenían casi todo el poder°, porque el gobierno° español les daba a ellos todos los puestos° políticos. Esta discriminación causaba resentimientos entre los criollos, y por eso eran inevitables los movimientos de independencia. En México el padre Miguel Hidalgo empezó la Revolución Mexicana; el general José de San Martín fue el jefe de las fuerzas° revolucionarias que lucharon° por la independencia de Argentina y Chile; y Simón Bolívar ganó la liberación del norte de Sudamérica. Para 1825 ya casi toda Hispanoamérica era independiente. Cuba y Puerto Rico son dos excepciones importantes. Aunque Bolívar quería unir° todos los países de Hispanoamérica para formar un solo país poderoso°, la unidad fue imposible y los países permanecieron° separados e independientes entre sí°. Muchas naciones pasaron a manos de dictadores. Aparentemente, la independencia política de España no fue una

Creoles
Poco... *Little by little / power / government positions*

forces / fought

unite
powerful
*remained / **entre...** among themselves*

Simón Bolívar   **El padre Miguel Hidalgo**

verdadera liberación para la mayoría° de los países de Hispanoamérica. Sin   *majority*
embargo°, varios países han tenido elecciones relativamente libres° en los últimos   *However / free*
años (Argentina, Uruguay, Paraguay, Bolivia, etc.) y los dictadores o juntas militares
anteriores han sido reemplazados por° gobiernos democráticos. En las fotos de arriba°   **han...** *have been*
se ve a Simón Bolívar y al padre Miguel Hidalgo, respectivamente.   *replaced by /*
    above

EJERCICIO

Match the people or groups on the left with the appropriate items on the right.

1. Simón Bolívar
2. los toltecas
3. los incas
4. el padre Hidalgo
5. los aztecas
6. los criollos
7. José de San Martín
8. los mayas

a. sabían mucho sobre medicina y tenían un sistema social bastante «socialista»
b. jefe de las fuerzas revolucionarias que lucharon por la independencia de Argentina y Chile
c. tenían un sistema de escritura con símbolos jeroglíficos
d. blancos nacidos en América
e. tenían un gran imperio cerca de Teotihuacán y tenían muchos enemigos
f. construyeron ciudades imponentes y precedieron a los aztecas
g. una persona muy importante en la Revolución Mexicana
h. ganó la liberación del norte de Sudamérica y quería unir todos los países sudamericanos para formar una sola nación

I. COMMANDS

React to the following statements with commands, as in the models. Use object pronouns whenever possible.

Modelos   Tú no haces tu trabajo. **Hazlo.**
Usted me lo pide. **No me lo pida.**

1. Ustedes hablan de su viaje.
2. Tú estudias con Ramón hoy.
3. Usted los apoya.
4. Tú no te vas ahora, Rosa.
5. Usted es pesimista.
6. Usted no me pasa la sal.
7. Ustedes están tristes.
8. Tú no le dices la verdad.
9. Tú me llamas muy temprano.
10. Tú no vienes a clase.
11. Usted no me trae una cerveza.
12. Tú no tienes cuidado.
13. Ustedes no me esperan.
14. Usted no se viste a la moda.

II. THE PAST TENSES

A. Change the verbs in the following sentences from the present to the preterit.

Modelo   Felipe va al centro. **Felipe fue al centro.**

1. Tienen que aprender inglés.
2. ¿Qué pides?
3. Ya los veo.
4. Se lo damos a ellos.
5. ¿Quién pierde? ¿Quién gana?
6. No tienes tiempo de ver el partido.
7. Simón Bolívar quiere unir (*unite*) toda Sudamérica.
8. Los árabes traen a España una rica cultura.
9. Salgo temprano.
10. Fernando se va a casa a dormir.
11. Se divierten mucho.
12. No nos quiere ver.
13. Conocen a María.
14. Sabe la verdad.
15. Me levanto a las ocho.

B. Change the verbs in the following sentences of Exercise A to the imperfect: 1, 5, 6, 7, 11, 12, 13, 14, and 15.

Modelo   Felipe va al centro. **Felipe iba al centro.**

C. Change the verbs in the following sentences of Exercise A to the present perfect: 2, 3, 4, 5, 6, 10, and 11.

Modelo   Felipe va al centro. **Felipe ha ido al centro.**

D. Complete the paragraph with the appropriate past-tense (i.e., preterit, imperfect, present perfect, or past perfect) form of the verbs in parentheses.

Ayer, mientras yo (esperar) _____ el autobús, (ver) _____ a Juan, un amigo muy querido. Recuerdo que en 1980, cuando él y yo (conocerse) _____, los dos (querer) _____ ser pintores famosos. Él (admirar) _____ profundamente a Goya y (tener) _____ un cuadro que (heredar) (*inherit*) _____ de una tía rica. No (ver) _____ a Juan desde 1987. Cuando lo (ver) _____, (llevar) _____ un traje elegante y zapatos muy caros. Yo le (decir) _____ que (estar) _____ muy contento de verlo y le (preguntar) _____ si (seguir) _____ obsesionado por las obras de Goya. Me (decir) _____ que ya no, que ahora (dedicarse) _____ a viajar y a visitar casinos por todo el mundo. Juan me (contar) _____ que en 1986 (conocer) _____ a una mujer admirable, (enamorarse) _____ de ella y en menos de un mes ellos (decidir) _____ casarse. La mujer (tener) _____ mucho dinero porque (ser) _____ la única hija de un millonario italiano. Me contó mi amigo que él y su esposa (vivir) _____ muy felices hasta la semana pasada, cuando el doctor de la familia (descubrir) _____ que su esposa (tener) _____ cáncer. La tragedia de mi amigo me (dejar) _____ muy triste pero (inspirar) _____ este cuadro, que yo (empezar) _____ hace unas horas y cuyo título (*whose title*) va a ser «Los dólares todavía no (poder) _____ curar todos los dolores del mundo».

III. THE REFLEXIVE

Restate the following, changing the pronouns and verbs from the plural to the singular.

> **Modelo**   ¿Nos sentamos aquí? **¿Me siento aquí?**

1. Siempre nos divertimos con Andrea y Tomás.
2. Ellos se van de aquí mañana.
3. ¿Se lavan ustedes la cara? (Give both singular forms.)
4. Nos levantamos de la mesa.
5. ¿Cómo se llaman tus mejores amigos?
6. Siéntense, por favor. (Give both singular forms.)
7. Nos acostamos a las once.
8. Ustedes se despiertan temprano. (Give both singular forms.)

IV. USEFUL EXPRESSIONS

Give the Spanish equivalent of the following expressions.

1. What's new?   **2.** Glad to meet you.   **3.** Congratulations!   **4.** Can you tell me how to get to the Hotel Internacional?   **5.** Cheers!   **6.** You're welcome.   **7.** Where are shoes sold?   **8.** What time do the stores open?   **9.** Bring me a (cup of) coffee, please.   **10.** What do you wish to order?   **11.** The check, please.   **12.** Excuse me (I beg your pardon).   **13.** What a shame (pity)!   **14.** Enjoy the meal!   **15.** What do you recommend (to us)?

unos huevos de chocolate

un pavo

unas tarjetas

FELICES PASCUAS

un árbol de Navidad

los Reyes Magos*

un desfile

de cumpleaños

un candelabro

Fiestas y aniversarios 13

Extending Invitations
Accepting Invitations
Declining Invitations
Making a Toast
Making Introductions

EJERCICIO

Complete the sentences with an appropriate word or words.

1. El sábado próximo es el _____ de mamá; vamos a hacerle una
_____ para celebrarlo.
2. El 12 de octubre (Día de la Raza) va a haber un _____ en el centro
en honor a Cristóbal Colón.
3. ¿Dónde están los adornos para el _____ de Navidad?
4. Nuestros amigos judíos tienen un _____ de Janucá.
5. En los Estados Unidos mucha gente come _____ para celebrar el Día
de Acción de Gracias (*Thanksgiving*).
6. Andresito les va a pedir muchos regalos a los _____; en
Hispanoamérica los niños no le piden regalos a Santa Claus.*
7. Comprémosles _____ a los niños para las Pascuas (*Easter*).
8. Siempre les envío _____ de Navidad a mis amigos.

PREGUNTAS

1. ¿Cuándo es su cumpleaños (el de usted)? ¿Cómo lo celebra?   **2.** ¿Cuál es su día
de fiesta favorito? ¿Por qué?   **3.** ¿Envía muchas tarjetas a sus amigos? ¿Cuándo? ¿Se
las envían ellos también a usted? ¿Cuándo?   **4.** ¿Come pavo su familia el Día de
Acción de Gracias? ¿Y en Navidad?

---

*In Spain, and in most Latin American countries, children receive presents on January 6, Epiphany,
rather than on Christmas.

 # The present subjunctive of regular verbs

Un 15 de diciembre, en la ciudad de México.

RAMONA ¡Ay, Carmen, el instructor de baile quiere que yo *baile* con Carlos°! Pero yo no quiero bailar con él. ¡Él y yo no bailamos bien juntos!

CARMEN ¡Qué suerte tienes! Yo siempre le pido que me *permita* bailar° con Carlos, pero él manda que yo *practique* y *trabaje* con Luis.° Prohíbe que nosotros *bailemos*° con otra persona.

RAMONA ¡Qué injusticia! ¿Sabes que Luis y yo...?

CARMEN ¡Claro que lo sé°! ¡Todo el mundo lo sabe... y creo que el instructor también! Probablemente por eso° él prohíbe que tú y Luis *bailen* juntos. ¿Por qué no te quejas?

RAMONA Pues, porque no quiero que él le *diga* algo a Carlos°. ¡Pobre Carlos! Él no tiene la culpa°.

CARMEN Te comprendo. Además, ya sabemos que el instructor no va a cambiar de idea°. Ahora quiere que *practiquemos* durante las Posadas.* Y como una vez tú dijiste, si el instructor quiere que *bailes* con una mesa, lo haces y si nos pide que *asistamos* a clase en Navidad o en Año Nuevo, entonces tal vez nosotros también...

---

1. ¿Dónde están Ramona y Carmen? ¿Qué día es?   2. ¿Qué quiere el instructor? ¿Está de acuerdo Ramona? ¿Por qué?   3. ¿Qué le pide siempre al instructor Carmen? ¿Qué manda él?   4. Según su opinión, ¿qué relación hay entre Luis y Ramona? ¿Son hermanos? ¿amigos? ¿novios?   5. ¿Por qué no quiere quejarse Ramona?   6. ¿Qué dice Carmen de la situación?   7. Según las dos amigas, ¿es el instructor una persona buena y simpática? ¿Cómo es él? Descríbalo con dos o tres adjetivos.   8. ¿Conoce usted a alguien como este instructor? ¿Quién?

---

quiere... Carlos *wants me to dance with Carlos*
le pido... bailar *ask him to let me dance ("that he let me dance")*
él manda... Luis *he tells me to practice ("orders that I practice") and work with Luis*
Prohíbe... bailemos *He won't allow us to dance ("prohibits that we dance")*
¡Claro que lo sé! *Of course I know it!*   **por eso** *that's why ("for that reason")*
no quiero... Carlos *I don't want him to say anything to Carlos*
Él... culpa. *It's not his fault.*   **no va... idea** *(the instructor) won't change his mind*

---

* *See* **Nota Cultural 1** of this chapter.

So far in this text, the verb tenses presented have been in the indicative mood, except commands, which are in the imperative mood. In this chapter, the subjunctive mood is introduced. Whereas the indicative mood is used to state facts or ask direct questions and the imperative mood is used to give commands, the subjunctive is used:

1. For indirect commands or requests.

My boss requests that I *be* at work at eight o'clock sharp.
Fred's mother asks that he *celebrate* Christmas with the family.

2. For situations expressing doubt, probability, or something hypothetical or contrary to fact.

If I *were* rich, I would go to Seville for the Easter celebrations.
Be that as it *may* . . .

3. For statements of emotion, hope, wishing, or wanting.

May you *succeed* at everything you *do.*
Sally wishes that Tom *were going* to the party.

4. For statements of necessity.

It is necessary that he *do* the honors and *make* a toast.

5. For statements of approval or disapproval, permission, or prohibition.

Father forbids that she even *think* about going to Mexico for Christmas.
It's better that we *stay* home.

The subjunctive is used in Spanish far more than it is in English, and the discussion of the uses of the subjunctive in Spanish will be continued in Chapters 14 and 15. In this chapter, its use will be limited to indirect requests and commands with four verbs: **mandar** (*to order*), **pedir** (*to ask, request*), **querer** (*to wish, want*), and **prohibir** (*to prohibit, forbid*). First, you'll see how the subjunctive of regular verbs is formed.

A. To form the present subjunctive of regular **-ar** verbs, drop the ending **-o** from the first-person singular (**yo**) form of the present indicative and add the endings **-e**, **-es**, **-e**, **-emos**, **-éis**, **-en**. For **-er** and **-ir** verbs, add the endings **-a**, **-as**, **-a**, **-amos**, **-áis**, **-an**.

hablar		comer		vivir	
hable	hablemos	coma	comamos	viva	vivamos
hables	habléis	comas	comáis	vivas	viváis
hable	hablen	coma	coman	viva	vivan

Mis padres quieren que celebremos Nochebuena en casa de mis tíos.
Le pido que me presente a los invitados.

My parents want us to celebrate Christmas Eve at my aunt and uncle's.
I'm asking him (her, you) to introduce me to the guests.

Nos mandan que asistamos a clase.	*They're ordering us to attend class.*
El doctor prohíbe que yo fume* o que coma sal.	*The doctor forbids me to smoke or to eat salt.*
Quiero que le compres un regalo de cumpleaños a tu madrina.	*I want you to buy a birthday present for your godmother.*
¿Quiere el profesor que terminemos la lectura la próxima semana?	*Does the teacher want us to finish the reading next week?*

B. You may have noticed that the **usted** and **ustedes** forms of the present subjunctive are the same as the **usted** and **ustedes** command forms and that the **tú** form is like the negative **tú** command form. Compare the following sentences.

Lean el periódico.	*Read the newspaper.*
Quiero que ustedes lean el periódico.	*I want you to read the newspaper.*
No llame a los invitados hoy.	*Don't call the guests today.*
No quiero que llame a los invitados hoy.	*I don't want you to call the guests today.*
No mires el desfile.	*Don't watch the parade.*
Prohíben que mires el desfile.	*They forbid you to watch the parade.*
No te quejes.	*Don't complain.*
Te pido que no te quejes.	*I'm asking you not to complain.*

In an indirect command or request, there is an implied command, as you can see.

C. There are a number of things to notice about the structure of the sentences with the subjunctive that you have just seen. One is that the verb **mandar** or **pedir** or **prohibir** or **querer** is in the indicative in a clause that could (grammatically) stand alone as a sentence; for instance: **Piden.** (*They request.*) This clause is called an *independent clause.* The independent clause is followed by **que** (*that*) plus another clause that contains a verb in the subjunctive. This clause with **que** is called a *dependent clause*; it cannot stand alone as a sentence. For example, in the sentence **Piden que asistamos a clase**, the phrase **que asistamos a clase** (*that we attend class*) is not a complete sentence. The **que** is essential in the Spanish sentence, although *that* is not always used in English. In English, an infinitive construction is frequently used.

El doctor prohíbe que ella fume.	{ *The doctor forbids that she smoke.* { *The doctor forbids her to smoke.*

If the subject of the independent clause is different from the subject of the dependent clause, the subjunctive must be used in Spanish rather than an infinitive construction. However, an infinitive must be used in Spanish when there is no change of subject. Compare:

Quiero celebrar el Día de la Madre con tía Celia.	*I want to celebrate Mother's Day with Aunt Celia.* (no change in subject)

---

* The verb **fumar** means *to smoke.*

Quiero que nosotros celebremos el Día de la Madre con tía Celia.	*I want us to celebrate* ("I want that we celebrate") *Mother's Day with Aunt Celia.* (change in subject)
No quieren levantarse a mediodía.	*They don't want to get up at noon.* (no change in subject)
No quieren que sus hijos se levanten a mediodía.	*They don't want their children to get up at noon.* ("They don't want that their children get up at noon.") (change in subject)
Quieren reunirse en el Café Sol.	*They want to meet in Café Sol.*
Quieren que nos reunamos en el Café Sol.	*They want us to meet in Café Sol.*

EJERCICIOS

A. Por favor, ¡usen el subjuntivo! Restate the sentences, changing them to requests from a different person (or persons), following the model.

Modelo   Hablo con los niños. Me pide que...
Me pide que hable con los niños.

1. Pedrito nos invita a su cumpleaños. Quiero que...
2. Tus hijos miran el desfile. ¿No quieres que...?
3. Vivimos cerca de la universidad. Nos piden que...
4. Leo esta revista. ¿Prohíbes que...?
5. Toman vino con la comida. No quiero que...
6. Le escribo una carta a mi tía. ¿Quiere que...?
7. Estudian el capítulo trece. Manda que...
8. Comes sólo frutas y pescado. ¿Te pide que...?
9. Recibimos a los estudiantes. Mandan que...
10. Teresa y Jorge hablan por teléfono. Prohíben que...

B. El aniversario de los Gómez. Play the role of Mrs. Moreno. She's talking to Miguel, her husband. Add the words in parentheses to describe the **fiesta sorpresa** (*surprise party*) she's preparing for the wedding anniversary of her friends, Marta and Jorge Gómez.

Modelo   Marta y Jorge llegan aquí antes de las seis. (no querer)
No quiero que Marta y Jorge lleguen aquí antes de las seis.

1. Todos nos reunimos aquí a las cinco.   (querer)
2. Los invitados fuman en la casa.   (prohibir)
3. Tú y Marisa preparan el pavo.   (pedir)
4. Los niños pasan la tarde con la abuela.   (mandar)
5. Los amigos de la oficina compran el vino y la cerveza.   (querer)
6. Tú escribes algo estúpido en la tarjeta.   (prohibir)
7. La gente come la torta antes de comer el pavo.   (no querer)
8. Tú recibes a los invitados.   (pedir)
9. Nadie habla de religión ni de política.   (mandar)
10. Los Gómez abren sus regalos después de la cena.   (querer)

C. En acción. Describe what's happening in each of the following drawings, according to the models.

Modelos

Anita / querer / comer los chocolates, pero...
su mamá / prohibir / ella / comerlos / ahora

Anita quiere comer los chocolates, pero su mamá prohíbe que ella los coma ahora.

el señor Martínez / querer / descansar, pero...
los niños / pedirle / (él) / ayudarlos / con la piñata

El señor Martínez quiere descansar, pero los niños le piden que (él) los ayude con la piñata.

1. Alicia / querer / pasar unos días en Acapulco, pero...
   su novio / no querer / ella / viajar / allí sola

2. Susana / no querer / bailar con nadie, pero...
   Enrique / pedirle / (ella) / bailar / con él

3. Ernesto / querer / fumar uno o dos cigarrillos, pero...
   su esposa / prohibir / él / fumar / en la casa

4. los niños / querer / jugar en el patio, pero...
   su mamá / mandarles / (ellos) / comer / el almuerzo antes

5. el profesor Gris / querer / hablar del pasado de México, pero...
   sus estudiantes / querer / él / hablarles sólo del presente

que les hable

6. Marta / no querer / abrir su maleta, pero...
   el agente de aduana / mandarle / (ella) / abrirla

le manda que la abra

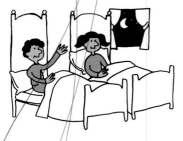

7. los niños / querer / ver sus regalos de Navidad, pero...
   sus padres / no querer / ellos / levantarse / antes de las 8:00 A.M.

que se levanten

8. la señora Vera / no querer / llegar tarde a la fiesta, pero...
   su marido / pedirle / (ella) / esperarlo / unos minutos más...

le pide que lo espere

D. Traducción. Give the Spanish equivalent of the following sentences.

1. I want you (**tú**) to send a birthday gift to your grandmother.
2. She is asking us to read the book.
3. The teacher is ordering Rodrigo to study more.
4. We want you (**ustedes**) to call us tomorrow. *Nos queremos que uds. llamen*
5. They always prohibit us from writing in the books. *Siempre nos prohiben que escriban*
6. Elena, I am asking you to drink your milk!
7. My parents forbid me to stay at my friend's house.
8. He wants you (**ustedes**) to attend his birthday party.
9. I'm asking them not to complain. *Les pido que no se quejen*
10. They want us to meet at the restaurant "La Cazuela". *Quiere nos encontremos EN el restaurante*

PREGUNTAS

1. ¿Quiere usted que sus padres lo (la) escuchen más?, ¿que celebren su cumpleaños?, ¿que le manden más dinero? **2.** ¿Quieren sus padres que usted les escriba más?, ¿que usted los visite todas las semanas? **3.** ¿Les pide usted a sus amigos que lo (la) acompañen al cine?, ¿que lo (la) ayuden con sus estudios? **4.** ¿Qué les pide a sus amigos?, ¿a su compañero(-a) de cuarto?

The present subjunctive of irregular, orthographic-changing, and stem-changing verbs

En casa de Alicia.

ALICIA	Mamá, quiero que *conozcas* a John°. Llegó hace unas horas de California.
MADRE	Mucho gusto, John. ¿Qué tal el viaje?
JOHN	Fue un poco largo, pero interesante.
ALICIA	¿Quieres que *salgamos*° para ver la ciudad?
JOHN	¡Sí, con mucho gusto! Sabes que tengo que volver el viernes.
MADRE	¿Ah, sí°? ¡Qué lástima! El sábado empiezan las Posadas.
JOHN	Es que...° mis padres quieren que *vuelva* pronto.
MADRE	¿Por qué no les pides que te permitan quedarte unos días más?
ALICIA	¡Sí, John! Quiero que los llames y les *digas* que estás invitado a pasar Navidad con nosotros.
JOHN	De acuerdo... Buena idea. ¡No veo la hora de saber° cómo son las Posadas!

---

1. ¿A quién quiere Alicia que su madre conozca?   2. ¿De dónde es él?   3. ¿Qué quiere Alicia que John y ella hagan?   4. ¿Cuándo debe volver John? ¿Por qué?   5. ¿Cuándo empiezan las Posadas?   6. ¿Qué quiere Alicia que haga su amigo?

---

quiero... John *I want you to meet John*   **¿Quieres... salgamos...?** *Do you want us to go out...?*   **¿Ah, sí?** *Oh, really?*   **Es que...** *It's just that...*
¡No... saber...! *I can't wait to find out...!*

A. Verbs that have an irregularity in the first-person singular of the present indicative maintain this irregularity in the present subjunctive. The endings, however, are regular.

decir		conocer		tener	
dig**a**	dig**amos**	conozc**a**	conozc**amos**	teng**a**	teng**amos**
dig**as**	dig**áis**	conozc**as**	conozc**áis**	teng**as**	teng**áis**
dig**a**	dig**an**	conozc**a**	conozc**an**	teng**a**	teng**an**

Other verbs that follow this pattern are:

construir*	**construy-**	poner	**pong-**	venir	**veng-**
hacer	**hag-**	salir	**salg-**	ver	**ve-**
oír	**oig-**	traer	**traig-**		

B. The following verbs are irregular:

dar		estar		haber	
dé	demos	esté	estemos	haya	hayamos
des	deis	estés	estéis	hayas	hayáis
dé	den	esté	estén	haya	hayan

ir		saber		ser	
vaya	vayamos	sepa	sepamos	sea	seamos
vayas	vayáis	sepas	sepáis	seas	seáis
vaya	vayan	sepa	sepan	sea	sean

C. Most stem-changing **-ar** and **-er** verbs retain the same pattern of stem change in the present subjunctive that they have in the indicative.

encontrar		poder	
enc**ue**ntre	encontremos	p**ue**da	podamos
enc**ue**ntres	encontréis	p**ue**das	podáis
enc**ue**ntre	enc**ue**ntren	p**ue**da	p**ue**dan

entender		pensar	
ent**ie**nda	entendamos	p**ie**nse	pensemos
ent**ie**ndas	entendáis	p**ie**nses	penséis
ent**ie**nda	ent**ie**ndan	p**ie**nse	p**ie**nsen

---

* **Construir** means *to build* or *construct*. A **y** is inserted before any ending (except future-tense and conditional endings) that does not begin with **i**: **construyo**. An **i** changes to **y** between two vowels: **construyó**.

D. Stem-changing **-ir** verbs that have a change in stem of **e** to **ie**, **e** to **i**, or **o** to **ue** in the present indicative follow the same pattern in the subjunctive, with one additional change: in the **nosotros** and **vosotros** forms, the **e** of the stem is changed to **i**; the **o** is changed to **u**.

sentir		morir		dormir	
si**e**nta	si**n**tamos	m**ue**ra	m**u**ramos	d**ue**rma	d**u**rmamos
si**e**ntas	si**n**táis	m**ue**ras	m**u**ráis	d**ue**rmas	d**u**rmáis
si**e**nta	si**e**ntan	m**ue**ra	m**ue**ran	d**ue**rma	d**ue**rman

pedir		vestirse	
p**i**da	p**i**damos	me v**i**sta	nos v**i**stamos
p**i**das	p**i**dáis	te v**i**stas	os v**i**stáis
p**i**da	p**i**dan	se v**i**sta	se v**i**stan

E. To preserve the sound of the stem when subjunctive endings are added, certain changes in spelling are sometimes necessary.

1. **c** changes to **qu** before **e**:
   que yo bus**qu**e, sa**qu**e, to**qu**e

2. **g** changes to **gu** before **e**:
   que yo jue**gu**e, lle**gu**e, pa**gu**e

3. **z** changes to **c** before **e**:
   que yo almuer**c**e, empie**c**e

Ana me pide que esté listo a las diez. Vamos a misa.	*Ana asks me to be ready at ten o'clock. We are going to mass.*
Mi madrina quiere que vayas con ellos al cine. — ¡Qué bien! Tengo toda la tarde libre.	*My godmother wants you to go with them to the movies. — Great! I have the whole afternoon free.*
El doctor prohíbe que te levantes o que te vistas.	*The doctor forbids you to get up or get dressed.*
Mandan que la compañía les construya una casa.	*They order the company to build them a house.*
¿Quieres que yo busque otra tarjeta?	*Do you want me to look for another card?*

A. Quiero que sean buenos, niños. Mrs. Gil is going to a party. Following the models, answer the questions that her children and the baby-sitter ask her before she leaves.

Modelos ¿Debo acostarme temprano? Sí, quiero que (tú)...
Sí, quiero que (tú) te acuestes temprano.

¿Debemos hacer eso? No, prohíbo que (ustedes)...
No, prohíbo que (ustedes) hagan eso.

1. ¿Debemos comer los huevos de chocolate? No, les pido que (ustedes) no...
2. ¿Debe hacer ejercicios Susana? No, no quiero que (ella)...
3. ¿Debo estar aquí hasta medianoche? Sí, quiero que (usted)...
4. ¿Deben saber eso ellos? No, prohíbo que (ellos)...
5. ¿Debo permitirles salir? No, le pido que (usted) no...
6. ¿Debemos ver ese programa? No, prohíbo que (ustedes)...
7. ¿Debo acostarme en el sofá? No, te pido que (tú) no...
8. ¿Deben ponerse pijama los niños? Sí, mando que (ellos)...

B. Completar las frases. Complete the sentences with the appropriate forms of the verbs in parentheses.

1. Quieren que nosotros (ir) —————— a su casa.
2. Te pido que (traer) —————— a tu novio a la fiesta del sábado.
3. Mis padres me prohíben que (pensar) —————— en esas cosas ahora.
4. Mamá nos manda que (hacer) —————— una torta.
5. Queremos que tú (seguir) —————— un curso con la señora Rodríguez.
6. ¡No pueden prohibirme que (volver) —————— tarde!
7. ¿Te pide ella que le (dar) —————— dinero por su cumpleaños?
8. El policía manda que usted le (decir) —————— dónde vive.

C. Entrevista. In pairs or small groups, interview each other about your wishes and complaints regarding your next vacation at home with your family. In particular, find out two or three things each person in your group would like his (her) family members to do for them and two or three things their family members won't allow them to do. Follow the model.

Modelos Estudiante 1: **¿Qué quieres que tus padres hagan por ti durante las próximas vacaciones?**

Estudiante 2: **Quiero que sean generosos conmigo, que tengan paciencia con mis amigos y que me den el auto los fines de semana.**

Estudiante 1: **¿Y qué te piden o prohíben tus padres?**
Estudiante 2: **Ellos no quieren que yo salga todas las noches; prohíben que oiga música después de las 11:00 p.m. y me piden que no fume en la casa.**

D. Traducción. Give the Spanish equivalent of the following sentences.

1. I want you to be good, Miguelito.
2. Carla asks her mother to give her ten dollars.
3. Do you (**usted**) want us to take something to the party?
4. Her mother prohibits her from going out at night.
5. Are you (**ustedes**) asking me to do you a favor?
6. The doctor asks him to get dressed.
7. The policeman orders her to tell the truth.
8. They are asking us to be here before the parade.

PREGUNTAS

1. ¿Quiere usted que sus compañeros de clase recuerden su cumpleaños? ¿Prefiere que lo ignoren? ¿Por qué? ¿Desea que lo celebren de alguna manera? ¿Cómo?   **2.** En general, ¿quieren los profesores que los estudiantes vengan a clase regularmente? ¿que sepan la lección? ¿que duerman en la clase? ¿Qué quiere su profesor(-a) que hagan ustedes en la clase de español?   **3.** ¿Deben los profesores prohibir que los estudiantes traigan radios a la clase?   **4.** ¿Qué quiere su profesor(-a) que usted haga para mañana?

Additional command forms

A fines° de diciembre, en casa de una familia mexicana.

PADRE	¿Qué quieren que les traigan los Reyes Magos, niños?
JUANITO	Mm... *pensemos°*...
PEPITO	No, mejor *escribámosles°* una carta.
PADRE	Bueno, pero no debe ser una carta muy larga, ¿eh?
JUANITO	No te preocupes por los regalos, papá. ¡Que *se preocupen* los Reyes°!

1. ¿Qué les pregunta el padre a sus dos hijos?   2. ¿Quién quiere que escriban una carta?   3. ¿Quiere el padre que la carta sea larga o corta?   4. Según Juanito, ¿quiénes deben preocuparse por los regalos?

A fines *Around the end*   **Mm... pensemos...** *Hmmm ... let's think ...*
No, mejor escribámosles *No, (better) let's write them*
¡Qué... Reyes! *Let the Wise Men worry about it!*

A. As you have seen, the **usted** and **ustedes** command forms are the same as the **usted** and **ustedes** forms of the present subjunctive, and the negative **tú** command forms are the same as the **tú** form of the present subjunctive. Similarly, the **nosotros** form of the present subjunctive is equivalent to the first-person plural command form; it corresponds to *Let's . . .* or *Let's not . . .* in English.

Hablemos con el dueño. (No hablemos con el dueño.)	*Let's speak with the owner. (Let's not speak with the owner.)*
Comamos pavo. (No comamos pavo.)	*Let's eat turkey. (Let's not eat turkey.)*
Escribamos tarjetas de Navidad. (No escribamos tarjetas de Navidad.)	*Let's write Christmas cards. (Let's not write Christmas cards.)*

One exception is the affirmative **Vamos** (*Let's go*). *Let's not go* is **No vayamos**. **Vamos a** + infinitive can also be used for the affirmative **nosotros** command form.

Vamos a cenar.⎫
Cenemos.⎭ *Let's eat dinner.*

Vamos a saludar a mi padrino.⎫
Saludemos a mi padrino.⎭ *Let's say hello to my godfather.*

Pronouns are added to the affirmative **nosotros** command forms just as they are added to other command forms; they precede the negative **nosotros** commands.

Celebrémoslo con una torta.	*Let's celebrate it with a cake.*
Comámosla pronto.	*Let's eat it soon.*
No la comamos ahora.	*Let's not eat it now.*

When **nos** is added to an affirmative command, the final **-s** of the verb is dropped.

Levantémonos. *Let's stand up.*   Vámonos. *Let's go.*

Note: In both cases, an accent mark must be written to preserve the original stress.

B. Indirect commands are commands given to someone else (indirectly). They usually follow the pattern **Que** + subjunctive + subject of the verb. Notice that object pronouns precede the affirmative indirect command.

Que les vaya bien.	*May all go well with you.*
¡Que terminen los niños de poner los adornos en el árbol de Navidad!	*Let (Have) the children finish putting the decorations on the Christmas tree!*
¡Que pasen todos al comedor!	*Have everyone go into the dining room!*
Que haga ella el papel de María.	*Let her play the role of María.*

A. En otras palabras... Restate the sentences following the models.

Modelos Vamos a saludar a Jorge.
Saludemos a Jorge.

Vamos a reunirnos hoy.
Reunámonos hoy.

1. Vamos a ver al dueño.
2. Vamos a servir la cena.
3. Vamos a celebrar nuestro aniversario.
4. Vamos a vestirnos de negro.
5. Vamos a traer una piñata.
6. Vamos a hacer una torta.

B. Entre niños. Luisito is asking his twin sister Anita whether they should or shouldn't do certain things. Answer his questions using affirmative **nosotros** commands, as Anita would. Use object pronouns whenever possible.

Modelo ¿Saludamos a los padrinos?
Sí, saludémoslos.

1. ¿Fumamos un cigarrillo?
2. ¿Escribimos a los Reyes Magos?
3. ¿Ponemos las tarjetas en la mesa?
4. ¿Nos vamos con Pepito?
5. ¿Visitamos a la abuela el día de su cumpleaños?
6. ¿Comemos los huevos de chocolate?

C. ¿Qué hacemos? It's Saturday afternoon, and Juan and María don't have any plans, yet they can't seem to agree on how to spend the rest of the day. Answer Juan's suggestions in the negative, as María would. Use **nosotros** command forms and object pronouns whenever possible, following the example.

Modelo ¿Vamos a visitar a Teresa?
No, no vayamos a visitarla.

1. ¿Hacemos la sopa?
2. ¿Nos reunimos con Ramón?
3. ¿Preparamos arroz con pollo para la cena?
4. ¿Nos sentamos en la sala?
5. ¿Pedimos una pizza grande?

D. No, gracias. Pablo is a polite but very shy boy. When he is asked to do something, he always suggests that someone else do it. Answer the questions with indirect commands, as Pablo would. Follow the model.

Modelo Pablo, ¿quieres romper la piñata? (los otros niños)
No, gracias. Que la rompan los otros niños.

1. ¿Quieres cantar «Guantanamera»? (Sonia y Luis)
2. ¿Quieres ir al desfile con Sonia? (Ernesto)
3. ¿Quieres ver *El padrino?* (mis hermanos)
4. ¿Quieres saludar a las muchachas? (mamá)
5. ¿Quieres poner los adornos en el árbol? (Anita)

1. ¿Qué quiere usted que hagamos hoy? ¿Quiere que leamos el diálogo o que conversemos por unos minutos? **2.** ¿Quiere usted que hagamos una fiesta aquí en la clase la semana próxima? ¿antes de terminar el semestre? **3.** ¿Qué quiere usted que hagamos mañana? ¿Quiere que hagamos muchos ejercicios? ¿que hablemos de algunas fiestas hispanas típicas? ¿que escuchemos algunas canciones en español?

Las posadas

Don Antonio, un español de 75 años, está en un pequeño pueblo de México de visita en casa de su hija Paula. Es época de Navidad. Varias familias se han reunido en la casa de unos vecinos para celebrar las Posadas.[1]

LA VECINA	Entren, por favor. Están en su casa.[2]
PAULA	¡Qué bonitos están los adornos y el nacimiento°!
LA VECINA	Gracias. Siéntese usted aquí, don Antonio; quiero que vea bien las Posadas.
DON ANTONIO	Muchas gracias, señora. Y como no sé mucho de esto, les pido que me expliquen el origen de la celebración.
PAULA	Es muy típica de México. Creo que viene de la época de los aztecas.
LA VECINA	¡Escuchen! Ya han empezado las canciones.

Una niña hace el papel de María en las Posadas.

Un niño golpea (*hits*) una piñata.

Dos hombres empiezan a cantar; uno hace el papel de San José y el otro hace el papel del dueño de la casa.

SAN JOSÉ   En nombre del cielo,
danos posada.
Ábrele la puerta
a mi esposa amada.

EL DUEÑO   Aquí no hay mesón.
Sigan adelante.
Ya no me hables más,
¡ladrón o tunante!³

Una hora después. Las canciones han terminado.

EL VECINO   Bueno, que pasen todos al comedor. La comida está lista.
LA VECINA   Sí, entremos y comamos. A ver..., ¡que traigan la piñata!⁴
PAULA   Me pregunto° quién va a ser el padrino el año que viene...
ROSITA   ¡Mira qué grande es la piñata, abuelo! ¿Tienen piñatas en España?
DON ANTONIO   No, mi tesoro°. No es nuestra costumbre.
PABLITO   ¡Pobres niños españoles!

---

nacimiento *nativity scene*   **Me pregunto** *I wonder*
mi tesoro *my dear* (literally, "my treasure")

1. ¿Para qué se han reunido varias familias mexicanas?   **2.** ¿Qué pide don Antonio que le expliquen? ¿Por qué no sabe mucho de esto?   **3.** ¿Cuáles son los papeles que hacen los dos hombres que cantan?   **4.** Después de las canciones, ¿adónde quiere el vecino que pasen todos? ¿Por qué?   **5.** ¿Qué manda la vecina que traigan? **6.** ¿Ha visto usted una piñata alguna vez? ¿Ha estado usted en México o en algún otro país hispano durante alguna celebración? ¿Cuál?

Notas culturales

1. The **Posadas** (literally, "the inns") are Christmas celebrations in Mexico commemorating the search of Joseph and Mary for lodging in Bethlehem. The festivities are held on nine consecutive nights, beginning on December 16 and ending on Christmas Eve. Nine families usually participate, with each family sponsoring one evening. The celebration begins around eight o'clock with prayers and songs; then, the company divides into two groups, one group acting as Joseph and Mary seeking lodging, the other acting as the innkeepers. The groups converse in song. At the end of each evening, the identity of those seeking shelter is revealed, they are admitted to the "inn," and there is much celebrating. For the first eight nights, there are fruits, nuts, candies, and punch; on Christmas Eve, the host family for that year (the **padrinos**) provides a large dinner after Midnight Mass (**Misa de gallo**). The origin of the custom is said to be an Aztec ceremony that a Spanish priest, Diego de Soria, adapted to Christian purpose.

2. This is the traditional greeting by which a host or hostess in the Hispanic world welcomes a guest into his or her home. It means *You are in your own house.*

3. *Saint Joseph:* In the name of heaven / give us shelter. / Open the door / to my beloved wife. / *Owner:* There is no inn here. / Continue (on your search). / Speak to me no further, / thief or rogue!

4. The **piñata** is a brightly colored figure, usually in the shape of an animal or toy, made of tissue paper, which covers a clay or cardboard container full of fruits, candies, and coins. The children take turns at being blindfolded and trying to break the **piñata** with a bat. When it is finally broken, the contents spill out, and all the children leap upon them happily. **Piñatas** are also used for children's parties in many countries.

FUNCIONES Y ACTIVIDADES

In this chapter, you have seen examples of some important language functions, or uses. Here is a summary and some additional information about these functions of language.

Extending invitations

¿Le (te) gustaría ir a... (conmigo)?	*Would you like to go to . . . (with me)?*
¿Qué le (te) parece si vamos a...?	*How do you feel about going to . . . ?*
Si está(-s) libre hoy, vamos a...	*If you're free today, let's go to . . .*
¿Quiere(-s) ir a...?	*Do you want to go to . . . ?*
¿Me quiere(-s) acompañar a...?	*Do you want to go with (accompany) me to . . . ?*

Accepting invitations

Sí, ¡con mucho gusto!	*Yes, gladly (sure)!*
¡Cómo no! ¿A qué hora?	*Sure! What time?*
¡Listo(-a)! Gracias por la invitación.	*I'm ready to go! Thanks for the invitation.*
Ah, sí ¡qué buena idea!	*Oh, yeah, what a good idea!*
No veo la hora de verte (de hablar con José, de comer, etcétera).	*I can't wait to see you (to talk to José, to eat, etc.).*
De acuerdo, ¡tengo todo el día libre!	*Okay, I have the whole day free!*

Declining invitations

Tengo (Es que tengo) mucho que hacer esta semana. La semana que viene, tal vez.	*I have a lot to do this week. Next week, perhaps.*
Me gustaría (mucho), pero (no puedo ir)...	*I'd like to (very much) but (I can't go) . . .*
Otro día tal vez; hoy estoy muy ocupado(-a).	*Another day, perhaps; today I'm very busy.*
¡Qué lástima! Esta tarde tengo que estudiar.	*What a shame! This afternoon I have to study.*

Making a toast

The most common way to make a toast is **¡Salud!** (*To your health!*), as you saw earlier. Three longer versions you may hear are:

Salud, amor y pesetas.	*Health, love, and money.*
Salud, amor y pesetas y el tiempo para gastarlos.	*Health, love, and money, and the time to enjoy (spend) them.*
Salud y plata y un(-a) novio(-a) de yapa.	*Health, money (silver), and a sweetheart besides.*

Making Introductions

If you are introducing yourself, you can say **Déjeme presentarme. Me llamo...** To introduce someone else to another person, you can say:

Esta es..., una amiga de México (California, etcétera).	*This is ..., a friend from Mexico (California, etc.).*
Quiero que conozca(-s) a...	*I want you to meet ...*
Quiero presentarle(-te) a...	*I want to introduce you to ...* (or: *I want to introduce ... to you.*)

As you have seen earlier, **Mucho gusto** is generally used for *Glad to meet you.*

A. Invitaciones. Working with a classmate, extend an invitation to do each of the following things. Your classmate should accept some of the invitations and decline others.

1. ir a un desfile
2. ir al zoológico
3. ir a un partido de jai alai
4. ir a misa el domingo
5. ir a una conferencia (*lecture*) sobre Centroamérica
6. ir al teatro
7. ir a un restaurante muy elegante
8. reunirse con unos amigos para (ir a) bailar
9. ir a una fiesta de cumpleaños para su mamá
10. ir a las montañas para esquiar
11. ir a una corrida de toros
12. ir con él (ella) de compras
13. ayudarlo(-la) a mudarse
14. ir a un concierto de música clásica
15. ir al barrio italiano para comer pizza

B. Role-play the following situations.

1. You and a friend are having dinner in a nice restaurant on Valentine's Day. You ask for some wine, which the waiter brings. You make a toast. Your friend tells you he or she had an interview for a job and the boss wants him or her to start work next week. You congratulate your friend. To celebrate his or her good luck, your friend wants to take you to the theater after dinner. You accept the invitation and say you'd be delighted.
2. An acquaintance of yours who is very selfish and difficult to be around is constantly inviting you out and won't take no for an answer. This time he (she) invites you to go to a movie on Friday. You say you're busy— you're going to a birthday party. He (She) then asks you about Saturday, then Sunday, etc. Each time, make up an excuse and decline the invitation (politely!).

C. In Spanish, make a list of five things you're interested in and would like to do: play a game of tennis, go to a rock concert, take dancing lessons, see a play, learn to cook Chinese food, etc. Then invite people in your class to join you. Try to find someone with the same interests you have. If you do, make plans in Spanish to get together. (You may even want to follow up on them!)

D. Situación. Consuelo and Manolo are guests at Graciela's house on Christmas Day. Play their roles, using the following ideas as guidelines.

GRACIELA	«Hola, Consuelo, ¡feliz Navidad! ¿Cómo estás?»
CONSUELO	Dice que está bien y que le encantan los adornos de la casa, etcétera.
GRACIELA	Le da las gracias y le dice que quiere que ella conozca a su vecino Manolo. Llama a Manolo.
MANOLO	Saluda a Graciela y le dice que la fiesta es muy agradable (*pleasant*), que la comida es muy rica, etcétera.
GRACIELA	Presenta a Manolo y a Consuelo.
MANOLO	Le pregunta a Consuelo si quiere que le traiga una copa de champaña.
CONSUELO	Dice que sí, que le gusta mucho el champaña y que entonces van a poder brindar (*toast*) por una feliz Navidad para todos.

E. El cumpleaños de Eduardo. Today is Eduardo's twenty-first birthday. Using the photo below, describe how he celebrates it. What are the people saying to him?

La Casa de los Azulejos (el famoso Sanborn) de la Ciudad de México

VOCABULARIO ACTIVO

Cognados

el aniversario
el candelabro
la celebración

el instructor, la
  instructora
la piñata

Verbos

celebrar	to celebrate
construir	to build
fumar	to smoke
mandar	to order, command; to send
permitir	to permit, allow
presentar	to introduce
quejarse	to complain
reunirse	to meet, get together
saludar	to greet

Fiestas y aniversarios

el adorno	decoration
el árbol	tree
el árbol de Navidad	Christmas tree
el comedor	dining room
el desfile	parade
Janucá	Chanukah
la madrina	godmother
la misa	mass
la Navidad	Christmas
la Nochebuena	Christmas Eve
el padrino	godfather

los padrinos	godparents; host family role
el papel	
hacer el papel (de)	to play the role (of)
el pavo	turkey
los Reyes Magos	Three Kings (Three Wise Men)
la tarjeta	card

Otras palabras y frases

el dueño (la dueña)	owner
la injusticia	injustice
¡Qué injusticia!	How unfair!
la lectura	reading
listo	ready; clever
medianoche	midnight
próximo	next
el vecino (la vecina)	neighbor

Expresiones útiles

No veo la hora de (+ inf.)	I can't wait (+ inf.)
Quiero que conozca(-s) a...	I want you to meet...

cabeza

La salud y el cuerpo   *14*

Expressing Doubt
Asking for Permission
Granting or Denying Permission
Giving Advice

EJERCICIO

Complete the sentences.

1. Una aspirina es una _____.
2. Cuando tengo una pregunta en la clase, levanto la _____.
3. Paco anda mucho en bicicleta; por eso tiene las _____ muy fuertes.
4. Pinocho (*Pinocchio*) tenía la _____ muy grande.
5. Esa muchacha tiene ojos azules y _____ negro.
6. Por favor, Miguelito, lávate la _____. Y no te olvides de tomar tus _____.
7. Voy a tomar mucho líquido hoy porque tengo dolor de _____.
8. «Ser el _____ derecho de alguien» quiere decir ser la persona de mayor confianza (*confidence*) de alguien.
9. Comí demasiado; tengo dolor de _____.
10. Vimos a una mujer india que llevaba a su hijo en la _____.

estómago

PREGUNTAS

1. ¿Qué parte del cuerpo usamos para ver? ¿para pensar? ¿para hablar? ¿para caminar? **2.** ¿Hace usted muchos ejercicios físicos? ¿Anda en bicicleta? ¿Nada? ¿Practica algún deporte regularmente? ¿Corre? ¿Tiene las piernas y los brazos fuertes? **3.** ¿Toma usted vitaminas todos los días? **4.** ¿Cuándo tiene usted más energía: por la noche o por la mañana? ¿el sábado por la noche o el lunes por la mañana? **5.** En general, ¿tiene usted dolor de cabeza durante un examen? ¿en una discoteca? ¿los domingos por la mañana? ¿en la clase de física?

aspirina

 ## Other uses of the definite article

En casa de una familia cubana, en Hialeah*, Florida.

RAMÓN	¿Qué tal *el* dolor de cabeza, mi amor?
EDUVIGES	Hoy fui *al* médico°. Me dio píldoras° de Anabufenol y otras medicinas. No sé qué son porque no sé leer latín. Después fui a *la* doctora Soya, que es experta en nutrición.
RAMON	¿Y qué te dijo ella?
EDUVIGES	Me dijo que *las* frutas y *las* verduras frescas son muy importantes para *la* salud° y que *el* café, *el* té y *el* chocolate son malos. Y me dio «Herbavor», que, según ella, cura todos *los* males.°
RAMÓN	¡Qué bien!°
EDUVIGES	Después, por *la* tarde, fui a una clase de yoga. *La* maestra me dijo que *la* tensión es *la* causa principal de *los* dolores de cabeza. Me enseñó algunos ejercicios como «*el* león» y «*la* cobra». Ahora me duele** mucho *la* espalda.°
RAMÓN	¡Qué lástima...!
EDUVIGES	Finalmente, fui a Madame Leona, *la* espiritista°. Ella me aconsejó quitarme *los* zapatos. Dijo que *los* zapatos pueden causar toda clase de dolores. Y que no debo salir *los* viernes porque soy del signo de Aries.
RAMÓN	Pero ahora, ¿cómo te sientes°?
EDUVIGES	No sé. Después de tantos consejos, ¡tengo un dolor de cabeza terrible!

---

1. ¿Qué problema tenía Eduviges?   2. ¿Qué le dio el médico?   3. ¿Qué le dijo la doctora Soya? ¿Qué le dio ella?   4. Según la maestra de yoga, ¿cuál es la causa principal de los dolores de cabeza? ¿Qué le recomendó ella a Eduviges?   5. ¿Qué le dijo Madame Leona a ella?   6. ¿Cómo se siente Eduviges después de todos esos consejos?

---

médico *doctor* **píldoras** *pills*	**para la salud** *for one's health*
cura... males *cures all (one's) ills*	**¡Qué bien!** *That's good!*
me... espalda *my back aches a lot*	**espiritista** *spiritualist*
¿cómo te sientes? *how do you feel?*	

---

* See **Nota cultural** 1.
** **Doler** (*to ache, hurt*) is an **o** to **ue** stem-changing verb. Like **gustar**, it is normally used with an indirect object pronoun.

Several uses of the definite article such as the article with titles (Chapter 1) and with dates and days of the week (Chapter 4), have already been presented. Other uses of the definite article are:

A. With parts of the body and articles of clothing when it is clear who the possessor is. The possessive adjective is not used in these instances.

El médico se lava las manos.	*The doctor is washing his hands.*
Ana se pone los zapatos.	*Ana is putting on her shoes.*
Ricardo se quitó el suéter.	*Ricardo took off his sweater.*
Dame la mano.	*Give me your hand.*
Me duele la cabeza. Tengo que descansar.	*My head aches. I have to rest.*
A Esteban le duelen los pies.	*Esteban's feet hurt.*

B. Before a noun used in a general sense as representative of its class or type. The noun can be singular or plural, concrete or abstract.

La salud es muy importante.	*Health is very important.*
Así es el amor.	*That's love.*
No me gustan los cigarros.	*I don't like cigars.*

C. With names of languages and fields of study, except after the preposition **en** and after **aprender**, **enseñar**, **estudiar**, **hablar**, and **leer**, when it is usually omitted.

Aprendo alemán. —El alemán es una lengua muy útil.	*I'm learning German. —German is a very useful language.*
Me gustan las ciencias en general.	*I like sciences in general.*
¿Hablas francés? —Sí, pero con dificultad.	*Do you speak French? —Yes, but with difficulty.*
¿Cómo se dice «buen viaje» en francés? —«Bon voyage.»	*How do you say "Have a good trip" in French? —"Bon voyage."*

D. For rates and prices.

Aquí se venden huevos a setenta centavos la docena.	*Eggs are sold here for seventy cents a dozen.*
Compré un vino excelente a cuarenta pesos el litro.	*I bought an excellent wine for forty pesos a liter.*
¿Ese queso cuesta quinientos pesos el kilo? —No tengo la menor idea.	*Does that cheese cost 500 pesos a kilo? —I don't have the slightest idea.*

EJERCICIOS

A. **¿Qué se puso Anita?**   Anita is getting ready to go meet her boyfriend downtown. Describe what she put on before she left, following the model.

Modelo   blusa / blanco
   Anita se puso la blusa blanca.

1. traje / rojo
2. falda / blanco
3. suéter / azul
4. zapatos / negro
5. chaqueta / nuevo
6. sombrero / gris

B. ¿Qué no le gusta a Luis?   Luis is telling his girlfriend some of the things he doesn't like. Describe them as he would, following the model.

Modelo   comidas / picante
No me gustan las comidas picantes.

1. café / negro
2. vinos / italiano
3. chocolate / blanco
4. películas / cómico
5. música / clásico
6. conciertos / moderno

C. ¿Qué le duele?   You are going to see a doctor because you ache everywhere. Describe your aches and pains, following the model.

Modelo   garganta / ojos
Me duele la garganta y también me duelen los ojos.

1. nariz / espalda
2. pies / piernas
3. manos / brazos
4. cuello / boca
5. cabeza / cuerpo
6. orejas / estómago

D. Completar las frases.   Complete the sentences, using a definite article if needed.

1. Teresa abre _____ ojos.
2. Orlando lleva el pasaporte en _____ mano.
3. Miguel se ponía _____ pantalones.
4. Ana se quitó _____ zapatos.
5. Me duelen _____ orejas.
6. _____ tiempo es oro.
7. A Jaime no le gustan _____ películas italianas.
8. _____ español es una lengua muy útil.
9. Compré un buen vino a veinte pesos _____ litro.
10. ¿Cómo se dice «Cheers!» en _____ español?—Se dice «*¡Salud!*»
11. ¿Habla usted _____ alemán?
12. Aquí venden huevos a setenta centavos _____ docena.

E. Traducción.   Give the Spanish equivalent of the following sentences.

1. Two very important languages are Spanish and French.
2. In the United States many people speak Spanish.
3. She put on her shoes.
4. Give me your hand.
5. Children need milk.
6. My arm hurts a lot.

PREGUNTAS

1. Cuando usted se despierta por la mañana, ¿abre los ojos fácilmente o con mucha dificultad?   **2.** ¿Le duele a usted a veces la cabeza? ¿el estómago? ¿la garganta? ¿Qué toma o qué hace usted entonces?   **3.** ¿Qué ropa se pone usted cuando hace frío? ¿cuando hace calor? ¿cuando llueve?   **4.** ¿Le interesa a usted el arte? ¿la política? ¿la literatura?

The subjunctive with certain verbs expressing emotion, necessity, will, and uncertainty

Una doctora
habla con su paciente.

En la Clínica Asociación Cubana de Miami.

LA DOCTORA Primero quiero que la enfermera le *tome* la temperatura.°
LA ENFERMA° Ya lo hizo, doctora, y no tengo fiebre°. Pero me siento* muy mal.
LA DOCTORA No me sorprende que *se sienta* mal°. Quiero que usted *vaya*° al hospital ahora mismo°.
LA ENFERMA Pero, doctora, ¿qué tengo?
LA DOCTORA No estoy segura. Por ahora° sólo sé que su aspecto físico° es horrible. Mírese en ese espejo°. Usted está muy pálida°, tiene los ojos nublosos, la nariz°...
LA ENFERMA ¡Basta ya!° ¡Tampoco usted es una Venus!

---

1. ¿Qué quiere la doctora que haga la enfermera?   2. ¿Cómo se siente la enferma?   3. ¿Qué quiere la doctora que haga la enferma?   4. ¿Sabe la doctora qué tiene la enferma?   5. ¿Qué hace usted cuando se siente muy mal?

---

quiero... temperatura *I'd like the nurse to take your temperature*   **enferma** *patient*
no tengo fiebre *I don't have a fever*   **No... mal.** *I'm not surprised that you feel bad.*
Quiero... vaya *I want you to go*   **ahora mismo** *right away*
Por ahora *Right now*   **aspecto físico** *physical appearance*   **espejo** *mirror*
pálida *pale*   **tiene... nariz** *your eyes are blurry, your nose*   **¡Basta ya!** *That's enough!*

***Sentirse** (**ie**) + adjective means *to feel* (*good, bad. etc.*); **sentir que** usually means *to be sorry that*: **Siento que Juan no esté aquí**. (*I'm sorry* [*that*] *Juan isn't here*.)

A. You have seen that many sentences are composed of two or more clauses, or groups of words containing a subject and a verb. For instance, in the sentence *We wish that he were coming*, *We wish* is an independent, and *that he were coming* is a dependent clause. The subjunctive is used in Spanish in dependent clauses after verbs expressing:

1. An order or request; for example, **insistir (en)**, **pedir**, **decir**.

Insiste en que su hijo estudie medicina.	*He insists that his son study medicine.*
Le pido al niño que no ponga los pies en la mesa.	*I am asking the child not to put his feet on the table.*
¡Te digo que levantes la mano!	*I'm telling you to raise your hand!*

2. Will, desire, preference; for example, **querer**, **desear**, **preferir**.

No quiero que usted pierda el tiempo.	*I don't want you to waste time.*
Deseo que vengan a visitarme.	*I want you to come visit me.*
Eduviges prefiere que su esposo no fume cigarrillos.	*Eduviges prefers that her husband not smoke cigarettes.*

3. Hope, emotion, and feeling; for example, **ojalá**, **tener miedo**, **alegrarse (de)**, **sorprender**, **sentir**.

Ojalá que Susana se sienta bien.	*I hope Susana will feel well.*
Tengo miedo que los niños se enfermen.	*I'm afraid that the children will get sick.*
Me alegro (de) que no tengas fiebre.	*I'm glad you don't have a fever.*
No me sorprende que Ernesto esté enfermo porque no come bien.	*It doesn't surprise me that Ernesto is sick because he doesn't eat well.*
Siento que Juan tenga un resfrío.	*I'm sorry Juan has a cold.*

4. Approval, permission, prohibition, or advice; for example, **gustar**, **permitir**, **prohibir**, **aconsejar**, **recomendar**.

Me gusta que Ana diga eso.	*I'm pleased (It pleases me) that Ana says that.*
Mamá no permite que hablemos con la boca llena.	*Mom doesn't allow us to talk with our mouths full.*
El doctor le prohíbe que se levante de la cama.	*The doctor forbids him (her) to get out of bed.*
Te aconsejo que llegues a las nueve en punto.	*I advise you to arrive at nine o'clock on the dot.*
El médico recomienda que tomes mucha agua y otros líquidos.	*The doctor recommends that you drink a lot of water and other liquids.*

5. Necessity; for example, **necesitar**.

Necesitan que alguien los lleve al hospital.	*They need someone to take them to the hospital.*

6. Doubt or uncertainty; for example, **dudar**, **no estar seguro(-a)**.

Dudo que encuentren la cura para esa enfermedad.

I doubt they will find the cure for that disease.

No estoy seguro que el doctor sepa hacerlo.

I'm not sure the doctor knows how to do it.

B. The verbs **creer** and **pensar** require the subjunctive in interrogative or negative sentences when surprise or doubt is implied. The indicative is used in affirmative sentences or when there is no uncertainty in the speaker's mind.

¿Crees que Alicia esté embarazada?

Do you think that Alicia is pregnant? (doubt implied)

¿Crees que Alicia está embarazada? —No tengo la menor idea.

Do you think that Alicia is pregnant? (simple question) —*I don't have the slightest idea.*

No creo que Alicia esté embarazada.

I don't believe that Alicia is pregnant.

¿Piensas que Ramón sea feliz?

Do you think Ramón is happy? (doubt implied)

No pienso que Ramón sea feliz.

I don't think that Ramón is happy. (The speaker thinks he probably isn't.)

Pienso que Ramón es feliz.

I think that Ramón is happy.

C. Remember that **que** is always used in these expressions, although in English *that* can be omitted or an infinitive used.

Espero que ellos hablen con el médico.

I hope (that) they talk to the doctor.

Quiero que Juanito tome estas vitaminas.

I want Juanito to take these vitamins.

Remember also that the subjunctive is used only when there is a change of subject; when the subject of the main and dependent clauses is the same, an infinitive is used.

Queremos ir a pescar mañana.

We want to go fishing tomorrow.

Necesito comprar unas medicinas.

I need to buy some medicines.

A. Doctora por un día...   Anita and a friend are playing "doctor and patient." Play Anita's role as the doctor and tell your "patient" what you want (advise, expect, request, etc.) him or her to do or not do, as Anita would. Follow the models.

Modelos   querer / abrir la boca
Quiero que abras la boca.

aconsejarte / no fumar los cigarrillos de tu papá
Te aconsejo que no fumes los cigarrillos de tu papá.

1. no creer / tener mucha fiebre
2. esperar / seguir todos mis consejos
3. aconsejarte / acostarte temprano esta noche
4. prohibirte / ver a otro(-a) doctor(-a)
5. aconsejarte / no ir a clase mañana
6. pedirte / pagarme hoy
7. querer / venir a verme otra vez la semana próxima
8. esperar / sentirte mejor muy pronto

B. Completar las frases.   Complete the sentences with the correct form of the verbs in parentheses.

1. (llegar) ¡Ojalá que la enfermera _____ pronto!
2. (conocer) Queremos que tú _____ a Magdalena.
3. (dar) Le pido que no le _____ aspirinas al niño.
4. (volver) ¿Dudas que el doctor _____ mañana?
5. (saber) Esperamos que ellas _____ hacerlo.
6. (venir) No creo que él _____ porque tiene dolor de garganta.
7. (tener) ¿Te sorprende que yo _____ un resfrío?
8. (ser) ¿No creen que ella _____ mi hermana?
9. (estar) Sentimos que usted _____ enferma.
10. (trabajar) ¿No le gusta que su esposa _____ en el hospital?
11. (descansar) El médico aconseja que tú _____ más.
12. (ir) Recomiendo que ustedes _____ en bicicleta.

C. ¿De veras...?   Working in pairs, make five statements in the present, saying things about yourself (or someone you know) to your partner. Some of your statements should be true and some false. Take turns. Start your responses with either «**¿De veras? Dudo que...**» or «**¡Qué interesante! No dudo que...**», as appropriate. How many times does your classmate guess correctly?

Modelos   Estudiante 1:   **Mis abuelos viven en Cuba. (Conozco al presidente de México. Sé hablar italiano.)**
Estudiante 2:   **¿De veras? Dudo que tus abuelos vivan en Cuba (que conozcas al presidente de México, que sepas hablar italiano).**

D. Traducción. Give the Spanish equivalent of the following sentences.

1. I hope (that) he helps the family.
2. I want him to help the family.
3. She believes you (**usted**) are at the hospital.
4. She doubts that you (**usted**) are at the hospital.
5. They don't believe that you (**usted**) are at the hospital.
6. Do you (**tú**) think he has a fever?
7. I think he has a fever.
8. We don't think he has a fever.
9. I advise you (**tú**) to arrive early.
10. The doctor forbids Mrs. López to do exercises now.

PREGUNTAS

1. ¿Cree usted que los médicos generalmente les dicen la verdad a sus pacientes?
2. ¿Necesita usted que el doctor le dé una dieta especial? ¿Qué tipo de dieta?
3. ¿Piensa usted que las vitaminas son necesarias? ¿Por qué sí o por qué no?

Una farmacia hispana

 ## The subjunctive with impersonal expressions

En casa de los Hernández, en Miami.

SR. HERNÁNDEZ   Si piensa casarse con mi hija, es importante que me *diga*° qué hace y cuánto gana°.

EL NOVIO   Pues mire, señor Hernández, yo trabajo en el Hospital Victoria y gano doscientos dólares por semana. Soy enfermero... Es preferible que su hija *sea* feliz° y no rica, ¿verdad...?

SR. HERNÁNDEZ   Sí, usted tiene razón. Sin embargo°, es posible que se *mueran de hambre*° aunque también es verdad que mi hija va a estar bien cuidada° con un enfermero en casa...

---

1. ¿Qué quiere saber el señor Hernández?   2. ¿Cuánto gana el novio? 3. Según el señor Hernández, ¿qué es posible que les pase a los novios después de casarse? ¿Por qué?   4. ¿Piensa él que su hija va a estar bien o mal cuidada? ¿Por qué?

---

es... diga *it's important that you tell me*   **cuánto gana** *how much you earn*
Es... feliz *It's preferable for your daughter to be happy*   **Sin embargo** *However*
es... hambre *it's possible that you might die from hunger*
es... cuidada *it's true that my daughter is going to be well taken care of*

A.   Impersonal expressions have no obvious subject, and equivalent English expressions often begin with the pronoun *it*. The subjunctive is used after many impersonal expressions of doubt, emotion, expectation, permission or prohibition, and personal judgment. Some of the more commonly used impersonal expressions that require the subjunctive in a following clause are:

Es bueno. *It's good.*	**Es (una) lástima.** *It's a pity.*
Es malo. *It's bad.*	**Es probable.** *It's probable.*
Es mejor. *It's better.*	**Es dudoso.** *It's doubtful.*
Es peor. *It's worse.*	**Es necesario.** *It's necessary.*
Es imposible. *It's impossible.*	**Es ridículo.** *It's ridiculous.*
Es posible. *It's possible.*	**Está bien.** *It's all right (okay).*
Es importante. *It's important.*	**Está prohibido.** *It's forbidden.*

¿Es bueno que ellos hagan ejercicios?	*Is it good that they exercise?*
Es mejor que me vaya.	*It's better for me to leave.*
Es importante que tomes vitaminas.	*It's important that you take vitamins.*
No es posible que sea tan difícil.	*It's not possible that it's so difficult.*
¿Está bien que te acompañemos?	*Is it all right if we go with you?*
Está prohibido que los estudiantes fumen en la sala de clase.	*It's forbidden for students to smoke in the classroom.*

All of the preceding impersonal expressions are followed by the subjunctive in dependent clauses in affirmative, negative, or interrogative sentences.

B. The following expressions require the indicative when used in the affirmative but the subjunctive when used in the negative. They take the subjunctive in interrogative sentences only if doubt is strongly implied.

Es cierto	*It's true.*	**Es seguro.**	*It's certain.*
Es (Está) claro.	*It's clear.*	**Es verdad.**	*It's true.*

No es verdad que todo se vaya a arreglar.*	*It's not true that everything is going to turn out all right.*
¿Es verdad que todo se vaya a arreglar?	*Is it true that everything is going to turn out all right?* (doubt implied)
¿Es verdad que todo se va a arreglar?	*Is it true that everything is going to turn out all right?* (simple question)
Es verdad que todo se va a arreglar.	*It's true that everything is going to turn out all right.*
No es cierto que esa enfermedad sea incurable.	*It's not true that that disease is incurable.*

C. The expressions **tal vez** and **quizás**, which both mean *perhaps*, normally require the subjunctive. They are followed by the indicative if the speaker or writer wants to express belief or conviction.

Quizás fume demasiado.	*Perhaps he smokes too much.* (The speaker is not sure.)
Quizás fuma demasiado.	*Perhaps he smokes too much.* (The speaker thinks he probably does.)
Tal vez Enrique lo sepa.	*Maybe Enrique knows about it.* (The speaker is not sure.)
Tal vez Enrique lo sabe.	*Maybe Enrique knows about it.* (The speaker thinks he probably does.)

*****Arreglar** means *to fix*, *repair*, or *arrange*; **arreglarse** is *to be okay*, *turn out all right.*

A. ¿Es necesario, doctor? Mrs. Ramos is pregnant with her first child and goes to see the family doctor. Form sentences with the following elements, starting with **Es necesario que**, as the doctor would.

Modelo usted / tomar mucha leche
Es necesario que usted tome mucha leche.

1. su esposo / ayudar más en la casa
2. usted / dormir ocho horas por día
3. usted y su esposo / querer tener este bebé
4. usted / comer bien y tomar vitaminas
5. ustedes / buscar un buen hospital
6. usted / no fumar
7. usted / no tomar bebidas alcohólicas
8. usted / volver aquí la próxima semana

B. Es mejor que practiquemos... Create new sentences, replacing the words in italics with **que** + a clause. Use the word or words in parentheses as subjects.

Modelo Es bueno *ser bilingüe*. (Tomás)
Es bueno que Tomás sea bilingüe.

1. Es una lástima *no llegar temprano*. (Eduardo y Carolina)
2. Es importante *no trabajar demasiado*. (tú)
3. Es posible *tener fiebre*. (la hija del doctor)
4. Es mejor *no hacerlo*. (nosotros)
5. Es ridículo *decir esas cosas*. (usted)
6. Es necesario *ver al doctor regularmente*. (yo)
7. ¿Está prohibido *hablar inglés en esta clase*? (los estudiantes)
8. Está bien *ponerse la ropa ahora*. (la enferma)

C. ¿Verdadero o falso? Professor Bonilla is very popular because all his exams are true/false. Today he's giving a quiz on Cuba. Follow Tomás' train of thought as he ponders each question. Follow the models.

Modelos No hay enfermos de SIDA en Cuba. (Es dudoso que...)
Es dudoso que no haya enfermos de SIDA en Cuba.

En Hialeah viven muchísimos cubanos. (Es cierto que...)
Es cierto que en Hialeah viven muchísimos cubanos.

1. Florida está al norte de Cuba. (Es verdad que...)
2. La mayoría de los cubanos habla ruso (*Russian*). (No es verdad que...)
3. «La esquina de Tejas» es un famoso restaurante cubano de Miami. (Es cierto que...)
4. El ochenta por ciento de los cubanos no sabe leer. (Es imposible que...)
5. Hay pocos médicos buenos en Cuba. (Es dudoso que...)
6. Todos los cubanos saben bailar la rumba. (Es imposible que...)

D. Quizás... In pairs, make three to five statements using **quizás** or **tal vez**; tell your partner what you or people you know may do this weekend. Then report the information to the class.

PREGUNTAS

1. ¿Es importante o no que uno vea al doctor regularmente? ¿Por qué? **2.** ¿Es posible que en el futuro exista la posibilidad de vivir eternamente? ¿Le gusta o no la idea de no morir? ¿Por qué sí o por qué no? **3.** ¿Cree usted que es probable que los científicos descubran alguna cura para el cáncer? ¿para el SIDA? **4.** ¿Es probable que podamos llegar a Marte (*Mars*) en esta década (*decade*)? ¿que podamos hablar con habitantes (*inhabitants*) de otros planetas? **5.** ¿Es posible que no tengamos guerras (*wars*) en el futuro? ¿problemas económicos? ¿enfermedades?

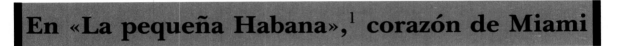

En «La pequeña Habana»,¹ corazón de Miami

Georgina visita a su papá en el Hospital Victoria de «la pequeña Habana», en Miami. A don Pedro lo habían operado del corazón° hacía unos días...

GEORGINA ¿Cómo te sientes después de la operación, papá...?
DON PEDRO Un poco mejor, mi hija, pero estoy muy solo y sin noticias. Hace tres días que no leo el periódico...
GEORGINA Pues... tengo una sorpresa para ti. Teresa estuvo en La Habana² la semana pasada. Fue a un Festival Internacional de Teatro que hubo allí y te trajo *Granma*³...

La Calle Ocho, en la «Pequeña Habana» de Miami

arroz con frijoles blancos

319

DON PEDRO	¿Qué dices...? ¿...que Teresa trajo a tu abuela aquí...? ¡Qué estupidez!° ¡Tu amiga debe estar loca...!
GEORGINA	¡No, papá...! Te trajo unos artículos de *Granma*...
DON PEDRO	¡Ah...! Me hablas de ese periódico comunista, lleno de mentiras°... Dudo que allí haya algo que pueda interesarme.
GEORGINA	Pues creo que éstos te van a interesar... Por ejemplo, aquí hay uno que habla de Mario Kid[4]...
DON PEDRO	¿De don Mario, el campeón de boxeo° que después fue masajista° de Hemingway? ¿Estás segura, Georgina...?
GEORGINA	Sí, papá... Aquí tienes el artículo. Lo puedes leer tú mismo. (*Le da el artículo y don Pedro lo lee rápidamente.*)
DON PEDRO	¡Qué increíble! Así que don Mario todavía vive... ¿Sabías que él y papá—tu abuelo—eran muy buenos amigos?
GEORGINA	Sí, lo sabía. Creo que me lo contó la abuela cuando fui a visitarla hace dos años. También sabía que los dos trabajaron como enfermeros en el mismo lugar durante varios años.
DON PEDRO	Así fue. Cuando papá se enfermó, don Mario venía a verlo y a cuidarlo todos los días. Después murió papá, me casé con tu mamá, naciste tú, vino la Revolución[5], nosotros salimos de Cuba y nunca más supimos de don Mario°... hasta ahora... ¡Qué linda noticia me has traído, Georgina...!
GEORGINA	Pues... esta noticia se la debemos a *Granma*...
DON PEDRO	Bueno, es natural que de vez en cuando publiquen° allí algo interesante, ¿no...? ¿Qué otros artículos me trajo Teresa?
GEORGINA	Estos dos... y uno de ellos está indirectamente relacionado conmigo. Como vas a leer, en agosto va a haber en Cuba un Congreso de Naciones Unidas°... Yo voy como periodista del *Diario de las Américas*° y Nicolás también va. Queremos pasar nuestro octavo° aniversario de casamiento en Varadero[6], donde nos conocimos hace diez años...
DON PEDRO	¡Dios mío...! ¡Hoy sí que estoy lleno de noticias...!
LA ENFERMERA	(*En ese momento entra la enfermera.*) ¡...Y de noticias buenas, espero! Yo también le traigo una y creo que le va a gustar: el doctor Benítez dice que puede volver a su casa hoy mismo...
DON PEDRO	¡Qué bien! ¡Otra noticia más! ¡Y la verdad es que ésta es para mí la mejor de todas! Vamos, Georgina, llévame a casa y tal vez tu mamá y yo viajemos con ustedes a Cuba en agosto... Tengo ganas de ver a don Mario y a tu abuela...

A don Pedro... corazón *Don Pedro had had a heart operation (literally, been operated on his heart)*
¡Qué estupidez! *What a stupid thing to do!*   **lleno de mentiras** *full of lies*
campeón de boxeo *boxing champion*   **masajista** *masseur*
nunca... Mario *we did not hear from Don Mario again*
es... publiquen *it's natural that from time to time they'd publish*
Naciones Unidas *United Nations*
como... Américas *as a journalist for* Diario de las Américas *(newspaper published in Miami, in Spanish)*   **octavo** *eighth*

1. ¿A quién visita Georgina? ¿Dónde? ¿Por qué está don Pedro allí?   **2.** ¿Cómo se siente don Pedro? ¿Por qué?   **3.** ¿Quién estuvo en La Habana recientemente? ¿Por qué fue ella allí?   **4.** ¿Qué le trajo Teresa de Cuba a don Pedro? ¿Qué creyó él que ella le había traído? ¿Por qué piensa usted que él se confundió (*got confused*)?   **5.** ¿Qué piensa don Pedro del periódico *Granma*? Según usted, ¿por qué tiene él esa opinión?   **6.** ¿Por qué cree Georgina que estos artículos le van a interesar a su papá?   **7.** ¿Quién es Mario Kid? ¿Lo conoce don Pedro? ¿Se conocieron ellos recientemente o hace muchos años? ¿Dónde?   **8.** ¿Qué sabía Georgina con respecto a la relación entre Mario Kid y su abuelo? ¿Qué más le cuenta don Pedro al respecto?   **9.** ¿Adónde va a viajar Georgina en agosto? ¿Para qué? ¿Quién va a ir con ella? ¿Por qué?   **10.** ¿Cuál es la buena noticia que le da la enfermera a don Pedro? ¿Está él muy contento con la noticia? ¿Cómo sabemos que él está feliz?

Notas culturales

1. La pequeña Habana is a section of the city of Miami, west of the downtown area. Since the early 1960s it has been a center of the Cuban immigrants' economic and social life, especially for the older generation (those who came to the United States in their thirties or forties). Business transactions here are dominated by Cuban merchants and customers. Since the influx of Nicaraguan immigrants after the fall of Anastasio Somoza in 1979, this portion of the city has attracted the newer Spanish-speaking community. However, it continues to be predominantly Cuban. **Hialeah** is a city northwest of the greater Miami area. Most of its population is of Cuban descent. The local economy relies heavily on the garment industry, which employs a great number of Hispanics, especially women. In both cities, Miami and Hialeah, Cubans hold seats in the City Council and have elected Cuban-born mayors.

2. La Habana is the capital of Cuba, one of the three Spanish-speaking countries in the Caribbean, together with Puerto Rico and the Dominican Republic. **La Habana** is the nation's economic, political, and cultural center and one of the historic cities of the New World. The city lies toward the western end of the long northern coast of the island of Cuba, around one of the Caribbean's finest harbors.

3. *Granma* is the title of a Cuban newspaper of wide circulation. It is published daily in Havana, but it has an international edition which appears weekly in four languages: Spanish, English, French, and Portuguese. ***Granma*** is named after the yacht that landed Fidel Castro and his fellow revolutionaries in Cuba in 1956.

4. Mario Sánchez Cruz, better known as Mario Kid, was a well-recognized Cuban boxing champion in the 1930s. After he retired from boxing in 1935 (with 100 victories versus 10 defeats total), he became Ernest Hemingway's masseur. He worked for the famous American novelist until 1960, when the latter left Cuba to return to the United States after residing twenty-two years on the island.

5. The reference here is to the Cuban Revolution of 1959. Fidel Castro, the present Cuban head of state, was the leader of the **Movimiento 26 de julio**, which for three years (1956–1959) was involved in guerrilla warfare against the government of Fulgencio Batista, finally overthrowing it on January 1, 1959.

6. **Varadero** is a very popular Cuban beach on the Atlantic coast, in the province of Matanzas, approximately 50 to 60 kilometers east of Havana.

FUNCIONES Y ACTIVIDADES

In this chapter, you have seen examples of some important language functions, or uses. Here is a summary and some additional information about these functions of language.

Expressing doubt

You don't know how to respond to someone because you don't know or can't decide something.

No sé.	*I don't know.*
No se sabe.	*No one knows.* (Literally, "It's not known.")
¿Quién sabe?	*Who knows?*
¿Qué sé yo?	*What do I know?* (informal)
No tengo la menor idea.	*I don't have the slightest idea.*

You have a response, but you are doubtful about it.

No estoy seguro(-a) que (+ subj.)...	*I'm not sure that . . .*
Es posible (probable) que (+ subj.)...	*It's possible (probable) that . . .*
Puede (Podría) ser.	*It could be.*
Tal vez..., Quizá(s)... (+ subj. or ind.)	*Perhaps . . .*
Que yo sepa... (+ ind.)	*As far as I know . . .*
Creo que sí (no).	*I believe so (not).*
Creo que (+ ind.)..., No creo que (+ subj.)...	*I believe that . . . , I don't believe that . . .*
Pienso que sí (no).	*I think so. (I don't think so.)*
Pienso que (+ ind.)..., No pienso que (+ subj.)...	*I think that . . . , I don't think that . . .*

Asking for permission

¿Me permite (+ inf.)...?	*May I...? (Will you allow me to...?)*
¿Se permite (+ inf.)... ? ¿Se debe (+ inf.)...?	*May one (we, I)...?*
¿Se puede (+ inf.)...?	*Can one (we, I)...?*
¿Está bien que (+ subj.)...?	*Is it okay to...?*

Granting or denying permission

Sí, está bien que (+ subj.)...	*Yes, it's okay to...*
Sí, estoy seguro(-a) que puede(-s)...	*Yes, I'm sure you can...*
No, no está bien que (+ subj.)...	*No, it's not okay to...*
No, está prohibido que (+ subj.)...	*No, it's prohibited to...*
Se prohíbe (+ inf.)...	*It's prohibited (forbidden) to...*
No se permite (+ inf.)...	*It's not permitted to...*
Eso no se hace.	*That's not done (allowed).*
¡Ni hablar!	*Don't even mention it!*

Giving advice

Usted debe (Tú debes)...	*You should...*
Le (Te) aconsejo que (+ subj.)...	*I advise you to...*
Es mejor que usted (tú) (+ subj.)...	*It's better for you to...*
Recomiendo que usted (tú) (+ subj.)...	*I recommend that you...*

A. Dudas. Juanita reads a lot about health, but she doesn't always get her facts straight. Express doubt as she tells you the following things, which she has incorrectly interpreted. Use as many different expressions of doubt as you can.

> Modelo   Hacer muchos ejercicios siempre es malo para el corazón.
> **No estoy seguro(-a) de que siempre sea malo para el corazón.**

1. El chocolate puede causar cáncer.
2. La persona que sale de la casa con el pelo mojado (*wet*) se enferma.
3. Las pulseras de cobre (*copper bracelets*) curan la artritis.
4. La vitamina C cura el cáncer.
5. La leche es buena para todo el mundo.
6. Es bueno para el pelo si uno se lo lava con huevos y cerveza.
7. Dos o tres días sin comer, tomando (*drinking*) sólo jugo de lechuga, cura todos los males.
8. Si uno tiene fiebre, es mejor no comer; si uno tiene un resfrío, se debe comer mucho.
9. La persona que come mucha cebolla (*onion*) va a vivir mucho.

B. No, mi amor... Manuel's wife, Sara, is pregnant for the first time, and he is overly protective. She asks if she can do various things, and he says no, since he is worried about her health. Take their roles and follow the model. Use as many different expressions to ask for permission as possible.

Modelo   tomar un café (es importante que no...)
    Sara: **¿Está bien que tome un café?**
    Manuel: **No, es importante que no tomes café.**

1. tomar una copa de vino (el doctor prohíbe que...)
2. fumar un cigarrillo (insisto en que no...)
3. hacer algunos ejercicios (te digo que no...)
4. llevar cuatro libros grandes de un lugar a otro (no quiero que...)
5. comer unos chocolates (no me gusta que...)
6. acostarse muy tarde (te pido que no...)
7. aumentar de peso (no está bien que...)

C. La espiritista. Tina has a lot of problems and goes to Madame Leona, a spiritualist. In pairs, role-play their conversation using the cues provided.

TINA	Dice que últimamente se siente mal, que siempre tiene dolores de cabeza y que está muy nerviosa. Le pregunta qué puede ser.
MME. LEONA	Le hace varias preguntas sobre su rutina diaria: a qué hora se levanta, a qué hora se acuesta, qué come, etcétera.
TINA	Dice que no duerme mucho y que tampoco come mucho porque no tiene tiempo. Trabaja unas dieciocho horas por día.
MME. LEONA	Le hace algunas preguntas sobre su vida social: si tiene novio, etcétera.
TINA	Describe a su novio.
MME. LEONA	Le da los siguientes consejos:

No es bueno:
    tomar café
    seguir viendo (*keep seeing*) a su novio
    salir los martes
    trabajar tantas horas al día
    ? (add two items of your own)

También le dice que es bueno:
    hacer más ejercicios
    dormir más
    comer tres comidas al día
    leer su horóscopo todos los días
    salir más para conocer a más muchachos
    ? (add two items of your own)

D. Consejos.   In pairs, take turns giving each other advice. One person states a problem, real or imaginary. The other tells him or her what to do.

Modelo   Siempre estoy cansado(-a).
   Te aconsejo que descanses más (que tomes vitaminas, etcétera).

E. ¿Qué dicen?   Tell what the people shown are probably saying, using expressions for asking, granting, and denying permission. You might want to use some of the following vocabulary: **cerrar**, **quitarme el sombrero**, **usar su lápiz**, **pescar**, **abrir**, **presentarle a mi amigo Adolfo**, **fumar**, **sentarme aquí**, **sacar una foto**, **entrar**.

Modelo

¿Podría sentarme aquí?

1.

2.

3.

4.

5.

No fumar

NO PESCAR

VOCABULARIO ACTIVO

Cognados

la energía	**posible**	**la temperatura**	**la vitamina**
humano			

Verbos

alegrarse (de)	to be glad (about)
andar	to walk
andar en bicicleta	to ride a bicycle
arreglar	to fix, arrange
arreglarse	to be okay, turn out all right
curar	to cure
descansar	to rest
doler (ue)	to ache, hurt
dudar	to doubt
enfermarse	to get sick
pescar	to fish
sentir (ie)	to feel; to sense
sentir que	to be sorry that
sentirse + adj.	to feel a certain way
sorprender	to surprise

El cuerpo humano

la boca	mouth
el brazo	arm
la cara	face
el cuello	neck
el cuerpo	body
la espalda	back
la garganta	throat
la nariz	nose
la oreja	ear
el pelo	hair
el pie	foot
la pierna	leg

La salud (*Health*)

el aspecto (físico)	(physical) appearance
la cama	bed
el cigarrillo	cigarette
el cigarro	cigar
la cura	cure
la enfermedad	illness
el enfermero, la enfermera	nurse
el médico, la médica	doctor
la píldora	pill
el resfrío	cold

Adjetivos

embarazada	pregnant
enfermo	sick
fresco	fresh; cool
libre	free, at liberty
pálido	pale

Otras palabras y frases

ahora mismo	right away
¡Basta!	That's enough!
la costa	coast
demasiado	too much
la dificultad	difficulty
la docena	dozen
el espejo	mirror
el miedo	fear
tener miedo (de) que	to be afraid that
Ojalá que...	I hope (It is to be hoped) that ...
perder (el) tiempo	to waste time
¿Qué te pasa?	What's wrong? (What's the matter with you?)

Expresiones útiles

No tengo la menor idea.	I don't have the slightest idea.
Quizás (+ ind. or subj.)...	Perhaps ...
Tal vez (+ ind. or subj.)...	Perhaps ...

> **Don't forget**
> Impersonal expressions, page 328

Las fiestas

Representación de la Conquista en Guatemala

La Semana Santa en Sevilla

A los hispanos les gustan las fiestas y los espectáculos. Celebran muchas fiestas religiosas y nacionales. En muchos pueblos de Guatemala los indios se visten de conquistadores o de jefes indios y participan en una representación de la conquista. Así pueden olvidar su vida de trabajo y pobreza y recordar las ricas tradiciones del pasado.

Como la mayoría° de la gente hispana es católica, las fiestas católicas son muy importantes, tanto en España como en Hispanoamérica. Por esa razón, muchos pueblos y ciudades celebran el día de su santo patrón. También por eso, muchas personas celebran el día de su santo. Por ejemplo, si alguien se llama Teresa, es muy probable que celebre—además de su cumpleaños—el quince de octubre, día de Santa Teresa de Jesús. Pero una de las festividades religiosas más importantes del mundo hispano es la celebración de la Semana Santa. En Sevilla, España, se adornan las casas y hay procesiones lentas y silenciosas de enormes «pasos», que son plataformas decoradas con estatuas que representan escenas religiosas. Después de las Pascuas°, hay una gran celebración con bailes, música y fuegos artificiales°. En la foto se ve parte de una procesión en Sevilla durante la Semana Santa.

En las fiestas religiosas de los pueblos pequeños de Hispanoamérica se encuentra, muchas veces, una mezcla° curiosa de cristianismo y paganismo. Así, por ejemplo, en algunas partes del Perú y de Bolivia, la gente honra° simultáneamente a la Virgen María y a la Pachamama o Madre Tierra. En la Fiesta de la Diablada, los indios bolivianos llevan máscaras° que representan el bien y el mal en forma de ángeles y diablos, o máscaras de los antiguos demonios de los Andes. Hay bailes dramáticos y la celebración generalmente termina con una ceremonia religiosa.

majority

*Easter / **fuegos...** fireworks*

mixture
honor

masks

EJERCICIO

Pretend that a Spanish-speaking student is visiting you; you are curious about his or her favorite holiday. Prepare a list of six questions you might ask, beginning with **¿Qué día de fiesta te gusta más?**

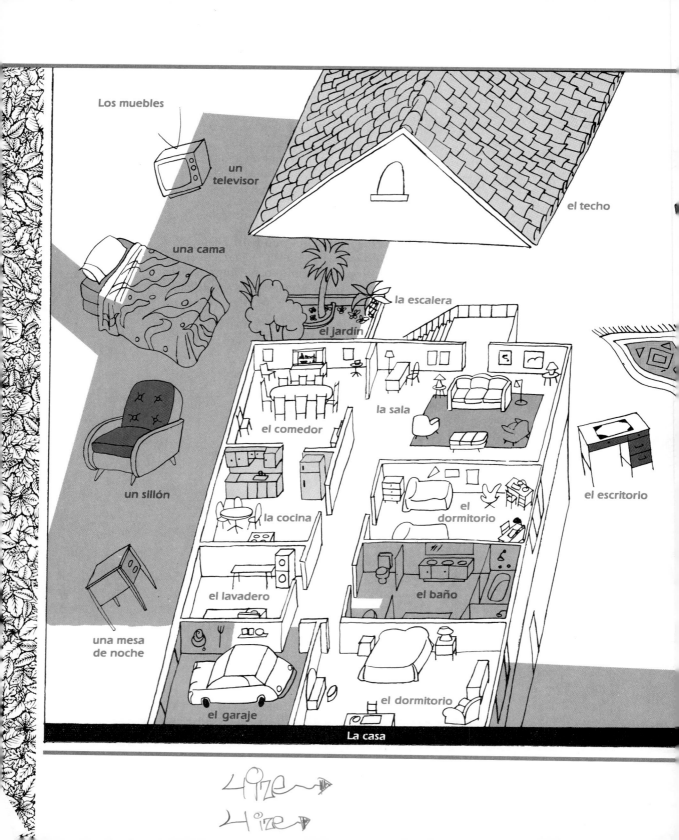

Los muebles

un televisor

el techo

una cama

la escalera

el jardín

la sala

un sillón

el comedor

el escritorio

la cocina

el dormitorio

el lavadero

el baño

una mesa de noche

el garaje

el dormitorio

La casa

una silla

estante
ra libros

una lámpara

una alfombra

una mesa

un sofá

Los muebles

En casa _____ *15*

Making Deductions
Stating Intentions
Expressing Probability and Possibility

EJERCICIO

Match the room with the activity described.

1. el dormitorio	a. cocinar
2. el comedor	b. dormir
3. la cocina	c. lavar la ropa
4. el lavadero	d. bañarse (*to bathe*), lavarse
5. la sala	e. comer
6. el baño	f. mirar televisión, leer

PREGUNTAS

1. Usted acaba de comprar la casa y los muebles (*furniture*) que se ven en estas dos páginas. ¿Dónde va a poner usted el sofá? ¿la cama? ¿el sillón? ¿la mesa de noche?   **2.** ¿Qué muebles va a poner usted en el comedor? ¿en la sala?   **3.** ¿Qué muebles no se usan nunca en el dormitorio?   **4.** ¿Adónde va usted para tomar sol? ¿para jugar a los naipes? ¿para preparar la comida?   **5.** ¿Qué hay que subir o bajar para ir de un piso (*floor*) a otro?   **6.** ¿Dónde guarda usted (*do you keep*) el coche?

 # The future tense

En un hotel de Quito, Ecuador.

GERENTE Sí, señorita, tenemos un cuarto muy lindo. Venga conmigo y se lo *enseñaré.°* (...) Mire, da al parque°.

SEÑORITA Sí, la vista es linda. ¿Tiene agua caliente°?

GERENTE Ahora no; sólo agua fría, pero *tendrá°* agua caliente en unas semanas.

SEÑORITA ¿Y qué le pasó a esta puerta?

GERENTE ¡Oh!... *estará* rota°. *Tendremos°* que arreglarla.

SEÑORITA ¡Uf!° ¡Qué calor hace aquí! ¿Tiene aire acondicionado la habitación°?

GERENTE No, pero *abriré°* la ventana. (...) ¡Oh!, casi nunca hay tanto ruido° aquí.

SEÑORITA (*En voz alta*) ¿Cómo? No lo puedo oír.

GERENTE Nada. Mire, señorita, aquí tiene una cama muy cómoda, un estante para libros°, un escritorio, un sillón°...

SEÑORITA ¿Se puede alquilar° el cuarto por semana?

GERENTE No, sólo por mes. Y *querré°* un depósito.

SEÑORITA Pues, necesito tiempo para pensarlo. Lo *llamaré°* mañana, ¿de acuerdo?

---

1. ¿Cómo es el cuarto? ¿Da a la calle? ¿Tiene agua caliente? ¿aire acondicionado? ¿Qué tiene? 2. ¿Se puede alquilar la habitación por semana? ¿Hay que dejar un depósito? 3. ¿Cree usted que la señorita va a alquilar el cuarto o no? 4. Describa su cuarto (el de usted). ¿Tiene alguna vista? ¿Qué muebles tiene? ¿Qué adornos tiene? (Por ejemplo, ¿hay fotos, cuadros o carteles [*posters*]? ¿De qué o de quién?) ¿Está limpio y ordenado (*neat*) su cuarto o está un poco desordenado (*messy*)? ¿A usted le gusta su cuarto, en general? ¿Por qué sí o por qué no?

---

enseñaré *I'll show* **da al parque** *it faces the park* **caliente** *hot* **tendrá** *it will have*
qué le pasó *what happened* **estará rota** *it must be broken* **Tendremos** *We'll have*
¡Uf! *Whew!* **habitación** *room* **abriré** *I'll open* **ruido** *noise*
estante para libros *bookcase* **sillón** *armchair* **alquilar** *rent*
querré *I'll want* **Lo llamaré** *I'll call you*

A. To form the future tense, add to the infinitive the endings **-é, -ás, -á, -emos, -éis, -án**. The endings are the same for **-ar, -er**, and **-ir** verbs. Except for the first-person plural, **nosotros**, all forms have written accents.

hablar		comer		vivir	
hablar**é**	hablar**emos**	comer**é**	comer**emos**	vivir**é**	vivir**emos**
hablar**ás**	hablar**éis**	comer**ás**	comer**éis**	vivir**ás**	vivir**éis**
hablar**á**	hablar**án**	comer**á**	comer**an**	vivir**á**	vivir**án**

Te acompañaré a comprar los muebles.

I'll go with you to buy the furniture.

¿Crees que el vendedor los convencerá de que compren esa propiedad?

Do you think the salesman will convince them to buy that property?

El miércoles próximo iremos a Quito.

Next Wednesday we will go to Quito.

B. Some verbs are irregular in the future. However, the irregularity is only in the stem; the endings are the same as those for regular verbs. The following are several types of verbs that show an irregularity in the future.

1. Verbs that drop the vowel of the infinitive ending.

   habr- (haber)
   podr- (poder)
   querr- (querer)
   sabr- (saber)

2. Verbs that replace the vowel of the infinitive ending with **d**. (Note that these are the same verbs that have a **g** in the present tense **yo** form.)

   pondr- (poner)
   saldr- (salir)
   tendr- (tener)
   vendr- (venir)

3. Verbs that drop the stem consonant, plus a vowel.

   dir- (decir)
   har- (hacer)

Jaime no querrá quedarse en una casa tan desordenada.

Jaime will not want to stay in such a messy house.

¡Limpia el piso!* —Lo haré mañana.

Clean the floor! —I'll do it tomorrow.

Tendrán que esperar un rato.

They'll have to wait a while.

Podremos quedarnos en un cuarto cómodo con dos camas, televisor, baño y una buena vista.

We'll be able to stay in a comfortable room with two beds, a television, a bath, and a good view.

---

* **El piso** means *floor* (of a room), as opposed to **el cielo raso** (*ceiling*); a floor or story of a building is also **el piso**. **El suelo** means *floor* or *ground*, as opposed to **el techo** (*roof*).

C. The future tense can also be used to express probability or doubt in the present.

¿Qué hora será?	*What time can it be? (I wonder what time it is.)*
Serán las ocho.	*It must be eight o'clock. (It is probably eight o'clock.)*
¿Dónde estará Tomás?	*Where can Tomás be? (Where might Tomás be?)*
Tomás estará en su dormitorio.	*Tomás is probably (must be) in his room.*

EJERCICIOS

A. Vacaciones futuras.   Mr. and Mrs. Villalba are discussing their family's plans for next summer. Form sentences in the future, as Mrs. Villalba would when describing them to her husband.

Modelo mamá y papá / ir a Lima y a Machu Picchu
Mamá y papá irán a Lima y a Machu Picchu.

1. nosotros / viajar a Europa en junio
2. yo / tener una fiesta para Susanita
3. ella / pasar las vacaciones con sus tíos
4. Susanita y sus primos / ver a Ramón en julio
5. tus padres / venir a visitarnos en agosto
6. mamá / visitar muchos museos peruanos
7. Isabel y Rogelio / hacer un viaje por América Central
8. tú y tu papá / divertirse mucho en Madrid

B. Planes futuros.   Complete the following paragraph with the appropriate future forms of the verbs in parentheses.

El próximo verano mi familia y yo _____ (ir) a México. Primero _____ (visitar) la ciudad de Monterrey, donde papá _____ (ver) a un amigo. Después, mamá y él _____ (ir) a Guanajuato. Allí tenemos varios parientes y mis padres _____ (sentirse) muy felices de verlos. Sé que todos _____ (querer) tenerlos en su casa, pero estoy seguro de que papá y mamá _____ (preferir) estar solos en algún hotel. Ellos _____ (necesitar) un dormitorio cómodo con una cama grande. Durante ese tiempo, mi hermano y yo _____ (viajar) y _____ (conocer) muchos lugares interesantes. _____ (hacer) una visita a Guadalajara, donde mi hermano _____ (poder) ver algunos cuadros de Orozco, el famoso pintor mexicano, y yo _____ (divertirse) en la Plaza de los Mariachis. Finalmente, los cuatro _____ (encontrarse) en la ciudad de México. Mis padres _____ (llegar) allí en auto desde Guanajuato y nosotros en avión desde Guadalajara.

C. En el año 2020.   In five sentences, describe how you envision life in the year 2020.

Modelo **En el año 2020 no tendremos que trabajar; la gente viajará más y los viajes costarán menos; se podrá curar el SIDA y otras enfermedades hoy día incurables, etc.**

D. Cuentos progresivos. In groups, prepare a story. The first person starts the story with a phrase such as **Mañana saldré de casa temprano...** Then another person repeats what the first one said and adds another sentence to the story. Continue in this fashion until each student in the group has added at least one sentence. Some possible first lines are:

1. Mañana me despertaré a las seis y...
2. El año que viene mis amigos y yo iremos a México y...
3. En el verano le daré mis muebles viejos al Ejército (*Army*) de Salvación y...
4. Mi novio(-a) y yo nos casaremos el año proximo y...

E. ¡Los muebles hablan! They say that a piece of furniture can reveal the personality of its owner. Below you'll find drawings of several items. What do you think of their owners? Say a couple of things about the person who might own each of them, following the model.

Modelo

La dueña será una persona vieja, tal vez una profesora; tendrá unos setenta años.

1.

2.

3.

4.

5.

F. Traducción. Give the Spanish equivalent of the following sentences.

1. You (**tú**) will find the things you need in my room.
2. Hernando will buy all the furniture that we'll need.
3. We'll meet her family next week.
4. Next time they'll bring more money.
5. It must be two o'clock.
6. Where can Alicia be?

PREGUNTAS

1. ¿Qué hará usted el próximo domingo? ¿Se quedará en su casa o irá a alguna parte? ¿Adónde?   **2.** ¿A qué hora se acostará usted esta noche? ¿A qué hora se levantará mañana?   **3.** ¿Va a viajar usted el próximo verano? ¿Adónde irá? Si no va a viajar a ninguna parte, ¿qué hará?   **4.** ¿Qué hora será ahora?   **5.** ¿Dónde estará su mamá en este momento? ¿su papá? ¿su novio(-a)?

The conditional mood

En el apartamento de Pablo y Marisa.

MARISA ¿Recuerdas la promesa que me hiciste la semana pasada mientras pintábamos las paredes de la sala°?

PABLO ¿La semana pasada? ¡Ah!, te dije que *iríamos*° al cine, ¿no?

MARISA No, dijiste que *harías*° algo que me *gustaría muchísimo*°.

PABLO ¿Qué te *prometería* yo?° ¡No lo recuerdo! Tal vez dije que *limpiaría* las alfombras°... o que *compraría*° algo para la sala... ¿un sillón nuevo, tal vez...?

MARISA ¡No! ¡Me prometiste que no *fumarías más*°!

PABLO ¡Y no fumo más, Marisa! Fumo exactamente *igual que siempre*°, querida.

1. ¿Recuerda Pablo su promesa?   2. ¿Le prometió él a Marisa que irían al cine? ¿que limpiaría la sala?   3. ¿Cuál fue la promesa de Pablo?   4. Según Marisa, ¿cuándo prometió Pablo que no fumaría más?   5. ¿Fuma más Pablo?

---

sala *living room*   **iríamos** *we would go*   **harías** *you would do*
me gustaría muchísimo *I would like very much*   **¿Qué... yo?** *What could I have promised you?*
limpiaría las alfombras *I would clean the carpets*   **compraría** *I would buy*
no fumarías más *you wouldn't smoke any more*   **igual que siempre** *the same as always*

A. To form the conditional mood, add to the infinitive the endings **-ía**, **-ías**, **-ía**, **-íamos**, **-íais**, **-ían**. The endings are the same for **-ar**, **-er**, and **-ir** verbs.

hablar		comer	
hablar**ía**	hablar**íamos**	comer**ía**	comer**íamos**
hablar**ías**	hablar**íais**	comer**ías**	comer**íais**
hablar**ía**	hablar**ían**	comer**ía**	comer**ían**

vivir	
vivir**ía**	vivir**íamos**
vivir**ías**	vivir**íais**
vivir**ía**	vivir**ían**

The conditional is used to express what would happen in a certain situation. It usually conveys the meaning *would* in English.*

Él no compraría una casa sin seis habitaciones, dos baños y un comedor grande.	*He wouldn't buy a house without six bedrooms, two bathrooms and a big dining room.*
Yo no alquilaría esa propiedad.	*I wouldn't rent that property.*
No aceptarían ese cambio.	*They wouldn't accept that change.*

B. The conditional often refers to an action that was projected as future or probable from the perspective of some time in the past.

Prometieron que traerían el sofá y los sillones antes de las dos.	*They promised they would bring the sofa and the armchairs before two o'clock.*
No sabíamos si el gerente llegaría hoy o mañana.	*We didn't know if the manager would arrive today or tomorrow.*
Dijo que alquilaría la casa que da al parque.	*He said he would rent the house that faces the park.*

A SOLO **1,591,999**
Sala modelo MONARCA-4, consta de sofá, love seat y sillón, tapizada en terciopelo, con respaldo y brazos seccionados, asientos reversibles, casco reforzado, en varios colores.
PRECIO NORMAL 2,274,995
AHORRE 682,996
Pago efectivo

GARANTIZAMOS
• LO ARREGLAMOS
• SE LO CAMBIAMOS
• O LE DEVOLVEMOS SU DINERO
Sin Compromiso Con Ud.

SALINA ROCHA

---

* Remember that the imperfect in Spanish can also be translated as *would* when referring to a repeated event in the past: **Durante el verano comíamos en el patio todos los días.** (*During the summer we would eat on the patio everyday.*)

C. The verbs that have irregular stems in the future also have the same irregular stems in the conditional. The endings are the same as those for verbs with regular stems.

dir-	(decir)	**pondr-**	(poner)	**saldr-**	(salir)
habr-	(haber)	**querr-**	(querer)	**tendr-**	(tener)
har-	(hacer)	**sabr-**	(saber)	**vendr-**	(venir)
podr-	(poder)				

¡Lucía no diría eso de tu jardín, mamá!	*Lucía wouldn't say that about your (flower) garden, Mom!*
Pedro prometió que pondría sus cosas y la lámpara en su cuarto.	*Pedro promised he would put his things and the lamp in his room.*
Creo que ellos podrían ayudarte a arreglar el techo y la escalera.	*I think they could (would be able to) help you fix the roof and the stairs.*

D. The conditional may be used to express probability in the past.

¿Qué hora sería cuando ellos llegaron?	*What time was it (probably) when they arrived?*
Serían las nueve.	*It must have been (was probably) nine o'clock.*
¿Qué edad tendría Pepito cuando fueron a España?	*Approximately how old was Pepito when they went to Spain?*
Tendría once o doce años.	*He was around eleven or twelve years old (he must have been eleven or twelve years old).*

E. The conditional may also be used to indicate an attitude of politeness or deference. (You have seen the forms **podría** and **gustaría** in the **Funciones y actividades** sections, since they are frequently used in many expressions of request, permission, etc.)

¿Me podría decir usted cómo llegar al Hotel Continental?	*Could you tell me how to get to the Continental Hotel?*
El concierto empieza en diez minutos. Por lo tanto, deberían tomar un taxi, ¿no?	*The concert starts in ten minutes. Therefore, you should take a taxi, right?*

EJERCICIOS

A. ¡Luisa tenía razón! In spite of Luisa's advice, Marisa rented an apartment by phone, without seeing it. Now she regrets it because she hates the apartment! Take Marisa's role and tell what her friend had warned her against, as Marisa would. Use the conditional forms of the verbs provided.

Modelo   Luisa me dijo que...
(gustar) ...no me __**gustaría**__ el barrio.

1. (ser) ...los cuartos _____ muy pequeños.
2. (tener) ...no _____ una linda vista.

3. (haber) ...en ese lugar _____ mucho ruido.
4. (dar) ...la ventana de la sala _____ a la calle.
5. (hacer) ...allí _____ mucho frío en el invierno.
6. (estar) ...yo _____ muy lejos de todo y de todos.
7. (poder) ...por eso, (yo) no _____ vivir sin auto.
8. (deber) ...ella y yo _____ alquilar un apartamento en el centro.

B. Castillos en el aire. (*Castles in the air.*) Mr. Benítez is telling his wife Leonor how he would spend his money and how their life would change if he suddenly became a millionaire. With the elements given, form sentences in the conditional, as Mr. Benítez would.

Modelo   yo / dar dinero a los pobres
Yo daría dinero a los pobres.

1. tú y yo / viajar por todo el mundo
2. nuestros hijos / asistir a una buena universidad
3. yo / comprarte un Mercedes
4. nosotros / vivir en una casa muy grande
5. nuestra casa / tener ocho dormitorios y cuatro baños
6. Anita / poder tener mucha ropa linda
7. yo / hacer muchas cosas que ahora no puedo hacer
8. todos / ser muy felices

C. ¿Por qué no irían? Last night Mario had a wonderful party, but many of his friends didn't show up. Using the conditional, give possible reasons why they didn't come.

Modelo   Marisa / limpiar su nuevo apartamento
Marisa limpiaría su nuevo apartamento.

1. Camilo / tener que trabajar hasta tarde
2. Luisa / estar enferma o cansada
3. Alfonso y Susana / ir a otra fiesta
4. Rosa / no poder dejar sola a su abuelita
5. Rafael y Luis / deber estudiar para algún examen
6. María / querer acostarse temprano
7. Miguel / no sentirse bien
8. Ramón y Teresa / no saber llegar a casa de Mario

D. Otro don Quijote. After reading a few chapters of *Don Quijote*, you are starting to see things the way the famous Spanish character did. You believe you must change the world. In five sentences, describe what changes you would make.

Modelo   **Yo eliminaría la pobreza: daría trabajo a todo el mundo y haría todo lo posible por socializar la medicina, etc.**

1. ¿Dónde le gustaría vivir? ¿ Por qué?   **2.** ¿Viviría en Rusia o en algún otro país comunista? ¿Por qué sí o por qué no?   **3.** ¿Tiene muchos amigos? ¿Le gustaría tener más? ¿Por qué?   **4.** ¿Daría su vida por un amigo o una amiga?   **5.** ¿Querría ser rico(-a)? ¿Qué haría con un millón de dólares?   **6.** ¿Le gustaría tener una casa en Ecuador? (¿en Acapulco? ¿en Sevilla? ¿en Buenos Aires?) ¿Le gustaría vivir allí o sólo pasaría sus vacaciones en ese lugar? ¿Por qué?   **7.** ¿Podría describir cómo sería su casa ideal? ¿Tendría muchos cuartos? ¿Cuántos dormitorios? ¿baños? ¿Tendría sala? ¿cocina? ¿patio? ¿jardín? ¿garaje? ¿Para cuántos autos? ¿Qué más tendría?

The present participle and the progressive tenses

Dos amigos se encuentran en lo alto° de una montaña.

MANUEL Alberto, ¿qué *estás haciendo* aquí?°
ALBERTO *Estoy admirando°* esta vista estupenda, *descansando°* y *respirando°* aire puro... Hace más de dos horas que *estoy haciendo* planes para el futuro, *pensando°* que sería muy lindo tener una casa en este lugar... Y tú, ¿por qué viniste aquí?
MANUEL Es que en casa había mucho ruido cuando salí: mi hijo *estaba leyendo°* un poema en voz alta, mi hija *estaba escuchando°* a Madonna, mi esposa *estaba cantando°*... ¡Y la verdad es que tanto ruido a mí me *estaba volviendo* loco°! Por eso estoy aquí...

1. ¿Qué está haciendo Alberto en lo alto de la montaña?   2. ¿Cuánto tiempo hace que él está allí?   3. ¿Por qué está allí Manuel?   4. ¿Va usted a las montañas de vez en cuando? ¿Para qué? ¿Está pensando pasar unos días en las montañas? ¿Cuándo? ¿Qué piensa hacer allí?

en lo alto at the top   **¿qué estás haciendo aquí?** *what are you doing here?*
admirando *admiring*   **descansando** *resting*   **respirando** *breathing*
pensando *thinking*   **estaba leyendo** *was reading*   **escuchando** *listening*
cantando *singing*   **me... loco** *was driving me crazy*

A. To form the present participle of most Spanish verbs, **-ando** is added to the stem of the infinitive of **-ar** verbs and **-iendo** to the stem of the infinitive of **-er** and **-ir** verbs.*

hablando	*speaking*
comiendo	*eating*
viviendo	*living*

Hablando de viajes, ¿cuándo sales para Guayaquil?	*Speaking of trips, when are you leaving for Guayaquil?*

B. Present participles of verbs with a stem ending in a vowel take the ending **-yendo** rather than **-iendo**, since in Spanish an unaccented **i** between two vowels becomes a **y**.

creyendo	(creer)	leyendo	(leer)
oyendo	(oír)	trayendo	(traer)

C. Stem-changing **-ir** verbs show a change in the stem of the present participle from **e** to **i** or **o** to **u** (as they do in the third-persons singular and plural of the preterit).

diciendo	(decir)	pidiendo	(pedir)
prefiriendo	(preferir)	siguiendo	(seguir)
sirviendo	(servir)	durmiendo	(dormir)
muriendo	(morir)		

D. A form of **estar** in the present tense can be combined with a present participle to form the present progressive tense. This tense is used to emphasize that an action is in progress—taking place—at a particular moment in time. It is used only to stress that an action is occurring at a specific point in time; otherwise, the present tense is used.

Estoy limpiando la cocina.	*I'm cleaning the kitchen.*
Estamos jugando al tenis ahora.	*We're playing tennis now.*

E. A form of **estar** in the imperfect tense can be combined with a present participle to form the past progressive tense, a tense that indicates that an action was in progress at a given moment in the past.

Estaba leyendo tu carta (cuando tuve la idea).	*I was reading your letter (when I had the idea).*
Entre paréntesis, ellos estaban comiendo (cuando llegué).	*Incidentally, they were eating (when I arrived).*
Mi esposa estaba cantando (a las seis de la mañana).	*My wife was singing (at six o'clock in the morning).*
Los niños estaban jugando en el patio.	*The children were playing on the patio (in the yard.)*

---

* The present participle of **ir** is **yendo**.

A. Imaginación y lógica. It's Christmas Eve, and you have a house full of relatives who are spending the holidays with you. Combining elements from all three columns, form logical sentences in the present progressive to describe what is happening this evening. (Add an indirect object pronoun, if needed.)

Modelos **Paco y yo estamos admirando este árbol de Navidad.**
Marta les está escribiendo tarjetas a sus amigos.

		para salir depués
	admirar	tarjetas a sus amigos
Marta	leer	rápidamente
ustedes	mirar	un álbum de fotos
Paco y yo	acostumbrarse	en su dormitorio
tú	escribir	los muebles nuevos
Rosita y tú	hacer	una torta deliciosa
yo	abrir	pasar las fiestas con parientes
Eva su novio	vestirse	las maletas
	comer	este árbol de Navidad
		una carta importante

B. Contestando una carta. Marisa is answering a letter to a friend. Change the following sentences to the present progressive, as Marisa would.

Modelo Carlos busca trabajo.
Carlos está buscando trabajo.

1. Mamá admira su jardín.
2. Los chicos aprenden francés.
3. Alberto y Susana viajan por América del Sur.
4. Yo sigo dos cursos de literatura española.
5. Aquí hace mucho frío hoy.
6. ¿Nieva mucho allí en estos días?
7. Nosotros queremos viajar a Chile en enero.
8. ¿Piensas ir a alguna parte durante tus vacaciones?
9. Alberto y Susana nos escriben cada semana.

C. Todos estábamos haciendo algo. Teresa, an exchange student from Mexico, is telling her Ecuadorean "sister" what people she knows were doing during the last big earthquake in Mexico City. Restate what she says, changing the verbs from the imperfect to the past progressive, as in the example.

Modelo Mi hermana mayor le escribía a su novio.
Mi hermana mayor le estaba escribiendo a su novio.

1. Yo desayunaba en casa.
2. Una de mis amigas hacía ejercicios en la sala.

3. Mis vecinos viajaban a Quito.
4. Los Bonilla salían de su casa para ir al trabajo.
5. Mis dos hermanos hacían mucho ruido en su cuarto.
6. Papá y mamá todavía dormían.

D. ¿Qué están haciendo?   Look at the drawings and describe what the people shown are doing at this moment.

Modelo

Pablo y Ana...
Pablo y Ana están cantando y tocando la guitarra.

1. Ernesto...

2. Tía Celia...

3. Pedrito y su hermano...

4. Jorge...

5. Papá...

6. Teresa y Alberto...

7. Osvaldo...

8. Pepito...

9. La señora Brítez...

E. Un poco de pantomima...   A few students will pantomime actions, and the class will try to guess what he (she) is doing. Follow the model.

Modelo   Profesor(-a):   **¿Qué está haciendo** (name of student)?
Estudiante 1:   **Está caminando.**
Profesor(-a):   **¿Estás caminando,** (name of student)?
Estudiante 2:   **Sí, está caminando.** or **No, no está caminando.**

F. Mini-drama.   Imagine you were not here (in class or on campus) last week. Transport yourself mentally to a specific setting and describe in three or four sentences where you were, what you were doing, etc.

Modelo   **Yo estaba hablando con unos amigos en un hotel de Quito. Estaba contándoles... cuando llegó mi novio(-a)...**

PREGUNTAS

1. ¿Qué está haciendo usted en este momento?   **2.** ¿Estaba mirando por la ventana? ¿pensando en sus próximas vacaciones? ¿Está pensando viajar a alguna parte? ¿Adónde?   **3.** ¿En qué (quién) estaba pensando usted hoy cuando entró a clase? ¿anoche cuando se acostó?   **4.** ¿Le gusta estar fuera de su casa haciendo deportes (nadando, corriendo, jugando al tenis, por ejemplo) o prefiere estar en su cuarto leyendo (escuchando música, tocando la guitarra, etc.)?

Quito: La ciudad de la eterna primavera

En el restaurante del Hotel Colón, en Quito.[1]

LAURA   Así que están pensando mudarse a Quito. ¡Qué bien! Pero, ¿cuándo...?

PEDRO   Pues, nos gustaría estar aquí para Año Nuevo. Yo me jubilo° el mes próximo, ¡por fin! Por ahora, estamos buscando casa...

LUIS   Realmente me sorprende que ya puedas jubilarte. ¡Todavía eres muy joven, Pedro!

ESTELA   Es que ya hace treinta años que él trabaja para la misma compañía. Estamos volviéndonos viejos°, Luis... ¡Cómo pasa el tiempo!, ¿no? La verdad es que no será fácil dejar Guayaquil[2] después de vivir tantos años allá. Susana, nuestra hija, daría cualquier cosa por convencernos de que no debemos mudarnos. Pero aquí siempre hace un tiempo magnífico, ¿no?

LAURA   Así es. Por algo llaman a Quito «la ciudad de la eterna primavera», ¿no? Estoy segura de que la vida aquí les gustará muchísimo. En general, no me gustan los cambios, pero en el caso de ustedes creo que un cambio les será muy beneficioso°.

Una plaza, en Quito, Ecuador

PEDRO	Eso espero. La verdad es que la vida debe ser un cambio constante. Por ejemplo, tenemos un amigo que no pasa más de dos años en el mismo lugar. Ya ha viajado por todo el mundo y, como resultado, tiene una casa que parece un museo. ¡Cómo lo envidio°!
ESTELA	Yo no. Para ti eso sería la felicidad° pero no para mí.
LUIS	Ni para mí tampoco. Eso de andar de hotel en hotel... ¡Ah!, ahora que recuerdo, ¿cambiaron la habitación del hotel que no les gustaba?
ESTELA	No. Pedí una habitación doble, con dos camas, pero no me la pudieron dar.
LAURA	Pues... «no hay mal que por bien no venga»°. Anoche justamente° me estaba diciendo que sería lindo tenerlos en casa. ¿Por qué no se quedan con nosotros...?
LUIS	¡Buena idea! Tenemos un dormitorio para huéspedes°, con baño y una sala pequeña.
ESTELA	Es que no nos gustaría molestar°...
LAURA	¡Por favor! Esa habitación les va a encantar y la pueden usar por el tiempo que quieran. ¿Aceptan?
PEDRO	Bueno, si no les causaremos problemas, ¡aceptamos! ¿Verdad, Estela?
ESTELA	¡Por supuesto que sí! Y un millón de gracias. Sé que con ustedes estaremos cien veces mejor.

Yo me jubilo *I will retire* **Estamos... viejos** *We're getting old* **beneficioso** *beneficial*
¡Cómo lo envidio! *How I envy him!* **felicidad** *happiness*
«no... venga» *"Every cloud has a silver lining."* (Literally, *"Nothing bad happens that doesn't lead to something good."*) **justamente** *precisely* **dormitorio para huéspedes** *guest room*
molestar *to bother (you)*

PREGUNTAS

1. ¿Qué están buscando Estela y Pedro en Quito? **2.** ¿Dónde están viviendo ellos ahora? ¿Cuándo piensan mudarse a Quito? **3.** ¿Qué le sorprende a Luis? ¿Por qué? **4.** ¿Cuánto tiempo hace que Pedro trabaja para la misma compañía? **5.** Según Estela, ¿será fácil para ellos dejar Guayaquil? ¿Por qué sí o por qué no? **6.** ¿Por qué llaman a Quito «la ciudad de la eterna primavera»? **7.** En general, ¿le gustan los cambios a Laura? ¿y a Pedro? ¿y a usted? ¿Por qué? **8.** ¿Le gusta viajar a Pedro? ¿y a Estela? ¿y a usted? ¿Por qué sí o por qué no? **9.** ¿Qué clase de habitación pidió Estela? ¿Se la dieron? **10.** Según su opinión, ¿por qué dice Laura que «no hay mal que por bien no venga»? (Por ejemplo, en este caso, ¿qué es lo «malo» y qué es lo «bueno» de la situación de sus amigos?) **11.** ¿Van a dejar el hotel Estela y Pedro? ¿Adónde van a ir? Describa el dormitorio para huéspedes que tienen Laura y Luis. **12.** ¿Le gusta a usted mudarse de casa constantemente o prefiere vivir siempre en el mismo lugar? ¿Por qué?

Notas culturales

1. Quito, the capital city of Ecuador (elevation: 9,500 feet), has been aptly called "a great outdoor museum" because of its numerous buildings in the ornate Spanish colonial style. The city was founded in 1534 on the site of the capital of the pre-Inca kingdom of the Scyris, which had fallen to the Incas shortly before the arrival of the Spaniards. Because it is so close to the equator (**ecuador** in Spanish), there is little seasonal variation of temperature.

2. Guayaquil and Quito strongly dominate the life of Ecuador. Quito, the government center, located high in the Andes, is cold in climate and colonial in the predominating tone of its architecture. Guayaquil, at sea level, is sultry, modern, and growing fast. Over 85 percent of Ecuador's trade pours through this great port, which is also the banking center of the country.

FUNCIONES Y ACTIVIDADES

In this chapter, you have seen examples of some important language functions, or uses. Here is a summary and some additional information about these functions of language.

Making deductions

Por eso...	*For that reason ...*
Por estas (esas) razones...	*For these (those) reasons ...*
Por lo tanto...	*Therefore ...*
Como consecuencia (resultado)...	*As a consequence (result) ...*
Será que...	*It must be that ...*
Sería que...	*It must have been that ...*

Stating intentions

In addition to using the future tense, you can state intentions with these expressions:

Pienso...	*I intend (plan) ...*
No pienso...	*I don't intend (plan) ...*
Voy a...	*I'm going to ...*
No voy a...	*I'm not going to ...*

Expressing probability and possibility

Besides the use of future and conditional forms to express probability and possibility, as you saw in this chapter, there are some other ways to express the same idea. The following are given in order, from most highly probable to least likely:

No hay duda de que (+ indicative)...	*There's no doubt that ...*
Seguramente (+ indicative)...	*Surely ... (also: Probably ...)*

Estoy seguro(-a) que (+ indicative)...	*I'm sure (positive) that...*
Es verdad (indudable, etcétera) que (+ indicative)...	*It's true (certain, etc.) that...*
Creo (Pienso) que (+ indicative)...	*I believe (think) that...*
Es probable que (+ subjunctive)...	*It's probable that...*
Es posible que (+ subjunctive)...	*It's possible that...*
Tal vez (Quizás) (+ subjunctive or indicative)...	*Perhaps...*
Es poco probable que (+ subjunctive)...	*It's unlikely that...*
No hay ninguna posibilidad de que (+ subjunctive)...	*There's no possibility that...*

For information on when to use the subjunctive and when to use the indicative with these forms, review Chapter 14.

A. En treinta años... The following sentences are predictions futurologists have made about the world in the near future. First, put each prediction in the future tense. Then express an opinion about how probable or possible you think each of the predictions is.

Modelo   En los países industrializados, casi todo el mundo **tendrá** (tener) un robot para limpiar la casa, cocinar, etcétera, y **será** (ser) muy común el uso de los robots en la industria.

Es posible que el uso de robots en la industria sea muy común; tal vez mucha gente también tenga robots en la casa.

1. Mucha gente _____ (vivir) y _____ (trabajar) en colonias en el espacio; esas colonias _____ (tener) su propio (*own*) sistema de producción de comida.

2. _____ (existir) órganos humanos artificiales de toda clase y el trasplante de órganos _____ (ser) algo muy común; también _____ (haber) sangre (*blood*) artificial que se _____ (poder) usar para cualquier persona—sin importar la clase de sangre que tenga (de tipo A, B, O, etcétera).

3. La gente _____ (hacer) sus compras por computadora; _____ (ser) posible seleccionar (*select*) algo entre una gran variedad de artículos y comprarlo sin salir de la casa. También, gracias al uso de las computadoras, mucha más gente _____ (trabajar) en su casa en vez de ir a la oficina.

4. La gente _____ (vivir) hasta la edad de cien años o más porque _____ (haber) curas para muchas enfermedades (como el cáncer, por ejemplo). Como consecuencia, mucha gente _____ (casarse) más de una vez, y la jubilación (*retirement*) _____ (ser) a una edad más avanzada.

5. El 20 por ciento de los animales y plantas que ahora existen no _____ (existir) dentro de treinta años, por las grandes cantidades de

anhídrido carbónico (*quantities of carbon dioxide*) que _____ (haber) en la atmósfera.

6. Se _____ (inventar) píldoras para mejorar (*improve*) la memoria, para curar el miedo a las alturas (*heights*) y otras fobias y para hacer crecer el pelo (*make hair grow*).

7. _____ (aumentar) dramáticamente el número de personas que vivan en nuestro planeta: la tierra _____ (tener) unos diez mil millones (10.000.000.000) de habitantes en el año 2030.

8. _____ (haber) menos gente «super-rica» y la situación económica del Tercer Mundo _____ (estar) peor que ahora.

9. Los futuros papás _____ (poder) seleccionar el sexo de sus hijos. Más padres _____ (quedarse) en su casa con los niños mientras las madres trabajen fuera de la casa.

10. Los trenes _____ (ir) a 300 millas por hora; los coches _____ (ser) mas pequeños y más rápidos; los aviones _____ (ser) de plástico.

11. En los Estados Unidos, el 60 por ciento de los jóvenes del futuro _____ (asistir) a una universidad o «college», en comparación con el 30 por ciento de ahora.

12. Los apartamentos y casas de los Estados Unidos y de otras partes del mundo _____ (ser) más pequeños, pero muchos muebles _____ (tener) más de un uso y las paredes _____ (ser) movibles.

B. Como consecuencia... Choose any two of the predictions about the future from Exercise A that you believe may be quite possible or probable. (Or choose predictions that you have read or heard about.) Assuming that these predictions turn out to be true, what consequences would there be? Make at least two statements using expressions in this chapter for making deductions.

Modelo **Mucha gente trabajará en su casa; por lo tanto, aumentará el número de madres que trabajen por dinero sin salir de la casa.**

C. Intenciones. In pairs, ask a classmate whether he or she intends or doesn't intend to do the following things this weekend; he or she answers and asks you a question in turn. Find out at least three things you are each going to do this weekend.

Modelo limpiar tu cuarto
¿Limpiarás tu cuarto? (¿Piensas limpiar tu cuarto? ¿Es posible que limpies tu cuarto?)

1. ir a un concierto de música «rock»
2. estudiar
3. trabajar en el jardín
4. jugar al vólibol
5. guardar una promesa o romper una promesa
6. celebrar un cumpleaños
7. hacer ejercicios
8. ir a alguna parte (a un sitio de interés, a un parque, etcétera)

D. ¿Dice la verdad el vendedor de propiedades? Imagine that a real-estate agent is trying to sell the house pictured at the beginning of the chapter to a couple who has three teen-age boys and two toddlers. Tell which parts of the agent's sales pitch seem true and which strike you as lies (**mentiras**) and explain why.

VENDEDOR Señores Smith, pronto entrarán en la casa de sus sueños y verán que esta casa es perfecta para todas sus necesidades. No importa que sólo tenga dos dormitorios. Así es mucho mejor porque eso permite mantener la unidad (*maintain the unity*) de la familia. Además, un baño es bastante para una familia como ustedes. Estoy seguro que no necesitarán más espacio porque la sala es grande. La cocina es pequeña pero eso no está mal; gracias a eso el piso que tendrán que limpiar será más pequeño. Créanme, señores: esta casa es un regalo porque el precio es muy razonable. Cuesta solamente 250.000 dólares.

VOCABULARIO ACTIVO

Cognados

la consecuencia	el garaje	el patio	el resultado
eterno			

Verbos

aceptar	to accept
alquilar	to rent
contar (ue) con	to count on
convencer	to convince
dar a	to face, be facing
estar por	to be about to
guardar	to keep
limpiar	to clean

La casa

la alfombra	rug, carpet
el baño	bathroom
el cielo raso	ceiling
la cocina	kitchen
el dormitorio	bedroom
la escalera	stairway
el estante para libros	bookcase

la habitación	room
el jardín	(flower) garden
la lámpara	lamp
el lavadero	laundry room
los muebles	furniture
el piso	floor, story
la sala	living room
el sillón	armchair
el suelo	floor, ground
el techo	roof
el televisor	television set

Otras palabras y frases

caliente	hot
cómodo	comfortable
desordenado	messy
le edad	age
¿Qué edad tiene(-s)?	How old are you?
el, la gerente	manager

igual	*the same, equal*
limpio	*clean*
ordenado	*neat*
la propiedad	*property, real estate*
el rato	*short time*
hace un rato	*a short while ago*
el repaso	*review*
el ruido	*noise*

Expresiones útiles

Como consecuencia (resultado)...	*As a consequence (result) . . .*
Estoy seguro(-a) que...	*I'm sure (positive) that . . .*
Pienso...	*I intend (plan) . . .*
Por eso...	*For that reason . . .*
Por lo tanto...	*Therefore . . .*

pone furiosa.

Sentimientos y emociones 16

Apologizing
Expressing Forgiveness
Expressing Relief
Expressing Surprise
Expressing Anger or Disappointment

EJERCICIO

Give the adjective that corresponds to each of the following nouns.

Modelo   el orgullo
          orgulloso

1. la tristeza
2. la alegría
3. la vergüenza
4. la depresión
5. el enojo
6. el susto
7. la desilusión
8. la furia

PREGUNTAS

1. ¿Cómo está (se siente) la persona que tiene un mes de vacaciones? ¿que dice o hace algo malo en público? ¿que descubre que su mejor amigo va a mudarse a otra ciudad? ¿que pierde su pasaporte y su dinero?   **2.** ¿Qué hace la persona que ve una película trágica? ¿que escucha un chiste (*joke*)?   **3.** ¿Cómo se siente la persona que está sola en la casa a medianoche y oye ruidos extraños?   **4.** ¿Cómo se siente usted cuando gana en un deporte o juego?   **5.** Cuando esperamos a una persona por mucho tiempo, ¿cómo nos ponemos?   **6.** ¿Cuándo llora usted?   **7.** ¿Cuándo tiene vergüenza usted? ¿Qué cosas le dan vergüenza?   **8.** ¿Hay cosas que le asustan (*frighten*) a usted? ¿Puede dar un ejemplo?

 ## The infinitive

La estación de trenes de Asunción, Paraguay

De Asunción a Encarnación, un pueblo al sur del Paraguay.

LA VIAJERA Señor, *¿es posible ir* a Encarnación en tren?

EL AGENTE Sí, señorita. *Puede tomar* el tren de las 6:00 A.M. (de la mañana) si *desea viajar* de día° o el expreso si no *teme viajar* de noche°. ¿Cuándo *quiere salir?*

LA VIAJERA Esta misma noche. *Espero estar* allí mañana antes de las 4:00 P.M. (de la tarde). ¡Estoy ansiosa *por ver* a mi familia!

EL AGENTE Pues, *vamos a ver...* Ahora son las doce menos cinco. *Acaba de salir* el expreso°... ¡Pero hoy es su día de suerte°, señorita! Dentro de diez minutos *va a salir* otro expreso para Encarnación...

LA VIAJERA ¡Qué alegría!° ¿Y a qué hora llega allí?

EL AGENTE	Mañana a las 2:15 P.M. Este lleva un coche-cama°. *Puede dormir unas horas, si quiere... y todo le va a costar sólo veinte mil guaraníes°.*
LA VIAJERA	¡Buena idea! Déme un pasaje de ida y vuelta, con cama. ¡Pero, dése prisa, por favor! ¡No *quiero perderlo°!*

1. ¿Es posible viajar de Asunción a Encarnación en tren?   2. ¿Qué tren debe tomar la viajera si quiere viajar de noche? ¿de día?   3. ¿A qué hora quiere estar la señorita en Encarnación? ¿Por qué?   4. ¿Perdió ella el expreso de las doce menos cinco? ¿y el de las doce y cinco?   5. ¿A qué hora llega ese expreso a Encarnación? ¿Lleva o no un coche-cama?   6. ¿Qué clase de pasaje quiere ella? ¿sólo de ida o de ida y vuelta?

de día *by day*   **de noche** *at night*   **Acaba... expreso** *The express (train) has just left*
su... suerte *your lucky day*   **¡Qué alegría!** *How happy I am!*
coche-cama *sleeping car*   **guaraníes** *monetary unit of Paraguay*   **perderlo** *to miss it*

In Spanish the infinitive can be used in the following ways.

1. As a noun: The infinitive is often used as the subject or object of a verb in much the same way that the *-ing* form of the English verb is used. It can be used with or without the definite article.

Creo que (el) viajar es estupendo.   *I believe that traveling is great.*

2. As a verb complement: Most verbs may be followed directly by an infinitive. Certain verbs require a preposition (most often **a** or **de**, but in some cases **en** or **con**) before the infinitive. **Tener** and **haber** are followed by **que** to express obligation.

Francisca puede reír y llorar de alegría a la vez.	*Francisca can laugh and cry from happiness at the same time.*
Fuimos a ver *La venganza del Zorro.*	*We went to see* The Revenge of Zorro.
Tratarán de llegar temprano. Tienen una sorpresa para ti.	*They'll try to arrive early. They have a surprise for you.*
Tenemos que comprar el pasaje. Hay que comprarlo hoy.	*We have to buy the ticket. It must be bought today.*

The expression **acabar de** is followed by the infinitive to mean *to have just* (done something.

Acabo de hablar con tus clientes. —¡Por fin!	*I have just spoken to your clients. —Finally!*
Acabamos de oír las malas noticias. —¡Esto es el colmo!	*We've just heard the bad news. —This is the last straw!*

3. As the object of a preposition:

Antes de comprender el problema, Marta lo leyó muchas veces.	*Before understanding the problem, Marta read it many times.*
Después de llorar casi una hora, Ana se calmó.	*After crying almost an hour, Ana calmed down.*
En vez de trabajar, él va a la playa todos los días.	*Instead of working, he goes to the beach every day.*
Sin mentir, le conté todo.*	*Without lying, I told him everything.*
Para ir a Asunción, hay que manejar dos horas.	*To go to Asunción, you have to drive two hours.*

4. With **al**: **Al** + infinitive expresses the idea of *on* or *upon* + the *-ing* form of the verb.

Al hablar con mamá, me di cuenta que estaba enojada. —Lo siento, le dije.	*Upon talking to Mom (When I talked to Mom), I realized she was angry.* —*"I'm sorry," I said to her.*
Al recibir la noticia, Pedro se sintió avergonzado.	*Upon receiving the news (When he received the news), Pedro felt embarrassed.*
Al saber que su esposo tenía una amante, Olga se puso furiosa.	*Upon learning that her husband had a lover, Olga became furious.*

5. On signs, as an alternative to an **usted** command form.

Usar la escalera.	*Use the stairs.*
No fumar.	*No smoking.*

EJERCICIOS

A. ¡Vamos a darnos prisa!   Lelia and Rolando are going over some last-minute details regarding a farewell party they have organized for Alicia, who is leaving town in the morning. Answer Lelia's questions using the cues provided, as Rolando would.

> **Modelos**   ¿Quién le da la sorpresa a Alicia?
> **Yo se la voy a dar.**
>
> ¿Quién trae la torta? (Marisa / prometer)
> **Marisa prometió traerla.**

1. ¿Quién compra el regalo? (Daniel / ir a)
2. ¿Quién habla con Sofía? (mi hermana / pensar)
3. ¿Quién le da el regalo a Alicia? (yo / querer)
4. ¿Quién trae los discos? (Ernesto y Mario / prometer)

---

* **Mentir** (*to lie*) is an **e** to **ie** stem-changing verb.

5. ¿Quién cuenta los chistes? (los Gómez / deber)
6. ¿Quién hace el postre? (Rogelio / tener ganas de)
7. ¿Quién busca a Alicia? (su novio / querer)
8. ¿Quién prepara la sangría? (los muchachos / prometer)
9. ¿Quién llama a los clientes de Alicia? (tú / deber)
10. ¿Quién toca la guitarra y canta? (tú y yo / poder)

Una invitación muy especial

Alberto Nogués

Embajador Adscripto a la Presidencia de la República

tiene el honor de invitar a Usted al

almuerzo que, en agasajo de los Señores Observadores Internacionales,

ofrecerá el día domingo 30 de abril a las 12.30 horas, en el

Yatch y Golf Club Paraguayo.

Abril de 1989.

Se ruega presentar esta tarjeta.

B. Sí, abuela, acabo de hacerlo. Answer Mrs. Bello's questions according to the example, as her grandson would. Use object pronouns wherever possible.

Modelo   ¿Viste a tu prima?
              Sí, acabo de verla.

1. ¿Terminaron el trabajo tus padres?
2. ¿Lavaste el auto?
3. ¿Les habló Lucía a ustedes?
4. ¿Recibiste mi carta?
5. ¿Leyeron mis chistes tus hermanos?
6. ¿Te contaron la sorpresa tus amigos?

C. Letreros del camino... José sees the following signs while traveling to visit his grandparents. What does each one mean?

Modelo   NO DOBLAR A LA DERECHA

D. Traducción. Give the Spanish equivalent of the following sentences.

1. I have just watched that program.
2. We left before eating.
3. Was he angry? He went away without saying anything.
4. Seeing is believing.
5. The clients have just arrived.
6. Why doesn't she laugh instead of cry?

PREGUNTAS

1. ¿Qué hizo usted anoche al llegar a su casa (apartamento, cuarto)? ¿Estaba cansado(-a)? ¿Por qué?   **2.** ¿Cómo se sintió usted al terminar sus estudios secundarios? ¿Por qué?   **3.** ¿Se sintió orgulloso(-a) o desilusionado(-a) (feliz o triste) al recibir la nota de su primer examen de español? ¿Por qué?   **4.** Cuando usted viaja, ¿prefiere viajar de día o de noche? ¿Tiene miedo de viajar en avión? ¿Por qué sí o por qué no?

The subjunctive in descriptions of the unknown, nonexistent, or indefinite

En un liceo° de Asunción.

SR. MÉNDEZ	¿Es usted la persona que quiere trabajar aquí?
SR. GÓMEZ	Sí, señor, yo soy profesor y busco un empleo° *que me guste.* Puedo enseñar historia, literatura o cualquier otro curso *que usted mande°.*
SR. MÉNDEZ	¡Qué bien! Por fin conozco a alguien que sabe más que *yo*... Dígame, ¿sabe usted quién mató° a Julio César?
SR. GÓMEZ	Pero señor, pregúntele eso a alguien *que sea detective.*
SR. MÉNDEZ	¡Bruto!°
SR. GÓMEZ	Esto es demasiado, señor. Por favor, sin ofender...

1. ¿Quién busca un empleo que le guste?   2. ¿Qué es el señor Gómez?   3. ¿Qué puede enseñar él?   4. Aparentemente, ¿sabe él quién mató a Julio César? 5. Según el señor Gómez, ¿a quién hay que preguntarle quién lo mató?   6. ¿Sabe usted quién fue Julio César?, ¿y Bruto?

liceo *high-school*   **empleo** *job*   **cualquier... mande** *any other course you like (literally "order")*   **mató** *killed*   **¡Bruto!** *Brutus! (also Brutus! Ignoramus!")*

A. A dependent clause that modifies a noun or pronoun is called an adjective clause.

Asunción es una ciudad *que tiene más de 400 años.*	*Asunción is a city* that is over 400 years old.
Me da rabia pensar en eso *que me dio tanta vergüenza.*	*It makes me angry to think of that (thing, circumstance)* that made me so ashamed.

The noun or pronoun being described is called the antecedent. In the preceding sentences, the antecedents are **ciudad** and **eso**. Pronouns that often appear as the antecedents of adjective clauses include **alguien** (*someone*), **algo** (*something*), and **alguno** (*some, someone*).

Sandra habló con alguien que conoce a un buen detective.	*Sandra spoke to someone who knows a good detective.*
¿Dije algo que te ofendió?	*Did I say something that offended you?*

B. The verb in an adjective clause may be indicative or subjunctive, depending on whether the antecedent is definitely known to exist.

1. Antecedent definitely exists and is known: indicative.

El alcalde es un abogado que sabe guaraní.*	*The mayor is a lawyer who knows Guaraní.*
La pobreza es algo que lo asusta.	*Poverty is something that scares him.*

2. Antecedent unknown, indefinite, uncertain, or nonexistent: subjunctive.

Necesitan un médico que sepa guaraní.	*They need a doctor who knows Guaraní.*
No hay nada que lo asuste.	*There isn't anything that scares him.*

Study the contrasts in the following examples.

¿Hay alguien aquí que comprenda la lengua de los guaraníes?	*Is there anybody here who understands the language of the Guaraní Indians?*
Sí, aquí hay alguien que la comprende.	*Yes, there's someone here who understands it.*
No, aquí no hay nadie que la comprenda.	*No, there's nobody here who understands it.*

C. The personal **a** is used before a direct object standing for a person when the speaker has someone definite in mind but not when the person is indefinite or unspecified. (However, when the pronouns **alguien, nadie, alguno,** and **ninguno** are used as direct objects referring to a person, the personal **a** is nearly always used, whether the person is known or not.)

Buscan un profesor que sea experto en lenguas indígenas.	*They're looking for a professor who is an expert on Indian languages.*

---

* See **Nota cultural**, 2, p. 368

Le pagan a un profesor que es experto en lenguas indígenas.	*They're paying a professor who is an expert on Indian languages.*
Necesitamos a alguien que sepa hablar español y guaraní.	*We need someone who knows how to speak Spanish and Guaraní.*
Encontramos a alguien que sabe hablar español y guaraní.	*We found somebody who knows how to speak Spanish and Guaraní.*

EJERCICIOS

A. El (La) candidato(-a) ideal.   The National University in Asunción is looking for someone who can teach the course "Guaraní for Foreigners" scheduled to be offered next semester. Imagine you are a member of the selection committee. What kind of candidate are you looking for?

Modelo   tiene buenas recomendaciones
Buscamos a alguien que tenga buenas recomendaciones.

1. sabe hablar inglés y guaraní
2. es experto(-a) en culturas indígenas
3. tiene mucha experiencia
4. nunca se enoja con nadie
5. no es una persona racista
6. puede trabajar largas horas
7. se lleva bien con los estudiantes

B. ¿Por qué se mudan?   The Riquelmes are thinking about moving. To find out why they want to move, complete Mr. Riquelme's comments with the present indicative or subjunctive of the verbs indicated, as appropriate.

Modelo   (gustar) Vivimos en un barrio que no nos **gusta** mucho.
                Buscamos un barrio que nos **guste** más.

1. (ser) Tenemos una casa que _____ muy pequeña.
    Necesitamos una casa que _____ más grande.
2. (estar) Los niños quieren jugar en un parque que _____ cerca de casa.
    Ahora juegan en un parque que _____ muy lejos.
3. (haber) Vivimos en una ciudad donde no _____ universidad.
    Buscamos una ciudad donde _____ universidad.
4. (interesar) En este lugar hay pocas actividades culturales que nos
    _____.
    En realidad, aquí no hay nada que nos _____.
5. (enseñar) Mi hija asiste a una escuela donde no _____ música.
    Quiere asistir a una escuela donde _____ música.

C. ¿No hay nadie que piense igual?   Use the words and phrases in parentheses to give Armando's wishes, needs, and comments, which never coincide with those of the people around him.

Modelo Quiero asistir a la conferencia que empieza a las diez. (una conferencia / más tarde)
Pues yo quiero asistir a una conferencia que empiece más tarde.

1. Queremos visitar las ruinas que son de la época colonial. (unas ruinas / época de los Jesuítas)
2. Necesito encontrar al señor que habla guaraní. (una persona / francés)
3. La compañía busca a los jóvenes que quieren trabajar aquí. (unos jóvenes / conmigo)
4. Vamos a la cafetería donde tienen buenos postres. (un restaurante / comida china)
5. Aquí hay alguien que sabe cuál es la capital del Perú. (no hay nadie / Bolivia)
6. Alfredo va a quedarse en el hotel que está cerca de la calle Palma. (buscar / un hotel / lejos del centro)
7. Quiero comprarle a Sonia los zapatos que le gustan. (un suéter)
8. Constancia y Alfredo van a leer el libro que describe la cultura maya. (querer leer / un libro / cultura guaraní)

D. Para completar. Complete the following sentences using adjective clauses in the indicative or subjunctive, as necessary. Follow the models.

Modelos Quiero comprar un disco que...
Quiero comprar un disco que tenga canciones paraguayas.

Jorge conoce a una persona que...
Jorge conoce a una persona que estuvo en Asunción durante las elecciones de 1989.

1. Busco un hotel que...
2. Tengo un libro que...
3. En Paraguay hay gente que...
4. En esta clase no hay nadie que...
5. Conozco a un señor que...
6. No hay detective que...
7. ¿Dónde está ese secretario que...?
8. En esta ciudad yo he visto casas que...

E. Su opinión personal. Complete the following sentences with a personal opinion.

1. Quiero casarme con un hombre (una mujer) que...
2. Quiero vivir en una casa que...
3. Quiero seguir dos o tres cursos que...
4. Quiero trabajar en un lugar que...
5. Quiero manejar un auto que...
6. Quiero comer en un restaurante que...
7. Quiero ir al teatro con alguien que...
8. Quiero escuchar unos discos que...

1. ¿Tiene usted amigos que viven cerca de su casa? ¿Prefiere que sus amigos (sus papás, sus profesores) vivan cerca o lejos de su casa? ¿Por qué? **2.** ¿Es usted amigo(-a) de alguien que sea muy interesante? ¿que tenga muchos problemas? ¿que siempre esté contento(-a)? **3.** ¿Conoce usted a alguien que tenga más de cien años? ¿que escriba poemas o cuentos? ¿que viaje mucho? **4.** ¿Prefiere usted ver películas que le den risa? ¿que le hagan llorar? ¿que le hagan pensar?

The subjunctive with certain adverbial conjunctions

En una casa paraguaya.

JANE	Discúlpeme°, doña Ramona. Me siento muy avergonzada. Creo que rompí este reloj.
DOÑA RAMONA	No importa°, Jane. Ya estaba roto, pero vamos a dejarlo aquí *para que Luis lo arregle° cuando llegue.* Él es muy bueno en estas cosas.
JANE	Oh, ¡qué alivio!°
DOÑA RAMONA	Pero pareces un poco deprimida. Debe ser por° el viaje... Entonces, *para que no pienses* en eso, ¿qué te parece si te enseño algunas palabras en guaraní *antes de que vuelvas* a tu país?
JANE	¡Sí, doña Ramona! Las despedidas° siempre me causan tristeza°. Pero puede empezar a enseñarme guaraní *cuando desee.* Por ejemplo, ¿cómo se dice «yo te quiero»? Quiero decírselo a Teddy *cuando lo vea.*
DOÑA RAMONA	Pues eso se dice «che ro jaijú». Sé que él se va a sentir muy feliz *tan pronto como° le digas* qué significa.

---

1. ¿Por qué está Jane un poco deprimida? 2. ¿Qué quiere aprender ella antes de volver a su país? 3. ¿Qué le causa tristeza a Jane? 4. ¿Qué le quiere decir Jane a Teddy cuando lo vea? 5. ¿Cómo se dice «yo te quiero» en guaraní?

Discúlpeme *Forgive me* **No importa** *It doesn't matter*
para... arregle *so that Luis will fix it* **¡qué alivio!** *what a relief!*
Debe ser por *It must be because of*
despedidas *farewells* **tristeza** *sadness*
tan pronto como *as soon as*

A. The following adverbial conjunctions always require the subjunctive in a clause that follows them; they indicate that an action or event is indefinite or uncertain (it may not necessarily take place):

a menos que *unless*
antes (de) que* *before*
en caso (de) que* *in case*

para que *so that*
sin que *without*

No voy a ir a menos que me sienta mejor.	*I'm not going to go unless I feel better.*
Sea cortés, para que no se ofendan.	*Be polite, so that they are not offended.*
¿Por qué no salen ahora, chicos, antes de que papá se ponga nervioso?	*Why don't you go out now, children, before Dad gets nervous?*
Vamos ahora en caso de que ellos tengan prisa.	*Let's go now in case they're in a hurry.*
Ana ve a Carlos todos los días sin que su familia lo sepa.	*Ana sees Carlos every day without her family knowing it.*

B. **Aunque** is followed by the subjunctive to indicate conjecture or uncertainty, but by the indicative to indicate fact or certainty.

Voy a salir, aunque llueva.	*I am going to go out even though it may rain.*
Voy a salir, aunque llueve.	*I am going to go out even though it is raining.*

C. Either the subjunctive or the indicative may follow these conjunctions of time:

cuando *when*
después (de) que* *after*
hasta que *until*

mientras (que) *while*
tan pronto como *as soon as*

The indicative is used if the adverbial clause expresses a fact or a definite event; for instance, a customary or completed action. However, if the adverbial clause expresses an action that may not necessarily take place or that will probably take place but at an indefinite time in the future, the subjunctive is used.

A Elena le va a dar mucha rabia tan pronto como lo sepa.	*Elena is going to be very angry as soon as she finds out.*
A Elena le dio mucha rabia tan pronto como lo supo.	*Elena got very angry as soon as she found out.*
Cuando les cuente el chiste, ellos van a morirse de risa.	*When I tell them the joke, they're going to die of laughter.*
Cuando les conté el chiste, ellos se murieron de risa.	*When I told them the joke, they (nearly) died of laughter.*
No le digamos eso al jefe hasta que se calme. Será otra desilusión más...	*Let's not tell the boss that until he calms down. It'll be yet another disappointment . . .*

---

*The **de** may be omitted.

No le dijimos eso al jefe hasta que se calmó.	*We didn't tell the boss that until he calmed down.*
Vamos a poner la mesa después que llegue Jorge.	*We are going to set the table after Jorge arrives.*
Pusimos la mesa después que llegó Jorge.	*We set the table after Jorge arrived.*

D. Some of the conjunctions just discussed are prepositions or adverbs combined with **que** (**para que, sin que, antes de que, hasta que, después de que**). These prepositions are often followed by infinitives if there is no change in subject.

Después de enojarse, Juan se puso muy triste.	*After getting angry, Juan became very sad.* (no change of subject)
Después de que ella se enojó, Juan se puso muy triste.	*After she got angry, Juan became very sad.* (change of subject)

EJERCICIOS

A. Para completar...   Complete the following sentences with the correct form of one of the verbs listed, adding other information, as appropriate.

Modelo   Voy a pasar la noche aquí para que...
Voy a pasar la noche aquí para que tú no estés solo.

1. Quieren irse antes de que...
2. Susana hace eso para que usted...
3. Pensamos llegar a las siete a menos que...
4. ¿Por qué no vamos al cine antes de que...?
5. Ellos van a clase a menos que...
6. ¿Piensan hacerlo sin que ella lo...?
7. El profesor habla lentamente para que nosotros lo...
8. ¿Realmente no puedes hacer nada sin que ellos...?

volver
ofenderse
estar
llover
entender
llegar
saber
levantarse

B. La historia de Inés.   Combine the sentences using the conjunction given in parentheses to find out about Inés' personal life. Follow the model.

Modelos   Inés vivió con sus padres. Compró un apartamento. (hasta que)
Inés vivió con sus padres hasta que compró un apartamento.

Inés y Bob van a trabajar. Ellos pueden casarse y mudarse a una casa grande. (hasta que)
Inés y Bob van a trabajar hasta que ellos puedan casarse y mudarse a una casa grande.

1. Su papá se puso furioso. Inés se fue de la casa. (cuando)
2. Ella no le habló más a su papá. Él se calmó. (hasta que)
3. Inés se va a poner feliz. Su padre la disculpa. (cuando)
4. Inés le escribió una carta. Su padre la llamó. (tan pronto como)
5. Su mamá se puso muy contenta. Ella supo la noticia. (después que)
6. Inés quiere mucho a su novio. Él es mucho mayor que ella. (aunque)

C. Imaginación y lógica. Combining elements from all three columns, form logical sentences with the indicative or subjunctive, as appropriate. Use each of the conjunctions in the second column at least once.

Modelos **Lo hacen mientras los niños duermen.**
Debes comer para que ellos no se enojen.

debes comer	mientras	Sergio / volver
vamos a estar tristes	aunque	ellos / no enojarse
lo hacen	tan pronto como	ustedes / irse
pienso esperar aquí	cuando	tú / no tener hambre
siempre vamos al cine	hasta que	los niños / dormir
se pone furioso(-a)	para que	su novio(-a) / mentirle
van a sentirse felices	a menos que	sus amigos / mudarse
en general, estudio	antes (de) que	yo / escribir
		los Pérez / estar lejos

D. Consejos. Work with a classmate and give each other advice. One of you mentions a problem, real or imaginary; the other says what to do or not to do.

Modelos Estudiante 1: **Siempre estoy cansado(-a) cuando me despierto por la mañana.**

Estudiante 2: **Debes tomar vitaminas (bañarte, hacer ejercicios) tan pronto como te levantes, antes de venir a clase.**

Estudiante 1: **Nunca me va bien en los exámenes, aunque estudie mucho.**

Estudiante 2: **Debes hablar con tus profesores para que te ayuden (te den consejos, etc.)**

E. Traducción. Give the Spanish equivalent of the following sentences.

1. They will call me before they leave.
2. She is going to his birthday party, although she doesn't feel well.
3. I usually play the piano whenever I am a little depressed.
4. They are waiting for us until we arrive.
5. He is going to use the car without his father's knowing about it.
6. You (**tú**) can't sleep unless you are very tired, right?

PREGUNTAS

1. ¿Adónde piensa ir usted cuando termine esta clase? ¿cuando lleguen las vacaciones? ¿cuando complete sus estudios universitarios? **2.** ¿Qué quiere hacer usted cuando sepa hablar bien el español? ¿antes de que termine esta década (*decade*)? **3.** ¿Asiste usted a clase aunque llueva? ¿aunque esté muy cansado(-a)? **4.** ¿No puede estudiar usted a menos que tome café? ¿a menos que esté solo(-a)? **5.** ¿Qué cree usted que debe hacer un(-a) estudiante para que le sea más fácil aprender español?

Asunción:[1] El hombre y la mujer

Vista de Asunción, Paraguay

Dos mujeres se encuentran en la «Peluquería° Guaraní»[2] de Asunción, Paraguay.

GLORIA ¡Hola, Elena! ¡Cuánto me alegro de verte! ¿Cómo estás?

ELENA Muy bien, Gloria. ¡Qué sorpresa! Hacía tanto que no te veía. ¿Qué haces aquí?

GLORIA Vengo todos los meses para que me cambien el color del pelo. Hay una muchacha aquí que me lo hace muy bien, sin que nadie pueda notarlo°. No quiero que mi novio descubra que no soy rubia° natural. Me da vergüenza decírselo.

ELENA Pero cuando él sepa la verdad, se va a sentir desilusionado, ¿no lo crees?

GLORIA Tal vez sí, pero no importa. Por ahora no lo sabe y está contento.

Entra María, la peluquera°.

MARÍA Buenas tardes, señorita Martínez. Tan pronto como termine con la señora Ospina, la atiendo°.

GLORIA Gracias, María. No tengo prisa.

MARÍA (*a Elena*) ¿Y usted, señorita? ¿En qué puedo servirla?

ELENA Tengo que dar una charla° y necesito un peinado° que sea elegante y sencillo° a la vez.

MARÍA No hay ningún problema... si usted puede esperar unos veinte minutos hasta que termine con otra cliente.

ELENA	Cómo no... Francamente, Gloria, me parece triste que una mujer le tenga que mentir a su novio o a su esposo.
GLORIA	¿Por qué? Ellos nos mienten a nosotras. Hace algunos días—para darte un ejemplo—Olga me llamó por teléfono para contarme que su esposo tiene una amante°. Y tú sabes que han tenido otros problemas también. ¡Lloraba tanto la pobre!
ELENA	¡Qué barbaridad! ¿Y qué va a hacer?
GLORIA	Nada. ¿Qué puede hacer?
ELENA	Puede buscarse un amante ella también.
GLORIA	¿Para qué? La venganza° es estúpida.
ELENA	Entonces puede divorciarse.
GLORIA	Tampoco. Aunque su esposo no le es fiel°, Olga todavía lo quiere. Creo que cuando te cases, Elena, vas a pensar de otra manera°.
ELENA	Lo dudo. Es obvio que mis ideas sobre el matrimonio son muy diferentes a las que tienen ustedes dos... Además es difícil que me case aquí.[3]
GLORIA	¿No conoces a ningún hombre que te interese?
ELENA	Sí, pero no hay ninguno que me guste para esposo.
GLORIA	¡Qué increíble! Espero que no te mueras soltera.
ELENA	¿Por qué no? Mi abuela siempre decía que «más vale° estar solo que mal acompañado». Y en mi caso, realmente prefiero estar soltera que mal casada...

---

peluquería *beauty parlor*		**notarlo** *notice it*		**rubia** *blond*		**la peluquera** *hairdresser*	
la atiendo *I'll wait on you*		**charla** *talk*		**peinado** *hairdo*		**sencillo** *simple*	
amante *lover*	**venganza** *revenge*		**fiel** *faithful*		**de otra manera** *otherwise*		
más vale *it's better*							

PREGUNTAS

1. ¿Dónde se encuentran Gloria y Elena? **2.** ¿Por qué viene Gloria a este lugar todos los meses? **3.** Según Elena, ¿cómo se va a sentir el novio de Gloria cuando sepa la verdad? **4.** ¿Qué le parece triste a Elena? ¿Le parece triste eso a usted también? ¿Por qué sí o por qué no? **5.** ¿Qué le contó a Gloria su amiga Olga cuando la llamó por teléfono? **6.** ¿Qué va a hacer Olga? ¿Por qué no va a divorciarse? ¿Qué cree usted que ella debe hacer? **7.** ¿Piensa casarse Elena? ¿Por qué? **8.** ¿Está usted de acuerdo en que es mejor estar soltero(-a) que mal casado(-a)? ¿Por qué?

Notas culturales

1. **Asunción**, one of the oldest cities of South America (founded in 1537), is the capital city and port of Paraguay, on the eastern bank of the Paraguay River. The center of trade and government of the nation, it has a picturesque charm with its pastel-colored buildings and numerous orange trees.

2. **Guaraní** is the language of the Indians who inhabited Paraguay before the Spanish conquest. Paraguay is the only Latin American country that has adopted an Indian language as one of its own official languages. Almost all Paraguayans are **mestizo** and bilingual, and street signs, newspapers, and books often appear in both Spanish and **guaraní**. Spanish is the language used for instruction and business in general, but **guaraní** is favored for social discourse at all levels of society. The **guaraní** is also the monetary unit of the country.

3. In Paraguay the ratio of men to women is rather low because many men emigrate to nearby Brazil and Argentina, where there are more opportunities for work. The scarcity of males dates from the War of the Triple Alliance (1865–70), when President Solano López waged a war against Argentina, Brazil, and Uruguay that killed about half of Paraguay's population. Only 13 percent of the survivors were male, mostly old men and very young boys. It took many years for the sex ratio of young people of a marriageable age to return to an approximately even balance. It is said that some of the priests in those times went so far as to advocate polygamy.

FUNCIONES Y ACTIVIDADES

In this chapter, you have seen examples of some important language functions, or uses. Here is a summary and some additional information about these functions of language.

Apologizing

Lo siento (mucho).	*I'm (very) sorry.*
Siento mucho que (+ subj.)...	*I'm very sorry that . . .*
Perdón. Perdóneme. (Perdóname.)	*Excuse me. (Forgive me.)*
Discúlpeme. (Discúlpame.)	*Excuse me. (Forgive me.)*

Expressing forgiveness

Está bien.	*It's okay.*
No hay (ningún) problema.	*There's no problem.*
No importa.	*It doesn't matter.*
No hay pena.	*No need to be embarrassed.*
No hay de qué.	*It's nothing. (also: You're welcome.)*

Expressing relief

¡Qué bien!	*Good! (How nice!)*
¡Qué alivio!	*What a relief!*
¡Cuánto me alegro!	*How happy I am!*
¡Qué alegría!	*How wonderful! (How happy I am!)*
¡Por fin!	*Finally!* (when something good has finally happened)
Gracias a Dios.	*Thank God. (Thank goodness.)*

Expressing surprise

¡Qué sorpresa!	*What a surprise!*
¡Qué lindo (amable, etcétera)!	*How pretty (nice, etc.)!*
¡Qué increíble!	*How amazing!*

Expressing anger or disappointment

¡Esto (Eso) es el colmo!	*This (That) is the last straw!*
¡Esto (Eso) es demasiado!	*This (That) is too much!*
¡Qué barbaridad!	*Good grief! (How terrible! How absurd!)*
¡Qué desilusión!	*What a disappointment!*

A. **¿Qué se dice?**   Give an appropriate expression that you could use in each of the following situations.

> **Modelo**   El equipo de béisbol de su universidad perdió todos los partidos que jugó este año.
> **¡Qué barbaridad!**

1. Supo que su padre tuvo un accidente de auto, pero por suerte ya salió del hospital y está bien.
2. Recibió una A en un examen para el que (*for which*) usted sólo estudió diez minutos.
3. Recibió una F en un examen para el que usted estudió todo el fin de semana.
4. La semana pasada un compañero de clase le pidió un favor. Usted prometió hacérselo ese mismo día pero se olvidó... Ayer volvió a ver a su compañero.
5. Fue con un(-a) amigo(-a) a cenar a un restaurante; pidieron bistec y vino. Les trajeron un bistec delicioso y un buen vino francés. La cena estuvo excelente pero no supieron el precio hasta que llegó la cuenta... (¿El precio total de la cena...? ¡Cincuenta dólares!)
6. Su mamá lo (la) llamó para contarle que va a visitarlo(-la) este fin de semana.
7. Jugó al tenis con la raqueta de su compañero(-a) de cuarto y la perdió. No recuerda dónde la dejó... Su compañero(-a) está muy enojado(-a).
8. Recibió una carta de sus abuelos con un pasaje de avión y dos boletos para asistir al próximo campeonato mundial (*world championship*) de fútbol.

9. Ayer fue su cumpleaños (de usted) y creía que nadie lo sabía; cuando llegó a su casa por la noche, allí lo (la) esperaban treinta personas, con una torta de cumpleaños.
10. Le acaban de contar que vieron a su novio(-a) en el parque, besando a su mejor amiga(-o).
11. Le robaron la bicicleta.
12. Su compañero(-a) de cuarto le acaba de decir que siente mucho haberlo(-la) despertado a usted cuando llegó tan tarde anoche. Pero en realidad, no lo (la) despertó.

B. Situación. Role-play the following situation. Your boyfriend (girlfriend) calls you two hours after you had planned to go out. He (She) had forgotten all about the date. You mention that this is the second time this week that this has happened (**es la segunda vez que pasó esto esta semana**). You are furious and say so. He (She) apologizes profusely, but at first you refuse to forgive him (her). Eventually you give in and accept his (her) apology.

C. Refranes. (*Proverbs.*) Here are some Spanish proverbs on the subject of love and friendship. What does each one mean? Can you give an English equivalent?

Donde hay amor, hay dolor.
El amor es un egoísmo entre dos.
Ni el que ama ni el que manda quieren compañía.
Amores nuevos olvidan viejos.
Ni ir a la guerra (*war*) ni casar, se debe aconsejar.
Donde hay celos, hay amor.
Más vale (*It's better*) estar solo que mal acompañado.
Ojos que no ven, corazón que no siente.
El casado casa quiere.
Dime con quién andas y te diré quién eres.

D. Entrevista. Ask a classmate the following questions. Then report the information to the class.

1. ¿Qué cosas te dan rabia? ¿Te has enojado recientemente por alguna razón? ¿Por qué? ¿Cuándo fue la última vez que te enojaste?
2. ¿Cuál fue una de las sorpresas más lindas que has recibido últimamente?
3. A muchos hispanos la mujer norteamericana le parece «liberada», libre de hacer lo que quiera (*whatever she likes*). Según tu opinión, ¿está «liberada» la mujer norteamericana? ¿Crees que las mujeres de este país tienen los mismos derechos que los hombres, tanto en el trabajo como en la casa?
4. ¿Existe la «norteamericana típica» o no? Si crees que existe, descríbela.
5. ¿Crees que es mejor que una mujer con hijos se quede en su casa en vez de trabajar fuera de casa (*outside the home*)? ¿Por qué sí o por qué no?
6. ¿Piensas que son más felices las mujeres casadas que las solteras? ¿los hombres casados que los solteros? ¿Por qué?

VOCABULARIO ACTIVO

Cognados

ansioso	el, la detective	expreso	el picnic
cliente	experto	furioso	la sorpresa
la cultura			

Verbos

acabar de + inf.	to have just (done something)
asustar	to frighten, scare
asustarse	to be frightened, scared
darse cuenta de	to realize
disculpar	to forgive
enojarse	to become angry, get mad
llorar	to cry
manejar	to drive
matar	to kill
mentir (ie)	to lie, tell a lie
ofender	to offend
ofenderse	to take offense
ponerse + adj.	to become + adj.
reírse (i)	to laugh
tener prisa	to be in a hurry
tratar (de)	to try (to)

Sentimientos y emociones

alegre	happy
la alegría	happiness
asustado	frightened, startled
avergonzado	embarrassed, ashamed
deprimido	depressed
la desilusión	disappointment
desilusionado	disappointed
enojado	angry
el enojo	anger
orgulloso	proud
la rabia	anger, rage
la risa	laughter
el susto	fright
triste	sad
la tristeza	sadness
la vergüenza	shame
darle vergüenza a alguien	to make someone ashamed

Conjunciones

a menos que	unless
antes (de) que	before
aunque	although
en caso (de) que	in case
hasta que	until
mientras (que)	while
para que	so that
sin que	without
tan pronto como	as soon as

Otras palabras y frases

cualquier(-a)	any
el chiste	joke
la despedida	farewell, leave-taking
la noticia	news item
las noticias	news

Expresiones útiles

¡Cuánto me alegro!	How happy I am!
Discúlpeme.	Excuse me. (Forgive me.)
¡Esto es el colmo!	This is the last straw!
¡Esto es demasiado!	This is too much!
Lo siento.	I'm sorry.
No hay (ningún) problema.	There's no problem.
No importa.	It doesn't matter.
¡Qué alegría!	How happy I am! (I'm so happy!)
¡Qué alivio!	What a relief!
¡Qué increíble!	How amazing!
¡Qué sorpresa!	What a surprise!

La vida diaria

Un bautismo

En general, la familia tiene un papel más importante en la sociedad hispana que en la anglosajona. Es muy común que en la misma casa o apartamento vivan la mamá, el papá, los niños, uno o dos abuelos, una tía soltera, etcétera. Aunque se usa la palabra «niñero» o «niñera» para designar a la persona que cuida a los niños, este trabajo generalmente lo hace alguien que vive en la misma casa, algún pariente o algún amigo de la familia. Los equivalentes culturales de «baby-sitter» y «rest home» prácticamente no existen en la cultura hispánica.

Todos los miembros de la familia pasan mucho tiempo juntos. En los pueblos pequeños—y en otras partes, si el horario de trabajo lo permite—el padre y los niños regresan a casa a las doce para almorzar con toda la familia. El almuerzo es la comida principal del día. Después, es costumbre conversar o dormir la siesta antes de volver al trabajo, más o menos a las dos y media o a las tres. Sin embargo, cada día son más pocos los que pueden practicar esta costumbre ya que muchos negocios han adoptado el «horario continuo» (con una hora libre para el almuerzo) y los trabajadores en general trabajan de 8 a 5 o de 9 a 6, respectivamente. Después de salir del trabajo por la tarde, muchos empleados se reúnen con sus amigos a conversar o a tomar un café juntos, antes de volver a la casa a cenar. Durante estas horas se ve mucha gente por la calle. La cena se sirve generalmente a las diez en España y un poco más temprano, entre las ocho y las nueve, en Hispanoamérica.

En los pueblos pequeños del mundo hispano, la vida de la mujer todavía se limita° principalmente a la casa, a la familia y a un pequeño grupo de amigas. Entre los jóvenes, la separación de los sexos es grande y las relaciones entre muchachos y muchachas son relativamente formales. En general, los futuros novios se conocen en lugares públicos: la plaza, el mercado, la iglesia o en alguna fiesta del pueblo. Sólo después de mucho tiempo el novio visita a su novia (su futura esposa) en casa de ella.

se... *is limited*

Una fiesta de cumpleaños

Hoy día muchas costumbres tradicionales están cambiando, especialmente en las grandes ciudades. Aquí no hay tiempo para dormir la siesta. Y a veces ¡ni para almorzar! La mayoría de los negocios y oficinas públicas permanecen° abiertos a la hora de la siesta. Ahora, más mujeres trabajan fuera de la casa. En las grandes ciudades los jóvenes tienen más libertad, especialmente en el ambiente° más informal de la universidad. Muchos empleados de grandes compañías tienen que mudarse con frecuencia a otra ciudad y por eso no les es posible mantener relaciones muy estrechas° con los amigos. Por estas razones, la vida actual° en muchas ciudades hispanas—especialmente en ciudades industrializadas como Buenos Aires o Madrid—tiene mucho más en común con la vida en las ciudades de los Estados Unidos que en otros pueblos o ciudades hispanas menos industrializadas. Pero a unos cuantos° kilómetros de una gran ciudad todavía se puede encontrar la rica variedad de costumbres hispanas típicas.

remain

atmosphere

close / present

a... a few

PREGUNTAS

1. ¿Por qué cree usted que no hay equivalentes exactos de conceptos como «baby-sitter» o «rest home» en español? **2.** ¿A qué hora almuerza la familia hispana tradicional? ¿A qué hora cena? ¿Cuál es la comida principal del día? **3.** ¿Cómo es la vida de la mujer en los pueblos pequeños del mundo hispano? **4.** ¿Es común que un muchacho y una muchacha salgan solos en los países hispanos? ¿Dónde se conocen generalmente? **5.** Según esta lectura, las costumbres tradicionales están cambiando mucho en las grandes ciudades. ¿Cómo? ¿Por qué? **6.** Se dice que a causa del divorcio y de otros fenómenos sociales, la familia nuclear (inmediata) de los Estados Unidos está hoy día en peligro (*danger*). ¿Está usted de acuerdo? ¿Cree que es mejor el sistema social y familiar (de la familia) de los países hispanos? ¿Por qué?

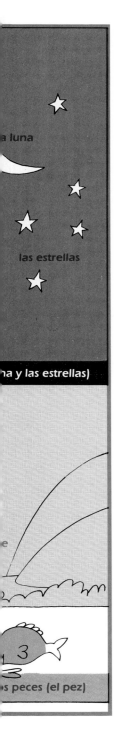

las estrellas

na y las estrellas)

peces (el pez)

La naturaleza 17

**Adding Information
Changing the Subject
Expressing Empathy**

EJERCICIO

Choose the word that does not belong.

1. la luna / el sol / la estrella / la flor
2. el cielo / el pájaro / el pez / el animal
3. la flor / la piedra / el árbol / la planta
4. el mar / el río / el valle / el océano
5. la nube / la lluvia / la niebla / la tierra

PREGUNTAS

1. ¿Cómo se llama la parte del día cuando empieza a salir el sol? ¿Sabe usted a qué hora salió el sol esta mañana? **2.** Una adivinanza (*riddle*): «¿Qué le dijo la luna al sol?» Respuesta: «¿Tan grande y no te dejan salir de noche?» ¿Qué sale de noche con la luna? **3.** ¿Cómo se llaman los «animales» que viven en los árboles y cantan? ¿los que viven en el agua? ¿Qué diferencia hay entre un pez y un pescado? (Para el pez, la diferencia es muy importante.) **4.** Describa cómo es el invierno donde usted vive. ¿Llueve mucho? ¿Nieva? (¿Hay nieve?) ¿Hay nubes? ¿niebla? ¿Qué le gusta del invierno? ¿de la primavera? ¿del verano? ¿del otoño?

 ## The neuter *lo*

Consuelo y Pepe hablan de sus planes para el fin de semana.

CONSUELO ¿Te gustaría ir de campamento° con nosotros este fin de semana, Pepe?

PEPE No, Consuelo. Realmente no tengo tiempo. *Lo* malo de° ir de campamento es que hay que dormir afuera... con los animales, los pájaros°, los insectos...

CONSUELO Por otra parte, *lo bueno*° es poder ver las estrellas° que salen al anochecer°, oír los pájaros que cantan por la mañana...

PEPE *Lo que*° no me gusta es que los pájaros me despierten de mañana temprano. Y no me gusta vivir sin comodidades°.

CONSUELO ¿Qué es *lo que* llamas «vivir sin comodidades»?

PEPE Pues, déjame pensar... estar sin mi piano de cola°, por ejemplo.

---

1. ¿Le gusta a Pepe ir de campamento? ¿Qué es lo malo de ir de campamento, según él?   2. Según Consuelo, ¿qué es lo bueno de ir de campamento?   3. ¿Qué es lo que Pepe llama «vivir sin comodidades»?   4. ¿Le gusta a usted ir de campamento o prefiere pasar la noche en casa de amigos o en algún hotel? ¿Por qué?

---

ir de campamento *to go camping*   **Lo malo de** *The bad thing about*
pájaros *birds*   **lo bueno** *the good thing*   **estrellas** *stars*
que... anochecer *that come out at dusk*   **Lo que** *What*
sin comodidades *without conveniences*   **piano de cola** *grand piano*

A. The neuter article **lo** can be used with a masculine singular adjective to express an abstract quality or idea.

Lo malo de vivir en la ciudad es que hay mucho ruido.

The bad thing about living in the city is that there is a lot of noise.

En cambio, lo divertido de vivir en la ciudad es que hay muchas cosas que hacer los fines de semana.

On the other hand, the fun thing about living in the city is that there are many things to do on the weekends.

Lo maravilloso de ir de campamento es el contacto con la naturaleza.

The wonderful part about going camping is the contact with nature.

B. **Lo** can replace an adjective or refer to a whole idea previously stated.

—¿Estás cansado? —Sí, lo estoy.   *"Are you tired?" "Yes, I am."*
—¿Es aburrida la vida del campo?   *"Is life in the country boring?"*
  —No, no lo es.   *"No, it isn't."*
—¿Sabes cómo se dice «pájaro» en   *"Do you know how to say 'pájaro' in*
  inglés? —Sí, lo sé: se dice «bird».   *English?" "Yes, I know: you say*
                                                   'bird.'"

C. **Lo que** can be used to express something imprecise or to sum up a preceding idea, but it must precede a conjugated verb.

Lo que más me gusta de Florida es el   *What I like most about Florida is the*
  clima.   *climate.*
Pedro vino a visitarnos ayer al   *Pedro came to visit us yesterday at dusk,*
  anochecer, lo que nos alegró   *which made us very happy.*
  mucho.

D. However, **el**, **la**, **los**, or **las** (**el que, la que, los que, las que**) must be used to refer to a specific person or thing, the gender of which is known.

Esta composición es la más larga que   *This composition is the longest one I wrote.*
  escribí. La terminé al amanecer.   *I finished it at dawn.*
—¿Tienes las plantas? —¿Cuáles? —Las   *"Do you have the plants?" "Which ones?"*
  que te di ayer.   *"The ones I gave you yesterday."*

EJERCICIOS

A. **Dos puntos de vista.** Almost everything has good and bad points. Tell what you think is good and bad about each of the following things.

Modelo   el verano
              Lo bueno del verano es el calor.
              Lo malo del verano son los insectos.

1. este país
2. la televisión
3. el campo
4. muchas ciudades
5. el fútbol americano
6. los viajes
7. la vida universitaria
8. este libro
9. el clima de esta región
10. los postres

B. ¿Le gusta o no...? Give your opinion about the following people and things. Tell why you do or don't like them.

Modelos   pintar / esos pintores
Me gusta lo que pintan esos pintores porque buscan inspiración en la naturaleza.

(yo) ver / por televisión
No me gusta lo que (yo) veo por televisión porque muchos programas son aburridos.

1. pasar / en el mundo
2. hacer / el presidente
3. decir / los expertos sobre la ecología
4. enseñar / algunos profesores
5. (yo) leer / en los periódicos
6. pensar / mis padres

C. Posibilidades múltiples. Complete each of the following sentences by underlining the appropriate article.

Modelo   Aquel pájaro, (lo, la, <u>el</u>) que tú quieres comprar, es muy caro.

1. Estas flores son (los, las, lo) más lindas que encontré.
2. Anoche llamaron las chicas, (la, lo, los) que nos alegró mucho.
3. Estos ejercicios son (los, las, el) más interesantes de este capítulo.
4. ¿Me preguntas si estoy cansado? Pues, ¡claro que (la, lo, los) estoy!
5. Tengo ganas de vivir en aquella casa, (el, lo, la) que está en el valle.
6. El amanecer será maravilloso, pero ¡el anochecer también (el, lo, la) es!

D. Traducción. Give the Spanish equivalent of the following sentences.

1. The good part about living in the city is that there are many cultural activities.
2. The bad thing about driving in the city is the traffic.
3. The best part about my house is the large living room.
4. Our friend is able to go camping with us, which pleases us very much.
5. What I want is for you to sit down and enjoy yourself at the party.

PREGUNTAS

1. ¿Qué es lo más interesante de la vida universitaria? ¿lo más aburrido? ¿lo más divertido?   **2.** ¿Qué profesores le gustan más a usted: los que divierten mucho a sus estudiantes o los que los hacen trabajar? ¿Por qué?   **3.** ¿Quién aprende más: el que lee mucho pero viaja poco o el que lee poco pero viaja mucho? ¿Por qué?   **4.** Para usted, ¿qué es lo mejor de la ciudad? ¿lo peor? ¿lo mejor de la vida del campo? ¿lo peor?   **5.** ¿Quién lleva una vida más tranquila: el que vive en la ciudad o el que vive en el campo? ¿Por qué?

Other uses of *por* and *para*

Teresa, profesora de español, llama a su amiga Luisa por teléfono.

LUISA   Hola.
TERESA   Hola, Luisa. Soy yo, Teresa. Te llamo *para* pedirte un favor. Estoy enferma y necesito que alguien enseñe *por* mí mañana.
LUISA   *Por* supuesto que cuentas conmigo.° Si quieres, más tarde paso *por* tu casa *para* que me expliques° qué hacer en clase.
TERESA   ¡Un millón de gracias, Luisa! Estoy *por* terminar° unos ejercicios de repaso°. Así no tienes que preparar nada.
LUISA   Como quieras.° ¿Qué te parece si voy *por* esos ejercicios a eso de las tres°?
TERESA   Buena idea. Estarán listos *para* esa hora°. Y gracias de nuevo° *por* ayudarme, Luisa.
LUISA   De nada, Teresa. Creo que *para* eso están los amigos°, ¿no?

---

1. ¿Para qué llama Teresa a su amiga?   2. ¿Qué hará Luisa por Teresa? ¿Por qué?   3. ¿Qué prepara Teresa para la clase?   4. ¿A qué hora piensa pasar Luisa por la casa de Teresa? ¿Tendrá Teresa listos los ejercicios para esa hora?   5. Según Luisa, ¿para qué están los amigos?

Por...conmigo. *Of course you can count on me.*   **para...expliques** *so that you can explain to me*
Estoy por terminar *I'm about to finish*   **ejercicios de repaso** *review exercises*
Como quieras. *As you like.*   **a eso de las tres** *at around three*
para esa hora *by that time*   **de nuevo** *again*   **para...amigos** *that's what friends are for*

In Chapter 7 you saw some common uses of **por** and **para**, both often translated as *for* in English. Here is a review and some additional uses of **por** and **para**.

A. **Por** is generally used to express:

1.   Cause or motive (*because of, on account of, for the sake of*).

Lo hizo por amor.
No hay ninguna posibilidad de que encontremos trabajo aquí. Por eso, vamos a mudarnos a la capital.

He (She) did it for (the sake of) love.
There's no possibility of our finding work here. That's why (Because of that) we're moving to the capital.

2. Duration, length of time, including parts of the day.

Los García irán a Cuzco por dos días.	*The Garcías will go to Cuzco for two days.*
Voy a trabajar en el jardín por la tarde.	*I'm going to work in the (flower) garden in the afternoon.*

3. Exchange (*in exchange for*).

Cambiamos nuestro televisor viejo por uno nuevo.	*We exchanged our old television set for a new one.*
Pagué cuatro mil pesos por ese pájaro.	*I paid four thousand pesos for that bird.*

4. *In place of, as a substitute for, on behalf of.*

Juan vendió las plantas por Manuel.	*Juan sold the plants for (on behalf of) Manuel.*
Trabajé por Ana hoy.	*I worked for (as a substitute for, instead of) Ana today.*

5. The equivalent of *through*, *along*, or *by* (often with means of communication or transportation).

Lo vimos por televisión ayer.	*We saw it on TV yesterday.*
Pase por el parque.	*Go through the park.*
Caminaban por la calle principal.	*They were walking along the main street.*
Los Castro piensan viajar por tren.*	*The Castros plan to travel by train.*

6. The object of an errand.

Pepe fue al mercado por papas.	*Pepe went to the market for potatoes.*
Vendré por ti a las siete.	*I'll come for you at seven o'clock.*

7. Number, measure, or frequency (*per*).

Venden huevos por docena.	*They sell eggs by the dozen.*
Van a ochenta kilómetros por hora.	*They are going eighty kilometers an (per) hour.*
Nos visitan tres veces por año.**	*They visit us three times a year.*

B. **Para** is generally used to express:

1. An intended recipient (*for someone or something*).

Trabajo para una compañía que vende computadoras.	*I work for a company that sells computers.*
Ana compró la corbata para su esposo.	*Ana bought the tie for her husband.*

2. Direction or destination.

Salieron para Quito ayer.	*They left for Quito yesterday.*

---

*The preposition **en** is often used for transportation also: **en avión, en tren.**
The definite article may also be used with time periods: **Nos visitan tres veces al año (a la semana, etcétera).

3. Purpose (*in order to*).

Voy a la florería para comprar unas flores. — *I'm going to the flower shop (in order) to buy some flowers.*

4. Lack of correspondence in an expressed or implied comparison.

Pedrito es muy inteligente para su edad. — *Pedrito is very intelligent for his age.*

Esa lámpara es muy grande para la mesa. — *That lamp is too big for the table.*

5. A specific event or point in time.

Tienen que regresar para el jueves. — *They have to return by Thursday.*

Iré a visitarte para Navidad. — *I'll go visit you for Christmas.*

6. The use for which something is intended.

Un sillón es para descansar. — *An armchair is to rest in.*

Esta taza es para café. — *This cup is for coffee.*

C. In Chapter 7, Section IV, you saw some commonly used expressions with **por**; here are some others (many of which you have already seen in this book):

estar por (+ inf.)   *to be about to*
por casualidad   *by chance*
por ciento   *percent*
por cierto   *surely, certainly*
por estas razones   *for these reasons*
por lo común   *commonly, usually*

por lo general   *in general*
por lo menos   *at least*
por lo tanto   *therefore*
por primera (última) vez   *for the first (last) time*
por todas partes   *everywhere*

EJERCICIOS

A. **¿Por o para?**   Substitute the expressions in italics with either **por** or **para**, as appropriate.

Modelos   Hoy trabajo *en lugar de* Juan Mario.
Hoy trabajo por Juan Mario.

Aunque es italiano, habla muy bien el inglés.
Para italiano, habla muy bien el inglés.

1. Esta tarde pienso pasar *a buscar* las plantas.
2. *Si quieres* sacar buenas notas, tienes que estudiar más.
3. *A pesar de* su edad, es muy alto. ¡Sólo tiene cinco años!
4. Mario vendrá *a llevar a* los niños después de las siete.
5. ¿Trabajaron en esa compañía *durante* diez años?
6. Me pagan quinientos dólares *al mes a cambio de* (*in exchange for*) mi trabajo.
7. Se fueron en avión *con destino* (*destination*) a Quito.
8. Rogelio y yo estamos *a punto de* (*about to, ready to*) salir.

B. La casa nueva. Complete the following paragraph with **por** or **para**, as needed.

Esta mañana Luisa me llamó _____ teléfono _____ invitarme a cenar en su casa nueva. Ella y Pepe están muy contentos porque _____ fin pudieron comprarse una casa. _____ eso, ellos quieren reunirnos a todos sus amigos esta noche _____ enseñarnos la casa y _____ celebrar juntos esa ocasión. No sé cuánto pagaron _____ la casa, pero sé que _____ poder comprarla tuvieron que pedir prestado (*to borrow*) mucho dinero del banco y de sus padres. Vivieron en un apartamento _____ más de seis años y pagaban unos $500,00 _____ mes. Decidieron buscar una casa sólo porque supieron que Luisa espera un bebé _____ agosto y el apartamento va a ser muy pequeño _____ los tres. Roberto, Luis, Tina, Paulina y yo decidimos contribuir $15,00 cada uno _____ comprarles un lindo regalo _____ la sala. También vamos a llevarles las bebidas y el postre _____ la fiesta. Los muchachos van _____ el vino y la cerveza; Sonia y Paulina pasan _____ la panadería _____ comprar un postre y yo debo ir _____ el regalo. Creo que les voy a comprar el cuadro que a Luisa le gustó tanto. Lo venden _____ $75,00.

C. En acción. Describe the situations and tell what the people are saying in the drawings below. Use **por** or **para**, as appropriate.

Modelo

Estos dos jóvenes están por casarse y por eso se ven mucho.
Aquí Pedro le trae algo a Lelia.
—¿Es para mí?
—Sí, por tu cumpleaños... ¡y porque te quiero mucho!

1.

2.

3.

(no image reference — drawing 3 with 80 K/H sign and car)

4.

5.

6.

Juan esta estudiando
Tiene que estudiar para su examen
Quiere se acuesta

7.

8.

9.

10.

El Sr. garcía se pone su siglo para ganar

D. Un viaje. In groups of three or four students, choose a place with which you are familiar and imagine you are going to take a trip there. Write at least five sentences describing your trip, using **por** and **para** as many times as possible. You might include answers to these questions:

1. ¿Para qué ciudad o región piensan ir?
2. ¿Cómo van? (¿por tren, por avión, etc.?)
3. ¿Por cuánto tiempo se quedan?
4. ¿Cuánto dinero piensan pagar por hoteles? ¿por comida?
5. ¿Tienen planes para hacer o ver algo en especial? ¿Qué?

PREGUNTAS

1. ¿Viene usted a alguna clase por la mañana? ¿por la tarde? ¿por la noche? ¿A qué hora sale de su casa? ¿vuelve para su casa?   2. ¿Cuántas veces por semana va usted al laboratorio de lenguas? ¿a la biblioteca?   3. ¿Cómo se informa usted (*do you become informed*) de las noticias? ¿Por radio? ¿Por televisión? ¿Por los periódicos? 4. ¿Para cuándo piensa usted terminar sus estudios?   5. ¿Ha viajado mucho por avión? ¿por tren? ¿Adónde ha viajado? ¿Por qué países le gustaría viajar en el futuro?

The passive voice *(for recognition only)*

La Catedral, en la Plaza de Armas de Lima

Querida Margarita:

Hace dos días que estoy en Lima. Llegué a esta histórica y bonita capital peruana el miércoles pasado y creo que me quedaré unos diez días más antes de volver a casa. Lima *fue fundada°* en 1535 por Francisco Pizarro y *fue bautizada°* con el nombre de Ciudad de los Reyes. Hay iglesias, jardines y pequeñas plazas por todas partes. La ciudad tiene magníficos edificios coloniales que *fueron construidos°* por los españoles en el siglo XVI. Hoy visité la catedral que *fue construida* en el mismo lugar donde Pizarro ordenó la construcción de la primera iglesia de Lima. Dentro de la catedral hay un ataúd de vidrio° donde están en exhibición pública los restos momificados° de Pizarro. ¡Eso parece increíble!, ¿no? ¿Sabías que él *fue asesinado°* en 1541, sólo seis años después de la fundación de Lima? Y aún más interesante, ¿sabías que el actual Palacio de Gobierno, residencia oficial del presidente del Perú, también *fue construido* en el mismo lugar donde estaba la casa de Pizarro? Desde allí *fueron gobernados°* los habitantes del Perú colonial y desde allí *son gobernados* los habitantes del Perú contemporáneo. Todavía no he visitado este «palacio» pero pienso hacerlo mañana. Después quiero visitar la Universidad de San Marcos, que *fue establecida* en 1551 y es la primera universidad del Nuevo Mundo... También quiero visitar algunos museos y ver más iglesias... ¡y hacer un viaje al Cuzco y a Machu Picchu...! ¡Es que aquí hay tanto que ver, Margarita...! Y todo es de lo más fascinante° para mí.

Bueno..., como te darás cuenta, ¡me encanta el Perú! y tal vez me quede un poco más de lo que pensaba... Te llamaré tan pronto como llegue a Boston, ¿O.K.?

Cariños°,
Diana

¿Verdadero o falso?

1. La capital del Perú fue fundada en 1535.
2. Francisco Pizarro fue el primer presidente del Perú.
3. En Lima hay muchos edificios coloniales que fueron construidos en el siglo XIV.
4. Pizarro fue asesinado en la Catedral de Lima.
5. El Palacio de Gobierno del Perú y la Casa Blanca de los Estados Unidos tienen funciones similares.
6. La Universidad de San Marcos es la universidad más antigua del Nuevo Mundo.
7. Diana no visitará Machu Picchu porque no tiene tiempo.
8. Ella volverá a Boston un poco antes de lo que pensaba.

---

fue fundada *was founded* **fue bautizada** *was baptized*
fueron construidos *were built* **ataúd de vidrio** *glass-walled coffin*
restos momificados *mummified remains* **fue asesinado** *was slain*
fueron gobernados *were governed* **de lo más fascinante** *most fascinating*
Cariños *Affectionately*

A. In Spanish, as well as in English, sentences can be either in the active voice or the passive voice. Compare:

Active voice:

Los incas construyeron Machu Picchu.	*The Incas built Machu Picchu.*
(**Ellos**) hicieron la guitarra en México.	*They made the guitar in Mexico.*

Passive voice:

Machu Picchu fue construido por los incas.

Machu Picchu was built by the Incas.

La guitarra fue hecha en México.

The guitar was made in Mexico.

The subjects of the sentences are shown in bold type. In the passive voice, the subject receives the action of the verb rather than performing it. In the active voice, the subject performs the action of the verb.

B. In Spanish, the passive voice is formed with a conjugated form of **ser** and a past participle, which must agree with the subject in gender and number. If an agent, or "doer," of the action is expressed, it is usually introduced by the preposition **por**.

subject	+ ***ser*** + *past participle* + ***por*** + *agent*
Machu Picchu	fue construido por los incas.

Las papas fueron descubiertas en América.

Potatoes were discovered in America.

Cambiando de tema, ¿sabías que los muros fueron pintados por los chicos?

To change the subject, did you know that the walls were painted by the boys?

El poema «Romance de la luna, luna» fue escrito por Federico García Lorca.

The poem "Romance of the Moon, Moon" was written by Federico García Lorca.

C. The true passive is not used as often in Spanish as the passive voice is in English. The active voice is preferred. When an agent is not expressed, the passive **se** is much more common than the true passive. Compare:

Las ruinas de Machu Picchu se descubrieron en 1911.

The ruins of Machu Picchu were discovered in 1911.

Las ruinas de Machu Picchu fueron descubiertas por Hiram Bingham en 1911.

The ruins of Machu Picchu were discovered by Hiram Bingham in 1911.

Guernica se pintó en 1937.

Guernica *was painted in 1937.*

Guernica fue pintada por Pablo Picasso en 1937.

Guernica *was painted by Pablo Picasso in 1937.*

El Palacio de Gobierno, en Lima

A. ¿Por quién...? Say who did or who does the actions described in the following sentences. Follow the models.

Modelos   La luna fue explorada por tres astronautas en 1969.
tres astronautas

Los muros del patio son pintados por Sandra.
Sandra

1. América fue descubierta por Colón en 1492.
2. Los problemas fueron resueltos por el profesor.
3. El *Quijote* fue escrito por Cervantes.
4. Las bebidas fueron traídas por Rogelio.
5. Las hermanas Vera fueron invitadas por Susana.
6. La mesa es puesta por los niños.
7. Tus amigos son oídos por todo el mundo.
8. Ese museo es visitado por miles de turistas todos los años.

B. Una fiesta en honor de la profesora Ledesma. The Department of Romance Languages is having a party in honor of Professor Ledesma, who has been teaching there for twenty years. Form sentences to describe the event by choosing an appropriate phrase from Column B and one from Column C for each phrase from Column A. Follow the model.

Modelo   **La fiesta fue organizada por tres profesoras.**

A	B	C
1. la lista de invitados	fue comprado	Esteban
2. las invitaciones	fueron ayudados	las secretarias
3. el vino	fue preparada	una amiga de Tina
4. la torta	fueron escritas	tres profesoras
5. la fiesta	fue traído	Laura y Tina
6. el regalo	fue hecha	Teresa y Ramón
7. los profesores	fue organizada	los estudiantes

C. Infórmese sobre el Perú. Choose **a** or **b** to complete the sentences below, as appropriate.

1. Lima _____ por Francisco Pizarro.
   a. fue fundada en 1535
   b. fue fundada en 1551
2. La primera iglesia de Lima y la casa de Pizarro _____ en el siglo XVI.
   a. fueron destruidas
   b. fueron construidas
3. Franciso Pizarro _____ en 1541.
   a. fue asesinado
   b. fue bautizado

4. Los restos de Pizarro _____, en un ataúd de vidrio.
   a. fueron puestos en la Catedral de Lima
   b. fueron puestos en el Palacio de Gobierno
5. La Universidad de San Marcos _____.
   a. fue establecida en 1535
   b. fue establecida en 1551
6. Hoy día los peruanos _____ desde el Palacio de Gobierno.
   a. son gobernados por Francisco Pizarro
   b. son gobernados por el presidente del Perú

D. ¿Cuál es la mejor traducción? Choose **a** or **b** to indicate the most appropriate translation of the phrases in italics.

1. Those plants *were bought and brought* here last week.
   a. fueron comprados y traídos
   b. fueron compradas y traídas
2. The party *was organized* by Raquel.
   a. fue organizado
   b. fue organizada
3. These short stories *were written* by a famous writer.
   a. fueron escritos
   b. fueron escritas
4. Those two banks *were built* before 1850.
   a. fueron construidos
   b. fueron construidas
5. New flowers and plants *are cultivated* every year.
   a. son cultivados
   b. son cultivadas
6. When *was* that cake *made*?
   a. fue hecho
   b. fue hecha

Machu Picchu: La misteriosa ciudad de los incas[1]

Eva y su novio están visitando las ruinas de Machu Picchu, en el Perú. Ella es pintora y está buscando inspiración para unos cuadros.

JUAN   ¿Qué haces, mi amor?

EVA   Estoy admirando estos muros imponentes.[2] Dicen que fueron construidos por los incas hace cientos de años pero no fueron descubiertos hasta 1911. Parecen más bellos ahora, sin turistas.

JUAN   ¿A qué hora saliste?

EVA   A las cinco. No te desperté porque estabas durmiendo como una piedra. Hace dos horas que espero el amanecer, pero creo que hoy no vamos a poder ver el sol por la niebla.

Vista de Machu Picchu

JUAN Mira aquella piedra. Parece una escultura moderna. Creo que es la que usaba el Inca para atrapar° el sol.[3]

EVA Sí, lo es. Conozco la leyenda°. Me la contó el muchacho indio que trabaja en el hotel. ¡Mira, allí está él!

TANO Muy buenos días, señores.

JUAN Buenos días. No sabía que hablabas español.

TANO En casa hablamos quechua,[4] señor, pero en la escuela nos enseñan español.

EVA ¿No tienes frío sin zapatos?

TANO No, señora, estoy acostumbrado al frío. Ustedes también se acostumbrarán pronto, dentro de dos o tres semanas...

EVA No podemos quedarnos... El martes salimos para Venezuela.

JUAN Yo ya no siento mucho el frío. Esta mañana tomé un té que fue hecho con hojas de coca.[5] Dicen que es bueno para que uno se caliente° y no sienta tanto la altura.°

EVA Sí, es difícil acostumbrarse a esta altura. Me estoy imaginando que estamos en el cielo.

JUAN No te lo estás imaginando. Esa niebla en realidad no es niebla. ¡Es una nube baja!

---

atrapar *to catch*   **leyenda** *legend*   **se caliente** *gets warm*   **altura** *altitude*

¿Cuál es la respuesta correcta?

1. ¿Qué busca Eva en las ruinas de Machu Picchu?
   a. hojas de coca
   b. inspiración
2. ¿A qué hora salió ella del hotel?
   a. a las cinco de la mañana
   b. a las cinco de la tarde
3. ¿Cuándo fue construida la ciudad inca de Machu Picchu?
   a. en 1911
   b. hace cientos de años
4. ¿Cuándo fueron descubiertas las ruinas de Machu Picchu?
   a. en 1911
   b. hace cientos de años
5. ¿Qué lengua hablan en la casa de Tano?
   a. español
   b. quechua
6. ¿Qué lengua aprende Tano en la escuela?
   a. español
   b. quechua
7. ¿Cuándo salen para Venezuela Eva y su novio?
   a. dentro de dos o tres semanas
   b. en una semana

Notas culturales

1. Machu Picchu is the ancient fortress city of the Incas, located high in the Andes not far from Cuzco, Peru, which was the capital of the Inca empire when the Spanish arrived. Because it cannot be seen from the valley below, Machu Picchu remained unknown to the outside world until 1911.

2. The city offers a unique glimpse into the life of the ancient Incas, with temples, stairways, walls, and houses still standing. The stones were precisely shaped and chiseled so that no mortar was necessary. Stones with as many as twelve sides fit so perfectly together that a razor blade cannot be inserted between them. Modern engineers are unable to explain how the Incas, who, like other American Indians, did not have the benefit of the wheel, were able to transport these stones over long distances.

3. According to the legend, the priests would tell the Inca emperor (who at that time was the only one called Inca) which day was to be the shortest of the year, and on that day he would go forth at sunset and ceremonially "tie" the sun to the earth, using this stone, called "the hitching post of the sun." This was supposed to prevent the sun from continuing to slip away from the earth. The proof came, of course, when the days that followed turned out to be longer, thus corroborating the general belief that the Inca was a direct descendant of the sun and had a special power over it.

4. Quechua, the language spoken by the Incas, was imposed upon all new members of the Inca empire after conquest. **Quechua** and **Aymará** are the most common Indian languages in Peru, and many Peruvians learn Spanish only as a second language.

5. Coca-leaf tea is made from the leaf of the coca plant, from which cocaine is extracted. The tea is strictly for medicinal purposes and does not have the effects of cocaine; it is sometimes served to tourists to prevent altitude sickness. The leaves of the coca plant, however, in combination with some other ingredients, are chewed as a narcotic by many Indians of the Peruvian and Bolivian sierra. The coca leaves impart a temporary feeling of well-being and enable the Indians to work despite the severe discomfort of the high altitude and intense cold. The prolonged use of coca causes whitish, cracked lips and, more important, mental deterioration. The Indians of the Andes thus find themselves trapped by the need to work in a harsh environment and by the destructive effects of the method that makes that work tolerable.

FUNCIONES Y ACTIVIDADES

In this chapter, you have seen examples of some important language functions, or uses. Here is a summary and some additional information about these functions of language.

Adding information

Además... *In addition . . . (Furthermore . . .)*

También... *Also . . . .*
Entre paréntesis... *Incidentally . . .*

Changing the subject

A propósito... *By the way . . .*
A propósito de... *Regarding . . .*
Cambiando de tema... *To change the subject . . .*

Por otra parte... *On the other hand . . .*
En cambio... *On the other hand . . .*
Por el contrario... *On the contrary . . .*
Sin embargo... *However . . .*

Expressing empathy

One of the most common language functions is the expression of empathy, indicating that you understand what someone is feeling or thinking. This, of course, is different from sympathy, discussed in Chapter 5. Here are some ways to express empathy:

¡Estará(-s) muy contento(-a)!
Debe(-s) estar muy desilusionado(-a).
Se (Te) sentirá(-s) muy orgulloso(-a).

You must be very happy!
You must be very disappointed.
You must feel very proud.

You might review the expressions of emotion from the **Vocabulario activo** of Chapter 15 for other words used in expressing feelings.

A. **Además...** See how much you remember from what you have read in this book. In pairs, one student reads the information below each drawing. The other student gives some additional information, using the passive voice and **además**.

Modelo

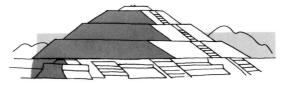

Ésta es la famosa Pirámide del Sol, que está cerca de la ciudad de México. No se sabe quiénes la construyeron. Ningún europeo la había visto hasta el siglo XVI.

Además, fue descubierta por Hernán Cortés.

1. Este acueducto está en Segovia. Todavía se usa para llevar agua a la ciudad.

2. El título completo de este libro es *El ingenioso hidalgo Don Quijote de la Mancha*. Se publicó en 1605.

3. Este cuadro se llama *Vista de Toledo*. Está en el Museo de Arte Metropolitano, en Nueva York.

4. La famosa Mezquita de Córdoba está en el sur de España. Se construyó en el siglo VIII.

B. **Reacciones.** Give a reaction to each of the following statements. (Use the **usted** form.)

Modelos Mi esposa está en el hospital. Va a tener un bebé.
Estará muy nervioso.

Le dieron a otra persona el trabajo que me habían prometido.
Estará furioso(-a).

1. Mi hija recibió un premio en química.
2. Mi mejor amiga va a mudarse a otra ciudad.

3. Es posible que mi esposo pierda su trabajo.
4. Mi novio me trajo flores y chocolates.
5. Hace mucho que trabajo doce horas por día.
6. Mi esposa me pidió el divorcio.
7. Tuve un accidente de automóvil. Aunque no tuve la culpa, tengo que pagar sesenta mil pesos para arreglar mi coche.
8. Compramos una casa muy linda, con vista al mar.

C. Cambiando de tema. In pairs, role-play this situation. Two friends are discussing a camping trip. "By the way," says the first one, "Ramón, Cecilia, and I are going camping this weekend." This person talks about all the things he or she likes about camping. The second person asks several questions about where the trip will be, when they are leaving, and so forth, and points out the disadvantages of camping, using words like *however* and *on the other hand* as transitions. Then he or she changes the subject and begins a new topic of conversation.

D. La naturaleza y los dichos populares. Try to guess which saying might be used by Hispanic people for each of the following situations. (The answers are below.)

a. Seis meses de invierno, seis meses de infierno (*hell*).
b. Está en la flor de la edad.
c. Está en la luna.
d. Después de la lluvia sale el sol.
e. Se está yendo (andando) por las ramas (*branches*).

1. Tomás no está pensando en lo que hace.

2. Maribel está celebrando su cumpleaños. Tiene 18 años.

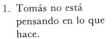

3. Federico está hablando de detalles (*details*) sin importancia y se está olvidando de lo principal (*main thing*).

4. Tenemos un clima extremo: o hace mucho frío o mucho calor.

5. Ana ha tenido muy mala suerte recientemente, pero pronto su suerte habrá cambiado.

Respuestas
1. c   2. b   3. e   4. a   5. d

VOCABULARIO ACTIVO

Cognados

la diferencia	el insecto	el silencio	el valle
extremo	la planta	tranquilo	

Verbos

ir de campamento	*to go camping*

La naturaleza

el amanecer	*dawn, daybreak*
el anochecer	*twilight, dusk*
el campo	*country (as opposed to city)*
el cielo	*sky; heaven*
el clima	*climate*
la estrella	*star*
la flor	*flower*
la grandeza	*grandeur*
la hoja	*leaf*
la luna	*moon*
la niebla	*fog*
la nube	*cloud*
el pájaro	*bird*
el pez (los peces)	*fish*
la piedra	*stone*
la tierra	*earth, land*

Adjetivos

bajo	*low; short*
bello	*beautiful*
imponente	*impressive*
maravilloso	*marvelous, wonderful*

Otra palabras y frases

adentro	*inside*
afuera	*outside*
bajo *adv.*	*beneath, under*
mientras tanto	*meanwhile*
mismo: lo mismo	*the same thing*
el muro	*wall*
por el contrario	*on the contrary*
por otra parte	*on the other hand*
la respuesta	*answer*
el tema	*subject*

Expresiones útiles

A propósito...	*By the way . . .*
A propósito de...	*Regarding . . .*
Entre paréntesis...	*Incidentally . . .*
Cambiando de tema...	*To change the subject . . .*

De compras _____ 18

Expressing Satisfaction and Dissatisfaction
Summarizing

EJERCICIO

Complete the sentences with an appropriate word or words.

1. Ese coche no es caro; al contrario, es _____. Sólo _____ cien mil pesos.
2. Rosario siempre _____ todo su dinero; nunca guarda nada en el banco.
3. Compre usted esta camisa, señor; es de buena _____.
4. Voy a _____ mil pesos y ponerlos en el banco.
5. A Enrique le debo los cincuenta pesos que me _____ la semana pasada.

PREGUNTAS

1. Cuando usted necesita ropa, ¿le gusta ir a almacenes grandes, a boutiques exclusivas o prefiere hacer sus compras en tiendas más baratas? ¿Dónde compra su ropa? **2.** Cuando va de compras, ¿busca ofertas o compra lo primero que ve? **3.** ¿Regateamos (*Do we bargain over prices*) cuando compramos ciertas cosas en este país? ¿Ejemplos? **4.** ¿Les debe usted mucho dinero a sus parientes o a sus amigos? ¿Les presta dinero a sus parientes o a sus amigos? **5.** ¿Ahorra usted dinero todos los meses? **6.** ¿En qué gasta más dinero: en la comida, en el alquiler (*rent*), en su auto, en libros, en diversiones, en su matrícula (*tuition*)...?

 ## The imperfect subjunctive

Una zapatería

En casa de los Bello.

RAÚL ¿Dónde estabas, Marta?

MARTA Ana me pidió que *fuera* de compras con ella. Quería que le *ayudara* a escoger unos zapatos para su entrevista en Caracas.

RAÚL ¿Encontraron algo que les *gustara*?

MARTA No, no compramos nada. A Ana no le gustaron los zapatos que estaban en oferta°. Buscaba algo que *hiciera* juego° con su traje nuevo.

RAÚL Total que° todavía no tiene zapatos para su entrevista... Sé que quiere conseguir ese puesto° en la capital.

MARTA Sí y yo le dije que tú no te opondrías°... Después de todo°, ¡es nuestra hija y hay que ayudarla!

RAÚL La verdad es que vamos a estar muy tristes y muy solos sin Ana. Tú sabes que siempre quise que *trabajara* en nuestra tienda, pero reconozco° que ella necesita hacer su propia vida°..., ¿no?

1. ¿Qué le pidió Ana a su madre?   2. ¿Por qué quería Ana zapatos nuevos?
3. ¿Qué le dijo Marta a Ana?   4. ¿Cómo van a estar Raúl y Marta sin Ana?
5. ¿Qué le gustaría a Raúl?   6. ¿Qué reconoce él?

en oferta *on sale*   **hiciera juego** *would match*   **Total que** *So*
conseguir ese puesto *to get that job*   **no te opondrías** *you would not be opposed*
Después de todo *After all*   **reconozco** *I recognize*   **su propia vida** *her own life*

A. To form the imperfect subjunctive of all verbs, remove the **-ron** ending from the third-person plural form of the preterit and add the imperfect subjunctive endings: **-ra, -ras, -ra, ´-ramos, -rais, -ran**. Notice that the **nosotros** form requires a written accent on the vowel preceding the ending.

hablar		comer	
habla**ra**	hablá**ramos**	comie**ra**	comié**ramos**
habla**ras**	habla**rais**	comie**ras**	comie**rais**
habla**ra**	habla**ran**	comie**ra**	comie**ran**

vivir	
vivie**ra**	vivié**ramos**
vivie**ras**	vivie**rais**
vivie**ra**	vivie**ran**

pensar		volver	
pensa**ra**	pensá**ramos**	volvie**ra**	volvié**ramos**
pensa**ras**	pensa**rais**	volvie**ras**	volvie**rais**
pensa**ra**	pensa**ran**	volvie**ra**	volvie**ran**

Verbs with spelling changes or irregularities in the third-person plural form of the preterit have the same changes in the imperfect subjunctive.

pedir		dormir	
pidie**ra**	pidié**ramos**	durmie**ra**	durmié**ramos**
pidie**ras**	pidie**rais**	durmie**ras**	durmie**rais**
pidie**ra**	pidie**ran**	durmie**ra**	durmie**ran**

Other verbs with irregular stems in the imperfect subjunctive are:

Infinitive	*Ustedes* **Form** Preterit	*Yo* **Form** Imperfect Subjunctive
andar	anduvieron	anduviera
construir	construyeron	construyera
creer	creyeron	creyera
dar	dieron	diera

(continued next page)

Infinitive	**Ustedes** Form Preterit	**Yo** Form Imperfect Subjunctive
decir	dijeron	dijera
estar	estuvieron	estuviera
haber	hubieron	hubiera
hacer	hicieron	hiciera
ir, ser	fueron	fuera
leer	leyeron	leyera
morir	murieron	muriera
poder	pudieron	pudiera
poner	pusieron	pusiera
querer	quisieron	quisiera
saber	supieron	supiera
tener	tuvieron	tuviera
traer	trajeron	trajera
venir	vinieron	viniera
ver	vieron	viera

B. The imperfect subjunctive is used in the same situations as the present subjunctive but usually when the verb in the main clause is in some past tense rather than in the present. Compare the following examples.

No quiero que usted gaste tanto dinero.	*I don't want you to spend so much money.*
No quería que gastara tanto dinero.	*I didn't want you to spend so much money.*
Es mejor que ahorres parte de tu sueldo... ¡o nunca serás rico!	*It's better that you save part of your salary . . . or you'll never get rich!*
Era mejor que ahorraras parte de tu sueldo.	*It was better that you saved part of your salary.*
El dependiente dice el precio claramente para que los turistas lo puedan entender.	*The salesclerk is saying the price clearly, so the tourists can understand it.*
El dependiente dijo el precio claramente para que los turistas lo pudieran entender.	*The salesclerk said the price clearly so that the tourists could understand it.*

Sometimes the verb in the main clause is in the present, but the imperfect subjunctive is used in the dependent clause to refer to something in the past.

¿Es posible que el tapiz valiera tanto?	*Is it possible that the wall hanging was worth that much?*
No, no es posible que costara 500.000 bolívares.	*No, it's not possible that it cost 500,000 bolivars.*

C. The imperfect subjunctive of **querer** is often used in requests, as you saw in Chapter 6.

Quisiera hablar con el gerente.   *I'd like to speak to the manager.*

EJERCICIS

A. Consejos. Jaime, a student from Venezuela, came to study engineering in the United States. When his parents found out that he was not taking good care of himself, they wrote him a long letter. Complete the sentences below to reconstruct what his parents told or advised him to do or not to do. Follow the models.

Modelos (dormía poco) Le pidieron que...
Le pidieron que durmiera más (se acostara más temprano, etc.).

(usaba cocaína) No querían que...
No querían que estuviera adicto a ninguna droga (usara drogas tan peligrosas, etc.).

1. (fumaba dos paquetes de cigarrillos por día)   Le dijeron que...
2. (miraba televisión todas las noches)   No les gustaba que...
3. (sólo comía sándwiches y papas fritas)   Le prohibían que...
4. (tomaba mucho café)   Querían que...
5. (se acostaba a las tres de la mañana)   Le pidieron que...
6. (salía muy poco)   Querían que...
7. (había aumentado más de veinte kilos)   No querían que...
8. (había recibido una «F» el semestre pasado)   Le pidieron que...

B. La historia se repite. Don Andrés retired two years ago, leaving his store to Ramón, his grandson. Take Don Andrés's role and react to Ramón's comments by telling him that what happens now also happened in the past.

Modelos Busco una persona que me ayude los sábados.
Antes yo también buscaba una persona que me ayudara los sábados.

Las leyes (*laws*) no permiten que vendamos ponchos importados (*imported*) aquí.
Antes las leyes tampoco permitían que vendiéramos ponchos importados aquí.

1. No puedo pagar buenos sueldos hasta que aumenten las ventas del negocio.
2. Siempre tengo cosas en oferta para que los clientes estén contentos.
3. Tengo miedo de que los precios sean muy altos.
4. Tampoco hay nadie que sepa regatear.
5. La ley no permite que tengamos joyas para vender.
6. No creo que los clientes quieran pagar tanto por una camisa.

C. Las noticias. Elvira read the following news items in the paper. React to each of them starting with a phrase such as **Me alegro...**, **Es una lástima...**, **Dudo...**, **Es posible...**, **Ojalá...**, etc. Follow the models.

Modelos Hace poco hubo un accidente de automóvil en El Paso pero no murió nadie.
Me alegro de que no muriera nadie.

Los antropólogos encontraron más ruinas aztecas en México.
Es interesante que ellos encontraran más ruinas aztecas.

1. El precio del petróleo (*oil*) bajó en Venezuela.
2. Ayer el presidente dio una conferencia y no fue nadie.
3. El año pasado murieron muchas personas en El Salvador.
4. Muchos turistas viajaron a Costa Rica el año pasado porque el dólar estaba fuerte allí.
5. El equipo de fútbol de la universidad Stanford ganó un partido importante ayer.
6. Los Juegos Olímpicos de 1988 tuvieron lugar en Seúl.

D. Entrevista. In pairs, interview each other on the following topics and/or on any others you might want to talk about. Then report to the class some of your partner's answers.

Modelos algo que usted (no) quería que pasara antes y algo que (no) quiere que pase ahora...
Antes quería que mis padres me dieran mucho dinero y ahora no quiero que ellos me den demasiados consejos.

el tipo de compañero(-a) de cuarto que buscaba y el (la) compañero(-a) que tiene ahora...
Buscaba un(-a) compañero(-a) que nadara o jugara al tenis y tengo un(-a) compañero(-a) que no tiene ningún interés en los deportes.

1. el tipo de casa que quería antes y el tipo de casa que quiere ahora...
2. el tipo de universidad que buscaba antes y la universidad a la que asiste ahora...
3. las cualidades que buscaba en su novio(-a) ideal y las cualidades que ahora busca en un(-a) novio(-a)... (*or*: ...tiene su novio(-a) real...)
4. algo que usted esperaba que pasara en su vida y algo que realmente pasó...
5. el tipo de auto con el que soñaba y el tipo de auto con el que sueña ahora...
6. el tipo de trabajo que le gustaba antes y el tipo de trabajo que le gusta (*or*: ...que tiene) ahora...

PREGUNTAS

1. Cuando usted era niño(-a), ¿querían sus padres que usted se acostara temprano? ¿que terminara toda la comida de su plato? ¿Qué otras cosas querían que hiciera?

2. ¿Le prohibían ellos que fuera al cine a ver películas violentas? **3.** ¿Le permitían que organizara fiestas en su casa? **4.** ¿Hacía usted muchas cosas sin que sus padres lo supieran? ¿Qué cosas? **5.** ¿Querían ellos que usted trabajara durante las vacaciones? ¿que ahorrara un poco? ¿Para qué? **6.** ¿Le prohibían sus padres que usted les prestara dinero a sus amigos? ¿Por qué?

If clauses

En un mercado de artesanos, en Caracas.

DOÑA CARLA	¿Cuánto cuesta este poncho, señorita?
VENDEDORA	Quinientos bolívares, señora. Es de lana pura, sabe...
DOÑA CARLA	¿Quinientos bolívares? No los tengo... y *si* los *tuviera* no lo podría comprar... ¡Es demasiado caro!
VENDEDORA	¿Y *si* se lo *vendiera* por cuatrocientos ochenta?
DOÑA CARLA	Pues, lo *preferiría* en otro color. Este no me gusta porque...
VENDEDORA	Es el último que me queda°. Hace unos diez minutos vendí uno rojo muy bonito. ¿Sabe que en las tiendas del centro estos ponchos cuestan el doble°? ¡Y en esos lugares tienen precios fijos°... ! Pero lléveselo por cuatrocientos cincuenta, señora...
DOÑA CARLA	*Si* me lo *diera* por cuatrocientos veinte, me lo llevaría.
VENDEDORA	Está bien. Se lo doy por cuatrocientos veinte.
DOÑA CARLA	¡De acuerdo! Muchas gracias.

1. ¿Cuánto cuesta el poncho? 2. ¿Cree doña Carla que el poncho es muy caro o muy barato? 3. Si ella tuviera quinientos bolívares, ¿compraría el poncho? 4. Si la vendedora le vendiera el poncho por cuatrocientos ochenta bolívares, ¿lo compraría? 5. ¿De qué color era el poncho que la vendedora había vendido unos minutos antes? 6. Según la vendedora, ¿cuánto cuestan esos ponchos en el centro? En general, ¿es posible regatear en las tiendas del centro? ¿Por qué sí o por qué no? 7. ¿Compraría ella el poncho si la vendedora se lo diera por cuatrocientos veinte bolívares?

---

me queda *I have left*　　**el doble** *double, twice as much*　　**precios fijos** *fixed prices*

A. When an *if* clause expresses a situation that the speaker or writer thinks of as true or definite, or makes a simple assumption, the indicative is used.

Si llueve, Carlos no va de compras.	*If it rains, Carlos isn't going shopping.*
Si llovió ayer, Carlos no fue de compras.	*If it rained yesterday, Carlos didn't go shopping.*
Si Manuel va al mercado, yo voy también.	*If Manuel goes to the market, I will go too.*

When the verb in an *if* clause is in the present tense, it is always in the indicative, whether the speaker is certain or not.

Si vienes, me alegraré.	*If you come, I'll be happy.*
Si esta bicicleta no funciona bien, vamos a devolverla.	*If this bicycle doesn't work well, we'll return it.*

B. However, when the *if* clause expresses something that is hypothetical or contrary to fact and the main clause is in the conditional, the *if* clause is in the imperfect subjunctive.

Esa cámara es estupenda; si tuviera dinero, la compraría.	*That camera is wonderful; if I had money, I would buy it.*
Luis y Mirta irían con nosotros si estuvieran aquí.	*Luis and Mirta would go with us if they were here.*
Si las frazadas fueran de mejor calidad, las compraríamos.	*If the blankets were of better quality, we'd buy them.*
Si fueras más cuidadoso, no romperías las cosas.	*If you were more careful, you wouldn't break things.*

C. The expression **como si** (*as if*) implies a hypothetical, or untrue, situation. It is followed by the imperfect subjunctive.

¡Regateas como si supieras lo que haces!	*You bargain as if you knew what you were doing!*
Andrés gasta dinero como si fuera millonario.	*Andrés spends money as if he were a millionaire.*
Elena se viste como si tuviera una fortuna.	*Elena dresses as if she had a fortune.*

EJERCICIOS

A. Si... Raquel is thinking about what she would do if things were different. Change the sentences following the model.

Modelo   Si hace buen tiempo, iremos al Parque Central.
Si hiciera buen tiempo, iríamos al Parque Central.

1. Si tía Julia me manda dinero, compraré un vestido nuevo.
2. Si Carmen y su hermano tienen tiempo, me acompañarán.
3. Si tenemos hambre, comeremos en un restaurante.
4. Si veo a mis amigos, los invitaré a almorzar con nosotros.

5. Si los precios están bajos, le diré a Ramón que se compre unas corbatas nuevas.
6. Si encontramos algunas ofertas, valdrá la pena gastar dinero.

B. Puros sueños. Complete the following sentences.

Modelo Si fuera actor (actriz), ...
Si fuera actor (actriz), saldría en muchas películas románticas.

1. Si tuviera un millón de dólares, ...
2. Si yo fuera dueño(-a) de una tienda, ...
3. Si yo volviera a nacer en otra forma, ...
4. Si yo fuera hombre (mujer), ...
5. Si yo tuviera tres días libres, ...
6. Si yo fuera invisible, ...
7. Si mañana fuera mi cumpleaños, ...
8. Si yo estuviera hoy en América del Sur, ...

C. ¡Buena suerte, Sr. Benítez! Mr. Benítez bought a lottery ticket and is thinking about all the wonderful things that could happen to him and his family if only he were to win. Form *if* clauses as he would, following the model.

Modelo si yo / ganar la lotería / (yo) / comprar un barco grande
Si yo ganara la lotería, (yo) compraría un barco grande.

1. si yo / tener un barco grande / mis hijos y yo / viajar mucho
2. si nosotros / viajar mucho / (nosotros) / conocer muchos países
3. si yo / conocer muchos países / (yo) / querer hablar muchas lenguas
4. si mi esposa e hijos / querer hablar otras lenguas / ellos y yo / asistir a clases de lenguas
5. si yo / poder ganar sólo parte de la lotería / (yo) / comprar una casa más grande
6. si nosotros / vivir en una casa más grande / mi esposa y mis hijos / estar muy contentos
7. y si ellos / estar contentos / yo también / sentirse muy feliz

D. Si así fuera... For each of the questions, choose one of the two possible answers and add one of your own. Follow the model.

Modelo ¿Qué haría usted si ganara el Premio Nobel?
    a. no lo aceptaría
    b. seguiría trabajando igual que antes
    c. ¿?
Si ganara el Premio Nobel, yo seguiría trabajando igual que antes y ahorraría el dinero para gastarlo en el futuro.

1. ¿Qué haría usted si fuera rico(-a)?
    a. viajaría por todo el mundo
    b. ayudaría a los pobres
    c. ¿?

2. ¿Qué haría usted si estuviera de vacaciones?
   a. esquiaría en las montañas
   b. me levantaría tarde todos los días
   c. ¿?
3. ¿Qué haría usted si recibiera malas notas?
   a. estudiaría más
   b. les pediría ayuda a mis profesores
   c. ¿?
4. ¿Qué haría usted si su novio(-a) se enamorara de su mejor amiga(-o)?
   a. lloraría mucho
   b. buscaría otro(-a) novio(-a) («Un amor se cambia por otro», ¿no?)
   c. ¿?
5. ¿Qué haría usted si pudiera viajar al pasado o al futuro?
   a. viajaría a 1492 para participar en el descubrimiento (*discovery*) de América
   b. volvería a visitar esta universidad en el año 2020
   c. ¿?

E. Entrevista. In pairs ask each other the following questions and then report the information to the class.

¿Qué harías si...?

1. tuvieras dolor de cabeza en este momento
2. fueras presidente de los Estados Unidos
3. recibieras una «D» en tu próximo examen de español
4. no estuvieras en clase hoy
5. quisieras ser famoso(-a)
6. pudieras cambiar el mundo
7. no tuvieras dinero para asistir a la universidad

PREGUNTAS

1. Si le pudiera dar un millón de dólares a alguien o a alguna organización, ¿a quién o a qué organización se los daría? ¿Por qué?   **2.** Si el médico le dijera que sólo tiene un año de vida, ¿qué haría?   **3.** Si estuviera en una isla desierta, ¿con quién le gustaría estar? ¿Qué le gustaría hacer?   **4.** Si hiciera un viaje por un año y sólo pudiera llevar tres libros, ¿qué libros llevaría?

 ## Long forms of possessive adjectives; possessive pronouns *(for recognition only)*

En el aeropuerto de Caracas.

ÓSCAR	Esta llave es *mía,*° ¿no?
RAÚL	Sí, es *tuya*°. Y dime, ¿es éste el pasaporte de Enrique?
ÓSCAR	Pues... sí, creo que es *el suyo*°. Pero... no veo mi maleta.
EMPLEADA	¿La maleta azul era de usted? ¡Yo creía que era de esos turistas franceses!
ÓSCAR	No, señorita, *la mía* era la única azul°. Las de ellos eran todas negras.
EMPLEADA	¡Dios *mío*! Vino un hombre con barba°, dijo que era amigo de ellos... ¡y se la llevó!

¿Verdadero o falso?

1. Óscar y Raúl están en el aeropuerto de Madrid.
2. Óscar busca su maleta pero no la encuentra.
3. Las maletas de los turistas franceses eran azules.
4. Óscar no pudo encontrar su maleta porque Raúl ya la había puesto en el auto.

Esta... mía *This key is mine* **tuya** *yours* **el suyo** *his*
la... azul *mine was the only blue one* **barba** *beard*

A. There are other forms of possessive adjectives besides those you learned in Chapter 5. These longer forms follow rather than precede the nouns they modify, and they agree with them in gender and number.

la camisa mía	*my shirt*
el sueldo tuyo	*your salary*
los cuadernos nuestros	*our notebooks*

The longer forms are often used for emphasis, that is, to emphasize ownership.

B. Possessive pronouns have the same forms as the long forms of the possessive adjectives and are usually preceded by a definite article. The article and the pronouns agree in gender and number with the noun referred to, which is omitted.

el auto mío, el mío	*my car, mine*
la maleta tuya, la tuya	*your suitcase, yours*
la casa nuestra, la nuestra	*our house, ours*

C. **Suyo(-a, -os, -as)** can have several different meanings, depending on the possessor: for instance, **la casa suya** could mean *his house, her house, your house* (of **Ud.** or **Uds.**), or *their house.* For clarity, a prepositional phrase with **de** is sometimes used instead.

—¿Y las llaves? —Las suyas no están aquí. (Las de usted no están aquí.)   *"And the keys?" "Yours aren't here."*

D. After the verb **ser**, the definite article is usually omitted.

—¿Es mío este refresco? —Sí, es tuyo.   *"Is this soft drink mine?" "Yes, it's yours."*

EJERCICIOS

A. ¿Con quiénes vamos? Your Spanish teacher has asked the whole class to visit a typical **mercado al aire libre** (*open-air market*) and then to write a composition about it. Tell who went with whom, by completing the sentences below, following the model.

Modelo   yo / amigos (mío, míos)
    Yo fui con unos amigos míos.

1. Miguel y Jorge / compañero (suyo, suyos)
2. Elsa y Susana / hermana (suya, suyas)
3. tú / primos (tuyo, tuyos)
4. usted / tías (suya, suyas)
5. nosotros / vecino (nuestro, nuestros)
6. el profesor Gómez / estudiantes (suyo, suyos)

B. ¡Qué coincidencias tiene la vida! Mr. Ruiz tells his son Alberto of his good old days. Play Alberto's role and say that things are the same today. Follow the model.

Modelo   Sr. Ruiz: Mi apartamento era grandísimo. (Lo mío / El mío)
           Alberto: **El mío es grandísimo también.**

1. Mis clases eran muy interesantes. (Las mías / Los míos)
2. Mi compañero de cuarto era peruano. (Lo mío / El mío)
3. Mis diversiones favoritas eran nadar y bailar. (Las mías / Los míos)
4. Pagaba muy poco por mi apartamento. (el mío / lo mío)
5. Mis profesores eran muy buenos. (Los míos / Las mías)

C. ¿Es tuyo esto?   Mrs. Ruiz is helping a friend unpack after a trip. Answer her questions in the affirmative, following the model.

Modelo   ¿Es tuyo este paraguas? (mío / mía)
Sí, es mío.

1. ¿Es tuya esta falda? (mío / mía)
2. ¿Son de Irene estas sandalias? (suya / suyas)
3. ¿Es de Luisito esta camisa? (suya / suyo)
4. ¿Son de los niños estas bicicletas? (suyos / suyas)
5. ¿Es de Luisa este poncho? (suyo / suya)
6. ¿Es de Luis esta maleta? (suyo / suya)
7. ¿Son de ustedes estos cuadros? (nuestros / nuestras)

Caracas: Diferencias entre padres e hijos

Un matrimonio° de un pequeño pueblo venezolano toma café con sus vecinos.

EL VECINO	No nos han dicho nada de su viaje a Caracas. ¿Qué les pareció la capital?
LA SEÑORA	¡Horrible!
EL SEÑOR	Una gran desilusión°. Todo era muy caro y de mala calidad. Además, las cosas tenían precios fijos y no se podía regatear. Nosotros hicimos el viaje principalmente para que los muchachos vieran los sitios importantes: los museos, la casa de Bolívar...[1]
LA SEÑORA	Pero también vieron otras cosas sin que lo pudiéramos evitar°.
LOS VECINOS	¿Qué cosas?
EL SEÑOR	Fuimos al Parque del Este[2] y vimos novios que se besaban en público, como si estuvieran solos en el mundo. En resumen, Caracas es un centro de perdición°...
EL VECINO	¡Qué escándalo!
EL SEÑOR	Pero eso no es todo... Había muchachos de once o doce años que fumaban en la calle.
LA VECINA	¡Como si no tuvieran otra cosa que hacer!
EL SEÑOR	Por eso regresamos pronto. Queríamos volver antes de que los muchachos empezaran a imitar° las malas costumbres°.

En otra parte de la casa, el hijo de catorce años y la hija de dieciséis toman refrescos con sus amigos.

EL AMIGO	¿Y el viaje a Caracas? ¿Qué les pareció la ciudad?
EL HIJO	¡Fabulosa! Allí todo es muy barato y de buena calidad. En las tiendas se venden miles de cosas.
LA HIJA	Sí, es un sueño. Los jóvenes se visten a la moda y tienen mucha libertad.

Vista de Caracas, Venezuela

EL HIJO	Los edificios son bellos y modernos.[3]
LA AMIGA	¿Vieron la Rinconada?[4]
EL HIJO	Sí, por fuera. Yo quería que entráramos, pero mi padre dijo que no.
LA HIJA	Es una lástima que no pudiéramos pasar más tiempo en las playas. Conocimos allá a un grupo de chicos que nos invitaron a una fiesta.
EL HIJO	Sí, pero mamá nos prohibió que aceptáramos la invitación.
LA AMIGA	¡Qué lástima! A mí me gustaría vivir algún día en Caracas.
EL HIJO	A mí también. Si yo pudiera vivir en esa ciudad, sería la persona más feliz del mundo.

matrimonio *married couple*   **desilusión** *disappointment*   **evitar** *to avoid*
perdición *eternal damnation*   **imitar** *to imitate*   **costumbres** *habits*

EJERCICIO

¿Cuál es la respuesta correcta?

1. ¿Les gustó Caracas a los señores de Díaz?
   a. Sí, les encantó.
   b. No, les pareció horrible.

2. ¿Qué vieron ellos en el Parque del Este?
   a. Vieron novios que se besaban en público.
   b. Vieron ponchos de muy mala calidad.
3. Según ellos, ¿qué edad tendrían los muchachos que fumaban en la calle?
   a. Tendrían ocho o nueve años.
   b. Tendrían once o doce años.
4. ¿Pasaron los Díaz mucho tiempo en Caracas?
   a. Sí, se quedaron un mes en Caracas.
   b. No, regresaron pronto.
5. ¿Qué les pareció Caracas a los hijos del matrimonio Díaz?
   a. Les pareció horrible.
   b. Les encantó la ciudad.
6. ¿Por qué no entraron a la Rinconada?
   a. Porque su padre no quiso que entraran.
   b. Porque ya era tarde y estaba cerrada.
7. ¿Dónde conocieron a los chicos que los invitaron a una fiesta?
   a. En la playa.
   b. En el Parque del Este.
8. ¿Por qué no fueron a la fiesta con los chicos?
   a. Porque preferían ir de compras.
   b. Porque su mamá les prohibió que aceptaran la invitación.

Notas culturales

1. Caracas is the birthplace of Simón Bolívar, one of South America's greatest heroes, and the site of the Bolívar Museum, which houses his personal effects and documents. Bolívar was born in 1783 and was a major figure in the movement for independence from Spain. He was a brilliant general and a greatly admired politician who dreamed of uniting the countries of South America as one nation. He died broken-hearted in 1830 without realizing his dream.

2. **El Parque del Este** in Caracas is a large park with artificial lakes, a zoo, playgrounds, and a train with fringe-topped cars. A great variety of orchids can be seen in its gardens, and in its excellent aviary there are specimens of the many tropical birds for which Venezuela is famous.

3. Caracas is a city of modern and ultramodern architecture. In the last several decades the government has sponsored many low-rent apartment complexes. The money for such projects comes from Venezuela's oil industry.

4. **La Rinconada** is one of the world's most luxurious racetracks, complete with escalators, an air-conditioned box for the president, and a swimming pool for the horses.

In this chapter, you have seen examples of some important language functions, or uses. Here is a summary and some additional information about these functions of language.

Expressing satisfaction and dissatisfaction

Here are some ways to express your pleasure or displeasure with something you have bought, seen, etc.

Esto es muy bueno (fabuloso, justo lo que nos faltaba, etcétera).	*This is very good (great, just what we needed, etc.).*
¡Eso es terrible (feo, malo, aburrido, insoportable)!	*That is terrible (ugly, bad, boring, unbearable)!*
Esto (no) es aceptable.	*This is (un)acceptable.*
Es demasiado...	*It's too ...*
Eso no funciona (no sirve).	*That doesn't work.*
(No) me gusta... porque...	*I (don't) like ... because ...*
Me gustaría devolver... porque...	*I would like to return ... because ...*

Summarizing

Here are some ways to conclude, to express that you are coming to the point.

Total que...	*So ...*
A fin de cuentas...	*After all ... (All things considered ...)*
Después de todo...	*After all ...*
Al fin y al cabo...	*In the end ... (To make a long story short ...)*
En resumen... (En conclusión...)	*In short ... (In conclusion ...)*

A. ¿Qué dicen?   Tell what these people are probably saying as they express satisfaction or dissatisfaction.

Modelo

Esta maleta no sirve. Me gustaría devolverla.

B. En conclusión. Give a concluding remark, in Spanish, for each of the following situations.

1. A lecturer has been talking for nearly an hour about prices and inflation. His thesis is that it's not a good idea to save money in times of high inflation (**en tiempos de mucha inflación**).
2. A friend of yours has been complaining about her roommates for ten minutes and comes to the conclusion that she is going to look for another place to live.
3. You're writing a short paper on bargaining in Latin America. You end by saying that bargaining is fine in markets; it's not good to bargain in most stores, where prices are fixed.

Now make a concluding remark about your Spanish class. Use a summary word.

VOCABULARIO ACTIVO

Cognados

la boutique	fabuloso	la generación	puro
la capacidad	la fortuna	el poncho	la responsabilidad
el experto, la experta			

Verbos

ahorrar	to save (time, money, etc.)
deber	to owe
devolver (ue)	to return (something)
funcionar	to work
gastar	to spend
pedir prestado	to borrow
rebajar	to lower
regatear	to bargain (over prices)
valer	to be worth

Compra y venta

el almacén	grocery store
barato	inexpensive, cheap
la calidad	quality
el, la dependiente	salesperson
fijo: precio fijo	fixed price
la oferta	sale, (special) offer
el sueldo	salary
la venta	sale, selling

Otras palabras y frases

fuera	outside
por fuera	from or on the outside
la lana	wool
el refresco	soft drink

Expresiones útiles

Después de todo...	After all ...
En resumen...	In short ... (In conclusion ...)
Es demasiado...	It's too ...
Total que...	So ...

I. USE OF THE SUBJUNCTIVE

Cross out the words that a Spanish speaker would not be likely to say.

Modelo ~~Es mejor~~ / *Es cierto* que yo estoy muy contento.

1. *Se alegró mucho de* / *No sabía* que se casaran.
2. *Sabe* / *Tiene miedo* que su equipo pierda el partido.
3. *Me sorprende* / *Creo* que ellos venden la casa.
4. *Dudo* / *Sé* que Susana vaya al cine hoy.
5. *Es cierto* / *No es cierto* que él tenga dolor de cabeza.
6. *No había nadie* / *Había alguien* allí que pudiera hacerlo.
7. *Supo* / *Esperaba* que ellos llegaron temprano.
8. El médico *cree* / *no cree* que Silvia esté enferma.

II. FORMS OF THE PRESENT SUBJUNCTIVE

Complete the following sentences with the present subjunctive of the verbs in parentheses. Remember that the subjunctive is used:

A. With verbs of expectations and feelings.
   1. Mamá tiene miedo que nosotros no _____ (estar) allí a las doce.
   2. Ojalá que él _____ (tener) las entradas.
   3. Esperamos que ellos no _____ (volver) tarde.
   4. Siento que Gustavo no _____ (poder) venir.
B. With verbs expressing an order, request, or plea.
   5. Le prohíbo que _____ (mentir).
   6. Te pido que _____ (traer) a tu hermana a la cena.
C. With verbs expressing will, desire, or preference.
   7. Preferimos que él no _____ (venir).
   8. Quiero que tú _____ (conocer) a Anita.
D. With verbs of approval, advice, or permission.
   9. Me gusta que ellos _____ (ganar) mil pesos más por mes.
   10. El médico no permite que yo _____ (fumar) y me aconseja que _____ (descansar) más.
E. With verbs of necessity.
   11. Necesitan que el señor Villa les _____ (hacer) un favor.
F. With verbs expressing doubt or uncertainty.
   12. Dudo que José _____ (comer) bien.
   13. No estamos seguros de que _____ (ser) ellos.
G. With **creer** and **pensar** in the negative or interrogative, when doubt is implied, and with **quizás** and **tal vez** normally.
   14. No pienso que Bárbara _____ (poder) ayudarte mucho.
   15. ¿Cree usted que nosotros _____ (tener) razón?

16. Tal vez Eduardo _____ (alquilar) un auto cuando vaya a Toledo, pero lo dudo.

H. With certain impersonal expressions.

17. No es bueno que ellos _____ (trabajar) tanto.
18. Es necesario que nosotros _____ (acostarse) temprano.
19. Es mejor que yo _____ (irse).

I. With **es verdad** (**cierto, seguro, claro**) in the negative or interrogative, when doubt is implied.

20. ¿Es seguro que Elena _____ (salir) mañana?
21. No es cierto que Felipe _____ (recibir) dinero de su padre.

J. With descriptions of the unknown or indefinite.

22. Busco una bicicleta que _____ (funcionar) bien y que _____ (ser) barata.
23. No veo a nadie que _____ (poder) ayudarme.

K. With certain adverbial conjunctions.

24. El señor Juárez piensa invitar a los Hernández sin que su esposa lo _____ (saber).
25. Vamos a cenar a las nueve a menos que ellos _____ (llegar) tarde.

III. POR AND PARA

Complete the following sentences with **por** or **para**. State the reasons for your choices.

1. Siempre camino _____ la Avenida Independencia.
2. El señor Ramírez maneja a 70 millas _____ hora.
3. Mamá dice que los chocolates son _____ mí.
4. Me gustaría viajar _____ las montañas de Sudamérica.
5. ¿Es verdad que usted estará en Europa _____ más de dos meses?
6. Fue a la playa _____ tomar sol.
7. ¿_____ qué estás tan triste?
8. Eduardo fue a la panadería _____ pan.
9. _____ republicano, el señor Díaz es muy liberal.
10. ¿Cuánto pagaste _____ el poncho que compraste _____ Isabel?

IV. THE FUTURE, CONDITIONAL, AND PROGRESSIVE TENSES

A. Change the following verbs from the present to the future tense.

Modelo   yo recuerdo
          yo recordaré

1. yo doy
2. él escribe
3. nosotros viajamos
4. tú haces
5. ellos ponen

6. ella va
7. nosotros pedimos
8. tú dices
9. yo me levanto
10. él duerme

B. Now change these same verbs to the conditional tense.

C. Now change them to the present progressive.

V. THE IMPERFECT SUBJUNCTIVE; SEQUENCE OF TENSES

Complete the sentences with the indicative or subjunctive, as required.

Present indicative or present subjunctive:

1. Se cree que esta costumbre (venir) _____ de la época de los aztecas.
2. Es ridículo que ustedes (perder) _____ el tiempo así.
3. Sé que nosotros (ir) _____ a tener que vender la casa.
4. Si los Balbuena (llegar) _____ hoy, vamos al lago.
5. No creo que mi hermana (querer) _____ casarse todavía.
6. Díganme si ustedes (ir) _____ al cine hoy.

Past indicative or imperfect subjunctive:

1. En cuanto su marido (saber) _____ la noticia, se alegró mucho.
2. Si tú (tener) _____ mucho dinero, ¿qué harías?
3. No vi a ninguna joven que (llevar) _____ ropa decente.
4. Tenía miedo que nosotros (estar) _____ solos allí.
5. Olga se encontró con una persona que la (tratar) _____ muy bien.
6. No le dijimos eso a María hasta que (calmarse) _____.

VI. USEFUL EXPRESSIONS

Give the Spanish equivalent of the following expressions.

1. I want to go shopping. Would you like to come with me?   **2.** Where is the post office?   **3.** "By the way, how did you like the city?" "It was wonderful!"   **4.** What time does the train leave for Madrid?   **5.** Give me a round-trip ticket, please.   **6.** Where can one change money?   **7.** Do you have a room with a bath?   **8.** Good grief! I've lost my three suitcases!   **9.** Good-bye. May all go well with you.   **10.** My head aches.   **11.** Is there a drugstore nearby?   **12.** I want to introduce you to my friend Rafael Márquez.   **13.** What a surprise! We thought you'd be arriving tomorrow, not today.

Appendix I

Word Stress

Word Stress (Emphasis of Syllables)

1. Most Spanish words are divided into syllables after a vowel or diphthong; diphthongs are not divided. A single consonant (including *ch*, *ll*, and *rr*) between two vowels begins a new syllable.

co-mo	mu-cho	a-diós
cla-se	va-lle	ai-re
Te-re-sa	gui-ta-rra	au-to

2. Where there are two consonants between vowels, the syllable is usually divided between the consonants, except in most words where *r* or *l* follows another consonant.

is-la	ar-tis-ta	Ca-li-for-nia
es-pa-ñol	u-ni-ver-sal	Jor-ge
a-gró-no-mo	ha-blar	a-tre-ver
a-brir	A-driá-ti-co	

3. In a combination of a strong vowel (**a**, **e**, or **o**) and a weak vowel (**i** or **u**) where the weak vowel is stressed, a written accent divides them into two syllables. (If the weak vowel is not stressed, the combination is a diphthong and is one syllable.)*

pa-ís	dí-a	fi-lo-so-fí-a

---

*Note that an accent is also used with a few words to distinguish between meanings: **sí** (*yes*), **si** (*if*); **él** (*he*), **el** (*the*).

Appendix II

Answers to Self-Tests

Self-Test I

I. **1.** conozco, sé **2.** buscan **3.** podemos **4.** pongo **5.** salgo; Vienes **6.** crees, soy **7.** debemos **8.** quieren **9.** tengo, tienes **10.** va **11.** tenemos **12.** vive **13.** digo, dice **14.** duerme **15.** vuelven **16.** veo

II. es, es, es, está, es, es, está, está

III. **A.** **1.** mi **2.** Tus **3.** sus **4.** Nuestro **5.** Su
   B. **1.** esta **2.** aquellos **3.** Este **4.** esos **5.** Esa

IV. **1.** Sí, yo la llevo. **2.** Sí, te puedo esperar unos minutos. **3.** Sí, yo les hablo. **4.** Sí, quiero preguntárselo. (*or*: Sí, se lo quiero preguntar.) **5.** Sí, te quiero. **6.** Sí, puedo decírselo. (*or*: Sí, se lo puedo decir.) **7.** Sí, quiero dárselos. (*or*: Sí, se los quiero dar.) **8.** Sí, Anita nos escribe mucho. **9.** Sí, me puedes visitar mañana. (*or*: Sí, puedes visitarme mañana.) **10.** Sí, se lo voy a dar. (*or*: Sí, voy a dárselo.)

V. **1.** Conoce, saber **2.** dice, Habla **3.** pido, pregunta **4.** están, Son

VI. **1.** Mucho gusto. **2.** Buenos días. **3.** Gracias. **4.** Por favor. **5.** Qué hora es? **6.** ¿Qué día es hoy? **7.** Tengo hambre. **8.** Buenas tardes. **9.** ¿Puedo reservar un cuarto para dos en este hotel? **10.** ¿Cuánto cuesta este reloj? **11.** Lo llevo. (*or*: Lo voy a llevar.) **12.** Hace calor. **13.** ¿Tiene(-s) calor? **14.** ¿De veras? **15.** ¡Por supuesto! (*or*: ¡Cómo no!) **16.** ¿Puede decirme dónde está el restaurante «La Cazuela» (*or*: ¿Me puede decir...?) **17.** Hasta mañana. (*or*: Nos vemos mañana.) **18.** ¡Qué lástima! **19.** ¡Cuidado!

Self-Test II

I. **1.** No hablen de su viaje. **2.** No estudies con Ramón hoy. **3.** No los apoye. **4.** Vete ahora, Rosa. **5.** No sea pesimista. **6.** Pásamela. **7.** No estén tristes. **8.** Dísela. **9.** No me llames muy temprano. **10.** Ven a clase. **11.** Tráigamela. **12.** Ten cuidado. **13.** Espérenme. **14.** Vístase a la moda.

II. **A.** Tuvieron que aprender inglés. **2.** ¿Qué pediste? **3.** Ya los vi. **4.** Se lo dimos a ellos. **5.** ¿Quién perdió? ¿Quién ganó? **6.** No tuviste tiempo de ver el partido. **7.** Simón Bolívar quiso unir toda Sudamérica. **8.** Los árabes trajeron a España una rica cultura. **9.** Salí temprano. **10.** Fernando se fue a casa a dormir. **11.** Se divirtieron mucho. **12.** No nos quiso ver. **13.** Conocieron a María. **14.** Supo la verdad. **15.** Me levanté a las ocho.
   B. **1.** Tenían que aprender inglés. **5.** ¿Quién perdía? ¿Quién ganaba? **6.** No tenías tiempo de ver el partido. **7.** Simón Bolívar quería unir toda Sudamérica. **11.** Se divertían mucho. **12.** No nos quería ver. **13.** Conocían a María. **14.** Sabía la verdad. **15.** Me levantaba a las ocho.
   C. **2.** ¿Qué has pedido? **3.** Ya los he visto. **4.** Se lo hemos dado a ellos. **5.** ¿Quién ha perdido? ¿Quién ha ganado? **6.** No has tenido tiempo de ver el partido. **10.** Fernando se ha ido a casa a dormir. **11.** Se han divertido mucho.

D. esperaba; vi; nos conocimos; queríamos; admiraba; tenía; había heredado; había visto (*or:* veía); vi; llevaba; dije; estaba; pregunté; seguía; dijo; se dedicaba; contó; conoció (*or:* había conocido); Se enamoró; decidieron; tenía; era; vivieron (*or:* vivían); descubrió; tenía; dejó (*or:* ha dejado); inspiró (*or:* ha inspirado); empecé; han podido (*or:* pueden)

III. **1.** Siempre me divierto con Andrea y Tomás.   **2.** Él se va de aquí mañana.   **3.** ¿Se lava la cara? (*or:* ¿Te lavas la cara?)   **4.** Me levanto de la mesa.   **5.** ¿Cómo se llama tu mejor amigo?   **6.** Siéntese, por favor (*or:* Siéntate, por favor.)   **7.** Me acuesto a las once.   **8.** Te despiertas temprano. (*or:* Se despierta temprano.)

IV. **1.** ¿Qué hay de nuevo?   **2.** Mucho gusto.   **3.** ¡Felicitaciones!   **4.** ¿Me puede(-s) decir cómo llegar al Hotel Internacional?   **5.** ¡Salud!   **6.** De nada (*or:* No hay de qué).   **7.** ¿Dónde se venden zapatos?   **8.** ¿A qué hora (se) abren las tiendas?   **9.** Tráigame un café, por favor.   **10.** ¿Qué desea (desean) pedir?   **11.** La cuenta, por favor.   **12.** Perdón.   **13.** ¡Qué lástima!   **14.** ¡Buen provecho!   **15.** ¿Qué (nos) recomienda?

Self-Test III

I. **1.** Se alegró mucho de que se casaran.   **2.** Tiene miedo que su equipo pierda el partido.   **3.** Creo que ellos venden la casa.   **4.** Dudo que Susana vaya al cine hoy.   **5.** No es cierto que él tenga dolor de cabeza.   **6.** No había nadie allí que pudiera hacerlo.   **7.** Supo que ellos llegaron temprano.   **8.** El médico no cree que Silvia esté enferma.

II. **A.** **1.** estemos   **2.** tenga   **3.** vuelvan   **4.** pueda
B. **5.** mienta   **6.** traigas
C. **7.** venga   **8.** conozcas
D. **9.** ganen   **10.** fume, descanse
E. **11.** haga
F. **12.** coma   **13.** sean
G. **14.** pueda   **15.** tengamos   **16.** alquile
H. **17.** trabajen   **18.** nos acostemos   **19.** me vaya
I. **20.** salga   **21.** reciba
J. **22.** funcione, sea   **23.** pueda
K. **24.** sepa   **25.** lleguen

III. **1.** por   **2.** por   **3.** para   **4.** por   **5.** por   **6.** para   **7.** Por   **8.** por   **9.** Para   **10.** por, para

IV. **A.** **1.** yo daré   **2.** él escribirá   **3.** nosotros viajaremos   **4.** tú harás   **5.** ellos pondrán   **6.** ella irá   **7.** nosotros pediremos   **8.** tú dirás   **9.** yo me levantaré   **10.** él dormirá
B. **1.** yo daría   **2.** él escribiría   **3.** nosotros viajaríamos   **4.** tú harías   **5.** ellos pondrían   **6.** ella iría   **7.** nosotros pediríamos   **8.** tú dirías   **9.** yo me levantaría   **10.** él dormiría
C. **1.** yo estoy dando   **2.** él está escribiendo   **3.** nosotros estamos viajando   **4.** tú estás haciendo   **5.** ellos están poniendo   **6.** ella está yendo   **7.** nosotros estamos pidiendo   **8.** tú estás diciendo   **9.** yo me estoy levantando   **10.** él está durmiendo

V. **1.** viene   **2.** pierdan   **3.** vamos   **4.** llegan   **5.** quiera   **6.** van
1. supo   **2.** tuvieras   **3.** llevara   **4.** estuviéramos   **5.** trató   **6.** se calmó

VI. **1.** Quiero ir de compras. ¿Te [*or:* Le(-s)] gustaría venir conmigo? (*or:* ¿Quisieras [Quisiera(-n)] venir conmigo?)   **2.** ¿Dónde está el correo?   **3.** A propósito, ¿qué te (*or:* le) pareció la ciudad? ¡Una maravilla!   **4.** ¿A qué hora sale el tren para Madrid?   **5.** Deme un pasaje (boleto) de ida y vuelta, por favor.   **6.** ¿Dónde se puede cambiar dinero?   **7.** ¿Tiene un cuarto (una habitación) con baño?   **8.** ¡Qué barbaridad! ¡He perdido mis tres maletas!   **9.** Adiós. Que te (*or:* le) vaya bien.   **10.** Me duele la cabeza.   **11.** ¿Hay una (*or:* alguna) farmacia cerca?   **12.** Quisiera (*or:* Quiero) presentarte [*or:* -le(-s)] a mi amigo Rafael Márquez.   **13.** ¡Qué sorpresa! Pensamos (*or:* Pensábamos) que llegaría(-s) (*or:* llegarían) mañana, no hoy.

Appendix III

The Future and Conditional Perfect Tenses

A. The future perfect tense is formed with the future tense of the auxiliary verb **haber** + a past participle. The past participle always ends in **-o** when used to form a perfect tense.

haber		
habré	habremos	
habrás	habréis	+ past participle
habrá	habrán	

The future perfect tense expresses a future action with a past perspective—that is, an action that will have taken place (or may have taken place) by some future time. It can also express probability, an action that must have or might have taken place.

En unas semanas me habré
  acostumbrado al frío.
Mañana a esta hora ya nos habremos
  ido al campo.
Creo que Mario ya habrá llamado.

In a few weeks I will have become accustomed
  to the cold.
Tomorrow at this time we will have already
  left for the country.
I think that Mario must (might) have called
  already.

B. The conditional perfect tense is formed with the conditional tense of the auxiliary verb **haber** + a past participle. It often corresponds to the English *would have* + past participle.

haber		
habría	habríamos	
habrías	habríais	+ past participle
habría	habrían	

Habrían llamado.
¿Qué habría hecho usted?
Habría sido mejor quedarnos adentro,
  porque ahora está nevando.

They would have called.
What would you have done?
It would have been better to stay inside,
  because it's snowing now.

The Present Perfect and Past Perfect Subjunctive

A. The present perfect subjunctive is formed with the present subjunctive of **haber** (**haya, hayas, haya, hayamos, hayáis, hayan**) + a past participle. It is used in a dependent clause that expresses an action that happened (or was supposed to have happened) before the time indicated by the verb in the main clause. Compare the following examples.

Espero que ellos lleguen.   *I hope they arrive.*
Espero que ellos hayan llegado.   *I hope they have arrived.*

Dudo que tengas tiempo.   *I doubt that you have time.*
Dudo que hayas tenido tiempo.   *I doubt that you have had time.*

Es una lástima que no coman bien.   *It's a shame they don't eat well.*
Es una lástima que no hayan comido   *It's a shame they haven't eaten well.*
bien.

B. The past perfect subjunctive is formed with the past subjunctive of **haber (hubiera, hubieras, hubiera, hubiéramos, hubierais, hubieran)** + a past participle.* Compare the following examples.

Esperaba que llegaran.   *I was hoping they might arrive (were going to arrive).*

Esperaba que hubieran llegado.   *I was hoping they had arrived.*

Ella dudaba que tuvieras tiempo.   *She doubted that you had time.*
Ella dudaba que hubieras tenido   *She doubted that you had had time.*
tiempo.

Fue una lástima que no comieran bien.   *It was a shame they weren't eating well.*
Fue una lástima que no hubieran   *It was a shame they hadn't eaten well.*
comido bien.

---

* The **-iese** variant (**hubiese, hubieses, hubiese, hubiésemos, hubieseis, hubiesen**) is commonly used in Spain, but the **-iera** form is more frequent in Spanish America.

Appendix IV
Verb Charts

Irregular, Orthographic-Changing, and Stem-Changing Verbs

(The numbers refer to verbs conjugated in the charts on pages 424–432.)

acostar(se) o > ue
  (*see* contar)
almorzar o > ue; z > c[1]
  (*see* contar)
andar (1)
atender e > ie
  (*see* perder)
buscar c > qu[2]
cerrar e > ie
  (*see* pensar)
comenzar e > ie; z > c[1]
  (*see* pensar)
conducir (2) c > zc, j
conocer (3) c > zc
construir y[3]
contar (4) o > ue
costar o > ue
  (*see* contar)
creer (5)
dar (6)
decir (7)
defender e > ie
  (*see* perder)
despertar e > ie
  (*see* pensar)

divertirse e > ie, i
  (*see* sentir)
doler o > ue
  (*see* volver)
dormir (8) o > ue, u
empezar e > ie, z > c[1]
  (*see* pensar)
encontrar o > ue
  (*see* contar)
entender e > ie
  (*see* perder)
estar (9)
haber (10)
hacer (11)
ir (12)
jugar (13)
leer i > y[4]
llegar g > gu[5]
llover o > ue
  (*see* volver)
mantener
  (*see* tener)
mentir e > ie, i
  (*see* sentir)

morir o > ue, u
  (*see* domir)
obtener
  (*see* tener)
oír (14)
pagar g > gu[5]
parecer c > zc
  (*see* conocer)
pedir (15) e > i
pensar (16) e > ie
perder (17) e > ie
poder (18)
poner (19)
preferir e > ie, i
  (*see* sentir)
probar o > ue
  (*see* contar)
provocar c > qu[2]
querer (20)
recordar o > ue
  (*see* contar)
repetir e > i
  (*see* pedir)
resolver o > ue
  (*see* volver)

saber (21)
salir (22)
seguir e > i; gu > g[6]
  (*see* pedir)
sentar(se) e > ie
  (*see* pensar)
sentir(se) (23) e > ie, i
ser (24)
servir e > i
  (*see* pedir)
tener (25)
tocar c > qu[2]
traducir c > zc, j
  (*see* conducir)
traer (26)
valer (27)
venir (28)
ver (29)
vestir(se) e > i
  (*see* pedir)
volver (30) o > ue

---

[1] In verbs ending in **-zar**, the **z** changes to **c** before an **e**: **almorcé, comencé, empecé.**

[2] In verbs ending in **-car**, the **c** changes to **qu** before an **e**: **busqué, provoqué, toqué.**

[3] In **construir**, a **y** is inserted before any ending that does not begin with **i**: **construyo**, etc. An **i** changes to **y** between two vowels: **construyó.**

[4] In **leer**, **i** changes to **y** between two vowels: **leyó, leyeron.**

[5] In verbs ending in **-gar**, the **g** changes to **gu** before an **e**: **llegué, pagué.**

[6] In verbs ending in **-guir**, the **gu** changes to **g** before **a** and **o**: **sigo, siga.**

Regular Verbs

Simple Tenses

INFINITIVE	INDICATIVE				
	Present	**Imperfect**	**Preterit**	**Future**	**Conditional**
hablar	hablo	hablaba	hablé	hablaré	hablaría
	hablas	hablabas	hablaste	hablarás	hablarías
	habla	hablaba	habló	hablará	hablaría
	hablamos	hablábamos	hablamos	hablaremos	hablaríamos
	habláis	hablabais	hablasteis	hablaréis	hablaríais
	hablan	hablaban	hablaron	hablarán	hablarían
comer	como	comía	comí	comeré	comería
	comes	comías	comiste	comerás	comerías
	come	comía	comió	comerá	comería
	comemos	comíamos	comimos	comeremos	comeríamos
	coméis	comíais	comisteis	comeréis	comeríais
	comen	comían	comieron	comerán	comerían
vivir	vivo	vivía	viví	viviré	viviría
	vives	vivías	viviste	vivirás	vivirías
	vive	vivía	vivió	vivirá	viviría
	vivimos	vivíamos	vivimos	viviremos	viviríamos
	vivís	vivíais	vivisteis	viviréis	viviríais
	viven	vivían	vivieron	vivirán	vivirían

Perfect Tenses

PAST PARTICIPLE	INDICATIVE			
	Present perfect	**Past perfect**	**Future perfect**	**Conditional perfect**
hablado	he hablado	había hablado	habré hablado	habría hablado
	has hablado	habías hablado	habrás hablado	habrías hablado
	ha hablado	había hablado	habrá hablado	habría hablado
	hemos hablado	habíamos hablado	habremos hablado	habríamos hablado
	habéis hablado	habíais hablado	habréis hablado	habríais hablado
	han hablado	habían hablado	habrán hablado	habrían hablado
comido	he comido	había comido	habré comido	habría comido
	has comido	habías comido	habrás comido	habrías comido
	ha comido	había comido	habrá comido	habría comido
	hemos comido	habíamos comido	habremos comido	habríamos comido
	habéis comido	habíais comido	habréis comido	habríais comido
	han comido	habían comido	habrán comido	habrían comido

Simple Tenses

	SUBJUNCTIVE	COMMANDS
Present	**Imperfect**	
hable	hablara(-se)	—
hables	hablaras(-ses)	habla (no hables)
hable	hablara(-se)	hable
hablemos	habláramos(-semos)	hablemos
habléis	hablarais(-seis)	hablad (no habléis)
hablen	hablaran(-sen)	hablen
coma	comiera(-se)	—
comas	comieras(-ses)	come (no comas)
coma	comiera(-se)	coma
comamos	comiéramos(-semos)	comamos
comáis	comierais(-seis)	comed (no comáis)
coman	comieran(-sen)	coman
viva	viviera(-se)	—
vivas	vivieras(-ses)	vive (no vivas)
viva	viviera(-se)	viva
vivamos	viviéramos(-semos)	vivamos
viváis	vivierais(-seis)	vivid (no viváis)
vivan	vivieran(-sen)	vivan

Perfect Tenses

	SUBJUNCTIVE
Present perfect	**Past perfect**
haya hablado	hubiera(-se) hablado
hayas hablado	hubieras(-ses) hablado
haya hablado	hubiera(-se) hablado
hayamos hablado	hubiéramos(-semos) hablado
hayáis hablado	hubierais(-seis) hablado
hayan hablado	hubieran(-sen) hablado
haya comido	hubiera(-se) comido
hayas comido	hubieras(-ses) comido
haya comido	hubiera(-se) comido
hayamos comido	hubiéramos(-semos) comido
hayáis comido	hubierais(-seis) comido
hayan comido	hubieran(-sen) comido

PAST PARTICIPLE / INDICATIVE

PAST PARTICIPLE	Present perfect	Past perfect	Future perfect	Conditional perfect
vivido	he vivido	había vivido	habré vivido	habría vivido
	has vivido	habías vivido	habrás vivido	habrías vivido
	ha vivido	había vivido	habrá vivido	habría vivido
	hemos vivido	habíamos vivido	habremos vivido	habríamos vivido
	habéis vivido	habíais vivido	habréis vivido	habríais vivido
	han vivido	habían vivido	habrán vivido	habrían vivido

PRESENT PARTICIPLE	INDICATIVE Present	Past	PRESENT PARTICIPLE	Present
hablando	estoy hablando	estaba hablando	comiendo	estoy comiendo
	estás hablando	estabas hablando		estás comiendo
	está hablando	estaba hablando		está comiendo
	estamos hablando	estábamos hablando		estamos comiendo
	estáis hablando	estabais hablando		estáis comiendo
	están hablando	estaban hablando		están comiendo

Irregular Verbs

INFINITIVE	INDICATIVE Present	Imperfect	Preterit	Future	Conditional
1. andar	ando	andaba	anduve	andaré	andaría
	andas	andabas	anduviste	andarás	andarías
	anda	andaba	anduvo	andará	andaría
	andamos	andábamos	anduvimos	andaremos	andaríamos
	andáis	andabais	anduvisteis	andaréis	andaríais
	andan	andaban	anduvieron	andarán	andarían
2. conducir	conduzco	conducía	conduje	conduciré	conduciría
	conduces	conducías	condujiste	conducirás	conducirías
	conduce	conducía	condujo	conducirá	conduciría
	conducimos	conducíamos	condujimos	conduciremos	conduciríamos
	conducís	conducíais	condujisteis	conduciréis	conduciríais
	conducen	conducían	condujeron	conducirán	conducirían

Perfect Tenses

SUBJUNCTIVE	
Present perfect	**Past perfect**
haya vivido	hubiera(-se) vivido
hayas vivido	hubieras(-ses) vivido
haya vivido	hubiera(-se) vivido
hayamos vivido	hubiéramos(-semos) vivido
hayáis vivido	hubierais(-seis) vivido
hayan vivido	hubieran(-sen) vivido

Progressive Tenses

	PRESENT PARTICIPLE	INDICATIVE	
Past		**Present**	**Past**
estaba comiendo	viviendo	estoy viviendo	estaba viviendo
estabas comiendo		estás viviendo	estabas viviendo
estaba comiendo		está viviendo	estaba viviendo
estábamos comiendo		estamos viviendo	estábamos viviendo
estabais comiendo		estáis viviendo	estabais viviendo
estaban comiendo		están viviendo	estaban viviendo

SUBJUNCTIVE		COMMANDS	PARTICIPLES	
Present	**Imperfect**		**Present**	**Past**
ande	anduviera(-se)	—	andando	andado
andes	anduvieras(-ses)	anda (no andes)		
ande	anduviera(-se)	ande		
andemos	anduviéramos(-semos)	andemos		
andéis	anduvierais(-seis)	andad (no andéis)		
anden	anduvieran(-sen)	anden		
conduzca	condujera(-se)	—	conduciendo	conducido
conduzcas	condujeras(-ses)	conduce (no conduzcas)		
conduzca	condujera(-se)	conduzca		
conduzcamos	condujéramos(-semos)	conduzcamos		
conduzcáis	condujerais(-seis)	conducid (no conduzcáis)		
conduzcan	condujeran(-sen)	conduzcan		

	Present	Imperfect	Preterit	Future	Conditional
3. conocer	conozco	conocía	conocí	conoceré	conocería
	conoces	conocías	conociste	conocerás	conocerías
	conoce	conocía	conoció	conocerá	conocería
	conocemos	conocíamos	conocimos	conoceremos	conoceríamos
	conocéis	conocíais	conocisteis	conoceréis	conoceríais
	conocen	conocían	conocieron	conocerán	conocerían
4. contar	cuento	contaba	conté	contaré	contaría
	cuentas	contabas	contaste	contarás	contarías
	cuenta	contaba	contó	contará	contaría
	contamos	contábamos	contamos	contaremos	contaríamos
	contáis	contabais	contasteis	contaréis	contaríais
	cuentan	contaban	contaron	contarán	contarían
5. creer	creo	creía	creí	creeré	creería
	crees	creías	creíste	creerás	creerías
	cree	creía	creyó	creerá	creería
	creemos	creíamos	creímos	creeremos	creeríamos
	creéis	creíais	creísteis	creeréis	creeríais
	creen	creían	creyeron	creerán	creerían
6. dar	doy	daba	di	daré	daría
	das	dabas	diste	darás	darías
	da	daba	dio	dará	daría
	damos	dábamos	dimos	daremos	daríamos
	dais	dabais	disteis	daréis	daríais
	dan	daban	dieron	darán	darían
7. decir	digo	decía	dije	diré	diría
	dices	decías	dijiste	dirás	dirías
	dice	decía	dijo	dirá	diría
	decimos	decíamos	dijimos	diremos	diríamos
	decís	decíais	dijisteis	diréis	diríais
	dicen	decían	dijeron	dirán	dirían
8. dormir	duermo	dormía	dormí	dormiré	dormiría
	duermes	dormías	dormiste	dormirás	dormirías
	duerme	dormía	durmió	dormirá	dormiría
	dormimos	dormíamos	dormimos	dormiremos	dormiríamos
	dormís	dormíais	dormisteis	dormiréis	dormiríais
	duermen	dormían	durmieron	dormirán	dormirían
9. estar	estoy	estaba	estuve	estaré	estaría
	estás	estabas	estuviste	estarás	estarías
	está	estaba	estuvo	estará	estaría
	estamos	estábamos	estuvimos	estaremos	estaríamos
	estáis	estabais	estuvisteis	estaréis	estaríais
	están	estaban	estuvieron	estarán	estarían

	SUBJUNCTIVE	COMMANDS	PARTICIPLES	
Present	**Imperfect**		**Present**	**Past**
conozca	conociera(-se)	—	conociendo	conocido
conozcas	conocieras(-ses)	conoce (no conozcas)		
conozca	conociera(-se)	conozca		
conozcamos	conociéramos(-semos)	conozcamos		
conozcáis	conocierais(-seis)	conoced (no conozcáis)		
conozcan	conocieran(-sen)	conozcan		
cuente	contara(-se)	—	contando	contado
cuentes	contaras(-ses)	cuenta (no cuentes)		
cuente	contara(-se)	cuente		
contemos	contáramos(-semos)	contemos		
contéis	contarais(-seis)	contad (no contéis)		
cuenten	contaran(-sen)	cuenten		
crea	creyera(-se)	—	creyendo	creído
creas	creyeras(-ses)	cree (no creas)		
crea	creyera(-se)	crea		
creamos	creyéramos(-semos)	creamos		
creáis	creyerais(-seis)	creed (no creáis)		
crean	creyeran(-sen)	crean		
dé	diera(-se)	—	dando	dado
des	dieras(-ses)	da (no des)		
dé	diera(-se)	dé		
demos	diéramos(-semos)	demos		
deis	dierais(-seis)	dad (no deis)		
den	dieran(-sen)	den		
diga	dijera(-se)	—	diciendo	dicho
digas	dijeras(-ses)	di (no digas)		
diga	dijera(-se)	diga		
digamos	dijéramos(-semos)	digamos		
digáis	dijerais(-seis)	decid (no digáis)		
digan	dijeran(-sen)	digan		
duerma	durmiera(-se)	—	durmiendo	dormido
duermas	durmieras(-ses)	duerme (no duermas)		
duerma	durmiera(-se)	duerma		
durmamos	durmiéramos(-semos)	durmamos		
durmáis	durmierais(-seis)	dormid (no durmáis)		
duerman	durmieran(-sen)	duerman		
esté	estuviera(-se)	—	estando	estado
estés	estuvieras(-ses)	está (no estés)		
esté	estuviera(-se)	esté		
estemos	estuviéramos(-semos)	estemos		
estéis	estuvierais(-seis)	estéis		
estén	estuvieran(-sen)	estén		

INFINITIVE		INDICATIVE			
	Present	Imperfect	Preterit	Future	Conditional
10. haber	he	había	hube	habré	habría
	has	habías	hubiste	habrás	habrías
	ha	había	hubo	habrá	habría
	hemos	habíamos	hubimos	habremos	habríamos
	habéis	habíais	hubisteis	habréis	habríais
	han	habían	hubieron	habrán	habrían
11. hacer	hago	hacía	hice	haré	haría
	haces	hacías	hiciste	harás	harías
	hace	hacía	hizo	hará	haría
	hacemos	hacíamos	hicimos	haremos	haríamos
	hacéis	hacíais	hicisteis	haréis	haríais
	hacen	hacían	hicieron	harán	harían
12. ir	voy	iba	fui	iré	iría
	vas	ibas	fuiste	irás	irías
	va	iba	fue	irá	iría
	vamos	íbamos	fuimos	iremos	iríamos
	vais	ibais	fuisteis	iréis	iríais
	van	iban	fueron	irán	irían
13. jugar	juego	jugaba	jugué	jugaré	jugaría
	juegas	jugabas	jugaste	jugarás	jugarías
	juega	jugaba	jugó	jugará	jugaría
	jugamos	jugábamos	jugamos	jugaremos	jugaríamos
	jugáis	jugabais	jugasteis	jugaréis	jugaríais
	juegan	jugaban	jugaron	jugarán	jugarían
14. oír	oigo	oía	oí	oiré	oiría
	oyes	oías	oíste	oirás	oirías
	oye	oía	oyó	oirá	oiría
	oímos	oíamos	oímos	oiremos	oiríamos
	oís	oíais	oísteis	oiréis	oiríais
	oyen	oían	oyeron	oirán	oirían
15. pedir	pido	pedía	pedí	pediré	pediría
	pides	pedías	pediste	pedirás	pedirías
	pide	pedía	pidió	pedirá	pediría
	pedimos	pedíamos	pedimos	pediremos	pediríamos
	pedís	pedíais	pedisteis	pediréis	pediríais
	piden	pedían	pidieron	pedirán	pedirían
16. pensar	pienso	pensaba	pensé	pensaré	pensaría
	piensas	pensabas	pensaste	pensarás	pensarías
	piensa	pensaba	pensó	pensará	pensaría
	pensamos	pensábamos	pensamos	pensaremos	pensaríamos
	pensáis	pensabais	pensasteis	pensaréis	pensaríais
	piensan	pensaban	pensaron	pensarán	pensarían

	SUBJUNCTIVE		COMMANDS	PARTICIPLES	
Present	*Imperfect*			*Present*	*Past*
haya	hubiera(-se)			habiendo	habido
hayas	hubieras(-ses)				
haya	hubiera(-se)				
hayamos	hubiéramos(-semos)				
hayáis	hubierais(-seis)				
hayan	hubieran(-sen)				
haga	hiciera(-se)		—	haciendo	hecho
hagas	hicieras(-ses)		haz (no hagas)		
haga	hiciera(-se)		haga		
hagamos	hiciéramos(-semos)		hagamos		
hagáis	hicierais(-seis)		haced (no hagáis)		
hagan	hicieran(-sen)		hagan		
vaya	fuera(-se)		—	yendo	ido
vayas	fueras(-ses)		ve (no vayas)		
vaya	fuera(-se)		vaya		
vayamos	fuéramos(-semos)		vayamos		
vayáis	fuerais(-seis)		id (no vayáis)		
vayan	fueran(-sen)		vayan		
juegue	jugara(-se)		—	jugando	jugado
juegues	jugaras(-ses)		juega (no juegues)		
juegue	jugara(-se)		juegue		
juguemos	jugáramos(-semos)		juguemos		
juguéis	jugarais(-seis)		jugad (no juguéis)		
jueguen	jugaran(-sen)		jueguen		
oiga	oyera(-se)		—	oyendo	oído
oigas	oyeras(-ses)		oye (no oigas)		
oiga	oyera(-se)		oiga		
oigamos	oyéramos(-semos)		oigamos		
oigáis	oyerais(-seis)		oíd (no oigáis)		
oigan	oyeran(-sen)		oigan		
pida	pidiera(-se)		—	pidiendo	pedido
pidas	pidieras(-ses)		pide (no pidas)		
pida	pidiera(-se)		pida		
pidamos	pidiéramos(-semos)		pidamos		
pidáis	pidierais(-seis)		pedid (no pidáis)		
pidan	pidieran(-sen)		pidan		
piense	pensara(-se)		—	pensando	pensado
pienses	pensaras(-ses)		piensa (no pienses)		
piense	pensara(-se)		piense		
pensemos	pensáramos(-semos)		pensemos		
penséis	pensarais(-seis)		pensad (no penséis)		
piensen	pensaran(-sen)		piensen		

INFINITIVE	INDICATIVE				
	Present	Imperfect	Preterit	Future	Conditional
17. perder	pierdo	perdía	perdí	perderé	perdería
	pierdes	perdías	perdiste	perderás	perderías
	pierde	perdía	perdió	perderá	perdería
	perdemos	perdíamos	perdimos	perderemos	perderíamos
	perdéis	perdíais	perdisteis	perderéis	perderíais
	pierden	perdían	perdieron	perderán	perderían
18. poder	puedo	podía	pude	podré	podría
	puedes	podías	pudiste	podrás	podrías
	puede	podía	pudo	podrá	podría
	podemos	podíamos	pudimos	podremos	podríamos
	podéis	podíais	pudisteis	podréis	podríais
	pueden	podían	pudieron	podrán	podrían
19. poner	pongo	ponía	puse	pondré	pondría
	pones	ponías	pusiste	pondrás	pondrías
	pone	ponía	puso	pondrá	pondría
	ponemos	poníamos	pusimos	pondremos	pondríamos
	ponéis	poníais	pusisteis	pondréis	pondríais
	ponen	ponían	pusieron	pondrán	pondrían
20. querer	quiero	quería	quise	querré	querría
	quieres	querías	quisiste	querrás	querrías
	quiere	quería	quiso	querrá	querría
	queremos	queríamos	quisimos	querremos	querríamos
	queréis	queríais	quisisteis	querréis	querríais
	quieren	querían	quisieron	querrán	querrían
21. saber	sé	sabía	supe	sabré	sabría
	sabes	sabías	supiste	sabrás	sabrías
	sabe	sabía	supo	sabrá	sabría
	sabemos	sabíamos	supimos	sabremos	sabríamos
	sabéis	sabíais	supisteis	sabréis	sabríais
	saben	sabían	supieron	sabrán	sabrían
22. salir	salgo	salía	salí	saldré	saldría
	sales	salías	salíste	saldrás	saldrías
	sale	salía	salió	saldrá	saldría
	salimos	salíamos	salimos	saldremos	saldríamos
	salís	salíais	salisteis	saldréis	saldríais
	salen	salían	salieron	saldrán	saldrían
23. sentir	siento	sentía	sentí	sentiré	sentiría
	sientes	sentías	sentiste	sentirás	sentirías
	siente	sentía	sintió	sentirá	sentiría
	sentimos	sentíamos	sentimos	sentiremos	sentiríamos
	sentís	sentíais	sentisteis	sentiréis	sentiríais
	sienten	sentían	sintieron	sentirán	sentirían

	SUBJUNCTIVE		COMMANDS	PARTICIPLES	
Present	Imperfect			Present	Past
pierda	perdiera(-se)		—	perdiendo	perdido
pierdas	perdieras(-ses)		pierde (no pierdas)		
pierda	perdiera(-se)		pierda		
perdamos	perdiéramos(-semos)		perdamos		
perdáis	perdierais(-seis)		perded (no perdáis)		
pierdan	perdieran(-sen)		pierdan		
pueda	pudiera(-se)			pudiendo	podido
puedas	pudieras(-ses)				
pueda	pudiera(-se)				
podamos	pudiéramos(-semos)				
podáis	pudierais(-seis)				
puedan	pudieran(-sen)				
ponga	pusiera(-se)		—	poniendo	puesto
pongas	pusieras(-ses)		pon (no pongas)		
ponga	pusiera(-se)		ponga		
pongamos	pusiéramos(-semos)		pongamos		
pongáis	pusierais(-seis)		poned (no pongáis)		
pongan	pusieran(-sen)		pongan		
quiera	quisiera(-se)		—	queriendo	querido
quieras	quisieras(-ses)		quiere (no quieras)		
quiera	quisiera(-se)		quiera		
queramos	quisiéramos(-semos)		queramos		
queráis	quisierais(-seis)		quered (no queráis)		
quieran	quisieran(-sen)		quieran		
sepa	supiera(-se)		—	sabiendo	sabido
sepas	supieras(-ses)		sabe (no sepas)		
sepa	supiera(-se)		sepa		
sepamos	supiéramos(-semos)		sepamos		
sepáis	supierais(-seis)		sabed (no sepáis)		
sepan	supieran(-sen)		sepan		
salga	saliera(-se)		—	saliendo	salido
salgas	salieras(-ses)		sal (no salgas)		
salga	saliera(-se)		salga		
salgamos	saliéramos(-semos)		salgamos		
salgáis	salierais(-seis)		salid (no salgáis)		
salgan	salieran(-sen)		salgan		
sienta	sintiera(-se)		—	sintiendo	sentido
sientas	sintieras(-ses)		siente (no sientas)		
sienta	sintiera(-se)		sienta		
sintamos	sintiéramos(-semos)		sintamos		
sintáis	sintierais(-seis)		sentid (no sintáis)		
sientan	sintieran(-sen)		sientan		

INFINITIVE		INDICATIVE				
		Present	**Imperfect**	**Preterit**	**Future**	**Conditional**
24. ser		soy	era	fui	seré	sería
		eres	eras	fuiste	serás	serías
		es	era	fue	será	sería
		somos	éramos	fuimos	seremos	seríamos
		sois	erais	fuisteis	seréis	seríais
		son	eran	fueron	serán	serían
25. tener		tengo	tenía	tuve	tendré	tendría
		tienes	tenías	tuviste	tendrás	tendrías
		tiene	tenía	tuvo	tendrá	tendría
		tenemos	teníamos	tuvimos	tendremos	tendríamos
		tenéis	teníais	tuvisteis	tendréis	tendríais
		tienen	tenían	tuvieron	tendrán	tendrían
26. traer		traigo	traía	traje	traeré	traería
		traes	traías	trajiste	traerás	traerías
		trae	traía	trajo	traerá	traería
		traemos	traíamos	trajimos	traeremos	traeríamos
		traéis	traíais	trajisteis	traeréis	traeríais
		traen	traían	trajeron	traerán	traerían
27. valer		valgo	valía	valí	valdré	valdría
		vales	valías	valiste	valdrás	valdrías
		vale	valía	valió	valdrá	valdría
		valemos	valíamos	valimos	valdremos	valdríamos
		valéis	valíais	valisteis	valdréis	valdríais
		valen	valían	valieron	valdrán	valdrían
28. venir		vengo	venía	vine	vendré	vendría
		vienes	venías	viniste	vendrás	vendrías
		viene	venía	vino	vendrá	vendría
		venimos	veníamos	vinimos	vendremos	vendríamos
		venís	veníais	vinisteis	vendréis	vendríais
		vienen	venían	vinieron	vendrán	vendrían
29. ver		veo	veía	vi	veré	vería
		ves	veías	viste	verás	verías
		ve	veía	vio	verá	vería
		vemos	veíamos	vimos	veremos	veríamos
		veis	veíais	visteis	veréis	veríais
		ven	veían	vieron	verán	verían
30. volver		vuelvo	volvía	volví	volveré	volvería
		vuelves	volvías	volviste	volverás	volverías
		vuelve	volvía	volvió	volverá	volvería
		volvemos	volvíamos	volvimos	volveremos	volveríamos
		volvéis	volvíais	volvisteis	volveréis	volveríais
		vuelven	volvían	volvieron	volverán	volverían

SUBJUNCTIVE		COMMANDS	PARTICIPLES	
Present	Imperfect		Present	Past
sea	fuera(-se)	—	siendo	sido
seas	fueras(-ses)	sé (no seas)		
sea	fuera(-se)	sea		
seamos	fuéramos(-semos)	seamos		
seáis	fuerais(-seis)	sed (no seáis)		
sean	fueran(-sen)	sean		
tenga	tuviera(-se)	—	teniendo	tenido
tengas	tuvieras(-ses)	ten (no tengas)		
tenga	tuviera(-se)	tenga		
tengamos	tuviéramos(-semos)	tengamos		
tengáis	tuvierais (-seis)	tened (no tengáis)		
tengan	tuvieran(-sen)	tengan		
traiga	trajera(-se)	—	trayendo	traído
traigas	trajeras(-ses)	trae (no traigas)		
traiga	trajera(-se)	traiga		
traigamos	trajéramos(-semos)	traigamos		
traigáis	trajerais(-seis)	traed (no traigáis)		
traigan	trajeran(-sen)	traigan		
valga	valiera(-se)	—	valiendo	valido
valgas	valieras(-ses)	val (no valgas)		
valga	valiera(-se)	valga		
valgamos	valiéramos(-semos)	valgamos		
valgáis	valierais(-seis)	valed (no valgáis)		
valgan	valieran(-sen)	valgan		
venga	viniera(-se)	—	viniendo	venido
vengas	vinieras(-ses)	ven (no vengas)		
venga	viniera(-se)	venga		
vengamos	viniéramos(-semos)	vengamos		
vengáis	vinierais(-seis)	venid (no vengáis)		
vengan	vinieran(-sen)	vengan		
vea	viera(-se)	—	viendo	visto
veas	vieras(-ses)	ve (no veas)		
vea	viera(-se)	vea		
veamos	viéramos(-semos)	veamos		
veáis	vierais(-seis)	ved (no veáis)		
vean	vieran(-sen)	vean		
vuelva	volviera(-se)	—	volviendo	vuelto
vuelvas	volvieras(-ses)	vuelve (no vuelvas)		
vuelva	volviera(-se)	vuelva		
volvamos	volviéramos(-semos)	volvamos		
volváis	volvierais(-seis)	volved (no volváis)		
vuelvan	volvieran(-sen)	vuelvan		

Vocabulario español-inglés

This vocabulary includes contextual meanings of all active vocabulary and idiomatic expressions as well as of most passive words not otherwise glossed where they appear in the text. It excludes most cognates which are not in the active vocabulary, diminutives, superlatives ending in **-ísimo**, most adverbs ending in **-mente**, most proper names, and most conjugated verb forms. The entries are arranged according to the Spanish alphabet. Stem changes are indicated for verbs: e.g., **acostar (ue)**. The number of the chapter where words or phrases in the active vocabulary first appear is listed. **CP** refers to **Capítulo preliminar**.

The following abbreviations are used.

adj	adjective	*inf*	infinitive
adv	adverb	*m*	masculine
contr	contraction	*pl*	plural
dir obj	direct object	*pres*	present
f	feminine	*pret*	preterit
fam	familiar	*pron*	pronoun
imp	imperfect	*rel pron*	relative pronoun
indic	indicative	*subj*	subject
indir obj	indirect object	*subjunc*	subjunctive

A

a at, to **1**; **a la derecha** on (to) the right **2**; **a la izquierda** on (to) the left **2**; **a la moda** in style, fashionable **7**; **a menos que** unless **16**; **a pesar de** in spite of **12**; **A propósito de...** Regarding... **17**; **A propósito...** By the way... **17**; **a tiempo** on time **11**; **a veces** sometimes **5**

abandonar to abandon **9**

abierto open

el **abogado**, la **abogada** lawyer **3**

abrazar to hug, embrace **10**

el **abrazo** hug, embrace **10**

el **abrigo** (winter) coat **7**

abril April **4**

abrir to open **3**

abstracto abstract **12**

la **abuela** grandmother **1**

el **abuelo** grandfather **1**

aburrido boring **2**

acá here

acabar de (+ *inf*) to have just (*done something*) **16**

aceptar to accept **15**

acompañar to accompany, go with **10**

acostar (ue) to put to bed **7**

acostarse to go to bed **7**
acostumbrarse to get used to **7**
activo active **CP**
el **actor** actor **10**
la **actriz** actress **10**
el **acueducto** aqueduct
acuerdo: ponerse de acuerdo to agree **12**; **¿de acuerdo?** okay?, all right?, agreed? **1**
adelante straight, straight ahead **11**; **Siga adelante.** Keep going straight. **11**
además moreover, besides **5**
adentro inside **17**
Adiós. Good-bye. **CP**
el **adjetivo** adjective **2**
¿Adónde? To what place? Where? **1**
adornar to adorn
el **adorno** decoration **13**
la **aduana** customs; customs house **11**
la **aerolínea** airline **1**
el **aeropuerto** airport **1**
el **aficionado**, la **aficionada** fan **8**
afuera outside **17**
la **agencia de viajes** travel agency **2**
el, la **agente de viajes** travel agent **2**
agosto August **4**
agradecido: Muy agradecido(-a). (I'm) very grateful. **6**
agregar to add
la **agricultura** agriculture
ahora now **1**; **ahora mismo** right away **14**
ahorrar to save (*time, money, etc.*) **18**
el **aire** air **2**
al (*contr of* **a + el**) to the **2**; **Al contrario...** On the contrary... **12**; **al lado (de)** beside, next to **2**

alegrarse (de) to be glad (about) **14**
alegre happy **16**
alegremente happily **8**
la **alegría** happiness **16**; **¡Qué alegría!** How happy I am! I'm so happy! **16**
alemán German **3**
la **alfombra** rug, carpet **15**
algo something **7**
alguien someone, anyone **7**
alguna parte somewhere **11**
algún, alguno(-s), alguna(-s) some, any **7**
alivio: ¡Qué alivio! What a relief! **16**
el **alma** *f* soul
el **almacén** department store **18**
almorzar (ue) to have lunch **6**
el **almuerzo** lunch **6**
alquilar to rent **15**
el **alquiler** rent
alto tall **8**
altruista altruistic **2**
allí (*or* **allá**) there **1**
amable nice, friendly, kind **2**
el **amanecer** dawn, daybreak **17**
el, la **amante** lover
amar to love **10**
amarillo yellow **7**
el **amigo**, la **amiga** friend **1**
el **amor** love **10**
anaranjado orange **7**
andar to walk **14**; **andar en bicicleta** to ride a bicycle **14**
la **anestesia** anesthesia
el **ángel** angel
anglosajón Anglo-Saxon
el **anillo** ring **10**
el **aniversario** anniversary **13**

anoche last night **8**
el **anochecer** twilight, dusk **17**
ansioso anxious, nervous **16**
anterior earlier, previous
antes first **6**; **antes de** before **6**; **antes (de) que** before **16**
antiguo ancient
la **antología** anthology **12**
la **antropología** anthropology **3**
el **año** year **3**
el **apartamento** apartment **5**
aprender to learn **3**
aquel, aquella *adj* that (*over there*) **3**
aquél, aquélla *pron* that (*over there*) **3**
aquello *neuter pron* that (*over there*) **3**
aquellos, aquellas *adj* those (*over there*) **3**
aquéllos, aquéllas *pron* those (*over there*) **3**
aquí here **CP**
árabe Arabian **9**
el **árbol** tree **13**; el **árbol de Navidad** Christmas tree **13**
argentino Argentine **2**
la **arquitectura** architecture **3**
arreglar to fix, arrange **14**
arreglarse to be okay, turn out all right **14**
el **arroz** rice **9**
el **arte** *f.* art **7**
el, la **artista** artist; actor, actress **12**
así like that **5**; **Así así.** So so. **CP**
asistir a to attend **8**
el **aspecto (físico)** (physical) appearance **14**
la **aspirina** aspirin **4**
asustado frightened,

startled **16**
asustar to frighten, scare **16**
asustarse to be frightened **16**
el, la **atleta** athlete **8**
aumentar to gain, increase **9**
aunque although **16**
el **autobús** bus **2**
el **autor**, la **autora** author **12**
avanzado advanced
la **avenida** avenue **1**
avergonzado embarassed, ashamed **16**
el **avión** airplane **1**
ayer yesterday **8**
la **ayuda** help **5**
ayudar to help **5**
azteca Aztec **3**
el **azúcar** sugar **9**
azul blue **7**

B

bailar to dance **6**
el **baile** dance **6**
bajar de to get off **2**
bajo *adv* beneath, under **17**; *adj* low; short **17**
la **banana** banana **9**
el **banco** bank **5**
el **baño** bathroom **15**; el **traje de baño** swimming suit **7**
barato inexpensive, cheap **18**
el **barco** ship, boat **11**
el **barrio** neighborhood, community **5**
básico basic
el **básquetbol** basketball **5**
¡Basta! That's enough! **14**
bastante rather; enough **3**
la **basura** garbage **5**

la **bebida** beverage, drink **9**
el **béisbol** baseball **8**
bello beautiful **17**
besar to kiss **10**
el **beso** kiss **10**
la **biblioteca** library **3**
la **bicicleta** bicycle **5**; **andar en bicicleta** to ride a bicycle **14**
bien okay; well **CP**; **estar bien** to be well **CP**; **Está bien.** It's all right (okay). **14**
la **bienvenida** welcome **11**; **darle la bienvenida a alguien** to welcome someone **11**
bienvenido welcome **2**
la **biología** biology **3**
el **bistec** (beef) steak **9**
blanco white **7**
la **blusa** blouse **7**
la **boca** mouth **14**
la **boda** wedding **10**
el **boleto** ticket **11**; el **boleto de ida y vuelta** round-trip ticket **11**
el **bolso** purse, pocketbook **6**
bonito pretty **2**
la **bota** boot **7**
la **boutique** boutique **18**
el **brazo** arm **14**
la **broma** joke; **¡Pero lo dice(s) en broma!** But you're saying it in jest! **8**; **¿Habla(s) en broma?** Are you joking? **8**
bueno good **2**; **¡Buen provecho!** Enjoy the meal! **9**; **¡Buena lección!** That's a good lesson for you! **5**; **Buenas noches.** Good night. **CP**; **Buenas tardes.** Good afternoon. **CP**; **estar bueno** to be delicious (good, tasty) **9**; **Es**

bueno. It's good. **14**; **Bueno...** Well... **7**; **Buenos días.** Good morning. Good day. **CP**
buscar to look for; to search **1**

C

cada each, every **3**
el **café** coffee; café **5**
el **calcetín** sock **7**
el **calendario** calendar **3**
la **calidad** quality **18**
caliente hot **15**
la **calle** street **5**
calmar to calm **11**
calmarse to calm down, be calm **11**
calor: tener calor to be warm (*a person or animal*) **4**
la **cama** bed **14**
la **cámara** camera **1**
la **camarera** waitress **3**
el **camarero** waiter **3**
cambiar to change, exchange **11**; **Cambiando de tema...** To change the subject... **17**
el **cambio** change **12**; **En cambio...** On the other hand... **12**
caminar to walk **11**; **Camine dos cuadras...** Walk two blocks... **11**
el **camino** road
la **camisa** shirt **7**
campamento: ir de campamento to go camping **17**
el **campo** country (*as opposed to city*) **17**
la **canción** song **6**
el **candelabro** candelabra **13**
cansado tired **4**

cantar to sing **6**

la **capacidad** capacity; capability **18**

la **capital** capital (city) **1**

la **cara** face **14**

¡Caramba! Good grief! **5**

cariñoso tender, affectionate **10**

la **carne** meat **9**; la **carne de vaca** beef **9**

caro expensive **7**

la **carta** letter **3**

la **casa** house; home **CP**; **en casa** at home **CP**

casarse (con) to get married (to) **10**

casi almost **8**

caso: en caso (de) que in case **16**

castaño chestnut (*color*)

la **catedral** cathedral **9**

católico Catholic **8**

catorce fourteen **1**

causar to cause

la **celebración** celebration **13**

celebrar to celebrate **13**

los **celos** jealousy **10**; **tener celos de** to be jealous of **10**

la **cena** dinner **6**

cenar to have dinner **7**

la **censura** censorship **12**

el **centro** downtown; center **4**

cerca (de) near **2**

cero zero **1**

cerrar (ie) to close **5**

la **cerveza** beer **9**

el **cielo** sky; heaven **17**; el **cielo raso** ceiling **15**

cien(to) one hundred **4**

la **ciencia** science; las **ciencias de computación** computer science **3**; las **ciencias políticas** political sciences **3**; las **ciencias sociales** social sciences **3**

cierto: Es cierto. It's true. **14**

el **cigarrillo** cigarette **14**

el **cigarro** cigar **14**

cinco five **1**

cincuenta fifty **1**

el **cine** movie theater, movies **6**

la **cinta** tape **6**

el **cinturón** belt **7**

la **cita** date, appointment **10**; **tener una cita** to have a date or an appointment **10**

la **ciudad** city **1**

claramente clearly **8**

claro clear, light **7**; certainly **12**; **¡Claro!** Of course! **3**; **Es (Está) claro.** It's clear. **14**

la **clase** class(room) **CP**

el, la **cliente** client **16**

el **clima** climate **17**

la **cocina** kitchen **15**

cocinar to cook **9**

cognado cognate **CP**

colectivo collective

el **colmo** the last straw **16**

colombiano Colombian **2**

el **color** color; **¿De qué color es?** What color is it? **7**

el **comedor** dining room **13**

comer to eat **3**

el, la **comerciante** businessperson **3**

la **comida** food; meal **2**

como as, since **9**; **Como consecuencia (resultado)...** As a consequence (result)... **15**; **tan** (+ *adj or adv* +) **como** as...as **8**; **tanto como** as much as **8**

¿Cómo? How? What? **1**; **Cómo no.** Of course. **10**; **¿Cómo se dice...?** How do you say...? **CP**; **¿Cómo se**

llama...? What is the name of...? **CP**

cómodo comfortable **15**

el **compañero** (la **compañera**) **de clase (cuarto)** classmate (roommate) **10**

la **compañía** company **11**

completamente completely **8**

la **composición** composition **5**

la **compra** purchase **comprar** to buy **6**

comprender to understand **3**

la **computadora** computer **6**

común common **9**

con with **CP**; **con mucho gusto** gladly **6**; **Con permiso.** Excuse me. (With your permission.) **10**

el **concierto** concert **6**

la **conjunción** conjunction **conocer** to be familiar with, to know **5**; to meet **13**

conquistar to conquer

la **consecuencia** consequence **15**

el **consejo** advice, piece of advice **6**

construir to build **13**

la **contaminación del aire (del agua)** air (water) pollution **5**

contaminado polluted **2**

contar (ue) to tell; to count **11**; **contar (ue) con** to count on **15**

contento content; happy **5**

contestar to answer **4**; **Conteste, por favor.** Answer, please. **CP**

contra against **5**

contrario: Al contrario... On the contrary... **12**

convencer to convince **15**

el **corazón** heart **9**
la **corbata** tie **7**
correcto right, correct **12**
el **corredor**, la **corredora** runner **8**
el **correo** post office; mail **11**
correr to run **8**
la **corrida de toros** bullfight **8**
cortés courteous, polite **2**
corto brief, short (*not used in reference to people*) **5**
la **cosa** thing **6**
la **costa** coast **14**
costar (ue) to cost **6**
creer to believe, think **3**; **No lo puedo creer.** I can't believe it. **8**; **No lo creo.** I don't believe it. **8**
el **crimen** crime **5**
el **criollo** Creole
cristiano Christian **10**
cruzar to cross **11**
el **cuaderno** notebook **CP**
la **cuadra** (city) block **11**
el **cuadro** painting **12**
¿Cuál? ¿Cuáles? Which? Which one(s)? What? **1**
cualquier(a) any **16**
¿Cuándo? When? **1**
¿Cuánto(-os)? How much?, How many? **3**; **¡Cuánto me alegro!** How happy I am! **16**
cuarenta forty **1**
el **cuarto** room **6**
cuatro four **1**
cuatrocientos four hundred **4**
cubrir to cover **12**
el **cuello** neck **14**
la **cuenta** bill, check **9**; **darse cuenta de** to realize **16**; **La cuenta, por favor.** The check, please. **9**

el **cuento** story **12**
el **cuerpo** body **14**
la **cuestión** issue, question **12**
¡Cuidado! Be careful! Watch out! **4**
cuidar to take care of **9**
cuidarse to take care of oneself **9**
la **culpa** guilt **5**; **Es su (tu) propia culpa.** It's your own fault. **5**
la **cultura** culture **16**
el **cumpleaños** birthday **4**; **feliz cumpleaños** happy birthday
el **cura** priest
la **cura** cure **14**
curar to cure **14**
curioso curious
el **curso** course **6**

CH

el **cheque** check **11**; el **cheque de viajero** traveler's check **11**
la **chica** girl, young person **2**
chicano Chicano, Mexican-American
el **chico** boy, guy, young person **2**
chileno Chilean **2**
el **chiste** joke **16**
el **chocolate** chocolate **9**

D

dar to give **6**; **dar a** to face, be facing **15**; **dar las gracias** to thank **6**; **dar un paseo** to take a walk **6**; **darle la bienvenida a alguien**

to welcome someone **11**; **darse cuenta de** to realize **16**
de of, from **CP**; **¿de acuerdo?** okay?, all right?, agreed? **1**; **de la mañana** A.M. **3**; **de la tarde (noche)** P.M. **3**; **de moda** in style, fashionable **7**; **De nada.** You're welcome. **10**; **¿De qué color es?** What color is it? **7**; **¿De qué es?** What is it made of? **7**; **¿De qué tamaño es?** What size is it? **7**; **¿De veras?** Really? **8**
deber should, ought to, must **3**; to owe **18**
los **deberes** homework **5**
decidir to decide **3**
decir (i) to say, tell **6**; **Se dice...** You say... **CP**; **¿Cómo se dice...?** How do you say...? **CP**
decorar to decorate
del (*contr of* **de** + **el**) from the; of the **2**
delicioso delicious, good, tasty **2**
demasiado too much **14**; **¡Esto es demasiado!** This is too much! **16**; **Es demasiado...** It's too... **18**
el **demonio** demon
dentro (de) inside, within **10**
depender (de) to depend (on) **7**
el, la **dependiente** salesperson **18**
el **deporte** sport **8**
deprimido depressed **16**
derecho *adv* straight, straight ahead **11**; **Siga derecho.** Keep going straight. **11**

el **desayuno** breakfast **6**
descansar to rest **14**
el, la **descendiente**
descendent
descortés impolite **2**
describir to describe **12**
descubrir to discover **3**
desde from, since **10**
desear to want, wish **1**
el **desempleo**
unemployment **5**
el **desfile** parade **13**
designar to designate
la **desilusión**
disappointment **16**
desilusionado
disappointed **16**
desordenado messy **15**
despacio slowly **3**; **Más despacio, por favor.**
Slower, please. **3**
la **despedida** farewell,
leave-taking **16**
despertar (ie) to
awaken (*someone*) **6**
despertarse (ie) to
awaken, wake up **7**
despierto awake,
alert **12**
después afterward **6**;
después de after **6**;
Después de todo...
After all... **18**
el, la **detective** detective **16**
detrás (de) behind **2**
devolver (ue) to return
something **18**
el **día** day **1**; **Buenos días.**
Good morning. Good
day. **CP**
la **diablada** devilry
el **diablo** devil
diariamente daily **8**
diario daily **7**
diciembre December **4**
dieciséis sixteen **1**
el **diente** tooth
la **dieta** diet **9**; **estar a dieta** to be on a diet **9**
diez ten **1**
la **diferencia** difference **17**
difícil difficult **2**

la **dificultad** difficulty **14**
el **dinero** money **5**
el **dios** god **3**; **¡Dios mío!**
my goodness! My
God! **1**
la **dirección** address **1**;
¿Cuál es la dirección de...? What's the
address of...? **11**
el **disco** record **6**
la **discriminación**
discrimination **5**
disculpar to forgive **16**;
Discúlpeme. Excuse
me. (Forgive me.) **16**
la **diversión** diversion;
amusement **6**
divertir (ie) to amuse,
entertain **7**
divertirse (ie) to enjoy
oneself, have a good
time **7**
doblar to turn **11**;
Doble a la izquierda (derecha). Turn left
(right). **11**
doce twelve **1**
la **docena** dozen **14**
el **doctor**, la **doctora**
doctor **2**
el **dólar** dollar **6**
doler (ue) to ache,
hurt **14**
el **dolor** pain; **tener dolor de cabeza (estómago)**
to have a headache
(stomachache) **4**
el **domingo** Sunday **4**
¿Dónde? Where? **1**
don, doña titles of
respect used with first
names **1**
dormir (ue) to sleep **6**
el **dormitorio** bedroom **15**
dos two **1**
doscientos two
hundred **4**
la **droga** drug **5**
dudar to doubt **14**
el **dueño**, la **dueña**
owner **13**
durante during

durar to last

E

económico economical
7
la **edad** age **15**; **¿Que edad tienes?** How old
are you? **15**
el **edificio** building **5**
egoísta selfish **2**
el **ejemplo** example; **por ejemplo** for example **3**
él *subj* he **CP**
el the **1**
la **elegancia** elegance **7**
elegante elegant **2**
ella *subj* she **CP**
ellos, ellas *subj* they **CP**
embarazada
pregnant **14**
la **emoción** emotion
emocionante exciting **8**
el **emperador** emperor
empezar (ie) to begin,
start **5**
el **empleado**, la **empleada**
employee
el **empleo** employment **5**
en in, on, at **1**; **en casa**
at home **CP**; **en caso (de) que** in case **16**;
En fin... Finally...;
Well... (*as an expletive*)
10; **en punto** on the
dot **3**; **En resumen...**
In short... (In
conclusion...) **18**; **en seguida** at once, immediately **11**; **¿En serio?** Really? **10**
enamorarse (de) to fall
in love (with) **10**
encantar to delight **9**;
Me encanta(n)... I
love... **9**
encontrar (ue) to find;
to meet **6**
el **enemigo**, la **enemiga**
enemy **9**

la **energía** energy **14**
enero January **4**
enfermarse to get sick **14**
la **enfermedad** illness **14**
el **enfermero**, la **enfermera** nurse **14**
enfermo sick **14**
enfrente (de) in front (of); across (from), opposite **2**
enojado angry **16**
enojarse to become angry, get mad **16**
el **enojo** anger **16**
enorme enormous
la **ensalada** salad **9**
entender (ie) to understand **5**
entonces then **6**
la **entrada** ticket **6**
entrar (en) to enter, go into **7**
entre between, among **7**; **Entre paréntesis...** Incidentally... **17**; **entre sí** among themselves
enviar to send **12**
la **época** epoch, era **10**
el **equipaje** luggage **11**
el **equipo** team **8**
la **escalera** stairway **15**
la **escena** scene
escocés Scot
escribir to write **3**
el **escritor**, la **escritora** writer **3**
escuchar to listen to **1**
la **escuela** school **3**; la **escuela secundaria** high school **12**
la **escultura** sculpture **12**
ese, esa *adj* that **3**
ése, ésa *pron* that **3**
eso *neuter pron* that **3**
esos, esas *adj* those **3**
ésos, ésas *pron* those **3**
la **espalda** back **14**
el **español** Spanish **CP**
especialmente especially **8**

el **espectáculo** spectacle
el **espectador**, la **espectadora** spectator **8**
el **espejo** mirror **14**
esperar to wait for; to hope; to expect **5**; **Es de esperar.** It's to be expected. **5**
la **esposa** wife **1**
el **esposo** husband **1**
el **esquí** skiing; ski **8**
el **esquiador**, la **esquiadora** skier **8**
esquiar to ski **4**
la **esquina** corner **11**
estar to be; **Está al norte (sur, este, oeste) de...** It's north (south, east, west) of... **11**; **Está nublado.** It's cloudy. **4**
la **estación** station **11**; season **4**
el **estadio** stadium **11**
el **estado** state **2**
el **estante: estante para libros** bookcase **15**
estar to be **CP**; **estar bien (mal)** to be well (unwell) **CP**; **estar bueno** to be delicious (good, tasty) **9**; **estar de vacaciones** to be on vacation **2**; **estar por** to be about to **15**; **Estoy seguro(-a) que...** I'm sure (positive) that... **15**
la **estatua** statue
el **estereotipo** stereotype
este, esta *adj* this **3**
éste, ésta *pron* this **3**
el **estilo** style **12**
esto *neuter pron* this **3**; **¡Esto es demasiado!** This is too much! **16**; **¡Esto es el colmo!** This is the last straw! **16**
estos, estas *adj* these **3**
éstos, éstas *pron* these **3**

la **estrella** star **17**
la **estructura** structure
el, la **estudiante** student **CP**
estudiar to study **1**
el **estudio** study **3**
estupendo great **3**
eterno eternal **15**
exacto exact **3**
el **examen** exam, test **2**
excelente excellent **CP**
el **exiliado** exile
experto expert **16**; el **experto**, la **experta** expert **18**
explicar to explain **8**
la **exposición** exhibit **2**
la **expresión** expression **CP**
expreso express, fast **16**
extra extra **9**
extremo extreme **17**

F

fabuloso fabulous **18**
fácil easy **2**
fácilmente easily **8**
la **falda** skirt **7**
falso false **1**
faltar to be missing or lacking **9**; **Me falta(n)...** I need... **9**
la **familia** family **CP**
famoso famous **2**
la **farmacia** pharmacy **1**
fascinante fascinating **11**
el **favor** favor **6**; **Por favor.** Please. **CP**
favorito favorite **4**
febrero February **4**
la **fecha** date **4**
¡Felicitaciones! Congratulations! **10**
feliz happy **10**; **feliz cumpleaños** happy birthday
la **fiebre** fever; **tener fiebre** to have a fever **4**
la **fiesta** party, holiday **3**

fijo: precio fijo fixed price **18**

la **filosofía** philosophy **3**

el **fin** end; el **fin de semana** weekend **1**; **Feliz fin de semana.** Have a good weekend (*literally*, Happy end of week). **1**; **En fin...** Finally ...; Well ... (*as an expletive*) **10**; **por fin** finally **7**

la **física** physics **3**

el **flan** caramel custard **9**

la **flor** flower **17**

formar to form

la **fortuna** fortune **18**

la **foto(grafía)** photograph **6**

el **fotógrafo,** la **fotógrafa** photographer **12**

el **francés** French **1**

franco frank

la **frase** phrase **CP**

fresco fresh; cool **14**

los **frijoles** beans **9**

el **frío** cold; **tener frío** to be cold (*a person or animal*) **4**

frito fried **9**

la **fruta** fruit **9**

el **fuego** fire

fuera outside **18**; **por fuera** from or on the outside **18**

fuerte strong **8**

fumar to smoke **13**

funcionar to work **18**

fundar to found

furioso furious **16**

el **fútbol** soccer **8**; el **fútbol americano** football **8**

el **futuro** future **3**

G

ganar to win; to earn **8**

ganas: tener ganas de

(+ *inf*) to feel like (*doing something*) **3**

el **garaje** garage **15**

la **garganta** throat **14**

gastar to spend **18**

el **gato** cat **6**

el **gazpacho** cold soup made of tomatoes, cucumbers, onions **9**

la **generación** generation **18**

generalmente generally **8**

generoso generous **10**

la **gente** people **4**

el, la **gerente** manager **15**

el **gobierno** government **Gracias.** Thank you. **CP**; **Mil gracias.** Thank you very much (*literally*, A thousand thanks). **6**; **Muchas gracias.** Thank you. Thank you very much. **6**; **dar las gracias** to thank **6**

gran great

grande (**gran** *before a masculine singular noun*) big, tall; great **2**

la **grandeza** grandeur **17**

gris gray **7**

el **grupo** group **7**

el **guante** glove **7**

guapo handsome, good-looking (*said of men and women*) **7**

guardar to keep **15**

guatemalteco Guatemalan

la **guerra** war

la **guitarra** guitar **6**

gustar to please, be pleasing **9**; **Me gusta(n)...** I like ... **9**; **A mí me gustaría tomar (comer)...** I would like ... to drink (eat). **9**

el **gusto** pleasure **6**; **con mucho gusto** gladly **6**; **¡Qué gusto!** What a

pleasure!; **Mucho gusto.** Glad to meet you. **CP**; **Hago... con mucho gusto.** I'll do... with pleasure. **6**

H

haber: hay (*impersonal*) there is, there are **1**; **hay que** it's necessary; one (we, you, and so on) must **4**

la **habitación** room **15**

el, la **habitante** inhabitant

hablar to talk, speak **1**; **¡Ni hablar!** Don't even mention it! **12**

hacer to do; to make **3**; **Hace buen (mal) tiempo.** The weather is nice (bad). **4**; **Hace calor (fresco, frío, sol, viento).** It is warm (cool, cold, sunny, windy). **4**; **hace un rato** a short while ago **15**; **hace... que** (+ *pres*) to have been -ing for... **10**; **hace... que** (+ *pret* or *imp*) ago **10**; **hacer ejercicios** to do exercises **3**; **hacer el papel (de)** to play the role (of) **13**; **hacer la maleta** to pack one's suitcase **3**; **hacía... que** (+ *imp*) had been -ing for... **10**; **Hago... con mucho gusto.** I'll do... with pleasure. **6**

el **hambre** *f* hunger **5**; **tener hambre** to be hungry **4**

la **hamburguesa** hamburger **9**

hasta until; **Hasta luego.** See you later. **1**; **Hasta mañana.** See you tomorrow. **1**; **hasta que** until **16**

hay there is, there are (*see* **haber**) **1**; **¿Qué hay de nuevo?** What's new? **8**; **No hay de qué.** You're welcome. (It's nothing.) **10**; **hay que** (*from* **haber**) it's necessary; one (we, you, *and so on*) must **4**

el **helado** ice cream **9**

la **hermana** sister **1**

el **hermano** brother **1**

hermoso beautiful **7**

la **hija** daughter **1**

el **hijo** son **1**

hispano Hispanic **2**

la **historia** history **3**

la **hoja** leaf **17**

Hola. Hello. Hi. **CP**

el **hombre** man **1**

la **hora** hour **3**; **No veo la hora de** (+ *inf*). I can't wait (+ *inf*). **13**; **¿Qué hora es?** What time is it? **3**

el **horario** schedule **12**

el **hospital** hospital **CP**

el **hotel** hotel **1**

hoy today **1**

la **huelga** strike **5**

el **huevo** egg **9**

humano human **14**

I

ida: de ida y vuelta round-trip **11**

la **idea** idea **2**

idealista idealist **2**

la **iglesia** church **10**

igual the same, equal **15**

el **imperio** empire **1**

el **impermeable** raincoat **7**

imponente impressive **17**

la **importancia** importance **3**

importante important **6**; **Es importante.** It's important. **14**

importar to matter **16**

imposible impossible **8**; **Es imposible.** It's impossible. **14**

inca Inca

increíble incredible **8**; **¡Qué increíble!** How amazing! **16**

indígena native

indio Indian **2**

la **inflación** inflation **5**

la **influencia** influence

la **información** information **1**

la **ingeniería** engineering **3**

el **ingeniero**, la **ingeniera** engineer **3**

el **inglés** English **1**

la **injusticia** injustice **13**

inmediato immediate

el, la **inmigrante** immigrant **4**

el **insecto** insect **17**

insensible insensitive **2**

insistir (en) to insist (on) **11**

insociable unsociable **2**

el **instructor**, la **instructora** instructor **13**

intelectual intellectual **2**

inteligente intelligent **2**

el **interés** interest; **sitio de interés** point (site) of interest **11**

interesante interesting **2**

interesar to interest **9**; **Me interesa(n)...** I am interested in . . . **9**

internacional international **2**

interrogativo interrogative **1**

invadir to invade

el **invierno** winter **4**

el **invitado**, la **invitada** guest **9**

ir to go **4**; **ir a** (+ *inf*) to be going to (+ *inf*) **4**; **ir de campamento** to go camping **17**; **ir de compras** to go shopping **4**; **ir de vacaciones** to go on vacation **4**; **ir en auto (autobús, avión, tren)** to go by car (bus, plane, train) **4**; **¡Qué va!** Oh, come on! **8**; **Vaya derecho hasta llegar a...** Go straight until you get to . . . **11**

irlandés Irish

irresponsable irresponsible **2**

irse to go away; leave **7**

italiano Italian **2**

J

el **jai alai** jai alai **8**

jamás never, not ever **7**

el **jamón** ham **9**

Janucá Chanukah **13**

el **jardín** garden **15**

los **jeans** jeans **7**

el **jefe**, la **jefa** leader; boss **9**

el **jerez** sherry

el **jogging** jogging **8**

joven young **2**

la **joya** jewel **10**

las **joyas** jewelry **10**

judío Jewish **10**

el **jueves** Thursday **4**

el **jugador**, la **jugadora** player **8**

jugar (ue) a to play (sport or game) **6**

el **jugo** juice **9**

la **juguetería** toy store **11**

julio July **4**

junio June **4**

la **junta** junta; council

juntos together **7**

L

la the **1**; *dir obj* her, it, you **5**

el **lado** side; **al lado (de)** beside, next to **2**

el **lago** lake **4**

la **lámpara** lamp **15**

la **lana** wool **18**

el **lápiz** pencil **CP**

largo long **7**

las the **1**; *dir obj* them, you **5**

la **lástima** pity; **¡Qué lástima!** What a pity (shame)! **1**; **Es (una) lástima.** It's a pity. **14**

latino Latin

el **lavadero** laundry room **15**

lavar to wash **7**

lavarse to wash oneself **7**

le *indir obj* (to, for) you, him, her, it **6**

la **lección** lesson **CP**

la **lectura** reading **13**

la **leche** milk **9**

la **lechuga** lettuce **9**

leer to read **3**

lejos (de) far (from) **2**

la **lengua** language **12**

lentamente slowly **8**

lento slow **8**

les *indir obj* (to, for) you, them **6**

el **letrero** sign

levantar to raise **7**

levantarse to get up, stand up **7**

la **ley** law

la **liberación** liberation **1**

la **libertad** freedom **12**

libre free, at liberty **14**

la **librería** bookstore **3**

el **libro** book **CP**

limpiar to clean **15**

limpio clean **15**

lindo beautiful **2**

listo ready; clever **13**

la **literatura** literature **3**

lo *dir obj* him, it, you **5**; **Lo siento.** I'm sorry. **16**

los the **1**; *dir obj* them, you **5**

la **lucha** fight, struggle **5**

luchar to fight

luego then, next **6**; **Hasta luego.** See you later. **1**

el **lugar** place; room (*space*) **5**

la **luna** moon **17**

el **lunes** Monday **4**

LL

llamar to call **2**

llamarse to be called, to be named **7**; **¿Cómo se llama...?** What is the name of...? **CP**; **Me llamo...** My name is... **CP**

llegar to arrive **1**

llevar to carry; to take **1**; to wear **7**

llevarse (bien, mal) con to get along (well, poorly) with **10**

llorar to cry **16**

llover (ue) to rain **6**; **Llueve.** It's raining. **4**

la **lluvia** rain **4**

M

la **madera** wood **2**

la **madre** mother **1**

la **madrina** godmother **13**

el **maestro**, la **maestra** teacher, master, scholar **10**

magnífico great, magnificient **12**

el **maíz** corn **9**

la **maleta** suitcase **3**

malo bad; sick **2**; **estar**

mal to be unwell **CP**; **Es malo.** It's bad. **14**

la **mañana** morning **4**; *adv* tomorrow **1**; **de la mañana** A.M. **3**; **por la mañana** in the morning **3**; **Hasta mañana.** See you tomorrow. **1**.

mandar to order, command; to send **13**

manejar to drive **16**

la **manifestación** demonstration **12**

la **mano** hand **5**

mantener to maintain

la **manzana** apple **9**

el **mapa** map **11**

el **mar** sea **4**

maravilloso marvelous, wonderful **17**

el **marisco** shellfish **9**

marrón brown **7**

el **martes** Tuesday **4**

marzo March **4**

más (que) more (than) **8**; el **más** the most **8**; **más o menos** more or less; so-so **CP**; **¡Qué mundo más pequeño!** What a small world! **4**

matar to kill **16**

las **matemáticas** mathematics **3**

maya Maya **3**

mayo May **4**

mayor older **8**

el, la **mayor** oldest, eldest **8**

la **mayoría** majority

me *dir obj* me **5**; *indir obj* (to, for) me **6**

la **medianoche** midnight **13**

las **medias** stockings **7**

la **medicina** medicine **3**

el **médico**, la **médica** doctor **14**

medio half **10**; **en medio de** in the middle of **11**; **...y media** half past...

el **mediodía** noon **12**
mejor better **8**; el, la **mejor** the best **8**; **Es mejor.** It's better. **14**
menor younger **8**; el, la **menor** the youngest **8**
menos (que) less (than) **8**; el **menos** the least **8**; **más o menos** more or less; so-so **CP**; **a menos que** unless **16**
mentir (ie) to lie, tell a lie **16**
el **mercado** market **11**
el **mes** month **3**
la **mesa** table **CP**
mestizo person of mixed Indian and European ancestry
mexicano Mexican **2**
mi my **5**
el **miedo** fear **14**
el **miembro** member
mientras while **6**; **mientras (que)** while **16**; **mientras tanto** meanwhile **17**
el **miércoles** Wednesday **4**
mil one thousand **4**; **Mil gracias.** Thank you very much (*literally*, a thousand thanks). **6**
un **millón (de)** million **4**
mineral mineral **9**
la **minoría** minority **5**
el **minuto** minute **9**
mirar to look at **1**
la **misa** mass **13**
mismo same **6**; **ahora mismo** right away **14**; **lo mismo** the same thing **17**; **al mismo tiempo** at the same time **6**
misterioso mysterious **10**
la **moda** fashion, style **7**; **a la moda (de moda)** in style, fashionable **7**
moderno modern **2**

el **momento** moment **3**
la **montaña** mountain **4**
moreno brunet
morir (ue) to die **8**
el **moro** Moor
mostrar (ue) to show **6**
el **movimiento** movement
la **muchacha** girl **3**
el **muchacho** boy **3**
mucho much; many; a lot **1**; **Mucho gusto.** Glad to meet you. **CP**; **Muchas gracias.** Thank you. Thank you very much. **6**
mudarse to move, change residence **7**
los **muebles** furniture **15**
la **mujer** woman **1**
mulato mulatto
el **mundo** world **4**; **todo el mundo** everyone **4**
el **muro** wall **17**
el **museo** museum **2**
la **música** music **6**
el, la **músico** musician **3**
musulmán Moslem
muy very **1**; **Muy agradecido(-a).** (I'm) very grateful. **6**; **Muy bien.** Very good (well). **CP**

N

nacer (zc) to be born **8**
la **nacionalidad** nationality **4**
nada nothing, not anything **7**; **De nada.** You're welcome. **10**
nadar to swim **4**
nadie no one, not anyone **7**
el **naipe** (playing) card **6**
la **naranja** orange **9**
la **nariz** nose **14**
la **naturaleza** nature **4**

la **Navidad** Christmas **13**; **el árbol de Navidad** Christmas tree **13**
necesario necessary **4**; **Es necesario.** It's necessary, **14**
necesitar to need **1**
el **negocio** business **11**
negro black **7**
nervioso nervous **1**
nevar (ie) to snow **5**; **Nieva.** It's snowing. **4**
ni... ni neither . . . nor **7**; **¡Ni hablar!** Don't even mention it! **12**; **¡Ni por todo el dinero del mundo!** Not for all the money in the world! **12**
nicaragüense Nicaraguan
la **niebla** fog **17**
la **nieve** snow **4**
ningún, ninguno(-s), ninguna(-s) none, not any, no, neither (of them) **7**; **ninguna parte** nowhere **11**
la **niña** girl, child **1**
el **niñero**, la **niñera** baby-sitter
el **niño** boy, child **1**
no no; **No hay (ningún) problema.** There's no problem. **16**; **No hay de qué.** You're welcome. (It's nothing.) **10**; **No importa.** It doesn't matter. **16**; **No veo la hora de** (+ *inf*). I can't wait (+ *inf*). **13**
la **noche** night **4**; **por la noche** at night **3**; **de la noche** P.M. **3**; **Buenas noches.** Good night **CP**
la **Nochebuena** Christmas Eve **13**
el **nombre** name **4**
norteamericano North American **2**

nos *dir obj* us **5**; *indir obj* (to, for) us **6**

nosotros, nosotras *subj* we **CP**

la **nota** grade **10**; **sacar una nota** to get a grade **10**

la **noticia** news item **16**

las **noticias** news **16**

novecientos nine hundred **4**

la **novela** novel **12**

noventa ninety **1**

la **novia** girlfriend **7**

noviembre November **4**

el **novio** boyfriend **7**

la **nube** cloud **17**

nublado cloudy; **Está nublado.** It's cloudy. **4**

nuestro our **5**

nueve nine **1**

nuevo new **2**; **¿Qué hay de nuevo?** What's new? **8**

el **número** number; el **número de teléfono** telephone number **1**

nunca never, not ever **7**

O

o or; **o...o** either . . . or **7**

la **obra de teatro** play **6**

obsesionado obsessed

occidental western

octubre October **4**

ocupado busy **12**

ochenta eighty **1**

ocho eight **1**

ochocientos eight hundred **4**

ofender to offend **16**

ofenderse to take offense **16**

la **oferta** sale, (special) offer **18**

la **oficina** office **1**

el **oficio** job **3**

---

oír to hear **9**; **Oiga, señor(-a)...** Excuse me sir (madam) . . . (*literally*, Listen, sir (madam) . . .) **11**

Ojalá que... I hope (it is to be hoped) that . . . **14**

el **ojo** eye

la **ola** wave

olvidar to forget **12**

once eleven **1**

la **ópera** opera **2**

la **operación** operation

la **oportunidad** opportunity **5**

optimista optimistic **2**

ordenado neat **15**

la **oreja** ear **14**

organizar to organize **10**

orgulloso proud **16**

el **origen** origin **4**

el **oro** gold **2**

os *dir obj* you **5**; *indir obj* (to, for) you **6**

oscuro dark **7**

el **otoño** fall **4**

otro other, another **2**; **otra vez** again, once more **2**

P

el **padre** father **1**

los **padres** parents **1**

el **padrino** godfather **13**

los **padrinos** godparents; host family **13**

la **paella** dish with rice, shellfish, chicken, and vegetables **9**

pagano pagan

pagar to pay (for) **8**

la **página** page **CP**

el **país** country **2**

el **pájaro** bird **17**

la **palabra** word **CP**

---

el **palacio** palace

pálido pale **14**

el **pan** bread **9**

el **pantalón** pair of pants **7**

los **pantalones** pants **7**

la **papa** potato **9**

el **papel** paper **CP**; role **13**; **hacer el papel (de)** to play the role (of) **13**

para for; in order to **1**; **para que** so that **16**; **¿Para qué sirve?** What do you use it for? **7**

el **paraguas** umbrella **7**

parar to stop **11**

parecer (zc) to seem **10**

la **pared** wall **CP**

la **pareja** pair, couple **10**

los **paréntesis** parentheses; **Entre paréntesis...** Incidentally . . . **17**

el **pariente** relative (*family*) **1**

el **parque** park **5**

la **parte** part **11**; **la mayor parte** most; **alguna parte** somewhere **11**; **ninguna parte** nowhere **11**

participar to participate **8**

el **partido** match, game **8**

el **pasado** past **3**

el **pasaje** ticket; fare **11**

el **pasajero,** la **pasajera** passenger **2**

el **pasaporte** passport **1**

pasar to pass; to spend time **1**; to happen **5**; **¿Qué te pasa?** What's wrong? What's the matter with you? **14**

el **pasatiempo** pastime **6**

pasear to stroll, walk **10**

el **paseo** trip, outing **11**; **dar un paseo** to take a walk **6**

el **patio** patio **15**

patrón patron

el **pavo** turkey **13**

la **paz** peace **1**

pedir (i) to ask, ask for; to order (*in a restaurant*) **6**; **pedir prestado** to borrow **18**

la **película** film **5**

peligroso dangerous **8**

pelirrojo redhead

el **pelo** hair **14**

la **pelota** ball **8**

pensar (ie) to think; to plan; to intend **5**; **pensar de** to think about, have an opinion **5**; **pensar en** to think about, reflect on **5**; **Pienso...** I intend (plan) . . . **15**

peor worse **8**; el, la **peor** the worst **8**

el **pepino** cucumber **9**

pequeño small, little **2**

perder (ie) to lose; to miss (train, plane, etc.); to waste (*time*) **5**; **perder (el) tiempo** to waste time **14**

perdido lost **2**

Perdón. Excuse me. **10**

perdonar to forgive, pardon **11**

el **periódico** newspaper **12**

permanecer to remain

el **permiso** permission; **Con permiso.** Excuse me. (With your permission.) **10**

permitir to permit, allow **13**

pero but **1**; **¡Pero lo dice(s) en broma!** But you're saying it in jest! **8**; **¡Pero no habla(s) en serio!** But you're not serious! **8**

la **persona** person **2**

el **pescado** fish **9**

pescar to fish **14**

pesimista pessimistic **2**

el **pez**, los **peces** fish **17**

el **piano** piano **6**

picante hot, spicy (*said of foods*) **9**

el **picnic** picnic **16**

el **pie** foot **14**

la **piedra** stone **17**

la **pierna** leg **14**

el **pijama** pajamas **7**

la **píldora** pill **14**

la **pimienta** (black) pepper **9**

pintar to paint **12**

el **pintor**, la **pintora** painter **12**

la **pintura** painting **12**

la **piña** pineapple **9**

la **piñata** piñata, hanging pot filled with candy which is broken with a stick at a party **13**

la **pirámide** pyramid

el **piso** floor, story **15**

la **pizarra** blackboard **CP**

la **planta** plant **17**

la **plataforma** platform

el **plato** plate; dish **2**

la **playa** beach **4**

la **plaza** plaza, square

la **pluma** pen **CP**

la **población** population

pobre poor **8**; **¡Pobrecito!** Poor thing! **5**

la **pobreza** poverty **5**

poco little **5**

pocos few **5**

poder (ue) to be able, can **6**; **¿Me podría dar (pasar, prestar, etc.)..., por favor?** Could you give (pass, loan, etc.) me . . . , please? **6**; **No puede ser.** It can't be. **8**; **¿Nos puede traer...?** Can you bring us . . . ? **9**; **Le (te) puedo (+ inf)...?** May I . . . to (for) you? **6**; **No lo puedo creer.** I can't believe it. **8**;

¿En qué puedo servirlo(-la)? How can I help you? **6**

poderoso powerful

el **poema** poem **6**

la **poesía** poetry **12**

el **policía**, la **mujer policía** police officer **3**

el, la **político** politician **8**

el **pollo** chicken **9**

el **poncho** poncho **18**

poner to put **3**; **poner la mesa** to set the table **9**

ponerse to put on (*clothing*) **7**; **ponerse (+ adj)** to become (+ adj) **16**; **ponerse de acuerdo** to agree **12**

popular popular **2**

por by; for; through; because of **1**; **estar por** to be about to **15**; **¿Por dónde va uno a...?** How do you get to . . . ? **11**; **por ejemplo** for example(-s) **3**; **por el contrario** on the other hand **17**; **por esas razones** for those reasons **7**; **Por eso...** For that reason . . . **15**; **Por favor.** Please. **CP**; **por fin** finally **7**; **por la mañana** in the morning **3**; **por la noche** at night **3**; **por la tarde** in the afternoon **3**; **Por lo tanto...** Therefore . . . **15**; **por otra parte** on the other hand **17**; **¿Por qué?** Why? **1**; **por suerte** luckily **7**; **por supuesto** of course, naturally **4**; **por todas partes** everywhere **5**

porque because **1**

posible possible **14**; **Es posible.** It's possible. **14**

posiblemente possibly **8**

el **postre** dessert **9**

practicar to practice **3**

práctico practical **3**

preferir (ie) to prefer **5**

la **pregunta** question **1**

preguntar to ask **2**

el **premio** prize **12**

preocuparse (de) to worry (about) **11**

preparar to prepare **2**

presentar to introduce **13**

el, la **presidente** president **2**

prestado: pedir prestado to borrow **18**

prestar to loan **6**

la **primavera** spring **4**

primero first **4**

el **primo**, la **prima** cousin **1**

probable: Es probable. It's probable. **14**

probablemente probably **8**; **Probablemente no. (Es probable que no.)** Probably not. **12**; **Probablemente sí. (Es probable que sí.)** Probably. Probably so. **12**

el **problema** problem **16**

la **procesión** procession

la **profesión** profession **3**

el **profesor**, la **profesora** professor **CP**

el **programa** program **3**

programar to program **6**

el **progreso** progress **2**

prohibido prohibited; **Está prohibido.** It's forbidden. **14**

la **promesa** promise **6**

prometer to promise **6**

pronto soon; fast **3**; **tan pronto como** as soon as **16**

la **propiedad** property, real estate **15**

propio own; **Es su (tu) propia culpa.** It's your own fault. **5**

el **propósito** purpose; **A propósito de...** Regarding . . . **17**; **A propósito...** By the way . . . **17**

próspero prosperous

el **provecho** benefit; **¡Buen provecho!** Enjoy the meal! **9**

próximo next **13**

la **psicología** psychology **3**

el **público** public **10**

el **pueblo** town; people **12**

el **puente** bridge

la **puerta** door **CP**

el **puerto** port **11**

puertorriqueño Puerto Rican **5**

Pues... Well . . . **7**

el **punto** point **8**

puntual punctual **11**

puro pure **18**

Q

que *rel pron* that **4**; which, who, **9** **¿Qué?** What? **1**; **¿Por qué?** Why? **1**; **¡Qué alegría!** How happy I am! I'm so happy! **16**; **¡Qué alivio!** What a relief! **16**; **¡Qué barbaridad!** Good grief (*literally,* What barbarity!) **5**; **¿Qué es esto?** What is this? **CP**; **¡Qué escándalo!** What a scandal! **10**; **¿Qué espera(s)?** What do you expect? **5**; **¡Qué gusto!** What a pleasure!; **¿Qué hay de nuevo?** What's new? **8**; **¿Qué hora es?** What time is it? **3**; **¡Qué horror!** How horrible! **5**; **¿Qué importancia tiene?** What's so important (about that)? **5**; **¡Qué increíble!** How amazing! **16**; **¡Qué injusticia!** How unfair! **13**; **¡Qué lástima!** What a shame (pity)! **1**; **¡Qué mala suerte!** What bad luck! **5**; **¡Qué mundo más pequeño!** What a small world! **4**; **¿Qué nos recomienda?** What do you recommend (to us)? **9**; **¡Qué sorpresa!** What a surprise! **16**; **¡Qué suerte!** What luck! **CP**; **¿Qué tal el examen?** How was the exam? **CP**; **¿Qué tal?** How are things? **CP**; **¿Qué te pasa?** What's wrong? What's the matter with you? **14**; **¿Qué tiempo hace?** What's the weather like? **4**; **¡Qué tontería!** What nonsense! **12**; **¡Qué va!** Oh, come on! **8**

quedar to be left, remain **7**

quedarse to stay **7**

quejarse to complain **13**

querer (ie) to want, to love **5**; **querer decir** to mean **6**

el **queso** cheese **9**

quien *rel pron* who, whom **9**

¿Quién? ¿Quiénes? Who? Whom? **1**

la **química** chemistry **3**

quince fifteen **1**

quinientos five hundred **4**

Quisiera... I would like . . . **6**

quitarse to take off (clothing) **7**

quizás perhaps **2**; **Quizás** (+ *indic or subjunc*)... Perhaps... **14**

R

la **rabia** anger, rage **16**

la **radio** radio **1**

rápidamente rapidly **8**

la **raqueta** racket **8**

raramente rarely **8**

raso: el cielo raso ceiling **15**

el **rato** short time **15**; **hace un rato** a short while ago **15**

la **raza** race

la **razón** reason; **tener razón** to be right **4**; **por esas razones** for those reasons **7**

la **realidad** reality; **en realidad** in reality, really **4**

realista realist **2**

realmente really **8**; **¿Realmente lo cree?** Do you really believe it? **5**

rebajar to lower **18**

el, la **rebelde** rebel

el, la **recepcionista** receptionist **6**

recibir to receive **3**

recientemente recently **8**

recomendar (ie) to recommend **9**

recordar (ue) to remember **6**

el **refresco** soft drink **18**

el **refugiado**, la **refugiada** refugee

el **regalo** gift **1**

regatear to bargain **18**

el **régimen** regime

regresar to return, go back **5**

regularmente regularly **8**

el **reino** kingdom

reírse (i) to laugh **16**

el **reloj** watch; clock **2**

el **repaso** review **15**

repetir (i) to repeat **6**; **Repitan.** Repeat. **CP**; **Repita, por favor.** Repeat that, please. **3**

el **reportero**, la **reportera** reporter **4**

representar to represent **3**

el **resentimiento** resentment

reservar to reserve **6**

el **resfrío** cold **14**

respetar to respect, esteem **10**

la **responsabilidad** responsibility **18**

responsable responsible **2**

la **respuesta** answer **17**

el **restaurante** restaurant **1**

el **resultado** result **15**

resumen: En resumen... In short... (In conclusion...) **18**

el **retrato** portrait **12**

reunirse to meet, get together **13**

la **revista** magazine **12**

el **rey** king **10**; los **Reyes Magos** Three Kings (Three Wise Men) **13**

rico rich (*in property*) **8**; delicious, good, tasty **9**

ridículo ridiculous **8**; **¡Qué ridículo!** How ridiculous! **8**; **Es ridículo.** It's ridiculous. **14**

la **risa** laughter **16**

el **robo** theft, robbery **5**

rojo red **7**

romano Roman

romper to break **10**; **romper con** to break up with **10**

la **ropa** clothing **7**

la **rosa** rose

rubio blond

el **ruido** noise **15**

la **ruina** ruin **11**

la **rutina** routine **7**

S

el **sábado** Saturday **4**

saber to know, know how to **5**; **¿Sabías que...?** Did you know that...? **10**

el **sabio**, la **sabia** sage; scholar

sabroso delicious **9**

sacar to take (out) **10**; **sacar fotos** to take pictures **6**; **sacar una nota** to get a grade **10**

la **sal** salt **9**

la **sala** living room **15**; la **sala de clase** classroom **CP**

salir to leave, go out **3**

la **salud** health; **¡Salud!** Cheers! Gesundheit! (*literally*, Health!) **10**

saludar to greet **13**

salvadoreño Salvadoran

la **sandalia** sandal **7**

el **sandwich** sandwich **9**

la **sangre** blood

la **sangría** sangría, drink made with fruit and wine **9**

el **santo**, la **santa** saint

el **secretario**, la **secretaria** secretary **3**

secundario secondary **12**; la **escuela secundaria** high school **12**

la **sed** thirst; **tener sed** to be thirsty **4**

seguida: en seguida at once, immediately **11**

seguir (i) to continue, to follow **6**; **seguir un curso** to take a course **6**; **Siga adelante (derecho).** Keep going straight. **11**

según according to **2**

segundo second

seguro sure; **Estoy seguro(-a) que...** I'm sure (positive) that ... **15**; **Es seguro.** It's certain. **14**; **¿Está usted seguro?** Are you sure? **4**

seis six **1**

seiscientos six hundred **4**

la **semana** week **1**

el **semestre** semester **10**

sensible sensitive **2**

sentarse (ie) to sit down, be seated **7**

el **sentimiento** feeling

sentir (ie) to feel; to sense **14**; **sentir que** to be sorry that **14**; **Lo siento.** I'm sorry. **16**

sentirse (ie) (+ *adj*) to feel a certain way **14**

el **señor** man; sir; Mr. **CP**

la **señora** lady; ma'am; Mrs. **CP**

la **señorita** young lady; miss; Miss **CP**

ser to be **2**; **No puede ser.** It can't be. **8**; **Es...** It's ... **CP**; **Es de esperar.** It's to be expected. **5**; **Es demasiado...** It's too ... **18**; **Es que...** The thing is that ... **7**; **¿De qué es?** What is it made of? **7**

serio serious; **¡Pero no habla(s) en serio!** But you're not serious! **8**; **¿En serio?** Really? **10**

servir (i) to serve **6**; **¿En qué puedo servirlo(-la)?** How can I help you? **6**; **¿Para qué sirve?** What do you use it for? **7**

sesenta sixty **1**

setecientos seven hundred **4**

setenta seventy **1**

setiembre (septiembre) September **4**

si if, whether **3**; **Si quiere, podría...** If you like, I could ... **6**

sí yes **CP**

el **SIDA** AIDS (Acquired Immune Deficiency Syndrome) **5**

siempre always **3**

la **siesta** siesta, *afternoon nap or rest*

siete seven **1**

el **siglo** century **3**

significar to mean **12**

el **silencio** silence **17**

la **silla** chair **CP**

el **sillón** armchair **15**

el **símbolo** symbol

simpático nice **2**

simultáneo simultaneous

sin without; **sin embargo** however; **sin que** without **16**

el **sistema** system

el **sitio** place **11**; **sitio de interés** point (site) of interest **11**

la **situación** situation **1**

sobre on, about **1**

la **sociedad** society

el **sofá** sofa **10**

solamente only **6**

solo alone **9**

sólo only **7**

soltero single, unmarried **10**

el **sombrero** hat **7**

soñar (ue) con to dream about, to dream of **6**

la **sopa** soup **9**

sorprender to surprise **14**

la **sorpresa** surprise **16**; **¡Qué sorpresa!** What a surprise! **16**

su his, her, its, your, their **5**

subir to climb, go up **11**; **subir a** to get on **11**

el **sueldo** salary **18**

el **suelo** floor, ground **15**

la **suerte** luck **11**; **por suerte** luckily **7**; **¡Qué suerte!** What luck! **CP**

el **suéter** sweater **7**

supuesto: por supuesto of course, naturally **4**

el **sustantivo** noun **6**

el **susto** fright **16**

T

tal: Tal vez (+ *indic or subjunc*)... Perhaps ... **14**; **¿Qué tal?** How are things? **CP**

el **tamaño** size **7**; **¿De qué tamaño es?** What size is it? **7**

también also, too **1**

tampoco not either, neither **7**

tan so **8**; **tan** (+ *adj or adv* +) **como** as ... as **8**; **tan pronto como** as soon as **16**

tanto so much **8**; **tanto como** as much as **8**; **Por lo tanto...** Therefore ... **15**

tarde late **5**; la **tarde** afternoon; evening **4**; **por la tarde** in the afternoon **3**; **de la tarde** P.M. **3**; **Buenas tardes.** Good afternoon. **CP**

la **tarjeta** card **13**
el **taxi** taxi **11**
la **taza** cup **12**
el **té** tea **4**
  te *dir obj* you **5**; *indir obj* (to, for) you **6**
el **teatro** theater **2**
el **techo** roof **15**
el **teléfono** telephone **1**
la **televisión** television **1**
el **televisor** television set **15**
el **tema** subject, topic **17**
la **temperatura** temperature **14**
el **templo** temple
  temprano early **5**
  tener to have **3**; **tener que** (+ *inf*) to have to (+ *inf*) **3**; **tener calor (frío)** to be warm (cold) (*a person or animal*) **4**; **tener cuidado** to be careful **4**; **tener dolor de cabeza (estómago)** to have a headache (stomachache) **4**; **tener fiebre** to have a fever **4**; **tener ganas de** (+ *inf*) to feel like (*doing something*) **3**; **tener la oportunidad de** to have the opportunity to **9**; **tener miedo (de) que** to be afraid that **14**; **tener prisa** to be in a hurry **16**; **tener razón** to be right **4**; **tener... años** to be ... years old **4**; **No tengo la menor idea.** I don't have the slightest idea. **14**; **¿Qué edad tienes?** How old are you? **15**
el **tenis** tennis **6**
  tercero (*shortened form* **tercer**) third
  terminar to finish, end **5**

terriblemente terribly **8**
la **tía** aunt **1**
el **tiempo** time (*in a general sense*) **3**; weather **4**; **a tiempo** on time **11**; **¿Qué tiempo hace?** What's the weather like? **4**; **Hace buen (mal) tiempo.** The weather is nice (bad). **4**
la **tienda** shop, store **5**
la **tierra** earth, land **17**
el **tío** uncle **1**
  típico typical **2**
el **tipo** type **6**; (*slang*) guy **10**
  tocar to touch; to play (*music or a musical instrument*) **6**
  todavía still, yet **3**
  todo all, every **3**; **todo el mundo** everyone **4**
  todos all, every, everyone **3**; **todos los días** every day **4**; **todas las semanas** every week **4**
  tomar to take; to drink **4**
el **tomate** tomato **9**
la **tontería** nonsense **12**
el, la **torero** bullfighter **8**
el **toro** bull **8**
la **torta** cake **9**
la **tortilla** omelet **9**
  total: Total que... So . . . **18**
  trabajador hard-working **2**
el **trabajador**, la **trabajadora** worker
el **trabajo** work **5**
  traer to bring, carry **9**
el **tráfico** traffic **2**
el **traje** suit; outfit **7**; el **traje de baño** swimming suit **7**
  tranquilo tranquil **17**
  tratar (de) to try (to) **16**
  trece thirteen **1**

treinta thirty **1**
tres three **1**
trescientos three hundred **4**
la **tribu** tribe
el **trimestre** trimester **10**
triste sad **16**
la **tristeza** sadness **16**
triunfar to win
tú *subj* you (*fam*) **CP**
tu your **5**
la **tumba** tomb
el, la **turista** tourist **1**

U

último most recent, latest **5**
un, una a, an; one **1**
único unique; only **12**
la **unidad** unity
unir unite
la **universidad** university **1**
universitario university **3**
uno one **1**
unos, unas some; a few **1**
urgente urgent **5**
uruguayo Uruguayan **11**
usar to use **5**
usarse to be used
usted *subj* you (*formal*) **CP**
ustedes *subj* you (*formal pl*) **CP**
útil useful **CP**
utilizar use, utilize

V

la **vaca** cow; la **carne de vaca** beef **9**
las **vacaciones** vacation **1**; **estar de vacaciones** to

be on vacation **2**; **ir de vacaciones** to go on vacation **4**

valer to be worth **18**

el **valor** value, price **6**

el **valle** valley **17**

vanidoso vain **8**

la **variedad** variety

varios several, some **10**

el **vecino**, la **vecina** neighbor **13**

veinte twenty **1**

veintiuno twenty one **1**

el **vendedor**, la **vendedora** salesperson **3**

vender to sell **3**

venir to come **3**

la **venta** sale, selling **18**

la **ventana** window **CP**

ver to see **5**; **A ver.** Let's see. **7**; **No veo la hora de** (+ *inf*). I can't wait (+ *inf*). **13**

el **verano** summer **4**

veras: ¿De veras? Really? **8**

el **verbo** verb

la **verdad** truth **1**; **Es verdad.** It's true. **14**; **¿verdad?** right?, true? **1**

verdaderamente truly **8**

verdadero true; real **1**

verde green **7**

la **verdura** vegetable **9**

la **vergüenza** shame **16**; **darle vergüenza a alguien** to make someone ashamed **16**

el **vestido** dress **7**

vestir (i) to dress **7**

vestirse (i) to get dressed **7**

la **vez** time, instance **2**; **a veces** sometimes **5**

viajar to travel **1**

el **viaje** journey, trip **11**; el **viaje de negocios** business trip **11**

el **viajero**, la **viajera** traveler **11**

la **vida** life **3**

viejo old **2**

el **viernes** Friday **4**

el **vino** wine **9**

violento violent **8**

violeta violet **7**

el **violín** violin **6**

visitar to visit **1**

la **vista** view **9**

la **vitamina** vitamin **14**

vivir to live **3**

el **vocabulario** vocabulary **CP**

el **vólibol** volleyball **8**

volver (ue) to return, come back, go back **6**

vosotros, vosotras *subj* you (*fam pl*) **CP**

el **vuelo** flight **4**

la **vuelta** return; **de ida y vuelta** round-trip **11**

vuestro your **5**

Y

y and **CP**; **¿Y qué?** So what? **5**

ya already **9**; **ya no** no longer, not any longer **9**

yo *subj* I **CP**

Z

el **zapato** shoe **7**

el **zoológico** zoo **11**

Index of Grammar and Functions

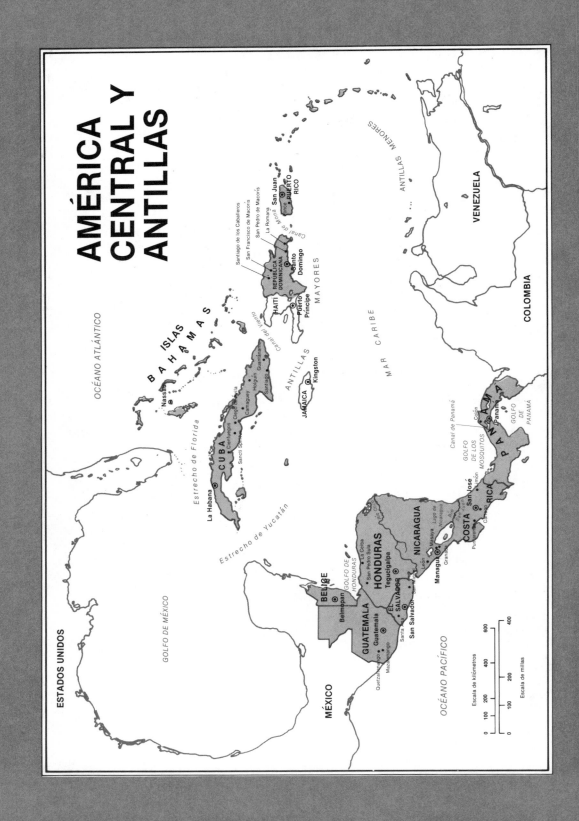

AMÉRICA CENTRAL Y ANTILLAS

ESTADOS UNIDOS

OCÉANO ATLÁNTICO

GOLFO DE MÉXICO

MÉXICO

ISLAS BAHAMAS

Nassau

Estrecho de Florida

La Habana
CUBA
Cienfuegos
Sancti Spíritus
Camagüey
Holguín
Santiago

Estrecho de Yucatán

ANTILLAS

JAMAICA
Kingston

MAR CARIBE

HAITÍ
Puerto Príncipe

REPÚBLICA DOMINICANA
Santiago de los Caballeros
San Francisco de Macorís
San Pedro de Macorís
La Romana
Santo Domingo

Canal de la Mona
Mona

SAN Juan
PUERTO RICO

MAYORES

ANTILLAS MENORES

VENEZUELA

COLOMBIA

GOLFO DE HONDURAS

BELICE
Belmopán

GUATEMALA
Guatemala
Quetzaltenango
Mazatenango
Santa María

EL SALVADOR
San Salvador
San Miguel

HONDURAS
San Pedro Sula
La Ceiba
Tegucigalpa

NICARAGUA
León
Managua
Masaya
Granada
Lago de Nicaragua

COSTA RICA
San José
Limón

GOLFO DE LOS MOSQUITOS

PANAMÁ
Colón
Panamá
Canal de Panamá

GOLFO DE PANAMÁ

OCÉANO PACÍFICO

Escala de kilómetros
0   100   200   400   600

Escala de millas
0   100   200   400